Creating Visual FoxPro Applications with Visual FoxExpress

Bob Archer
Dan Jurden

Hentzenwerke Publishing

Published by:
Hentzenwerke Publishing
980 East Circle Drive
Whitefish Bay WI 53217 USA

Hentzenwerke Publishing books are available through booksellers and directly from the publisher. Contact Hentzenwerke Publishing at:
414.332.9876
414.332.9463 (fax)
www.hentzenwerke.com
books@hentzenwerke.com

Creating Visual FoxPro Applications with Visual FoxExpress
  By Bob Archer and Dan Jurden
  Technical Editor: Mike Feltman
  Copy Editor: Farion Grove

Copyright © 2000 by Bob Archer and Dan Jurden

All other products and services identified throughout this book are trademarks or registered trademarks of their respective companies. They are used throughout this book in editorial fashion only and for the benefit of such companies. No such uses, or the use of any trade name, is intended to convey endorsement or other affiliation with this book.

All rights reserved. No part of this book, or the .CHM Help files available by download from Hentzenwerke Publishing, may be reproduced or transmitted in any form or by any means, electronic, mechanical photocopying, recording, or otherwise, without the prior written permission of the publisher, except that program listings and sample code files may be entered, stored and executed in a computer system.

The information and material contained in this book are provided "as is," without warranty of any kind, express or implied, including without limitation any warranty concerning the accuracy, adequacy, or completeness of such information or material or the results to be obtained from using such information or material. Neither Hentzenwerke Publishing nor the authors or editors shall be responsible for any claims attributable to errors, omissions, or other inaccuracies in the information or material contained in this book. In no event shall Hentzenwerke Publishing or the authors or editors be liable for direct, indirect, special, incidental, or consequential damages arising out of the use of such information or material.

ISBN: 0-930919-03-4

Manufactured in the United States of America.

I dedicate this book to my three children. So many times, when they asked me to "play a family game," my response was, "I have to work on the book." I am glad I won't have to say that to them much anymore. Also, to my wife, Lori, without whom I wouldn't have such a wonderful family and life. I love you.

—Bob Archer

To my wife, Ann, and four daughters, LeeAnn, Lane, Kara Beth and Kelly, for leaving daddy alone long enough to work on the book.

—Dan Jurden

Our Contract with You, The Reader

In which we, the folks who make up Hentzenwerke Publishing, describe what you, the reader, can expect from this book and from us.

Hi there!

I've been writing professionally (in other words, eventually getting a paycheck for my scribbles) since 1974, and writing about software development since 1992. As an author, I've worked with a half-dozen different publishers and corresponded with thousands of readers over the years. As a software developer and all-around geek, I've also acquired a library of more than 100 computer and software-related books.

Thus, when I donned the publisher's cap four years ago to produce the *1997 Developer's Guide,* I had some pretty good ideas of what I liked (and didn't like) from publishers, what readers liked and didn't like, and what I, as a reader, liked and didn't like.

Now, with our new titles for 2000, we're entering our third season. (For those who are keeping track, the '97 DevGuide was our first, albeit abbreviated, season, and the batch of six "Essentials" for Visual FoxPro 6.0 in 1999 was our second.)

John Wooden, the famed UCLA basketball coach, had posited that teams aren't consistent; they're always getting better—or worse. We'd like to get better...

One of my goals for this season is to build a closer relationship with you, the reader. In order for us to do this, you've got to know what you should expect from us.

- You have the right to expect that your order will be processed quickly and correctly, and that your book will be delivered to you in new condition.

- You have the right to expect that the content of your book is technically accurate and up-to-date, that the explanations are clear, and that the layout is easy to read and follow without a lot of fluff or nonsense.

- You have the right to expect access to source code, errata, FAQs, and other information that's relevant to the book via our Web site.

- You have the right to expect an electronic version of your printed book (in compiled HTML Help format) to be available via our Web site.

- You have the right to expect that, if you report errors to us, your report will be responded to promptly, and that the appropriate notice will be included in the errata and/or FAQs for the book.

Naturally, there are some limits that we bump up against. There are humans involved, and they make mistakes. A book of 500 pages contains, on average, 150,000 words and several megabytes of source code. It's not possible to edit and re-edit multiple times to catch every last misspelling and typo, nor is it possible to test the source code on every permutation of development environment and operating system—and still price the book affordably.

Once printed, bindings break, ink gets smeared, signatures get missed during binding. On the delivery side, Web sites go down, packages get lost in the mail.

Nonetheless, we'll make our best effort to correct these problems—once you let us know about them.

In return, when you have a question or run into a problem, we ask that you first consult the errata and/or FAQs for your book on our Web site. If you don't find the answer there, please e-mail us at books@hentzenwerke.com with as much information and detail as possible, including 1) the steps to reproduce the problem, 2) what happened, and 3) what you expected to happen, together with 4) any other relevant information.

I'd like to stress that we need you to communicate questions and problems clearly. For example…

- "Your downloads don't work" isn't enough information for us to help you. "I get a 404 error when I click on the **Download Source Code** link on www.hentzenwerke.com/book/downloads.html" is something we can help you with.

- "The code in Chapter 10 caused an error" again isn't enough information. "I performed the following steps to run the source code program DisplayTest.PRG in Chapter 10, and I received an error that said 'Variable m.liCounter not found'" is something we can help you with.

We'll do our best to get back to you within a couple of days, either with an answer or at least an acknowledgment that we've received your inquiry and that we're working on it.

On behalf of the authors, technical editors, copy editors, layout artists, graphical artists, indexers, and all the other folks who have worked to put this book in your hands, I'd like to thank you for purchasing this book, and I hope that it will prove to be a valuable addition to your technical library. Please let us know what you think about this book—we're looking forward to hearing from you.

As Groucho Marx once observed, "Outside of a dog, a book is a man's best friend. Inside of a dog, it's too dark to read."

Whil Hentzen
Hentzenwerke Publishing
November 2000

List of Chapters

Chapter 1: The Big Picture	1
Chapter 2: Before You Start	9
Chapter 3: VFE's IDE	21
Chapter 4: Data Storage and Classes	33
Chapter 5: Metadata	53
Chapter 6: Business Objects	65
Chapter 7: Presentation Objects	79
Chapter 8: Forms	93
Chapter 9: Your VFE Application	101
Chapter 10: How It Works	111
Chapter 11: Interface Controls	131
Chapter 12: Data Validation	147
Chapter 13: Working with Views	161
Chapter 14: Related Data and Forms	173
Chapter 15: Data Behavior Classes	201
Chapter 16: Extending the Framework	207
Chapter 17: VFE Security	215
Chapter 18: Outputting Data	231
Chapter 19: Client/Server	251
Chapter 20: Tips and Tricks	269

Table of Contents

Our Contract with You, The Reader	v
Acknowledgements	xxi
About the Authors	xxiii
How to Download the Files	xxv

Chapter 1: The Big Picture — 1

Codebook	1
Visual FoxExpress	2
The Visual FoxExpress IDE	2
Application Manager	2
Application Builder	2
Wizards and builders	2
Express Tools	3
The Visual FoxExpress framework	3
Starting at the back	3
Application design	4
The database	4
Metadata	4
Data classes	5
The data environment	6
Business object	7
Presentation object	7
Form class	8
Miscellaneous classes	8
Summary	8

Chapter 2: Before You Start — 9

Your development environment	9
ASSIST	12
Use a client/server mentality	13
Why views instead of tables	13
About grids and lists	15
Related tables vs. parameterized views	15
Relating tables	16
Parameterized views	16
Key generation for dummies	16
Primary key	17
Type of primary key	17

Naming conventions	19
Summary	19

Chapter 3: VFE's IDE — 21

Tutorial	21
Application Manager	23
Project directory	23
iLibs	24
What gets created?	24
Application Builder	25
Wizards	27
Builders	28
DBCX Explorer	28
Preferences	29
Express Tools	31
Component Gallery	31
Wizard Manager	31
Edit Default Menu choices	32
Summary	32

Chapter 4: Data Storage and Classes — 33

Create your physical database	33
Table requirements	33
Tutorial	34
Remote data	35
Create views	35
Tutorial data	35
Data classes	37
Tutorial	37
cDataEnvironment of cData.VCX	41
Cursors	41
InitialSelectedAlias	41
lPrivateDataSession	42
FindCursor()	42
GetCursor()	42
cCursor of cData.VCX	42
BOF	43
EOF	43
RecNo	43
RecordCount	43
VisibleRecordCount	43
cDeleteTriggerMessage	43
cInsertTriggerMessage	44
cUpdateTriggerMessage	44

IWritePrimaryKeyOnNew	44
IWritePrimaryKeyOnSave	44
NoDataOnLoad	44
Fields	44
Parameters	44
AddNew()	44
Cancel()	45
Update()	45
Delete()	46
Requery()	46
MoveFirst(), MoveLast(), MoveNext(), MovePrevious()	46
IsAdding(), IsChanged(), IsCursorEmpty(), IsNewAndEmpty()	47
Fields collection	47
View parameters collection	47
cAbstractDataItem	48
oBizObj	48
oCursor	48
oProperties	48
Value	49
cField of cData.VCX	49
IsChanged()	49
Revert()	49
Using the cursor and field objects	50
Summary	51

Chapter 5: Metadata   53

DBCX	53
VFE and DBCX	54
Tutorial	54
DBCX Explorer	58
Metadata storage	58
Explorer definition	59
Properties uncovered	60
Behavior page	60
Interface page	61
Structural page	62
Validation	62
Other	62
Default value generation	62
Code examples	63
Summary	64

Chapter 6: Business Objects — 65

- Tutorial — 65
- Business object class — 66
- Related business objects — 66
  - Parent business object — 67
  - Child business object — 67
- Data Environment Loader — 67
  - Business rules collection — 68
  - Business rules class — 68
- cBizObj of cBusiness.VCX — 68
  - cForeignKeyExpression — 68
  - cKeyField — 69
  - cParentBizObjName — 69
  - cRelationTag — 69
  - lAllowDelete, lAllowEdit, lAllowNew — 69
  - lConfirmOnDelete — 69
  - lNewOnParentNew — 69
  - lRequeryChildrenOnSave — 70
  - lSaveAllRows — 70
  - lWriteForeignKeyOnNew, lWriteForeignKeyOnSave — 70
  - oCursor — 70
  - oDataEnvironment — 70
  - oHost — 70
  - oParentBizObj — 71
  - oBizObjs — 71
  - RecNo, RecordCount, VisibleRecordCount — 71
  - AllowNew(), AllowDelete(), AllowEdit(), AllowSave() — 71
  - Cancel(), Cancel_Pre(), Cancel_Perform(), Cancel_Post() — 72
  - Delete(), Delete_Pre(), Delete_Perform(), Delete_Post() — 72
  - FindCursor() — 73
  - FindField() — 73
  - FindViewParameter() — 73
  - GetValues(), SetValues() — 73
  - GetRecordSet() — 74
  - IsAdding(), IsChanged(), IsDeleted(), IsCursorEmpty() — 74
  - New(), New_Pre(), New_Perform(), New_Post() — 74
  - OkToMove() — 74
  - Requery(), Requery_Pre(), Requery_Perform(), Requery_Post() — 75
  - Save(), Save_Pre(), Save_Perform(), Save_Post(), OnSaveNew() — 75
  - SetField(), SetParameter() — 76
- Creating your business rules — 77
- Summary — 77

Chapter 7: Presentation Objects — 79

- Control panel — 79
- Tutorial — 80
- Business Object Loader — 82
- cPresentationObj of cPresent.VCX — 83
  - cEditForm — 84
  - cListFields — 84
  - cMenuPad — 84
  - cSetFocusTo — 84
  - lActivateOnUIEnable — 84
  - lAllowDelete, lAllowEdit, lAllowFilter, lAllowList, lAllowNavigate, lAllowNew, lAllowOrder, lAllowPrint — 85
  - lConfirmDelete — 85
  - lDisplayNoRecordMessage — 85
  - lMain — 85
  - oBizObj — 85
  - AllowEdit(), AllowFilter(), AllowCancel(), AllowNavigate(), AllowNew(), AllowOrder(), AllowSave() — 85
  - Cancel(), Cancel_Pre(), Cancel_Post() — 86
  - Copy() — 86
  - Delete(), Delete_Pre(), Delete_Post() — 87
  - New(), New_Pre(), New_Post() — 87
  - IsAdding(), IsChanged(), IsDeleted(), IsCursorEmpty() — 88
  - Requery() — 88
  - Save(), Save_Pre(), Save_Post() — 88
  - Search(), GetCriteria() — 89
- Presentation Object Builder — 89
- Data binding options — 91
- Summary — 91

Chapter 8: Forms — 93

- Tutorial — 93
- Form class — 95
- Form manager — 96
- Session environment — 96
- cPresentationObjForm of cForms.VCX — 97
  - oPresentObj — 97
  - oPresentObjs — 97
  - AllowDelete(), AllowFilter(), AllowList(), AllowNavigate(), AllowNew(), AllowOrder(), AllowPrint(), AllowRequery(), AllowSave(), AllowSearch() — 98
  - FindBizObj(), GetBizObj() — 98
  - Data methods — 98
- Toolbars — 98
- Summary — 99

Chapter 9: Your VFE Application — 101

Building your application	101
Run your application	102
Splash screen	103
Options dialog	103
Database utilities	104
Error log	104
Security	104
Developers menu	105
Standard menus	106
Instructors form	106
Navigation and Tools menus	107
List tool	107
Add data	107
Summary	108

Chapter 10: How It Works — 111

System services	111
Application object	112
cApplication of cApp.VCX	112
Application startup	112
Init()	113
Do()	116
System classes	117
Application object: Part 2	118
cDataPath, cMetaPath, cLibsPath, cProgsPath, cOutPutPath,	
cMiscPath, cAdditionalPath, clLibsPath	118
cFactoryClass	118
cStartForm	118
IDisplayInterface	119
IMaximizeOnStartUp	119
lUseSecurity	119
GetClass(), Make()	119
GetMetaManager()	119
Init_Post(), Init_Pre()	119
SetSecurity()	120
Form instantiation	120
DoForm()	120
Form startup	120
Form load	121
oSessionEnvironmentLoader	121
oSessionEnvironment	121
oResizer	122
Controls	122

BizObjLoader	123
BizObj	123
oDELoader	124
oDataEnvironment	124
oCursor	124
oDataEnvironment Init()	124
oCursor Open()	125
oDataEnvironment, continued	126
oBizRules	127
oBizObj Init()	127
Presentation object Init()	128
Form Init()	128
BindControls()	130
Summary	130

Chapter 11: Interface Controls — 131

Data edit controls	131
cRightClickMenu	131
cField, cViewParameter	132
lNoValidate	132
lAlwaysDisable	132
lAlwaysReadOnly	132
oApplication	132
oField	132
oGlobalHook	133
Global hook class	133
cGlobalHook of Utils.VCX	133
Initialize()	133
ValidateControl()	133
LostFocusHook()	134
GetController()	134
RightClickHook()	134
BindControls()	134
Early vs. late binding	136
Builders	136
Quick-fill text box	138
Date text box	139
Grids	139
lGetHeaderCaptions	142
lPopulateOnInit	142
lRefreshParentOnRowChange	142
lRequeryChildrenOnRowChange	142
lSelectRecordOnDoubleClick	142
Action controls	142

Toolbars	143
Menus	145
Summary	146

Chapter 12: Data Validation — 147

Lookups	147
Look Up Cursor	149
Search Expression	149
Display Fields	150
Update Expression	151
Filter	151
Post Process Expression	151
Look Up Display Form	151
Look Up Add Form	151
Defined range	152
Value Is In List	152
Value Required	152
Mix and match	152
Table and field rules	153
When is data validated?	153
Validation trace	153
The trouble with lookups	154
Hand-code the validation	155
Parameterize the view	155
Summary	159

Chapter 13: Working with Views — 161

The View Designer	161
Filter tab	162
Creating parameters	162
Parameter uses	162
Parameter list	163
Relating views	164
Complex views	165
View Designer tip	166
Remote view tip	166
View parameter containers	167
Hand-code your views	168
Version control	170
eView	170
Summary	171

Chapter 14: Related Data and Forms — 173

- SET RELATION TO — 173
- Related views — 173
- Related business objects — 175
  - cForeignKeyExpression — 176
  - cKeyField — 176
  - cParentBizObjName — 176
  - cRelationTag — 176
- Related interfaces — 176
- Parent/child presentation object — 177
  - Create the parent/child presentation object — 180
- Single record modal add form — 185
- Multiple presentation object form — 189
  - Nits and gnats — 195
- Parent-child forms — 196
  - Is it n-tier? — 199
- Summary — 200

Chapter 15: Data Behavior Classes — 201

- Creating a behavior class — 201
- Specifying the behavior class — 201
- Custom validation — 202
- Lookup_Post() — 204
- Value_Access() — 205
- Raise an event — 205
- Summary — 206

Chapter 16: Extending the Framework — 207

- The I-layer — 207
  - What's it for? — 208
  - Making modifications — 208
  - Replacing code — 209
  - Don't use hooks — 209
- Subclassing — 209
- Factory class — 211
  - Making changes — 211
  - Using the factory — 212
- Implementation class — 213
- Third-party classes — 213
- Adding files to your project — 214
- Summary — 214

Chapter 17: VFE Security — 215

- Implementing security from the beginning — 216
  - Turning on security — 216
  - Adding security names — 218
  - Security in business objects — 219
  - Menu items security — 220
  - Child form security — 221
- Implementing security after creating the objects — 222
  - Turning on security — 222
  - Adding security names — 222
  - Business objects security properties — 222
  - Menu security — 222
  - Child form security — 223
- Field-level security — 223
- Creating security groups — 224
  - Creating group names — 224
  - Assigning security names and access rights to groups — 226
- Creating users — 228
- Security maintenance — 229
- Summary — 230

Chapter 18: Outputting Data — 231

- Report output class — 231
- Testing and modifying reports — 239
- Export output class — 242
- Controlling the tree view — 249
- Working with the report and export object classes — 249
  - SetFieldList() — 249
  - lUseCurrentData — 250
  - Executing reports from code — 250
- Summary — 250

Chapter 19: Client/Server — 251

- Why (not) client/server? — 251
  - Security — 252
  - Reliability (no more corrupt indexes) — 252
  - Speed — 252
  - Size restrictions — 253
- Tools used — 253
- Application database — 253
  - Creating the database and tables — 255
- ODBC/DSN — 255
- Creating your VFP database and remote views — 256
  - Add a connection — 258

Creating remote views	260
Creating VFE's objects	262
Lookups and data validation	262
SQL pass-through	263
Quick-fill text box	265
Upsizing local data	268
Summary	268

Chapter 20: Tips and Tricks — 269

Where's the project manager?	269
Drop the IDE	270
Accessing builders	270
DBCX Explorer	270
Running your application	270
Using VFP Builders	271
Where do I put the code?	271
Data manipulation	274
Mover alternative	274
Views only database	276
Create an edit mode	276
Debugging	277
UTILS.PRG	278
Team programming	279
Source control	279
Project files	279
Data	279
Metadata	280
Communicate	280
Remote data NewID()	280
Summary	281

Acknowledgements

First of all, I must thank Whil Hentzen for giving me, an unpublished programmer, a chance. When he told me how much work this book would be, I had no idea. Of course, I have to thank the wonderful folks at F1 Technologies for creating Visual FoxExpress. This is a fantastic product, and the more I use it, the more I learn about it. I also want to thank Dan Jurden, my co-author, for his great work on the chapters that I really didn't feel I had enough experience to write. Of course, now I'm deep into a SQL Server project with VFE, but that's another book. Thanks to Farion Grove for turning my scribbles into proper English and finding my stupid mistakes. Finally, thanks to the reader for buying the book—I hope you get as much out of it as I put into it.

—Bob

First, I would like to thank my wife Ann for having such patience and supporting me while I worked long evening hours. I would also like to thank my daughters LeeAnn, Lane, Kara Beth and Kelly for not complaining (too much) when daddy said he couldn't take them fishing on Saturday because he had "work to do." I love you all, and we can go fishing now!

Next, I would like to thank Mike and Toni Feltman for giving my name to Whil Hentzen as someone who would be a good person to help on this book project. Thank you, Whil, for contacting me. And thank you, Bob Archer, for allowing me to co-author this book with you.

—Dan

About the Authors

Bob Archer

Bob Archer has been programming computers since he was 14 years old, when he created a basic program on his Vic 20 that calculated statistics for the church's girls' softball team and stored them on cassette tape. He has worked with various PC languages and found his niche writing business applications, starting with Clipper and including FoxPro, Visual FoxPro, Visual Basic and SQL Server. Bob is currently a senior programmer at Geac Computers, Inc., where he's working on a VFP/VFE/SQL Server rewrite of their old FoxPro for Windows HR and Payroll application.

Bob can be reached at his personal e-mail address, pilotbob@akamail.com.

Dan Jurden

Dan Jurden is the Senior Application Developer at CICcorp, Inc., in College Station, Texas. He also does consulting, application development and project mentoring via his own consulting company. He has been working with Visual FoxPro since version 3.0 was released and with Visual FoxExpress since 1999. He has designed and developed several in-house applications for CICcorp using VFE and SQL Server, and a few commercial applications using VFE that use either VFP tables or SQL Server.

Dan can be reached at djurden@swbell.net.

Mike Feltman

Mike Feltman is the president and founder of F1 Technologies, the creators of Visual FoxExpress. Mike and his wife, Toni, designed and developed Visual FoxExpress. Mike has been the lead developer of the FoxExpress product line since its inception in 1990. Mike is also a frequent speaker at Developer Conferences and user groups and has been published in *FoxPro Advisor* and *FoxTalk*. Mike got his start in computers at the age of 15 as an assistant instructor at the University of Toledo and became an instructor at the University of Toledo at the age of 17. Prior to starting F1 Technologies, Mike worked at Fox Software, the original creators of FoxPro, in technical support, development and marketing.

Mike is also the proud father of William Michael "Mickey" Feltman III and the proud son of William Michael Feltman Sr. and Bobbie Feltman. When Mike is not chained to his keyboard, he enjoys hunting and fishing, Toledo Storm Hockey, and plays volleyball and softball.

Mike can be reached at mfeltman@f1tech.com.

How to Download the Files

There are two sets of files that accompany this book. The first is the source code referenced throughout the text, and the second is the e-book version of this book—the compiled HTML Help (.CHM) file. Here's how to get them.

Both the source code and the CHM file are available for download from the Hentzenwerke Web site. In order to obtain them, follow these instructions:

1. Point your Web browser to www.hentzenwerke.com.
2. Look for the link that says "Download Source Code & .CHM Files." (The text for this link may change over time—if it does, look for a link that references Books or Downloads.)
3. A page describing the download process will appear. This page has two sections:
   - **Section 1:** If you were issued a username/password from Hentzenwerke Publishing, you can enter them into this page.
   - **Section 2:** If you did not receive a username/password from Hentzenwerke Publishing, don't worry! Just enter your e-mail alias and look for the question about your book. Note that you'll need your book when you answer the question.
4. A page that lists the hyperlinks for the appropriate downloads will appear.

Note that the .CHM file is covered by the same copyright laws as the printed book. Reproduction and/or distribution of the .CHM file is against the law.

If you have questions or problems, the fastest way to get a response is to e-mail us at books@hentzenwerke.com.

Chapter 1
The Big Picture

So you want to learn more about Visual FoxExpress. You have made a great choice. There are many similar products on the market that you could select, but Visual FoxExpress has all the elements you need to build most business applications today. In this chapter we will take a brief look at the history of Visual FoxExpress, and then we'll present a brief overview of what's included in the package.

In order to appreciate what we have today, it's useful to examine history. With VFE, a bit of history will also help you to appreciate how it got where it is today—what design decisions were made, and generally "why it's like that."

Prior to version 3.0 of what is now called Visual FoxPro, we did not have an object-based development environment. Just as with COBOL or BASIC, you had to create every element from scratch. When Visual FoxPro 3.0 was released as an object-oriented product, many FoxPro programmers didn't know what to do.

Oh, don't misunderstand, we all knew the concepts of objects with attributes and behaviors that translated to properties and methods, but how did you build a class? What did it take to put together an application with the new paradigm? The FoxPro community needed some guidance.

Along came Y. Alan Griver from Flash with a groundbreaking book called *Codebook*.

Codebook

Codebook was published shortly after VFP 3.0 came out. It was described by one review as "more code than book." The first few chapters discussed business process engineering and application design. It introduced the concept of business objects to the FoxPro community for the first time. This was not a new concept in the object-oriented world by any means. The jewel of this book was in the CD that was included. Known as the Codebook Framework, it was the beginning and basis of many future works.

The Codebook Framework allowed you to build object-oriented programs with an n-tier mentality. (And from now on, when we refer to "Codebook," we mean the framework.) While the tiers in Codebook were only logical, the separation of business logic, data behavior and user interface code was well ahead of its time. In addition, Codebook supported a cursor class that allowed the developer to create an application that ran against local tables and SQL Server tables using the same code by doing nothing more than changing the setting of a single property.

The problem with Codebook was that it was sparsely documented and contained many bugs. Flash did make a small effort to put out a few fixes, but it was nowhere near the level that was needed. The business object class was also underpowered, and there were separate classes to build your business objects depending on whether it was a parent or child. This limited you to a single parent-child relationship, making more complex relations difficult to build with the existing classes.

When the users recognized what they had, an active user community developed and many documents and classes were released. There were also at least two commercial products based on Codebook that were developed by other software shops. There was one programmer who released his own business object class library.

Visual FoxExpress

F1 Technologies, known at the time as Neon Software, was one of the companies that released a commercial product based on Codebook. This product provided developers with many productivity tools that simplified building Codebook applications.

In addition to the new tools, F1 also added many classes to enhance the existing classes such as Security, Validation, Audit Trail and so forth. More importantly, the product was documented and supported. Developers could get help building their applications, and of course the company responded to bug reports with fixes much faster than Flash had.

At the time that the major first revision of Visual FoxExpress was released, physical n-tier applications were starting to become all the rage. While the code in Visual FoxExpress at this time was logically layered, it didn't really support a design that would allow for a physical three-tier deployment. F1 Technologies recognized this and embarked on a major rewrite of its current version.

If you already own VFE or are considering it, you probably already have a good handle on n-tier architecture and are well aware of its many benefits. F1 Technologies includes a discussion of the n-tier architecture and how it impacted the design of VFE in the VFE documentation under "n-tier applications and the Visual FoxExpress framework."

Released in April 1999, the current version of Visual FoxExpress, version 6, was virtually a new product. While you can still see some of the original designs, concepts and, yes, even code from the original Codebook, this is not your father's Codebook.

The Visual FoxExpress IDE

VFE is a Rapid Application Development (RAD) tool for Visual FoxPro 6.0. Using the VFE Integrated Development Environment, or IDE, a developer is removed from many of the mundane and repetitive tasks involved in creating an application with Visual FoxPro.

Application Manager

The Application Manager is a launching pad for the various VFE projects you have built. From the Application Manager, you can select an existing project or build a new one.

Application Builder

The Visual FoxExpress Application Builder is essentially an alternative interface for the Visual FoxPro Project Manager—it's essentially a project manager that's customized for working with the Visual FoxExpress framework. Behind the scenes, the Application Builder works with the Visual FoxPro Project object and manipulates the project just as if you were working with the Project Manager interactively.

Wizards and builders

In keeping with the theme of RAD, the VFE IDE provides dozens of wizards and builders. There is a wizard to create a subclass of each and every one of the major class types described later in this chapter. In addition, VFE has made the wizards data- and program-driven so you can modify them.

A builder is also provided for every control and visual class that you work with. These simplify your job and limit the amount of time spent wading through the properties window.

You can do *much* more with VFE than the wizards and builders provide. Don't fall into the trap that many VFE beginners fall into and assume that if there isn't a builder or wizard for it, it's not possible. This is still VFP, and using VFE in no way changes that or limits your use thereof.

Express Tools
Some of the less frequently used tools in the IDE are called the "Express Tools" on the Express menu. If you expand this menu selection, you will see the following items:

- The *Component Gallery* launches the Visual FoxPro Component Gallery with a VFE catalog built by F1 Technologies. This catalog contains all of the VFE framework classes.

- The *Wizard Manager* allows you to modify the behavior of the VFE wizards by modifying the database that drives their behavior.

- The *Edit Default Menu Choices* selection launches a menu editor that allows you to modify the menu structure that's used when a new application is created.

The Visual FoxExpress framework
Behind the scenes of the IDE's wizards and builders, you are actually creating subclasses of the classes provided by VFE. Once those subclasses are created, you'll set properties in order to tailor their behavior for your needs. While the IDE would be useless without the framework, the framework is the meat and potatoes of VFE. This is where the hundreds of prebuilt classes and thousands of lines of code reside that allow you to build a feature-rich program in less time than you thought possible.

The framework contains many layers. Each layer is designed to carry out a certain function. The layers are put one on top of another, much like a layer cake. Each layer generally only communicates with the layers it is connected to. For example, to build a maintenance screen in VFE, you would create a data file that's accessed by a cursor object, which is used by the business object, which provides services to a presentation object that contains the text boxes and other controls that show the data to the user.

Let's take a brief look at the major pieces you will use when building your application. Later we will actually get our hands dirty and build some of this stuff, but for now, just sit back and familiarize yourself with the basic pieces.

Starting at the back
Generally you will build the application from back to front. The back of the application would be the data, and the front would be the user interface. Of course, you don't have to do all of the back, then all of the middle, then the entire front—rather, you just build the layers

that build upon each other. So let's get to work and learn about the classes you are creating when you use this wonderful IDE.

Application design
You didn't think you were going to start coding yet, did you? Of course, the first step of any good application is the up-front design and specification. The majority of object-oriented programmers, ourselves included, prefer to utilize the Unified Modeling Language.

The Unified Modeling Language (UML) is the industry-standard language for specifying, visualizing, constructing and documenting the artifacts of software systems. With UML, programmers and application architects can make a blueprint of a project, which, in turn, makes the actual software development process easier.

Start with a solid application design and specification. If you are using UML, you would create use case documents, class diagrams, sequence diagrams and other design artifacts that document the entities and processes of your application. Don't skip this step or dismiss it as a waste of time. The time and effort you spend here will greatly enhance and simplify your implementation.

Of course, three paragraphs can't even begin to scratch the surface of program design and object modeling—these topics could take up several chapters of their own and are beyond the scope of this book. The good news is that those chapters have already been written, and you can find them in Markus Eggers' book, *Introduction to Object Oriented Programming in VFP 6.0*, from Hentzenwerke Publishing. We highly recommend it.

Now, on to the next layer.

The database
The first step in building your application will be to create your database. Of course, your database is derived from the database models you created in the design step of your project.

As you know, the database will contain the data relevant to your business domain. In other words, if you are writing a general ledger application, you need to store the ledger entries, chart of accounts, posting dates and so forth. Also, you'll be storing some application data—user names, lookup tables, user preferences and so on.

However, VFE isn't satisfied with the average amount of data. So, in addition to the data, you will also need to create metadata.

Metadata
Simply put, this is data about data. This is also referred to by some as a data dictionary. However, the framework needs to know a lot more about the data than the names of tables, columns and rows. During design time and run time, the framework and the IDE get a large amount of information from the metadata.

VFE uses a public domain metadata format known as DBCX. DBCX is short hand for DBC eXtensions. This standard was originally put together by F1 Technologies, Stonefield, Flash and MicroMega. VFE 6.0 uses the updated version 2 of this standard, known as DBCX2. Most of the DBCX2 upgrade was designed and written by Doug Hennig of Stonefield, with some assistance from F1 Technologies.

Basically, DBCX2 is a framework (a set of classes that work together) designed to build and maintain metadata. It is flexible and extendible, and F1 has created a specific DBCX2 manager, also known as the metadata manager, for VFE to maintain and manipulate the metadata that the framework and IDE use. As we discuss the features of the framework and IDE in more detail, you will see how various properties of the metadata are used and how you can modify them to change the behavior of your finished application without changing any code.

The metadata manager is actually more of a system-level service that all layers of the framework utilize to get information about the data, and is not specifically layered between the data and the data classes. If you would like to read more about DBCX2, the documentation is provided with your VFE install in \VFE6\HELP\DBCXREF.DOC.

Data classes
This actually brings us to the meat of the first layer of the framework—the data layer. The data layer basically consists of two classes that are used by the framework to manipulate data. You will generally write your code using methods and properties of the data classes rather than manipulating the data directly. This allows for more reusable and maintainable code. It also allows for the possibility of changing the data layer to access a completely different type of data, such as XML. Let's take a look at these data classes.

Cursor class
The first of the two data classes is the *cursor* class. As the name suggests, the cursor class allows you to manipulate a VFP cursor. However, because the data access has been encapsulated into the cursor class, the underlying cursor can be a local table, a remote view or even an ADO record set.

The main functionality of the cursor class is to perform create, retrieve, update and delete (CRUD) operations on the underlying data source. However, it doesn't stop there—in addition to adding a record, the cursor class will populate your primary key with a unique value, if that's what you want. So you can see the power of the cursor class already.

The cursor class maintains two collections (see the Note) of objects—a *fields* collection and a *view parameters* collection. These objects are very similar, as both the field class and the view parameter class are subclasses of the AbstractDataItem class.

> *Collections are heavily used in the VFE framework, and it is important for you to know what they are and how they work in order to understand much of the VFE architecture. A collection consists of many like objects grouped together. VFE includes a collection class that emulates the native collections you would find in Visual Basic or Java. The most common type you will find is what VFE calls a "reference collection," in which the collection object contains an array that holds all the references to the objects. All collections have a common interface you can use to access the contained objects. "Item" is an array property that you subscript with either the number of the object in the collection or the name.*
>
> *For example, let's assume that the object oCustomer has a phones collection. In order to reference the first phone number object in the collection, you would write the following:*

```
oPhone = oCustomer.Phones.Item(1)
```

(Because Item is an array, you could also use brackets instead of parentheses.) If you knew the name of the phone object you wanted to access, you could also specify it by name:

```
oPhone = oCustomer.Phones.Item['Home']
```

Once you understand this concept, VFE will be much easier for you. In a word, VFE is a collectionfest.

Abstract data item
The abstract data item is to a field or view parameter what the cursor class is to the cursor. The actual classes used are the field class and the view parameter class.

Field class
When the cursor class is instantiated, it will create an instance of the field class for each field in the cursor. This class will encapsulate all the access to that field. This sounds like a lot of overhead, but the init code is very minimal, so the field classes instantiate very quickly.

The field object knows what field it is connected to. This class will also contain all the metadata properties about that field, and it includes methods to update and validate the field's value as needed.

In keeping with the layered approach, the cursor object will talk to the field object. For example, prior to a record being saved to the underlying data source, the cursor object will ask each field object to validate itself. If all field objects return OK, the cursor object will then continue and save the record to disk.

View parameter class
The view parameter class is basically the same as the field class, except that it encapsulates all the actions that need to be taken with a view parameter. The main difference is that while the field class is primarily concerned with persistent data, the view parameter class is primarily concerned with manipulating values used for queries.

The data environment
Not unlike the data environment of a VFP form, VFE also contains a data environment (or DE) class. The difference is that the DE in the framework is a stand-alone class and acts as a container of cursor classes.

For example, if you have an Invoice form, you may want to build an Invoice data environment. This environment may contain the Invoice cursor and the InvoiceDetail cursor. This is mainly a design-time tool that simplifies specifying the cursors you will need for a specific use. The good thing is that the data environment class in VFE stands by itself as a reusable, encapsulated entity. The generic VFP approach requires you to define a form's data environment as part of the form that is then directly tied to a form. The VFE data environment has been separated from the form. For example, you could reuse your Invoice data environment for an Invoice report that requires the same data environment.

As you'll see later, VFE handles relations through business objects, so in general a data environment will contain a single cursor.

During run time, once the data environment object has loaded its cursors it may not be used by the application any further. However, the DE does contain methods to locate and return contained cursor references as well as the name of the "primary cursor," which you will learn about a little later.

As we continue, you'll recognize the distinct layers we are building upon the foundation of the data, and that we're working our way up to the user interface by creating reusable and well-encapsulated classes. Of course, the data environment provides services to the business object.

Business object

Unless you have been buried in a Y2K bunker for the past several years, you have undoubtedly heard the term "business object," or "bizobj" for short. A bizobj is the encapsulated representation of a real-world entity such as a customer, employee, invoice, contact, phone call or deposit.

You will create a bizobj class for each entity in your application. The bizobj will use the data environment you specify to instantiate the cursor objects. The bizobj class in the framework is one of the most powerful classes that you will use. It contains all the code needed to create, retrieve, update and delete your entities. In addition, the bizobj class contains code to relate itself to other business objects in order to create the entity relationships that you have created in your class model.

The CRUD methods in the bizobj class pass the message (or collaborate, in OOP talk) with the cursor class to actually carry out these functions. Generally, each business object has a primary cursor. The primary cursor is used by the bizobj to store information about the entity that it represents. If other cursors exist in the data environment, they are typically for lookup or validation purposes and aren't actually modified by the bizobj.

Presentation object

The presentation object is the first layer in the framework that actually contains a visual aspect. It is the presentation object that will contain your user interface controls such as text boxes, labels and buttons. In addition to the bizobj and cursor classes, this layer also contains the CRUD methods in its programming interface.

This may seem repetitive, but think of the presentation object as a control panel. The control panel has a small switch that's connected to a high-powered relay. When the switch of the control panel is activated, this activates the relay. The relay then sends power to a motor, which turns the wheels.

Think of the CRUD methods of the presentation object as similar switches. The save "switch" sends a message to (collaborates with) the bizobj to save, which sends the message to the cursor object to save. This continues until the correct layer handles the message. In addition to passing the message to save, each layer can also act on the message prior to passing it to the next layer. You'll find a more detailed explanation of this "chain of responsibility" in Chapter 10, "How It Works."

You will generally create a presentation object for each business object in your application, although this is not required. Presentation objects are reusable also. For example, you can create a customer presentation object that you use on the Customer form and on the Invoice form.

Speaking of forms, there's only one more major class to cover here—the form.

Form class

The form class is the container for your presentation object. A form may contain one or more presentation objects based on your needs and desires. The form is also the object that is called from the menu and connected to a specific toolbar.

Forms in VFE are fairly intelligent in that they are resizable and can also remember their last position if you so desire.

Miscellaneous classes

While we have covered the main building blocks to be used in your application, there are also many other classes in the VFE class libraries that, while less visible, are no less important. Brief descriptions of them follow.

Application object

This is actually the glue that holds the application together. The application object is a container that holds most of the miscellaneous classes. As the first object that is instantiated, the application object will instantiate many system-level classes. These classes provide many system-level services to all the framework classes. Examples of these application-level services include a forms manager, an error handler, a messaging class, a toolbar manager, a business object manager, a metadata manager and an abstract factory, among others.

Controls

From the users' perspective, the application is what they see. VFE has subclassed all of the VFP base class controls and enhanced them to work within the framework. The controls know how to bind to the VFE field objects, gather data from the metadata and integrate with the VFE security system, among many other things. There is also a toolbar class and controls designed to work in the toolbars.

You build VFE menus with the native VFP Menu Designer. However, when you generate the actual menu program, the result is an object-based menu, and this allows the menus to be integrated with the VFE security system in a much easier fashion. In addition, you can create custom menu classes.

Summary

This chapter has given you an overview of what makes up the product we know as Visual FoxExpress. You have learned that there are two major components of this product. The first is the Integrated Development Environment, which is a collection of tools, wizards and builders. The second consists of the classes that make up the framework of code with which you will build your application.

This chapter has given you an idea of what to expect from this book. We will cover each of the topics presented here in more detail, and explain how all the pieces work together and how you can use them to "Create Visual FoxPro Applications with Visual FoxExpress."

Chapter 2
Before You Start

In this chapter, we will take a look at how to set up your system to create a VFE application. There are also several methods you could use to complete certain tasks—we will discuss which of those methods we've chosen and why.

The first item of business is to install VFE 6.0. You are welcome to install it in any location on your computer you wish, but it will make it easier to use the source code that accompanies this book if you install the framework in the default directory of drive C:. If you don't do this, the classes in your files will not be able to locate their parent classes.

Second, it's recommended that you create a directory outside of the framework structure in which to store your applications. This is contrary to the VFE tutorial, but it makes it much easier to reinstall the framework if it becomes corrupted or you install an update incorrectly.

 Finally, be sure you have installed VFE Service Pack 2, which contains many bug fixes and enhancements to the original release. In addition, F1 Technologies has provided a database of all the fixes released since the service pack—you should install these also. The Developer Download files for this book, available at www.hentzenwerke.com, were created with VFE patched with Service Pack 2.

For your convenience, here are the URLs where you can obtain the VFE updates:

- Service Pack 2: http://www.f1tech.com/updates.htm

- Fixes Release after SP2: http://www.f1tech.com/Bugs

VFE also relies on many of the bug fixes that were made to Visual FoxPro in Visual Studio Service Pack 3. If you haven't installed Visual Studio Service Pack 3, it is highly recommended that you do so before continuing with VFE. It is also rumored that Visual Studio Service Pack 4 will be released very soon now, and it may be available at the time you are reading this book. Check the following locations for more information:

- Visual FoxPro homepage: http://msdn.microsoft.com/vfoxpro/

- Visual Studio Service Pack 3:
  http://msdn.microsoft.com/vstudio/sp/vs6sp3/default.asp

Your development environment

Even though we are using VFE as a tool, there is no reason to stop using all those other wonderful VFP tools that you've used in the past. You will still be able to use them as long as you plan in advance. Because the Application Builder is modal once it is running, you lose access to the command window and many menu options while running VFE.

We have created a startup program for VFP that's to be run prior to working in the VFE IDE. This program provides a few ways around the modality of VFE. Here's what it looks like:

10   Creating Visual FoxPro Applications with Visual FoxExpress

```
#DEFINE BOBPATH \vfp,\vfp\supercls,\vfp\stonefld\sdt,\vfp\stonefld\sdt\SOURCE

* This is a generic startup program to establish VFP development environment
* variable needed to check if the SDT menu option is already installed
LOCAL nBarCount,nCurBar,lRunSDT

CLOSE ALL
CLEAR ALL
SET CLASSLIB TO
SET LIBRARY TO
SET ASSERTS ON
ON ERROR
ON SHUTDOWN
POP KEY ALL

*-- Set up Hackers Guide on ALT-F1
ON KEY LABEL ALT-F1 RUN /N C:\WINNT\HH.EXE c:\vfp\books\hackfox.chm
* -- Set up HotKey to re-call this program
ON KEY LABEL ALT-S do \vfp\startup
* -- Set up HotKey to suspend VFE
ON KEY LABEL ALT-F10 suspend

SET PATH TO BOBPATH

* -- Call SDT if it is not on the Tools menu!
lRunSDT = .T.
nBarCount = CNTBAR('_MSM_TOOLS')
FOR nCurBar = 1 TO nBarCount
   IF 'STONE' $ UPPER( PRMBAR('_MSM_TOOLS', GETBAR('_MSM_TOOLS',nCurBar) ) )
     lRunSDT = .F.
     EXIT
   ENDIF
ENDFOR &&* nCurBar = 1 to nVarCount
IF lRunSDT
  DO sdt
ENDIF

* -- Call Super Class and dock on bottom toolbar
supercls(,,3)

* -- If this program was called from another program
*    exit here
IF PROGRAM(-1) > 1
  RETURN
ENDIF

* -- Run Visual FoxExpress
_GENMENU = ADDBS(CURDIR())+'tools\genmenux\genmenux.prg'
_INCLUDE = '\vfe6\vfeframe\include\vfe.h'
CD C:\VFE6
DO VFE.EXE
```

The comments are pretty self-explanatory, but let's take a quick look at what this little startup program does.

1. It defines a constant that holds the custom path. This path contains all the add-ons that are used with VFP and will remain in effect after loading VFE.

2. It sets some variables and cleans up the environment. We do this because not only is this the startup program, but it is also the cleanup program.

3. It sets a hot key to run the Hackers' Guide HTML Help file. This book includes more information about VFP than you will ever need to know, it's part of the Hentzenwerke Essentials collection.

4. A hot key (Alt-S) is set that can be used to call this program again. The full path is included because it is possible that the path to this program will no longer be in the menu after running or debugging the application.

5. Another hot key (Alt-F10) is set to suspend the running application. This is handy when you want to suspend the VFE Application Manager and use the command window.

6. At this point, it sets the path to the custom path constant built previously.

7. This next little bit of code will call the Stonefield Database Toolkit application. We basically look to see whether it is already added to the Tools menu. As nice as the SDT splash screen is, one can become tired of looking at it.

8. The final add-on that's called is Ken Levy's Super Class, which enables you to view method code of the parent class of the class you are editing from within the editor. It also has an IntelliSense-like interface that lists all the properties and methods of various objects in addition to all the VFP functions and their parameters.

9. The next bit of code will exit out of the program if it was called from another program. This allows you to press Alt-S and have the program run to this point and return. *Voilà*—startup and cleanup rolled into one.

10. Finally, some VFP system variables are set to the values required by VFE, and the VFE 6 executable is run.

At this point you may be wondering why we set up the _GENMENU and _INCLUDE system variables in our startup rather than in CONFIG.FPW, as suggested by F1 Technologies. Well, strangely enough, we don't create *all* of our applications with VFE, so using this method allows for the creation of several VFP configurations. Here's how this is accomplished.

Instead of setting a startup program in the Options page of VFP, we set up multiple desktop shortcuts, each of which has its own start directory and startup programs. In order to call the startup program, we add the name of it to the end of the Target field in the shortcut's Properties page (see **Figure 1**). You can also change the "Start in" field to the specific directory you wish to use for that configuration.

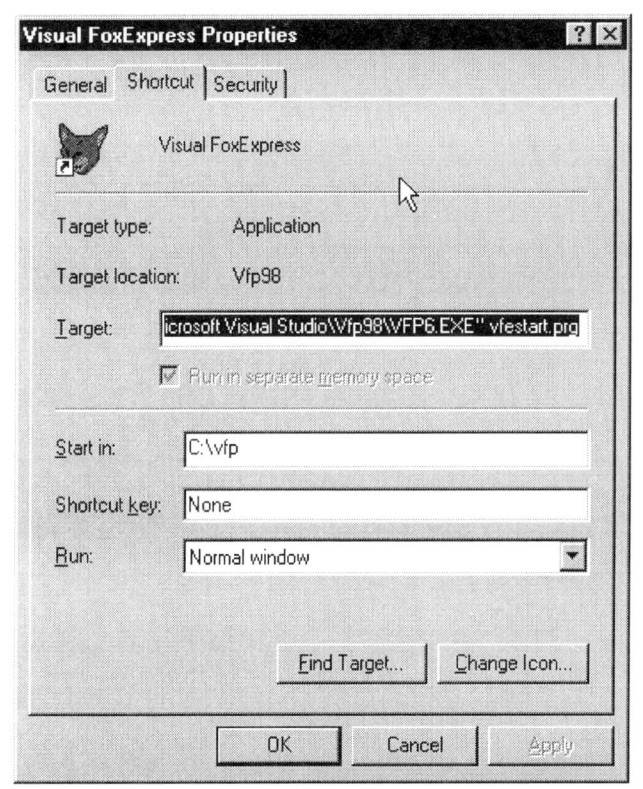

Figure 1. The Properties page of a VFP shortcut customized to run VFESTART.PRG at startup.

ASSIST

The default VFE install populates the _ASSIST system variable with VFE.EXE. The ASSIST command has been with us since the dBase III+ days. dBase III+ is a database management application upon which FoxPro was based, and it was command-compatible with dBase III+.

Typing the ASSIST command at the dot prompt of dBase III+ ran a menu system that was written in dBase III+ code. Because FoxPro was compatible with that software, the ASSIST command was also included in the language. However, the FoxPro application had menus available all the time, so the ASSIST command was extended to run whatever program you had populated the _ASSIST system variable with.

The makers of VFE figured no one was using ASSIST, so they decided it would be a nice idea to set up VFP during the VFE install so that when you typed ASSI in the command window, the VFE IDE would start up.

One of the authors of Visual FoxExpress, Mike Feltman, used to work at Fox Software and actually did some of the development work on a program called FoxCentral, which used to be mapped to the ASSIST command in FoxBase+—perhaps this is where the idea originated.

Use a client/server mentality

If you are 100 percent certain that your application will never, ever, possibly need to access a remote database, you can skip this section. If not, there are some basic guidelines you should follow when you are designing and building your application. Just remember, "never, ever" is a very long time!

- Never retrieve data you don't need. This seems like common sense, but you'd be surprised how often the support forums get questions like "Why is my combo box so slow with 20,000 records in it?"

- When you do retrieve data, only retrieve the least amount you need. This means not only restricting the depth of the data you query or the number of rows, but also restricting the width of the data you query, or the number of fields. For example, if you are presenting a pick list of customers, just query the name. Once you have the ID of the customer you need, you can retrieve all the fields of that one record.

- Lists should be empty until you have some idea of the data you need to display. For example, if you are writing an application for a company that creates assemblies and has a list of 30,000 parts, don't display all 30,000 parts in the list. Instead, ask them to somehow identify the part, so your query may only bring back 50 records for them to choose from. At this point you're probably thinking that your users insist on having a list of all the records, and that they want to be able to search through the list to find the record they're seeking. This may be the case because it's what your users are accustomed to; however, most users who thought they needed the whole list quickly realize that they are more productive if they're able to narrow the list down to a small set of records. F1 Technologies actually did studies with some of their consulting customers to verify this.

If you follow these guidelines, you should be able to avoid two potential problems if you do need to move to a remote database. The first is that your application's performance will still be outstanding, and it will not create a lot of network traffic. Second, and perhaps more important, your users will be conditioned to put parameters in for lists and search pages, as opposed to your putting all 30,000 parts in a grid.

Now, there are many fantastic things to say about VFE, but the lookup and validations implementation doesn't really follow these guidelines. Realistically, for F1 Technologies to be able to build these kinds of features into the framework, the framework would have to have domain-specific knowledge. The good news is that VFE is very easy to extend and modify; we'll look at some of these modifications in Chapter 12, "Data Validation."

The easiest way to accomplish all of these things is to use views.

Why views instead of tables

There is no doubt that in FoxPro 2.6, most people used tables and related them with indexes to get the data they needed. While this worked well, there were some problems. What did you have to do to create a grid to show the child data of a parent file? Many times we created a filter on a large record set. The slowest control in tarnation is a grid viewing filtered data.

Another problem we often dealt with was processing a group of records that met certain criteria. Once again the filter came to the rescue, or perhaps using SCAN FOR was your solution. Sometimes the conditions were a bit slow.

These days, many writings and articles seem to indicate that most people have moved to record set processing—that is, using a SELECT statement or a view to retrieve only the records the meet your parameters. All of a sudden your child grids are flying, and you are writing fewer IFs and FORs in your code, which makes it more readable and maintainable.

The bottom line is that VFE was designed with views in mind. Here are some of the main advantages of using views over tables:

- You can limit the number of records you are retrieving. This eliminates filters and valid record-checking code in your procedures.

- You can limit the number of fields you are retrieving. This will increase performance and lessen the amount of network traffic your application uses.

- You can order the fields without changing the physical layout of the file. This can allow your users to define the order in which they want a pick list to display the fields, without your having to modify any code.

- For child operations, particularly where grids are involved, views will work faster than tables. When a child table is included in a grid, internally VFP uses SET FILTER to only display the records for the current parent. During development, the performance difference is negligible when you're working with small data sets, but with large amounts of live data, child grids can be excruciatingly slow.

- Views allow fields from multiple tables to be contained in a single cursor. This is very handy when you need to present a list of records including a description of a foreign key. Of course, you can also do this with SET RELATION, but with SET RELATION you can't order by the description of the foreign key. You can with views.

- VFE provides the ability to create indexes on views, which allows for some very powerful features such as the ability of the views order to be changed on the fly without requerying, and Rushmore-optimizable searches within a view's record set, among others.

- Child tables must be ordered by the foreign key in order to be the target of RELATION in VFP. A child view can be ordered in any fashion you like, and its order can be changed on the fly.

- If you use row-level or field-level rules in the DBC, they can often cause problems when attempting to navigate within buffered data. Using views allows you to put these rules on the underlying tables and only deal with them when you are actually trying to commit the data.

- Views can be upsized to remote views to simplify the conversion to a remote data source.

Now, we're not going to tell you not to use tables, but often when you hit the wall using tables and ask F1 for help, their response is to use views. It's your choice. This book will basically concentrate on using views for all data access. As we mentioned earlier, you'll get better performance, simpler code and, heck, VFE was really designed with views in mind. The VFE support conference constantly contains questions from people trying to implement something difficult with tables that can easily be accomplished with views.

For more discussion on views vs. tables, see *Effective Techniques for Application Development with Visual FoxPro 6.0* by Booth and Sawyer.

About grids and lists

This might raise some hackles, but we're going to attack another old standard: the grid. Now, don't misunderstand, there's nothing wrong with the way grids present data; the spreadsheet is probably one of the most recognized and used data entry forms on the planet. But even in Excel, you don't actually enter the data on the grid, do you? Nope, you enter your data in that little text box at the top of the screen under the toolbars. So take a hint from Excel: Display your data in rows and columns, sure, but keep the data entry in text boxes and other controls outside of the grid.

Another problem with the VFP grid is that there is no way to bind it to an array. You bought VFE to create n-tier applications, didn't you? You eventually want to scale your application to multiple tiers, with the business layer in a separate physical middle tier. Well, the business layer returns data as a record set, but it will be in an array or an ADO record set—not a VFP cursor. Again, you can't bind a grid to an array or an ADO record set.

Why not use a list box control instead? The ActiveX list box, which ships with VFP, will support arrays and an ADO record set. In the current version of VFE, the framework's wizards and builders will use a grid control to implement a list of data, even if it is a read-only pick list. However, we have it on pretty good authority from F1 that the cListView class is almost plug-in compatible for cGrid and will give you much more functionality (to list records) than a grid will. Future releases will integrate this control into the builders and wizards also. The next time you look at your list of e-mail in Outlook, think about how you would do what its list box does with a VFP grid.

Related tables vs. parameterized views

One of the most pervasive interfaces found in most business applications involves related tables. There are three common types of related data you will find in business applications.

The first type of relationship is *one-to-many*, also called a *parent-child* relationship. In a one-to-many relationship, you will find that for each record (or row) in the parent table, there will be one or more rows in the child table. Examples of this are a Customer having multiple Addresses or a Customer having many Invoices.

The second type of relationship is *many-to-one*. In this relationship, you will find that many rows in a table are related to the same row in the related table. An example of the many-to-one relationship is the ID number of a part being stored in a Purchase Order table that identifies the one row in the Parts table. Many Purchase Orders could order this single part.

The third relationship, which is a bit more difficult to understand, is the *many-to-many* relationship. You should be able to deduce by now that many rows in table 1 would be related to many rows in table 2. In most cases, a third table, known as an association table, is created to link the many-to-many tables together. You will see an example of this in the data scheme for our tutorial: A Student table is related to a Course table. Each student is registered for many courses, and each course contains many students. The StudentCourse table will be the table that associates this many-to-many relationship.

You may also come across the term "one-to-one." This is the same as one-to-many; however, the many side is restricted to having one record for each record in the parent table (for example, each man has one wife).

Relating tables

In previous versions of FoxPro, the most popular method of implementing these types of relationships was to open both tables and set a relationship with the SET RELATION TO command. This command would direct FoxPro to automatically find the related record in the child file if you moved the file in the parent file. This was fine if there was only one matching record in the child file, but what if there were many?

If you were processing the "many" side of the relationship, you would perhaps use the SCAN WHILE command. This actually worked very well if you were processing all the child records. However, things became more complicated and processed more slowly if you only wanted to process particular child records. Most times you would add a FOR clause to the SCAN command. These techniques worked fairly well during processing. The main problem arose if you wanted to view these records.

The sad truth of the matter is that to display these records, we usually used the BROWSE command. As spoiled as we were with FoxPro and the Rushmore Optimization of the FOR clause in a SCAN, you had to use a filter to display those specific records in a BROWSE. This is where things slowed down.

Parameterized views

With the advent of VFP came the parameterized view. This allows you to create a cursor that contains only those records that meet your criteria. You can use a variable as a parameter that allows you to define the criteria at run time by modifying the value of the variable.

Working with a parameterized view greatly simplifies working with related files. Now the child side of the relationship only contains the records that are related. This greatly increases the performance of LOCATE, SUM, COUNT and other powerful commands found in VFP.

In addition, the performance of your user interface will also increase. There is no longer a need to use a SET FILTER to limit the records shown in a grid. (A grid is a fancy way to set up a browse in VFP.)

Using views to create relations has as many advantages over using related tables as using views has over using tables. It is due to this fact, and also the fact the VFE is strongly designed to use views, that we have devoted an entire chapter to creating and using views in VFE.

Key generation for dummies

As VFP programmers, we're taking advantage of the fact that you understand much about data design. We will also assume it to be a given that you, like most other database gurus, have come to accept that creating surrogate keys to identify each record in a database is the correct and only way to go when designing your data. If you haven't done this, you should consult

Booth and Sawyers' book *Effective Techniques for Application Development with Visual FoxPro 6.0*.

If you don't know anything about data or keys, we will give you a crash course and you can take us at our word, or you can spend weeks reading database design books until you are sick of hearing that surrogate keys are the de facto standard.

Primary key

A primary key is a field (or "column," in SQL-speak) or fields that uniquely define a record. They must contain unique values and cannot be null. Due to their importance in databases, primary keys are the most basic of all keys.

To continue the previous discussion, there are basically two places to get values with which to populate the fields of a primary key. One place where these values originate is from the business data. This is known as a business key. An example of a business key would be a phone number. The phone number belongs to the business data—hence the name, business key.

What's the problem, you ask? Everyone will have a phone number. Well, there are several problems that could arise:

- The phone number could change. If you have related files by putting the phone number in a child file, all those records would need to be changed. While it is fairly simple to implement the code to make these changes, it would be unnecessary if the phone number weren't used to identify the records for a person.

- Not everyone has a phone number. While this is unlikely in the year 2000, it is possible. Actually, it is more likely that people will have two or more phone numbers—which is used as the primary key?

- It is possible that the format or length of a phone number will change. Another possibility is that your business will move into a country that has a different phone number format. Primary keys must all be the same type and length.

It is for these and many other reasons that using a surrogate key has become pervasive. A surrogate key is a key that has no meaning or is in no way related to the business data. As a matter of fact, the user never sees them, interacts with them or even needs to know about them.

Type of primary key

As we begin to define default values for our primary keys, you will see that VFE gives us several methods to generate various types of keys. Each type of key has advantages and disadvantages, but VFE leaves it up to you to decide on the type. Here's a brief look at what VFE offers:

- *Expression*—This is not much different from saying, "Tell me what to use, and I'll use it." The expression you use will likely be a function that you have written. You might use this feature when you are dealing with legacy data and need to maintain its integrity with matching keys.

- *Incremental*—Here VFE will maintain the last number used. When you add a record to a table, VFE will get the last value and add one, and you'll have your new primary key value. You can choose to have VFE increment numbers or letters here if you're using a character field. For example, if you set the starting number to be AA000, VFE will increment it up to AA999 and then follow with AB000 and so on.

- *Base62*—This is similar to incremental; however, instead of sticking to the base 10 numeric system of numbers, the 26 letters of the alphabet are added. Wait, that's 26 + 10 = 36. Well, base 62 treats uppercase and lowercase letters as separate digits, so 26 + 26 + 10 = 62 digits used to create base 62 "numbers." Be careful if you use this and plan to upsize to SQL Server, which by default is set up to use a case-insensitive sort order.

- *GUID*—This is a 128-bit string generated by the operating system. The number is generated with a combination of the network card's MAC address (a unique number assigned to every Ethernet card made) and the current time. The number is said to be unique across space and time, and no two will be duplicated. The GUID is actually stored in hexadecimal form in a 16-bit binary field.

We originally decided to use integer keys, as these have been proven to provide the best performance. Mac Rubel did much testing of key types and published his results in *FoxPro Advisor* magazine—they gave indisputable evidence that queries and joins were faster when using integers as primary keys. However, after beginning to use the integer keys in VFE and considering other issues with using these key types, some problems arose.

So, after rethinking this decision and accepting that there were other criteria than performance to consider, it seemed that the GUID key type is generally better to use for generating keys when writing VFE applications. Of course, you are free to choose whichever key type you prefer. Here are the reasons we prefer GUID keys:

- With GUID, the concept of "losing" keys doesn't exist. With integer keys, many people have concerns about generating a key value in a view that ends up being discarded.

- The GUID can be generated at the client and the server. There is no need to communicate with another machine to generate a GUID value, which increases performance, especially in bulk data processing situations.

- No support file (AppIDs) is needed to maintain the last value used. In addition, because there is no support file to query, there are no multi-user performance or conflict issues.

- If you're dealing with a situation where data entry will take place offline, or if data from disconnected users will ultimately be combined, GUIDs will maintain their uniqueness.

- In a remote or distributed deployment, there is no network traffic generated, nor is there a back-end hit needed to create a GUID value.

Perhaps you will consider using GUID keys also.

Naming conventions

There's one final point we'd like to address in this chapter. We used to be sticklers for conventions: Write a list and follow your list. These days, we're a little more relaxed about this and prefer a few guidelines to a strict set of handcuffs.

This is especially true of code formatting. Thanks to the editor coloring and the beautify command, you can make anyone's code look the way you want. We have a standard beautify selection in which we like everyone to leave the code, so our source control doesn't see "beautify" as a code change.

We like to see Hungarian notation for variables, but we don't use it on properties. If you are looking for a nice list of naming conventions for your variables and objects, check out *Object Oriented Programming with Visual FoxPro 6.0* by Markus Egger (from Hentzenwerke Publishing); he provides a nice list of standards.

Here are a few guidelines we try to follow:

- Use descriptive names for classes, variables, properties and methods. VFP allows up to 255 characters for a variable name. While a 255-character name is a bit much, there is no need to use "x" or "y" in your code.

- Declare every variable local. This helps keep your black boxes from leaking and stepping on the code of others. Better to pass a variable by reference than to declare it private.

- Use object prefixes for objects, not classes. The prefix "txt" should be used for a text box object dropped on a form. The class should be named SocialSecurityNumberTextBox, not txtSSN.

- Write your comments before you write your code. This allows you to consider your logic prior to writing the code, and it comments your code without your having to go back and do it later. Try it. You will write better code, it will work the first time and your co-workers will enjoy maintaining it. Okay, maybe not "enjoy," but they won't shudder as much.

- Use the defined constants in VFE.h whenever possible. This makes your code much more readable for those of us who can't remember the key code and return value for everything.

Summary

Well, as you can see, this book puts forth some pretty strong opinions. But hopefully you've seen some solid reasoning to back up the choices presented here. Most of these recommendations come from working with VFP and VFE for thousands of hours, making a lot of mistakes and redoing a lot of things.

Someone once said, "A wise man learns from his mistakes, a very wise man learns from the mistakes of others."

Chapter 3
VFE's IDE

In this chapter, we will take a brief look at the elements of VFE's Integrated Development Environment. If you think of VFE as consisting of two major pieces—the toolbox and the building materials—the IDE would be the toolbox.

What you find when you look in the VFE toolbox is a plethora of tools to help you assemble the framework classes (which are the building materials) into an application. These tools enhance the VFP tools and are specifically aware of the framework classes.

As you learned in Chapter 1, "The Big Picture," there is a wide range of tools in the IDE. These include the Application Manager, Application Builder, wizards and builders. There are also some tools in the IDE that allow you to modify the behavior of the framework. We will briefly describe those here, and we'll take a closer look at some of them later in the book.

The Application Manager is the tool where you will start a new VFE project. So, let's get started and create our Tutorial application with the Application Manager.

Tutorial

At this point, you should have VFE installed on your computer, including Service Pack 2 and all subsequent fixes and updates published on the VFE Web site.

1. Start Visual FoxPro using your VFP shortcut with your VFE-specific startup program.

2. Start the Application Manager by choosing it from the Express menu, or by typing *assist* in the command window. At this point, the Application Manager should be centered in your VFP desktop. If not, refer to the VFE installation directions to see what might have gone wrong.

3. Press the Create button on the VFE Application Manager. This is the leftmost button with the icon that most applications use to designate "new." You will be presented with the first page of a wizard that will step you through the creation of the application project.

4. Click on the command button with the ellipses to create your project file. You will be presented with the VFP New Project dialog, with C:\VFE6 as the current directory. At this point, we will use the functionality of the New File dialog to create a directory in which to store our project, prior to creating the project.

5. Navigate up to the root directory of C:, and then create a new directory named "VFEBook." (If you have already copied the Developer Download files to your PC, the VFEBook directory will already exist on your C: drive; just navigate into it.)

6. Add a directory named "Tutorial" in the VFEBook directory. This will be the "root" directory for your application.

7. Double-click into the Tutorial directory.

8. In the file name field of the dialog, type "booktutorial" as the name of your project, and then click the Save button. You will then be brought back to the wizard, which will have your new project name with the path you created entered for you.

9. Press the Next button on the wizard, which is indicated by the right arrow icon. You will be presented with Step 2.

10. This step presents you with some directory information. We will use all the defaults except for one. Highlight "Intermediate Class Libraries" and press the Select Directory button, or just double-click the selection in the list. You will be presented with the Enter Directory dialog.

11. It would be nice if we were given an ellipses button here, but since we're not, we will have to do it the hard way. Enter "C:\VFEBook\Tutorial\iLibs" in this text box and press the OK button. An information dialog will be presented—read the section "iLibs" later in this chapter for more information on this. Click OK.

12. Press the Next button of the wizard, and you will be presented with Step 3.

13. Enter the information requested in this dialog. We used "Book Tutorial" for the application name. This information will be used to create a splash screen. Also, the name entered here is the name that will be displayed in the Application Manager. The "use local data" switch will be discussed in Chapter 19, "Client/Server." (Remember, you already defined the project/exe name in the first step.)

14. Press the Next button to move to Step 4. Enter the requested information. We left this section blank because we didn't have these files. You can always add these to your application at a later date.

15. Press the Next button on the wizard to move to Step 5. Select the defaults for this step, and then press the Next button to move to Step 6.

16. *Yeah!* VFE is ready to take what it learned in this interrogation and create your project directory structure and a starter or shell application. Press the Finish button.

After much whirring, buzzing, messages and status bars, VFE will complete its task. Your project has been created, and you will now be presented with the Application Builder, which is the main interface you will use to build your VFE application. At this point, you can even run your application following two simple steps:

1. Press the Build button. Make sure the "Build Project" action is selected, and then click the OK button.

2. Press the Run button. With a little luck, your application will run. The Options dialog will be present the first time you run a new app; just press OK, and then you can look around the menu and see which standard forms are already built for you.

For more information on your new application, see Chapter 9, "Your VFP Application." When you're done looking around, choose File | Exit from the menu.

Application Manager

As you can see in **Figure 1**, the Application Manager has eight buttons on it, which represent the functionality of this tool. The VFE documentation does a fine job of describing the basic function of each button; see the VFE documentation topic "The Visual FoxExpress Application Manager."

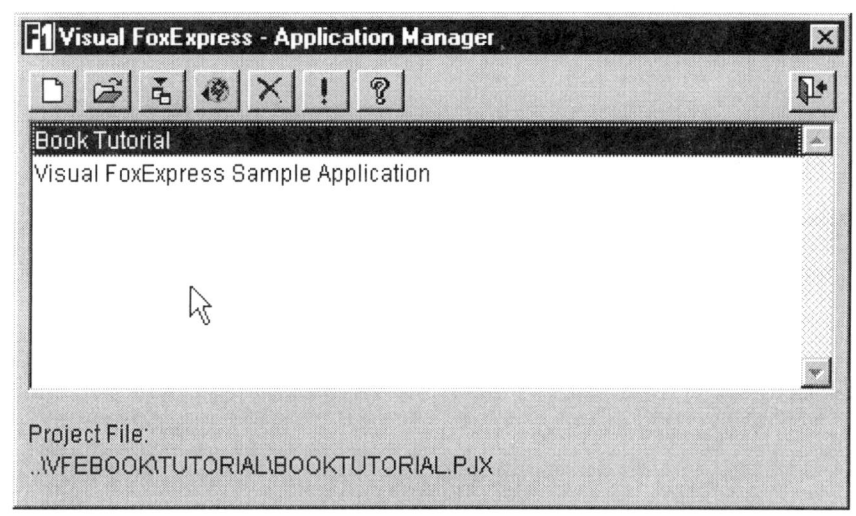

Figure 1. The VFE Application Manager.

By far the most important function of the Application Manager is new project creation. Now we'll explain why we made some of the choices we did when we ran the New Project wizard.

Project directory

If you followed the VFE tutorials, you were prompted to create a directory in a subdirectory beneath VFE6 to hold your VFP projects. While this approach works, we prefer to create a directory outside of the VFE directory to hold application projects.

The main reason for this decision is to allow for the possibility of something becoming corrupted or otherwise messed up inside the VFE6 directory. For example, what if you installed the service pack without telling WinZip to expand folders? All your files would have been placed into the VFE6 directory. Or, if you specified the wrong folder to unzip to, all the files would be in the incorrect directories.

In a situation like this, it would be much simpler to delete the VFE6 directory and reinstall from scratch. This is similar to installing VFP in the program files directory and building applications in a separate directory. Also, if you follow the common directory structure, you should be able to move your applications to a different directory, as there will be no direct references to the framework classes in your application classes.

iLibs

While most of the classes discussed here start with "C" and are in the ...\VFEFramework\Libs directory, the actual classes you use to build your application are the classes that start with "I" for intermediate.

The I-classes or I-layer give you a place to modify the functionality of the shipped VFE classes and still not lose or have to modify the shipped code. When creating applications, you can have all applications share a common set of iLibs, or you can create a new set for each application. Also, you could use a common set for some apps and another common set for other apps.

The reason you created a separate set for this application is because when you get to Chapter 16, "Extending the Framework," you may not want these changes in your apps—there won't be any conflicts because they wouldn't use these specific iLibs.

What gets created?

During all that whirring and buzzing, VFE is creating your new project and an application directory structure. For the most part the directories are empty, but some files are placed there. Let's see what directories are created and why.

1. A VFP project file is created. This project file is populated with all of the class libraries of the framework. VFE also creates some empty class libraries for you to store your classes in.

2. The following subdirectories are created under your project directory:

    a. *Data*—This is the directory where you are expected to store your database and table files.

    b. *Libs*—This is the directory where you are expected to store your class libraries.

    c. *iLibs*—If you specified a directory other than the default, this directory was created in your specified location, and all of the files from the \VFE6\iLibs directory were copied into it.

    d. *MetaData*—This is the directory in which VFE will create your metadata. See Chapter 5, "Metadata," for more information.

    e. *Misc*—A copy of the "default menu" is placed into this directory. You can read more about the default menu later in this chapter.

    f. *Output*—This is an empty directory in which you are expected to place your report layout files.

    g. *Progs*—This is an empty directory in which you are expected to place any PRG files you might create.

3. Perhaps most importantly, a subclass of VFE's application class was created and placed in the class library file AAPP.VCX, which was placed in the Libs directory of your project. The application class is the class that is instantiated to run your application. This class has properties that are populated based on

information you entered in the wizard, such as company name, icon files and so forth.

Application Builder

The Application Builder is the main component of the VFE IDE, and it's where you will spend most of your time (see **Figure 2**). The builder is actually a replacement for the VFP Project Manager. You will see later that the VFP project is actually open but hidden, allowing VFE to reference and update the project using a project hook class. The Application Builder contains three pages, labeled Project, Classes and Files.

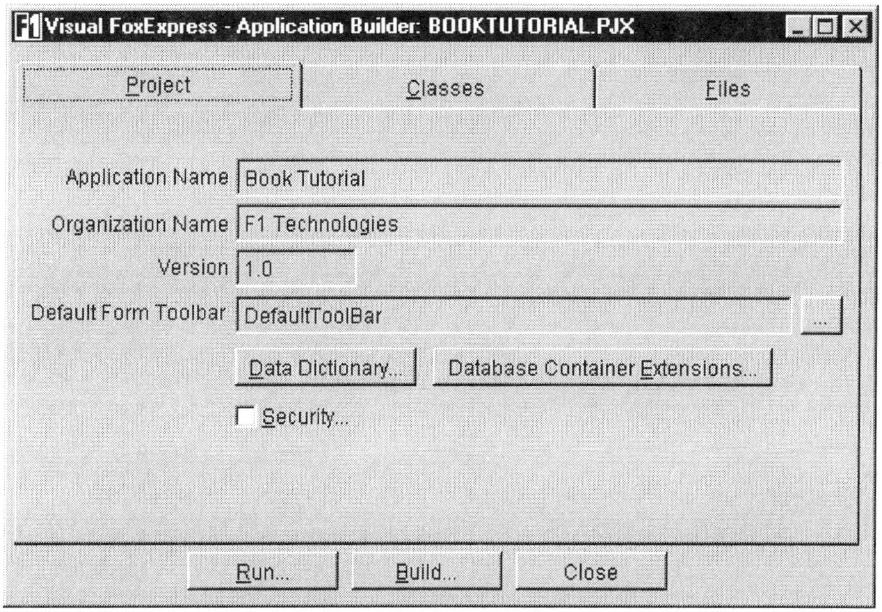

Figure 2. The Application Builder is command central while you are building your app.

The Classes page lists all of the classes you have created for your application. The classes are organized in a tree view that is similar to the Classes page of the VFP Project Manager. However, instead of being listed by class library file, VFE categorizes the classes based on the primary building block classes of the VFE framework, which are the cursor, data item, data environment, business object, presentation object, view parameter container, form, toolbar, output and other. The application object is found in the "other" object category.

We will discuss each of these classes as we work through the framework and build a small tutorial application.

Project page

The Project page lists general information about your project (see Figure 2). This page of the Application Builder is more informative than it is productive. It contains information such as the name of your application, version number and so forth. It is from this page that you also access the DBCX Explorer and the Security setup. We will discuss both of these in detail later in the book.

Classes page

The Classes page provides a categorized view of the classes you have built for your application (see **Figure 3**). You will spend most of your time in the Application Builder on the Classes page. This page is similar to the Files page; however, instead of grouping the files in your project by file name and directory, they are grouped by class.

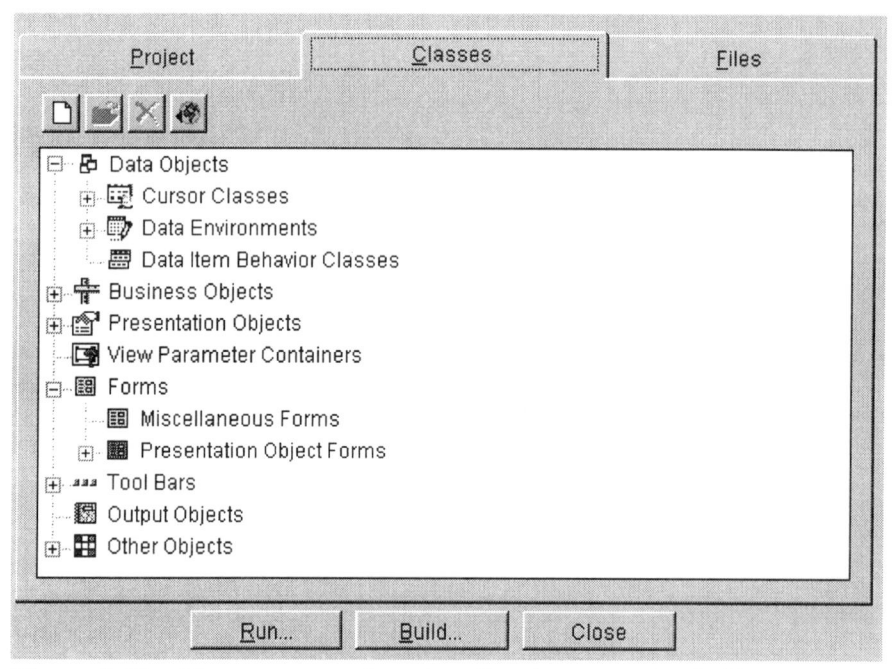

Figure 3. The Classes page categorizes the classes you've built.

There is a slight similarity between the Classes page of VFE's Application Builder and the VFP Project Manager's Classes page, as both list all the class libraries in your project. But VFE takes the organization of your project a step further by classifying the classes list by category. Each of the major nodes on the Application Builder's Classes page tree view corresponds to one of the major class types of VFE. There are five major class types included in the VFE framework that you will work with: the cursor object, data environment object, business object, presentation object and form object.

Files page

The Files page, shown in **Figure 4**, allows you to access all of the items in your project without leaving VFE; you can even open the framework class libraries from here. Here you'll see a tree view that contains all the files that are in the VFP project. As a matter of fact, this page is very similar to the All page of the VFP Project Manager.

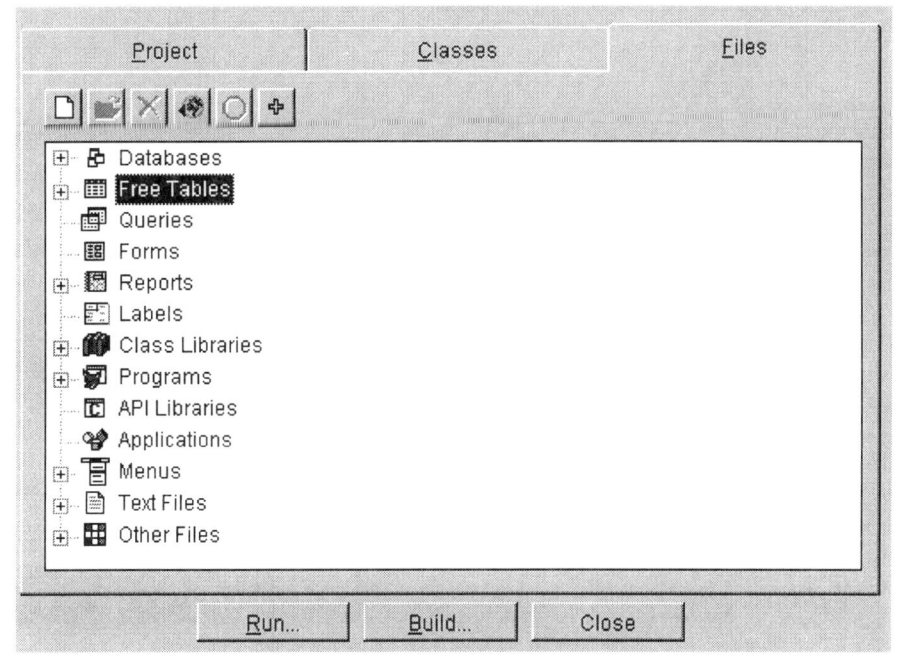

Figure 4. The Files page provides access to all files in your project, including the framework files.

If you need to access a specific file in your application, this page will give you access to it. One thing to remember is that this is the only page from which you can access your menu files. If you've worked with previous versions of VFE, you know that this is a huge improvement. The Files page allows you to access all of the items.

Wizards

If you take a look at the Classes page of the Application Builder (shown in Figure 3), you will see that there are many classes you will be building. VFE has provided a wizard to create each of these classes for you. The wizards bring you through a series of steps requesting the information needed to build the class you are working on. Your responses will be used to populate properties in the class and also to add other classes to your class.

For example, a presentation object is a container for the interface controls you need in order to edit your business object data. The wizard will present you with a list of fields in the business object. For each field you select, an interface control class will be added to a presentation object.

To run a wizard, you select the class type you want to build by highlighting a node on the tree view of the Classes page. Once the class type is highlighted, pressing the New button will bring up a wizard selection dialog. This dialog lists the wizards available for the class you selected. You see, you may want to build more than one type of form. You'll decide between the Modal Form wizard and the Business Object Form wizard.

One thing you should keep in mind is that the wizards are just tools to get you started. You don't *have* to use the wizards, and, by the same token, you are not limited to what the wizards build and how they build it. We will discuss this further in Chapter 16, "Extending the Framework."

Builders

Once you have created the classes with the wizards, you may want to edit them to your specific needs, or change them from how you originally specified them. Or you may want to modify the properties the wizard set when it built a class. Each class in the framework includes a builder. A builder is a small form/program that is written to set the properties and methods of a specific class.

You would launch a builder from the Class Designer. A builder provides access to commonly used properties and also may contain tools to simplify a certain task you need to perform to set up a control. The Grid Builder, for example, allows you to specify the columns you would like to be included in the grid (see **Figure 5**).

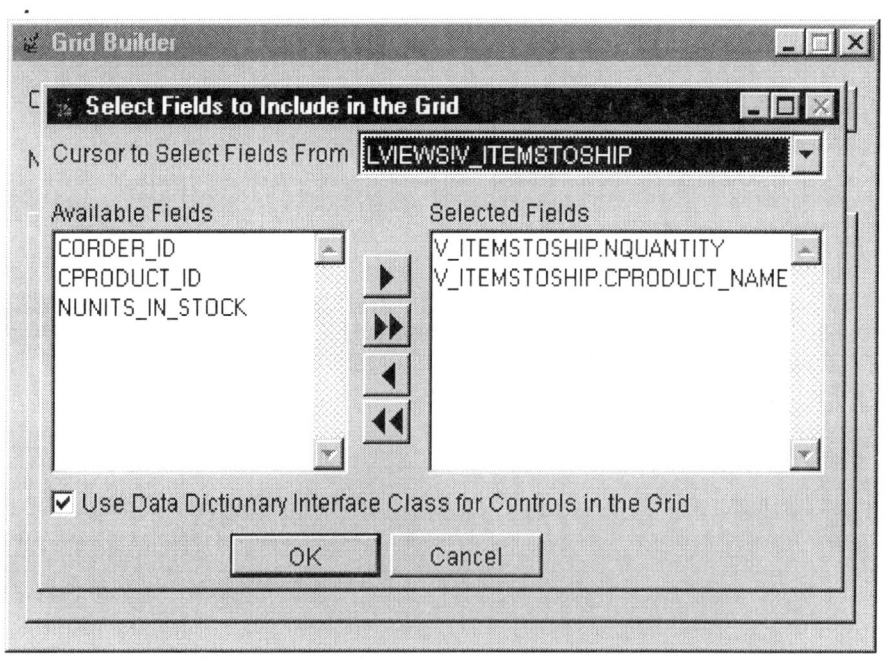

Figure 5. The Grid Builder contains a dialog that allows you to select and order the fields that will be used in the columns.

DBCX Explorer

An important part of the VFE framework is the metadata. Metadata is information stored about the data items in the application database. Both the IDE and the framework use this data at both design time and run time. The DBCX Explorer is a tool provided in VFE, which you will use to edit the metadata (see **Figure 6**).

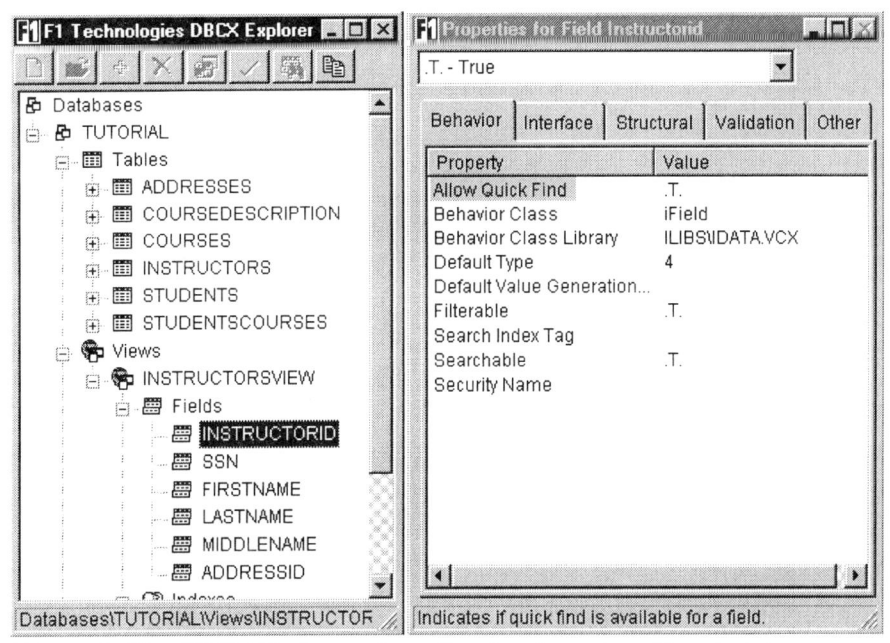

Figure 6. The DBCX Explorer allows the developer to edit metadata.

The DBCX Explorer is a stand-alone set of windows that you will use alongside the Application Builder. The left window of this tool displays the data items that have been created for the application. The window on the right displays the extended attributes that have been created. Each attribute holds information about the highlighted data item.

Preferences

After installing VFE and running the executable either with a startup program or directly from the command line, you should have an Express menu pad on your VFP menu bar. The menu gives you access to the Application Manager, VFE's Help and tutorials, and a Tools menu. What we'll concentrate on here is the Preferences menu item.

If you open the Preferences dialog (see **Figure 7**), the first page you'll see is the Objects page. This is the page you'll wish you knew about before you started building your application if you find that you need to make changes to it. This page lists the particular VFE control class that will be designated when a field is added to the metadata. For example, if you add a text field to a presentation object, the control class for that text box will be set up as "iTextBox." This provides the same functionality for the VFE wizards that the Field Mapping page of the VFP Options dialog provides when you are in the Form Designer.

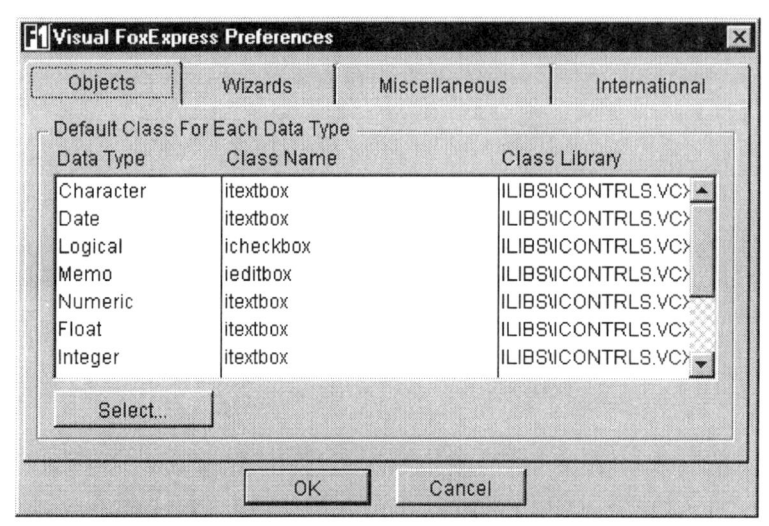

Figure 7. The Objects page of the VFE Preferences dialog displays the class that will be assigned to fields with the matching data type.

The Wizards page is pretty self-explanatory, so we'll skip to the Miscellaneous page (see **Figure 8**). You should be sure to visit this page prior to creating any VFE applications. The main check box you want to look at is "Assume Codebook Naming Conventions." When this is selected and you add a table to the metadata, VFE will chop off the first letter of each field name to populate the caption. We tend not to use Hungarian notation on field names, but if you do, you will always want to turn this check box on.

Figure 8. The Miscellaneous page of the VFE Preferences dialog has the all-important "Assume Codebook Naming Conventions" check box.

Express Tools
While these tools are the more common items with which you will become acquainted, there are a few more items of the IDE that we should take a look at. These items are loaded from the Express Tools menu pad of the Express menu.

Component Gallery
A feature that was added to Visual FoxPro, which was highly regarded by the programming community, was the Component Gallery. This program allows users to set up catalogs of files, grouping and organizing them as they see fit.

VFE has included a Component Gallery catalog that you can access for help when building your application. The gallery is fully functional and can be used when editing classes or writing code (see **Figure 9**).

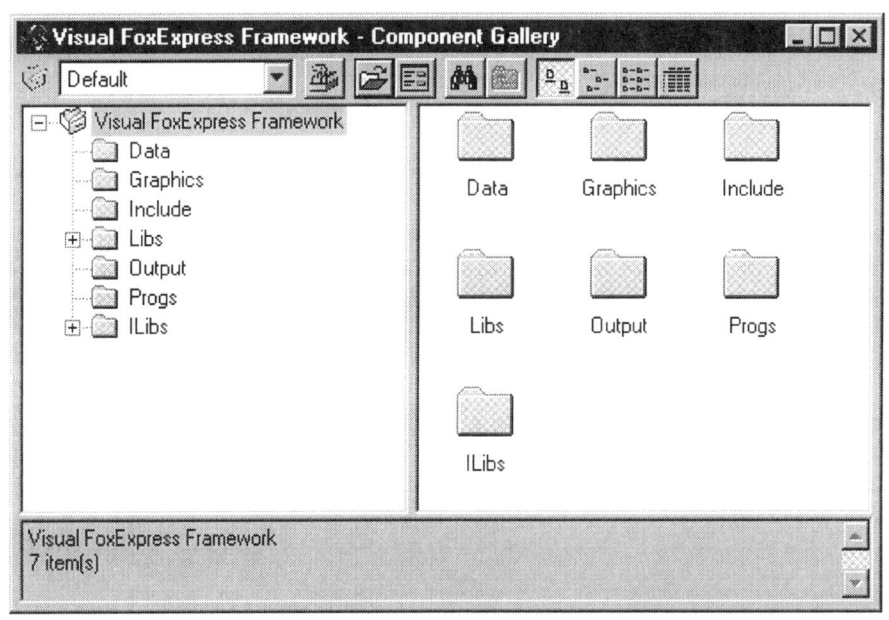

Figure 9. The Component Gallery provides quick and organized access to the framework classes.

Wizard Manager
The Wizard Manager is a tool that allows you to modify the definitions and behavior of the systems wizards. As we mentioned earlier, the wizards are data-driven; each step is defined in a database. The Wizard Manager can modify this database. With the ability to modify the wizards, the framework can be more seamlessly extended by outside programmers (see **Figure 10**).

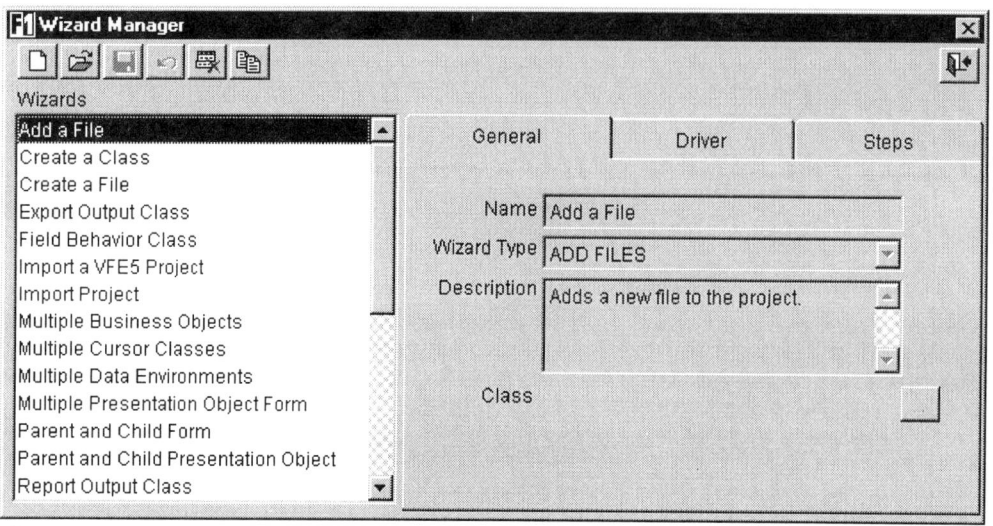

Figure 10. The Wizard Manager allows you to edit the data that drives VFE's wizards.

Edit Default Menu choices

Remember that when you created your first VFE application earlier, the default menu file was copied into the Misc directory of the project. Selecting "Edit Default Menu" from the Tools menu allows you to edit that default menu and customize it to your liking. Keep in mind that this is used for the default menu of all applications. The default is used if you don't change it; you are more than likely to change an application's menu once it has been created.

This function uses the standard VFP menu editor. The file is saved in the framework structure and copied to your application directory by the Application Manager while it is building your new project.

Summary

It's easy to see how using VFE is going to save you time and accelerate your productivity. The Application Manager provides a list of your projects, with tools to build and maintain the projects. The Application Builder gives you an interface that separates your work into categories used in the creation of a VFE application. As you work through the framework, you will recognize each of these categories as the main building block layers of the class libraries.

Finally, you are provided with tools to customize and modify the VFE IDE and framework to perform the way you want it to. It is not the intent of the framework to be an application cookie cutter where you stamp out similar applications. The customization tools are there so that you can insert your style and personality into the applications you build.

Now that you have peered into the toolbox, it's time to look at the building materials you will be molding with these tools. As many of us discover when visiting a home improvement store, you might find something that you didn't know existed before you entered but then decide that you just can't live without it.

Chapter 4
Data Storage and Classes

In this chapter, we will take a look at the requirements for defining and creating your physical data files. You will also learn how to create and use the data classes provided in the VFE framework.

If you have been working with FoxPro and/or Visual FoxPro for several years now, you are aware of the speed and flexibility of the data engine and the richness of the data manipulation language available to you.

However, even with the addition of views and buffering to Visual FoxPro, it is still not possible to pass data from one object to another. The VFE data classes provide an object wrapper around the cursor, fields and view parameters. These encapsulated objects provide a common interface to your data no matter what the underlying source is.

Create your physical database

You must provide a mechanism and location where application data will be physically stored. There are many options you can choose, and this may be dictated by your client or project requirements. A VFE application can access the same data sources supported by VFP. Also, because VFE performs all data access through a small set of classes, it is possible to create subclasses of the VFE data objects to access data, such as XML, that VFP normally wouldn't have direct access to and still use the framework on these types of data sources. Your data source will primarily be either *local data* or *remote data*.

- Local data refers to Visual FoxPro tables stored on disk as DBF files, either in a DBC or as free tables.

- Remote data refers to any ODBC-compliant data source for which there is a Windows ODBC driver. Examples of these databases would be SQL Server, Sybase and Oracle.

In Chapter 2, "Before You Start," you read about the advantage of using views to access your data vs. directly accessing tables. If you follow this advice, the only difference between a SQL Server application and an application that uses local data may be the tool you use to create your physical database. If you are using one of the several data design tools on the market that support more than one DBMS, you'll find the differences small indeed.

Table requirements

There is little restriction in how you design your physical layout. The only real requirement is that each table must have a primary key. Recall that in Chapter 2, we discussed the advantage of using a surrogate key as opposed to a business key.

It doesn't matter to VFE which type of key you select—in the case of legacy data, you may have no choice—as long as each table has a field or combination of fields that can be used to uniquely identify each record. VFE handles primary keys that are made up of a single field automatically throughout the framework; when a compound key is used, you may have to customize some of the methods, such as the WritePrimaryKey() method of the cCursor class.

Tutorial

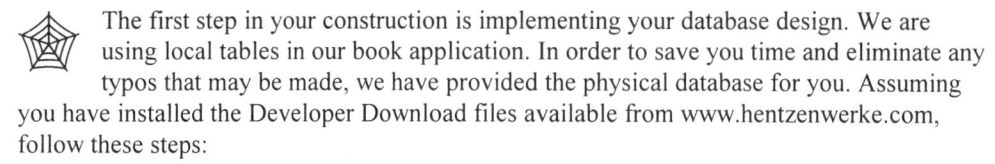

The first step in your construction is implementing your database design. We are using local tables in our book application. In order to save you time and eliminate any typos that may be made, we have provided the physical database for you. Assuming you have installed the Developer Download files available from www.hentzenwerke.com, follow these steps:

1. Using the method of your choice, copy all of the files in \VFEBook\Bob\Data to \VFEBook\Tutorial\Data.

2. Run Visual FoxPro with your VFE startup icon.

3. Start the VFE Application Manager. You can choose it from the Express menu or type ASSIST in the command window.

4. Open the VFE Book Tutorial application by double-clicking on it in the list box, or by highlighting it and pressing the Open button. (From this point on, we will assume you know how to open the tutorial application in the Application Builder.)

5. Click the Data Dictionary button on the Project page. VFE's DBCX Explorer will load. At this point, your screen should look similar to **Figure 1**.

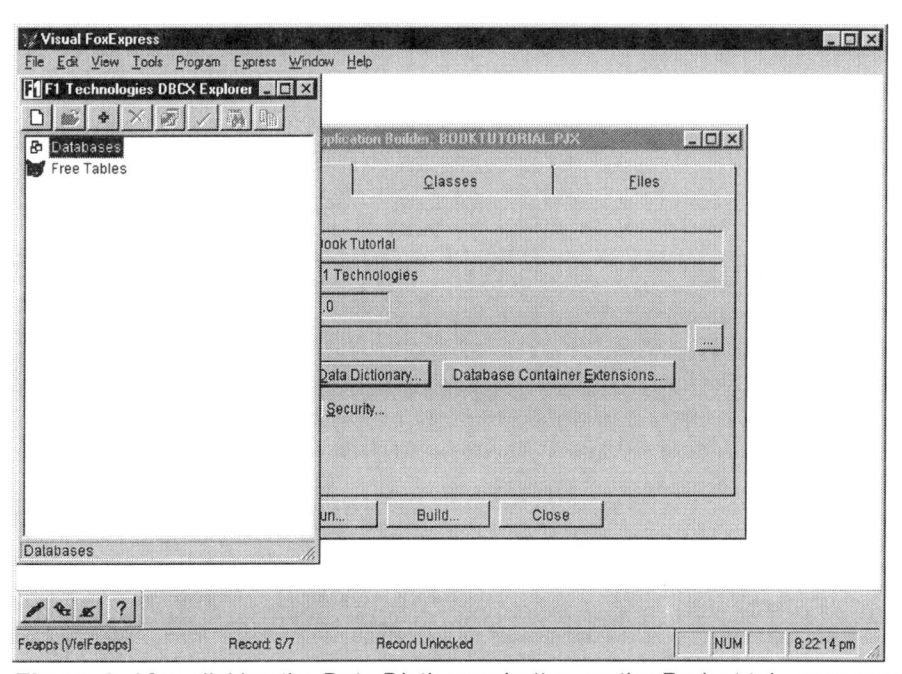

Figure 1. After clicking the Data Dictionary button on the Project tab, your screen will look similar to this.

6. The DBCX Explorer allows you to edit the metadata (see Chapter 5, "Metadata"). In order for the VFE framework to be aware of your database, it must be in the metadata. Make sure that the Database node of the tree view is highlighted in the DBCX Explorer, and then click on the Add button. A File Open dialog will appear.

7. Navigate to the Data directory by double-clicking on the Data folder in the Open dialog. At this point, you should see the TUTORIAL.DBC database container file that you copied in from the Developer Download files.

8. Add this database to the metadata by double-clicking on it, or by highlighting it and clicking the Add button.

9. VFE will display a message box asking whether you want to add the database container to the data dictionary (a.k.a. metadata). Click Yes.

After a few messages are displayed that indicate what items in the database are being processed, the name of the database container will be displayed in the Databases node of the DBCX Explorer. This indicates that the database was successfully added to the metadata. We will discuss the metadata in detail in the next chapter, but it is necessary to have the database in the metadata in order to create the views and the VFE data classes for our application—we'll tackle this next.

Remote data
At this point, if you are exclusively using a remote database there is no need to add it to the metadata because, in the current version, information on the remote tables is not created in the VFE data dictionary/metadata. You will, however, need to create a database container to hold the database connection information and Visual FoxPro view definitions.

For more detailed information on using remote data, take a look at Chapter 19, "Client/Server," which discusses creating client/server applications with VFE and SQL Server.

Create views
If you have chosen to use views with your application, you can define them at this point. As with the local tables, you will be able to modify your views from within the DBCX Explorer or directly from the VFP database editor. In a remote data application, you will only have views in your database container (DBC file).

Once again, if you have created the views outside of the VFE IDE, be sure to load the DBCX Explorer and validate your metadata as shown previously. We will fully discuss metadata and the Explorer in the next chapter. At this point, it's worth noting that VFE doesn't provide any tools to aid in the creation of views. It's generally easier to create the views outside of VFE, and then go into VFE and validate when the design work is finished.

Tutorial data
Let's now take a quick look at the sample data schema. We have tried to create a data structure that is small yet contains many relations, including linking tables for the many-to-many relationships that exist in this layout.

Displayed in **Figure 2** are the tables required to save the data for Tutorial U, a small school or university. The Students, Instructors and CourseDescriptions tables each contain a single record (or row) that will define one entity. The key icon in each table represents the primary key. Recall that the primary key is a unique value that identifies the entity. In this example, the primary keys are 16-byte, binary character data types that will hold GUID values.

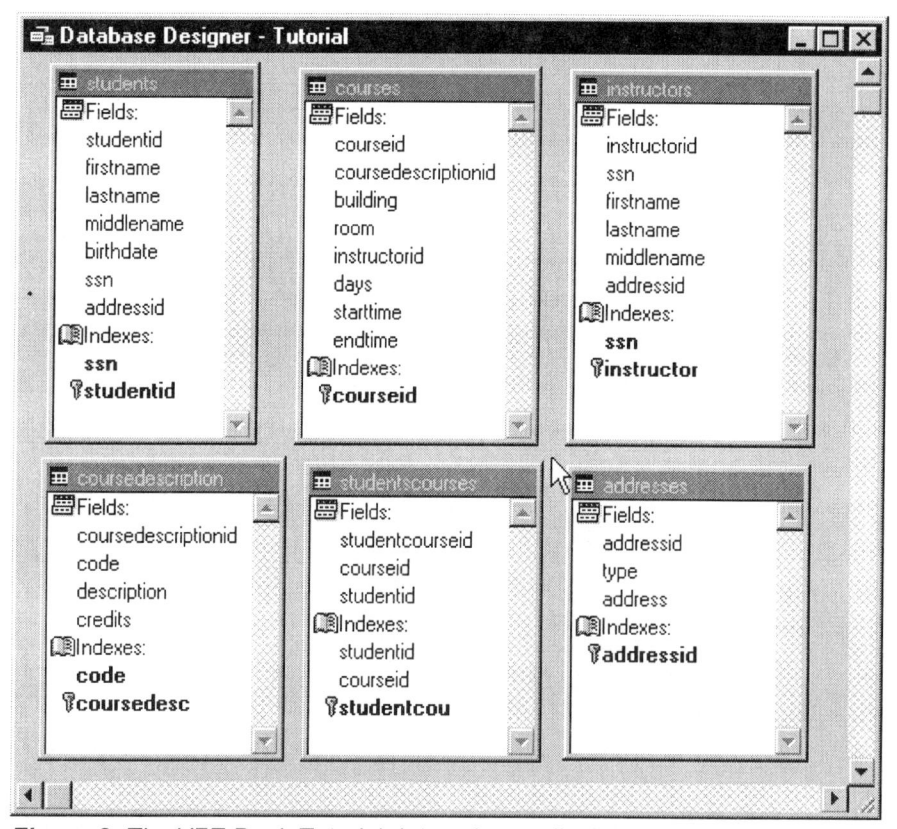

Figure 2. The VFE Book Tutorial data schema displayed in the VFP Database Designer.

There is a single table (Addresses) that will hold address data for both the students and instructors. This will allow for storing one or more addresses for each entity without the need to duplicate fields, while using the least amount of storage space. In other words, we don't need to use space unless there is an address to store. There is also a field named "type," which will allow the user to define what address is being stored, such as home, work, on-campus and so forth.

The CourseDescriptions table holds a list of all possible courses that will be taught at Tutorial U, while the Courses table holds the scheduling and location information for the CourseDescriptions that will be available to the students for registration. The Courses table also contains a foreign key, instructorid, which relates back to the primary key of the Instructors table. Notice that we use the same field name for the primary key and the foreign keys that are related to them. This makes it easier to join the tables, and you will see that the View Designer will also recognize this naming convention.

What isn't shown here is the view that we have created for which you will create a data class in this chapter. The view is the InstructorView, which contains all the fields of the Instructors table and has a view parameter attached to the lastname field. This parameter will allow you to follow our earlier recommendation to not retrieve data until it is needed. But how do we know which instructor record will be needed until the user interface is displayed and the user requests the record?

Data classes

The first layer you will create in a VFE application, the data layer, is made up of many data objects. There are two framework classes you will subclass when building an application: the cursor class and the data environment (DE) class. First, we'll walk through the steps to create two data classes for Tutorial U, and then we will look at each class in detail.

Tutorial

The initial goal of the tutorial is to create a single entity maintenance (or CRUD) form of your application. We will do this for the Instructors entity.

1. Open the VFE Book Tutorial application in the Application Builder, if you haven't already.

2. Select the Classes page in the Application Builder.

3. Expand the Data Objects node by clicking on the plus sign of the tree view next to the Data Objects label.

4. Highlight the Cursor Object node and press the New button. This will display the wizard selector. If at all possible, always use the "Single..." wizard when you are creating your application classes with the VFE IDE. If you select the "Multiple..." wizard, some steps will be skipped and you won't have as much control over the settings that are set by the wizard.

5. So, select the Single Cursor wizard and click the OK button. This will bring up Step 1 of the selected wizard.

6. At this point, you are directed to select the database that contains the view or table for which you would like to create a cursor class. There is also a selection for free tables, which are supported by VFE as well. Keep in mind that the databases listed are the DBC files that you have added to your metadata. If you are using remote data, those databases will not be listed—only the VFP database container you created to hold your remote views will be present. Because we only have one database, accept the default and press the Next button to move to Step 2 of the wizard.

7. Step 2 requests that you specify the cursor that will be opened and manipulated by your cursor class. You will see that the combo control lists all the tables and views contained in the database you selected in the previous step. If you're using views, be

sure to select the view and not the table. For our purposes, select the InstructorView and press the Next button.

8. Step 3 requests the default index to use when opening this cursor. VFE makes it simple to create indexes for views by defining them in the metadata; you will see this in the next chapter. Because we have not created any indexes for our view at this point, there are none to select. In this case, press the Next button.

> *You are not bound to the selections that you make in a VFE wizard. The wizard is just an interface to simplify creating a class and requesting some of the basic information required. This information is used to populate the properties of the class. You can always open the class in the Class Designer and modify those properties at a later date by using the property sheet or the builder that VFE has provided for each class.*

9. Step 4 of the wizard will be slightly different, depending on whether you selected a view or a table in Step 2. Our general recommendation is that you not implement any business rules at this level; it's preferable to do that at the business object level. So, if you wanted read-only access to this view, you could control that with bizobj properties. However, this is the only location where you can specify that you want "Exclusive" use. You certainly want the cursor opened when you create the cursor object and closed when you destroy it. The "No Data On Open" check box will only be available if you have put a parameter in the parameters list of the view. While "Alias" and "Buffermode" are self-explanatory, selecting the defaults certainly can't hurt. Okay, press the Next button.

> *Here's an example that demonstrates a tip about the read-only setting; it could save you hours of debugging. In this example, a view and cursor have been created for use in a grid-based form that was designed only to list people's names. Of course, this is a read-only function, so the cursor class's read-only property is set to True. However, the VFE grid class will see that the cursor is read-only and disable the columns, thus disabling the grid sorting and searching. Correcting this requires that the cursor, business object and presentation object all be set as normal and only the grid be set as read-only. After those changes, the control will work as expected. If you want to ensure that nothing gets saved to a view, it's better to de-select the "Send SQL Updates" switch in the View Designer's Update page. (Another related pitfall worth mentioning is that VFP does not allow Requery() to work with views that are opened read-only.)*

10. Step 5 requests the class name to create and the name of the class library to which the new class will be saved. The class name is derived from appending the word "Cursor" to the end of the alias name. You can change this if you like; however, sticking with this naming convention simplifies the naming of the next layers of classes you'll build with the wizards. You'll see how this works when we create the DE class. We recommend that you modify the class library name. You can certainly come up with

something more creative than ACURSOR. This becomes much more important if you are working with several developers. So, change the library name to "Instructor" and press the Finish button.

> *While the ability to store several classes in a single file makes VFP very workable, this is not the optimum situation for multiple developers and source control. There is no way we can recommend the best method for your project without knowing its structure or design goals. You can go to one extreme and store each class in its own library, or to the other extreme and store all classes in a single library. The VFE defaults have you put all of each type of class in a single library. We recommend that you put the classes for a single entity in a single library. This is what we have done here by creating the Instructor library for the Instructor cursor class. As we continue, we will store all the classes for the Instructor entity into that same library, creating other libraries as needed for other entities.*

After a bit of flashing and gyrating, VFE will have created the class and class library, and added the class library to the project. You will also see the new class in the Classes tree view under the Cursor node. What really happened here is that the VFE framework class iCursor was subclassed, and the properties were set based on the information that was provided in the wizard. If you like, you can open the Class Designer and take a look at your new class by double-clicking on the class name in the Application Builder, or by highlighting it and pressing the Open button.

At this point we can take a quick look at the Cursor Builder. Recall that a builder accompanies each class in VFE. You can open the builder while you have the cursor class open in the class editor. To do this, point to the class and press the right mouse button, and then select "Builder" from the shortcut menu (see **Figure 3**).

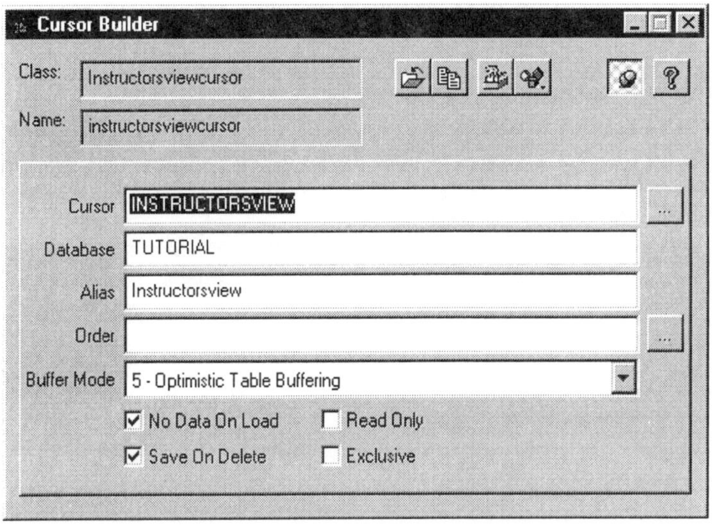

Figure 3. The Cursor Builder simplifies setting up the cursor object.

The next data class for our Instructor entity will be a data environment class. We'll create it now, and we will also explain this class in more detail later in this chapter.

1. From the Classes page of the Application Builder, highlight the Data Environments node and press the New button. The wizard selection dialog will appear. Once again, select the "Single…" wizard for assistance in building the class.

2. Step 1 of the DE wizard will list all of the cursor classes you have created up to this point. This is true even if the cursor class is included in another DE. This allows you to reuse the cursors in several DEs as needed. Move the only cursor class shown with the right arrow button, or by double-clicking on the name of the class in the list box. As you can see, you have the ability to put several cursors into the DE. Which cursors you put into the DE depends on application design and also the techniques you used to create it. Press the Next button of the wizard. (Often the class names are truncated in the moverlist for selecting a cursor class; the status bar displays the complete class name. This is true anyplace in the VFE wizards where the mover step is used.)

3. Step 2 of the wizard requests the name for your class and the class library in which to create it. VFE has used the name of the cursor class, removed the word "Cursor" and replaced it with the word "Environment." If you didn't accept the default name when creating the cursor class, the word "Environment" would have been appended to whatever the name of the class was. As we mentioned earlier, sticking to this standard makes using the wizards easier, especially in the event that you do choose the "Multiple…" wizards, which don't prompt for the names and just use the default rules. Be sure to select the Instructor class library to store this class, and then press the Finish button.

Once again, you will see the Class Designer as VFE creates a subclass of iDataEnvironment to create your specified class. Then an instance of each cursor class you specified will be dropped on the DE class. At this point, no properties are changed from the defaults of the parent class.

So far, you have been busy in the "Tutorial" sections of this chapter. You have created your database schema and imported it into VFE's metadata so that the VFE IDE is aware of it. From there, you created a cursor class and data environment class for the Instructor entity. You could see while using the wizards how the VFE IDE used the information in the metadata and the project to help you quickly build these classes by listing appropriate choices for the properties, views and classes required.

These two classes form the data layer that the application will utilize to communicate with the underlying Instructors table. Now we will describe the cursor and data environment classes, how they work and the key properties and methods you should be aware of.

cDataEnvironment of cData.VCX

The data environment class is a container that holds one or more cursor objects. For the most part, this class is a design-time convenience that saves you from writing code to instantiate each cursor object. The data environment also contains relation objects. A relation object is used to create a relation between two cursors after those cursors have been opened. Relation objects are not used much with view-based applications and are generally not used much with table-based applications either; VFE handles relations through business objects. VFE developers commonly attempt to use data environments with multiple cursors and relations in places where it's much easier to use related business objects. Using relations in the data environment should be considered a last resort.

A data environment class is instantiated by a business object, so you can say that the DE class creates the data environment for a business object. The DE then supplies the business object with a reference to the primary cursor, which is indicated by the InitialSelectedAlias property of the DE; we'll discuss this property shortly.

There are a few properties and methods of this class that you should be familiar with, as you may find yourself accessing or calling them for some reason or other.

Cursors

The cursors property is a collection of the cursor contained in the data environment. The cursor collection can be accessed, as can any collection, to reference a cursor in the collection. The reference contains class names. So, if you knew that the name of a cursor in the data environment was "Instructors," the following code would obtain a reference to the cursor:

```
LoInstructorCursor = Object.Cursors.Item['Instructors']
```

InitialSelectedAlias

The InitialSelectedAlias property contains the name of the cursor class that becomes the business object's primary cursor. This may not make sense, because we haven't covered business objects yet. Basically, each business object controls one cursor. One of the DE's responsibilities is to provide its business object with the reference to that cursor. If no cursor is specified in this property, and the DE contains multiple cursors, then the first cursor instantiated becomes the primary cursor.

IPrivateDataSession

This property is a logical value. If set to True, the DE class will instantiate the session class to create a private session in which its contained cursors are created. This property will generally be used when operating in a COM environment where there is no form hosting the DE. It can also be used when a business object that represents an event, such as posting GL entries, is opened from within another business object, such as the GL object when you want to provide the "posting" entity its own private data session for its data environment.

FindCursor()

This method will return a reference to a cursor object that controls the passed alias name. Here's the syntax:

```
Object.FindCursor( tcAlias )
```

Returns: Object
Argument: *tcAlias*—Specifies the alias name of the desired cursor class.

Remarks

FindCursor() will return a reference to the InitialSelectedAlias if none is specified. If the alias is not found in the cursor of the cursors collection, a NULL will be returned. Keep in mind that a NULL return doesn't indicate that the alias does not exist in the current data session, but only that it is not owned by any of the cursors in the DE's cursors collection. An example of this would be a lookup cursor, as lookup cursors are not added to the DE cursors collection. Be careful not to confuse this method with the GetCursor() method.

GetCursor()

This method returns the reference to the requested cursor class. Here's the syntax:

```
Object.GetCursor( tuIndex )
```

Returns: Object
Argument: *tuIndex*— Specifies the name or index (of the cursor collection) for the cursor reference requested.

Remarks

GetCursor() is a shortcut to the cursors collection of the DE object. The argument passed must be the name of a cursor class contained in the cursors collection. A NULL value will be returned if the cursor is not in the collection. Do not confuse this method with FindCursor(), which finds the cursor based on the alias, while GetCursor() finds the cursor based on the name of the class.

cCursor of cData.VCX

It is the cursor class's responsibility to manipulate the data at the cursor level. In addition to controlling the cursor, the cursor class has a fields collection. The fields collection is a collection of field objects that are responsible for manipulating the data at the field level.

To maintain the n-tier separation of layers that exist in the VFE framework, it is important that you not directly access the cursor and fields in your code. Notice that we said *important*, not *required*. There is a lot of code contained in the cursor objects to enhance and simplify the VFP commands that you may be accustomed to.

There is nothing stopping you, for example, from issuing the command "APPEND BLANK." This will still add a record to the current alias. However, if you send an Add message to the cursor object, it will do some other work for you. The cursor object will check to see whether the current record is dirty (has pending edits). Also, the cursor object will ensure that a record was added and, in addition, attempt to deal with any errors that may have occurred.

The decision is yours. Once again, we will cover what we feel are some of the more important properties and methods of the cursor class. Generally, though, you will not be calling these methods directly, but indirectly through the business objects. Do you see the thread here? The business object is the focus of dealing with an entity. Don't think of Instructors as a table, but rather as an entity that is represented by the business object.

BOF
This contains a True if the cursor is at the beginning of file. This property has an access method that will determine whether the cursor is at beginning of file.

EOF
This contains a True if the cursor is at the end of file. This property has an access method that will determine whether the cursor is at end of file.

RecNo
This contains the current record number of the cursor. This property has an access method that will determine the record number.

RecordCount
This contains the record count of the cursor. This property has an access method that will determine the record count.

VisibleRecordCount
This contains the number of records in the cursor that meet the current filter condition. This property has an access method that will determine the number.

cDeleteTriggerMessage
This determines the message that will be displayed when the cursor's delete trigger fails. If this is left empty, a default message will be displayed.

cInsertTriggerMessage
This determines the message that will be displayed when the cursor's insert trigger fails. If this is left empty, a default message will be displayed.

cUpdateTriggerMessage
This determines the message that will be displayed with the cursor's update trigger fails. If this is left empty, a default message will be displayed.

lWritePrimaryKeyOnNew
If this property is set to True, the cursor object will attempt to populate the primary key of the view with the default specified for the primary key of the table at add time. If you use this setting, there is no need to set a default value on the field for the view. However, setting this property to True leaves the possibility that you will lose keys if the user cancels prior to saving it. But, as you know, this is not an issue if you are using GUID values for your primary keys. When using this functionality, make sure that the primary key field of your view is set to be updatable, else a new value will be retrieved at save and your child records may be orphaned. By default this is set to True.

lWritePrimaryKeyOnSave

If this property is set to True, the cursor will attempt to populate the primary key of the view with the default specified for the primary key of the table at save time. As with the preceding property, this setting eliminates the need to add a default value to the primary key field of the view. Using this setting limits the number of incremental keys lost, as a key is not retrieved until the record that will use it is being saved. When using this functionality, make sure that the primary key field of your view is set to be updatable, else a new value will be retrieved at save and your child records may be orphaned. By default this is set to False.

NoDataOnLoad

This forces the cursor to open with the NODATA switch. You will generally set this if the view has a parameter, unless it is a "child file/view?". If you have a "child file/view?" and you set this to True, you will not see any child data for the parent record.

Fields

This is a reference to the fields collection of the cursor object. For more information on the field object, see information later in this chapter on the cField class.

Parameters

This is a reference to the view parameters collection of the cursor object. For more information on the view parameter object, see information later in this chapter on the cViewParameter class.

AddNew()

This method adds a record to the underlying cursor of the cursor class. Here's the syntax:

```
Object.AddNew( tcFields, tcValues )
```

Returns: A value represented by the following constants:
- FILE_OK
- FILE_CANCEL

Arguments: *tcFields*—A comma-delimited list of fields to populate as the record is added.
tcValues—A comma-delimited list of values to be used to populate the fields listed in tcFields.

Remarks

The AddNew() method will add a record to the underlying cursor of the cursor object. If using tcFields and tcValues, make sure that if the values are passed in variables or properties, they will all be in scope in the cursor object. The best idea is to evaluate them out into their final values in a character string to avoid problems. It is also just as easy and sometimes easier to send the AddNew() message and then populate the individual field values through the fields collection.

Cancel()

This method cancels the pending changes to a record. This only applies to a buffered cursor. Here's the syntax:

```
Object.Cancel( tlAllRows )
```

Returns: A value represented by the following constants:
- FILE_OK
- FILE_CANCEL

Argument: *tlAllRows*—Pass a True value to cancel all pending changes when table buffering is in effect; otherwise, only the changes in the current record are canceled.

Remarks
The Cancel() method will cancel any buffered changes made to the underlying cursor of the cursor object. Passing a True will cancel all buffered changes in the event that table buffering is being used.

Update()
This method saves changes to the underlying cursor of the cursor class. Here's the syntax:

```
Object.Update()
```

Returns: A value represented by the following constants:
- FILE_OK
- FILE_CANCEL
- FILE_ERRORHANDLED

Remarks
The Update() method will save the pending changes in the current record. The return of FILE_ERRORHANDLED indicates that the record did not pass validation. If being called from the normal chain of the UI classes, a message will be displayed. If you are accessing the Update() method directly, you will have to handle this error message.

Delete()
This method deletes a record of the underlying cursor of the cursor class. Here's the syntax:

```
Object.Delete()
```

Returns: A value represented by the following constants:
- FILE_OK
- FILE_CANCEL

Remarks
The Delete() method will delete the current record. If the lSaveOnDelete property of the cursor is True, the Update() method will be called to write the delete to the underlying table.

Requery()
This method refreshes the data in the cursor with records from the underlying table that match the criteria of the SELECT statement. Here's the syntax:

```
Object.Requery( tlAllowSelectAll )
```

Returns: A value represented by the following constants:
- REQUERY_SUCCESS
- REQUERY_ERROR

Argument: *tlAllowSelectAll*—Indicates to the cursor object whether it should query if there are no parameters or if all parameters are empty. Setting this to True will allow a query that would return all records. This parameter has no effect if the view does not have any parameters. When tlAllowSelectAll is True, the framework makes sure that at least one parameter has a value.

Remarks
The Requery() method will requery the underlying view of the cursor object. If there is an error requerying, a REQUERY_ERROR will be returned. Also, keep in mind that a REQUERY_SUCCESS indicates that no errors were returned, not that records were returned. Check the RecordCount property in order to determine how many rows the query brought back.

MoveFirst(), MoveLast(), MoveNext(), MovePrevious()
These methods move the record pointer as specified. Here's the syntax:

```
Object.MoveXXXX()
```

Returns: A value represented by the following constants:
- FILE_OK
- FILE_BOF
- FILE_EOF

Remarks
These methods basically perform as they are named, but be aware that if MoveLast() returns FILE_EOF, the cursor is not left at EOF. MoveLast will do a Skip –1 and leave the pointer on the record it was on originally. This is only a problem if you are not aware of it.

IsAdding(), IsChanged(), IsCursorEmpty(), IsNewAndEmpty()
These methods determine the specified information about the cursor object. Here's the syntax:

```
Object.IsXXXX()
```

Returns: Logical

Remarks
These methods basically perform as they are named. Each will determine the information of its namesake and return a logical result of True or False. These are helpful when you only want to allow certain things to happen at certain times. As the remarks for IsNewAndEmpty() say, be aware that the fields in the cursor could have values in them from defaults. This more accurately indicates New and Not Modified.

Fields collection
When the cursor object is created, it will create a field object for each field in the cursor. Each field object is added to the fields collection. Later sections in this chapter provide examples of how to navigate the fields collection.

The field information in the metadata is used to create these objects. Each field has a "data behavior" property. This property specifies the class to instantiate for each particular data item. Don't be confused by this fancy name; it is nothing more than a field class, as described later. You also have a head start on Chapter 15, "Data Behavior Classes," because you understand that it is a subclass of cField created to implement a specific behavior for that field object.

View parameters collection
In addition to the fields collection, there is the view parameters collection. As you might have already determined, this is built from the metadata for the cursor. However, there is a slight twist. A view parameter is only listed in the metadata if it is added to the view parameters list (see Chapter 13, "Working with Views").

This may or may not make sense to you. There is no need to represent a view parameter by an object if the value in the filter already exists in the environment of the view. Don't concern yourself with this too much at this point. Just be aware that only parameters included in the parameters list are created and added to the view parameters collection. The VFE documentation covers this in detail.

You've probably guessed what comes next. Yes, you can also define a behavior class for a view parameter. Just as the field has a data behavior property, so does the view parameter. Once again, like the field behavior class, the view parameter behavior class is nothing more than a subclass of cViewParameter implemented for a specific behavior.

cAbstractDataItem
Well, we promised we were going to look at the field and view parameter classes, and we are. Both of those classes are subclasses of the abstract data item class. This class has much of the functionality, as fields and view parameters are very similar. So, when we discuss the data item, remember that we're referring to field and view parameter objects.

The data item class encapsulates all the access to the field of the cursor. Don't mistake this class for other data classes that you may have seen or used. The data classes in VFE never store the value of the field. Instead, the value property of the data item has an access and an assign method connected to it. These methods go to the underlying field or parameter and populate or assign it with your data.

You will find all the methods needed to validate a field or view parameter in the cAbstractDataItem class. We won't detail all those methods here because for the most part you will not interface with these methods. The data object will read the validation information for the fields from the metadata and, based on the validation you have specified, verify that the data meets those rules. For more information on how to set up validation for a field or view parameter, see Chapter 12, "Data Validation," where it is covered in more detail. When you have time, you should use the class browser and go though the abstract data item class and the validation methods.

oBizObj
This property contains a reference to the business object that contains the cursor object that contains this data object. There will be times when you are writing code in a user interface control class when you need to know the business object that owns the cursors that own the data item you are dealing with. We use the word "contain" here, but there is no actual containership as we know it—if you are writing code in a data item object, you can't type "this.parent.parent" to get a reference to the business object, even though that is conceptually the ownership.

oCursor
Similar to the previous property, oCursor holds a reference to the cursor object that contains the data item.

oProperties
The oProperties property contains the reference to an object that contains the metadata property values of the field.

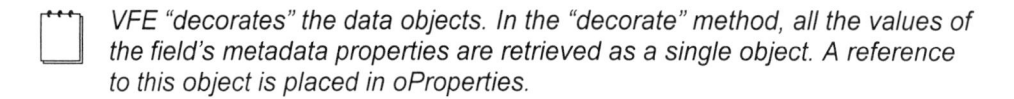

> *VFE "decorates" the data objects. In the "decorate" method, all the values of the field's metadata properties are retrieved as a single object. A reference to this object is placed in oProperties.*

Value
The value property contains the value of the underlying field. This property has an access method that retrieves the value from the field to return it. This property also has an assign method attached to it that populates the underlying field with the data you passed to it. (This explanation only really applies to fields, not view parameters.)

This property is likely the one that you will use most often. It is also the property that the user interface controls are bound to in order to display data item values.

cField of cData.VCX
As we stated earlier, the field class is a subclass of the abstract data item. For those of you who are new to object-oriented programming, this means that the class inherits all the properties and methods from its parent, cAbstractDataItem.

A field object is created for each field in a cursor. A reference to each field object is stored in a collection class. The cursor class has a property, "fields," that references the collection. The field class adds a small number of properties and methods that you should be aware of. There are two methods to consider that you may want to call in your code.

IsChanged()
This method indicates whether the field value has changed from its original value. Here's the syntax:

```
Object.IsChanged()
```

Returns: Logical

Remarks
This function can be useful if you need to rely on the fact that the value of a certain field has changed.

Revert()
This method sets a field back to its original value and marks the field as unmodified. Here's the syntax:

```
Object.Revert()
```

Returns: Logical

Remarks
This function sets the field back to the original value and sets it so that it will appear to have not been edited.

Using the cursor and field objects

One of the most frequent questions on the VFE support site is, "How do I access the field value with the cursor object?" As we mentioned earlier, the field objects are referenced by the fields collection of the cursor object. As you get further into this book, you will see that each class has a reference to the classes it owns or contains. So, depending on where you are writing your code, there are different ways to obtain a reference to the desired cursor object that contains your fields.

Let's assume that we have created a variable named "loCursor" and populated it with a reference to the cursor object. The fields collection is referenced with the field property of the cursor object. So loCursor.Fields would provide us with a reference to the fields collection.

If you have followed our advice and studied the collections class, you know that all collections have an Item array property. The Item array contains the actual references to the collected objects. You can use a numeric or character subscript for the item property to access your field objects.

You can follow along by running some of this code in the command window. Note that this code is provided to give you an understanding of how the cursor, fields and view parameters work; in your applications, code of this nature will typically reside in a business object. In order to instantiate our cursor class, we must have all the framework classes loaded and ready to work. The simplest way to accomplish this is by running your application, so open your application in the Application Builder and press the Run button. Once it is running, suspend it from the Suspend option on the Developers menu. You should have access to your command window now.

Let's instantiate the cursor class we created:

```
loCursor = createobj('InstructorsViewCursor')
```

You now have instantiated your cursor class and have a reference to the cursor object. Even though the cursor class has the responsibility of opening the cursor, it is not done by default. The DE class calls the Open() method of each cursor object it creates. So, we will do that manually. First, open the View window so you can see what's going on:

```
Set
```

Now call the Open() method of the cursor. This will open the cursor, which, in this case, is a local view. You should see the view open in the set window. You will also see the table open, because a local view is no more than a stored SQL statement.

```
? loCursor.Open()
```

We use the "?" in front of the call so the return value will be echoed to the screen. Let's look at some of the properties and methods of the cursor object while we are at this step. Try these commands:

```
? loCursor.RecNo
? loCursor.RecordCount
? loCursor.AddNew()
? loCursor.RecordCount
? loCursor.Cancel()
```

Now let's add a record, put some data in and make some changes, all programmatically. To see what's happening behind the scenes, browse the view so you can see the values we add. Size the browse window so that you can see it and the command window. First, we will add a record to the view:

```
? loCursor.AddNew()
```

If you click on the browse it will update, and you will see that a record has been added. Next, let's put a GUID into the primary key. The cursor class normally will do that for us, but we haven't defined the default value as a GUID in the metadata yet; that will happen in the next chapter. So, for the first time, we will access a field using the fields collection:

```
? loCursor.Fields.Item['InstructorID'].Value = Guid()
```

Okay, the preceding line is actually the correct code, but it didn't work. This is due to the fact that VFP does not fire access and assign methods in interactive or suspended mode. To trick VFP into running this code for us, put in the following commands:

```
Public poCursor
poCursor = loCursor
ON KEY LABEL F4 loCursor.Fields.Item['InstructorID'].Value = Guid()
Resume
```

Now that the program is running again, press the F4 key. This will run our code during normal execution, and the access method for the value property will fire. This access method will populate the data we passed to the value property to the field. Now, suspend your application by using the Developers menu, and click on your browse window. *Voilà*—the GUID value is in the InstructorsID field.

Finish out the record by putting values in the other fields. To make it easier on yourself, just type the values right into the browse. When you are done, close the browse window. At this point, the record is only buffered in the view. To write this data to the underlying table, we have to save the record. The following code will save the record using the cursor object. (We will have to use the public variable reference, since the private variable was released when we resumed the program.)

```
? poCursor.Update()
```

You should get a 0 returned, which indicates success. At this point, you can resume the program and then exit it from the menu. This will bring you back to the Application Builder or Manager, whichever you ran the program from or have your settings set for.

Summary

A lot of ground has been covered in this chapter. Everything we discussed here works together to form what is commonly referred to as the "data services" tier. This tier begins with the physical tables. These tables, either local VFP tables or SQL Server tables, store your business domain and system data. From there a cursor class is created for each table. The cursor objects are responsible for interacting with the VFP cursor. The cursor collaborates with the field and view parameter objects to manipulate the VFP fields and cursors. Finally, to simplify opening the cursors, a data environment class is created that is responsible for instantiating the cursors and holding a reference to each.

It's easy to see that if you were accessing the cursor classes over a remote connection using DCOM, it would be possible to manipulate data without accessing the physical tables directly. This is the first step to physical separation of tiers.

Did you also notice how many of the VFE framework classes are interrelated? It was very difficult to structure this book because in order for us to discuss cursor objects, you had to at least know what metadata was. However, you can't discuss metadata (data about data) until you have data. It seems that this is a drawback of explaining objects with a procedural language like English.

At this point, you may want to go back to the VFE documentation and read the description of these classes and look at the additional methods and properties; by no means were they all covered in this chapter. Also, if you are still fuzzy about what a collection is and how to access it, read more about them in this book, in the VFE documentation, in your MSDN library or from a variety of other resources.

In the next chapter, you will finally meet the metadata. You've heard about it, and you knew it was coming—it's finally time to shake its hand, so to speak. See you in Chapter 5.

Chapter 5
Metadata

In this chapter we will look at the VFE metadata, otherwise known as the data dictionary. But the VFE metadata contains much more information than your normal data dictionary. Let's take a look at how the metadata is stored, accessed and used in and by VFE.

If you've been reading this book from the beginning, you have seen the word "metadata" mentioned several times. Metadata is basically data about data. Metadata is often referred to as a "data dictionary." VFP gave us the first small hint of a data dictionary with the introduction of the database container, or DBC. This file holds information about each field in your database—data about data, or metadata.

While the DBC was a step in the right direction, it still didn't address some of the needs of the FoxPro community. One problem was that the DBC, which contained extended information about the fields, didn't contain any information about a table's indices. If an index was corrupted, there was no way to rebuild it from the data in the DBC. There was also no way to add your own properties to a DBC and ensure backward compatibility.

So, three vendors got together and decided that they wanted to solve this problem. One of those vendors was F1 Technologies (Neon Software at the time). It was decided that in order for their design to be widely adopted, it should be freely available. The result of this collaboration is what is known today as DBCX.

DBCX

DBCX is the public domain database container extension that resulted from that collaboration. It met all of the design ideas put forth by the team. While DBCX was not as wildly popular as it should have been, it was used by the originators in several products. Codebook and subsequently Visual FoxExpress used DBCX services to manage their metadata. Prior to the current release of Visual FoxExpress, DBCX2 (version 2) was released. The man primarily responsible for this updated version is Doug Hennig of Stonefield Technologies. We owe him many thanks. For full information and documentation, the DBCX2 manual is shipped with VFE. You will find the doc file in the \VFE6\Help folder.

Because the manual does an excellent job of explaining the technical details of DBCX, we will just give you an overview here. At some point you should read the manual in order to fully understand the powerful metadata services you have at your command.

Basically, DBCX is a set of class libraries that provide services to your application. The main class is DBCXMgr, also known as the MetaManager, or MetaMgr for short. This class is based on the "form" base class using a private data session that encapsulates the data and code within the object, allowing it to manage the metadata. There are several tables used by MetaMgr that store the metadata. The core public domain MetaMgr uses the table COREMETA.DBF to store the metadata. The design of DBCX2 also allows it to be extended by creating subclasses of the DBCXMgr class.

Each subclass of the MetaMgr can provide specific services for the application it is designed for. When you first instantiate the MetaMgr class, a field named DBCXREG.DBF is opened. DBCXREG.DBF is the manager registration table. This table contains information about all of the custom managers that will be used for the data. The MetaMgr instantiates each of these classes based on the registration information.

Each specialized manager is in control of certain extended properties. For example, the VFE MetaManager has a table named VFEMETA.DBF. Each field in this table is considered an extended property of the field. You should look at the structure of the VFEMETA.DBF table to become familiar with the data that is stored there. This data is not limited to the framework; you can access the data at any time using the DBCX functions and properties explained in the DBCX manual.

F1 Technologies created a manager subclass to manage the metadata used by VFE. This manager is automatically instantiated when your application is started, and you can use those services in your code if needed. For full information on using the programmatic interface to DBCX, see the DBCX manual.

VFE and DBCX

As you have seen in the previous chapters, the VFE IDE is highly integrated with the metadata. Most of the builders and wizards obtain information from the metadata to provide you with choices or set properties based on the metadata values. For example, when you created your cursor class, the Cursor Class wizard read the metadata to list the cursors that were available for you to select.

The framework is also highly integrated with the metadata at run time. In the previous chapter, you learned about the fields collection. When the cursor class is instantiated, the field object is built from the field information in the metadata. The metadata has an extended property for each field containing the name of the behavior class to instantiate. There are also many other extended property values used to "decorate" the fields. Remember, VFE "decorates" the field object by creating an object that contains all the DBCX properties and placing its reference into the oProperties property of the field object.

So, if this data is so important to VFE, there must be an easy way to create and modify it without having to browse tables and change values. Yes, there is. VFE provides an application for the developer to use called the DBCX Explorer. In this chapter, you'll use the DBCX Explorer to populate some metadata properties for our Tutorial U application, and then it will be time to go over all the gory details.

Tutorial

We will use the DBCX Explorer to populate some of the extended properties of certain tables, views and fields. These properties will be specific to the Tutorial U application that is being built. We briefly used the Explorer in a previous tutorial. We did this to create metadata for the existing database item.

At this point we recommend that you read the "DBCX Explorer" topic in the VFE documentation, which gives a brief overview of the sections of the Explorer. Now, let's populate some properties for our application.

1. Open the Book Tutorial application in the VFE Application Builder.

2. Press the Data Dictionary button to run the DBCX Explorer (from now on referred to as Explorer).

3. In the Explorer window, you will see a tree view that lists the databases and free tables that have been created in the metadata (see **Figure 1**). In the Databases node, you will see the Tutorial database. This is present because in the previous chapter we added the database to the metadata and "validated" the metadata. Validating the metadata reads all the information about the database and everything it contains and creates a record for each item in that database to each XXXMETA.DBF file.

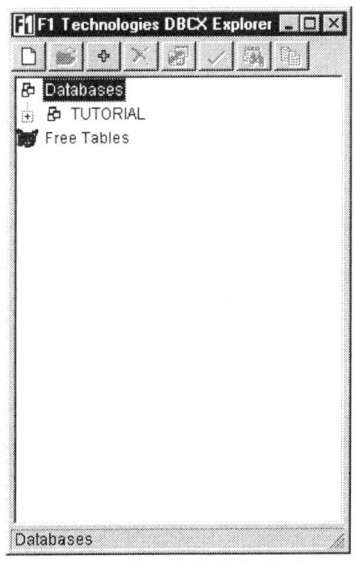

Figure 1. The DBCX Explorer tree view window. This window contains a list of databases and free tables that have been added to the metadata.

4. Expand the Tutorial database, and expand both the Tables and Views nodes. Once again, the tables and views of the database are shown as nodes of the tree view window.

5. If you highlight any of the data nodes, a second window will open to the right of the tree view window. This window is the *properties* window. The properties window contains different pages and items, depending on what type of entity you have highlighted in the left-hand window. Try it. Click on the database name, then a table name to see how this works. This demonstrates that everything in the properties window is an extended property for the item selected in the left-hand window.

6. If you haven't already, expand the Tutorial Databases node, then the Tables node. Now highlight the Instructors table and expand its node. Expand the Fields node for the Instructors table. Finally, highlight the InstructorID field so that the properties window is displaying the extended properties for that field. Your Explorer should look similar to **Figure 2**.

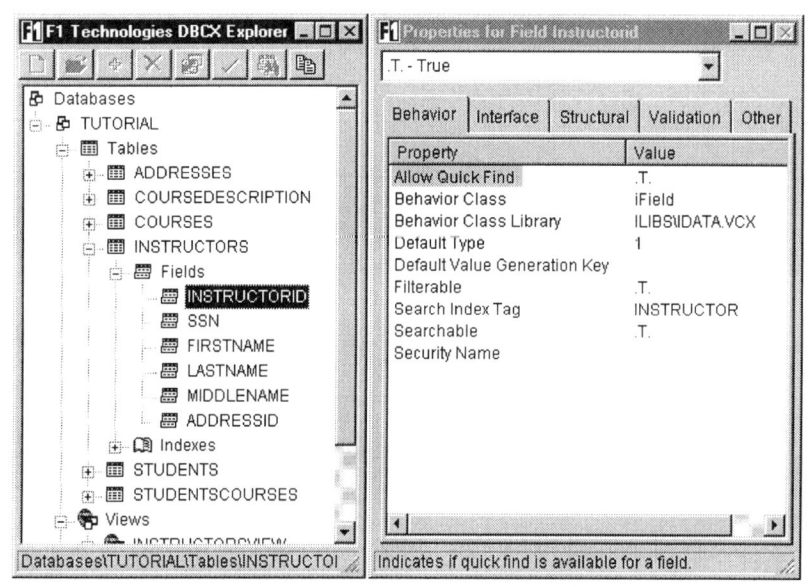

56   Creating Visual FoxPro Applications with Visual FoxExpress

Figure 2. The DBCX Explorer with the InstructorID field of the Instructors table selected in the tree view pane. In the properties pane, the title bar indicates "Properties for Field InstructorID."

7. In the properties pane, highlight the property name "Default Value Generation Key." This is the property where we tell VFE that we want a default value placed in this field every time a record is added. What VFE will do, depending on your selection, is populate the default property in the DBC.

8. After you have selected Default Value Generation Key, the Builder button will appear in the top right corner of the properties pane (it has a picture of bricks and a trawl). Press the Builder button. The Default Value Builder dialog will pop up (see **Figure 3**).

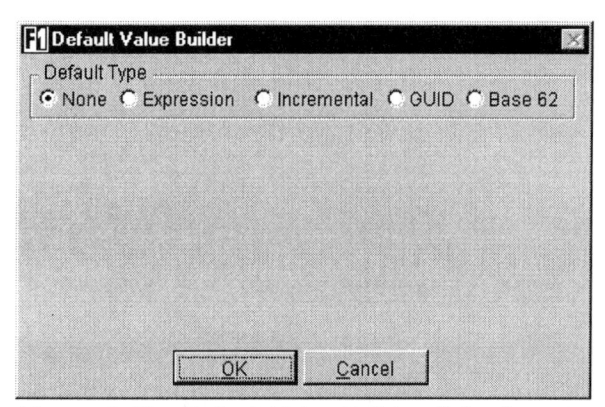

Figure 3. The Default Value Builder dialog is accessed by clicking the Builder button when the Default Value Generation Key property is selected in the Explorer's properties pane.

9. You should recognize the key types from our earlier discussion. Only the types available based on the field type will be enabled. Because we are using Binary Character field, all types show. Select the GUID radio button. A testament to using the GUID's simplicity is the fact that the dialog requests no additional information. If you were to select the Incremental or Base62 type, you would be prompted for additional information. See the Default Value Generation Key property explanation for more information.

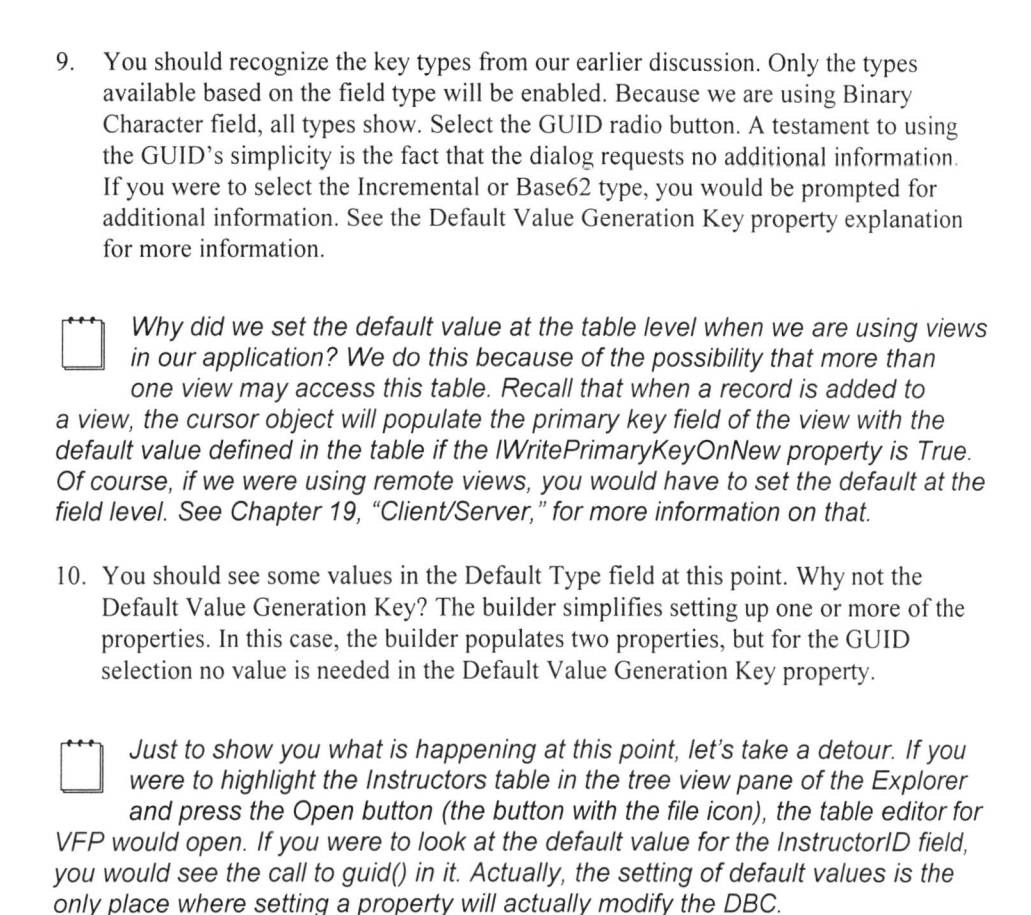

> *Why did we set the default value at the table level when we are using views in our application? We do this because of the possibility that more than one view may access this table. Recall that when a record is added to a view, the cursor object will populate the primary key field of the view with the default value defined in the table if the lWritePrimaryKeyOnNew property is True. Of course, if we were using remote views, you would have to set the default at the field level. See Chapter 19, "Client/Server," for more information on that.*

10. You should see some values in the Default Type field at this point. Why not the Default Value Generation Key? The builder simplifies setting up one or more of the properties. In this case, the builder populates two properties, but for the GUID selection no value is needed in the Default Value Generation Key property.

> *Just to show you what is happening at this point, let's take a detour. If you were to highlight the Instructors table in the tree view pane of the Explorer and press the Open button (the button with the file icon), the table editor for VFP would open. If you were to look at the default value for the InstructorID field, you would see the call to guid() in it. Actually, the setting of default values is the only place where setting a property will actually modify the DBC.*

11. There's just one more property to set at this time. Highlight the SSN field. In the properties pane, select the Interface page, and then highlight the Input Mask extended property and press the Builder button. Set the mask value to "999-99-9999" and check the "Ignore Input Mask" check box. Press the OK button.

You have now set metadata properties for the tutorial application. The default value will be used to automatically populate the primary key. The input mask will be used in any control in which you display the SSN field. This saves you from having to set the mask anytime you use the control, or even from creating a text box specifically for SSN that includes the correct input mask.

DBCX Explorer

Your experience has shown you that the Explorer is a user interface provided to the VFE developer to edit the metadata used by your application. At this point, we suggest that you read the following three topics in the VFE Help: "DBCX Explorer," "The Visual FoxExpress Data Dictionary" and "How the Framework Uses the Data Dictionary."

After reading these topics, you should have a good overview of how the Explorer is laid out and how to use it. You should also realize that there is an abundance of information in the metadata, and VFE makes use of most of it in many places. As a matter of fact, the author of the VFE documentation didn't even want to tackle explaining where and how every extended property is used.

Certainly, if VFE couldn't fully document 100 percent of the metadata, there is no way we could possibly do it here. Taking into account the constant changes and improvements being made to VFE, a new use is thought of for each property every now and then. Also, an update here and there will surely add some properties.

However, we'll take a shot at giving you a brief description of what each property does and what classes use them. Keep in mind that even though the one of the framework authors is editing this book and we have made every effort to be as accurate as possible, there may be a few assumptions here. For things we were unsure about, we consulted the source code before committing it to paper.

Metadata storage

Before we get into what each property is used for, you should be aware of where the metadata is stored. We hinted at this before, but we didn't look at it in detail. The VFE metadata manager uses the data stored in the VFEMETA.DBF table. This table is stored in the \Metadata folder of your project directory.

Of course, what we're going to cover here is all discussed, in detail, in the DBCX2 manual, but just in case you haven't had a chance to read that fascinating document, here goes. Take a look at the structure of VFEMETA.DBF (see **Figure 4**) so that we can investigate the field names and what they represent.

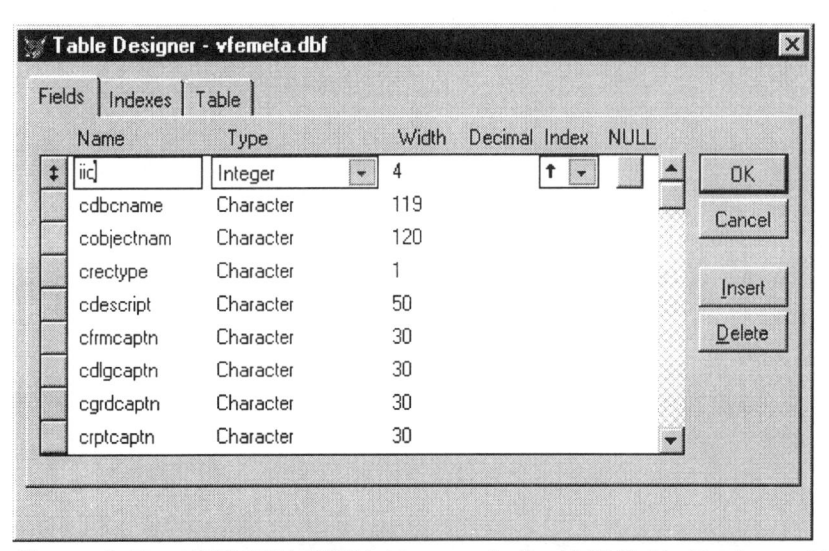

Figure 4. The VFEMETA.DBF table open in the VFE Table Designer. Here you can see that other than the first four fields, which are used for DBCX housekeeping, each field name is the name of an extended property, allowing information for that property to be stored for each entity in the database.

The first four fields in the list—iID, cDBCName, cObjectNam and cRecType—are used by DBCX to find the specific record in question. Each of the other fields represents an extended property in the metadata. To add a new property, you add a field to this table. Knowing this, you could add a property for your own purposes.

Looking at the structure, you'll see that cFRMCaptn is a character property with 30 bytes of space. Of course, this field will hold the form caption, or the caption to use for this field when it is placed on a form. Pretty cool stuff, eh? Now, let's take a look at another file. While it isn't part of the metadata, it makes using the metadata a bit easier for the everyday VFE developer.

Explorer definition

Knowing that VFE would grow and be improved upon, it was a simple deduction that the metadata would expand with it. As we showed earlier, this is easily accomplished with the metadata by modifying its table structure. F1 Technologies took that a bit further and made the Explorer data-driven also. So placing a new record in its definition file was all that would be needed for Explorer to display the property.

If you open and browse the C:\VFE6\DBCX Explorer\Data\PROPMAP.DBF table, you will see all the information used by the DBCX Explorer. There is a column to specify what page to place the property on, a column to specify whether the property is read-only and so forth. We'll leave this table to you to figure out. Where would the fun be if we revealed all the secrets?

Be that as it may, you would be able to add information about your own property to the PROPMAP table if you wanted to add your properties to it. If you own Stonefield Database Toolkit by Doug Hennig and Stonefield Technologies, you will see that he includes a PROPMAP file that you can append to the VFE PROPMAP table so you can edit the SDT extended properties with the DBCX Explorer if you wish.

Properties uncovered

Okay, here is where we'll attempt to list all or most of the VFEMETA properties. Once again, due to the dynamic nature of the framework and software in general, these are not set in stone. So, please, as Ronald Reagan would say, "Trust but verify."

There is actually a set of properties for each entity—Database, Table/View and Fields. We will only list the properties for Fields here. The Database and Table/View have fewer properties, and generally they are for caption information. The only exception to this is that the Table/View Behavior page has a place to specify a cursor class. This is the cursor class that will be instantiated for the Table/View if the framework needs to open a table or view without a cursor class being in existence already.

Behavior page

Table 1 shows the properties and usage available on the Behavior page.

Table 1. The Behavior page properties and usage.

Property	Usage
Allow Quick Find	This is a logical field that specifies whether Quick Find is available for that field. Quick Find is run by right-clicking on a control and choosing "Quick Find..." When working with views, Quick Find will find the value entered in the current record set; it will not go to the underlying table.
Behavior Class	As stated in Chapter 4, "Data Storage and Classes," this is a fancy name for a cField or cViewParameter class you have created with specific behavior programmed into it. This property will hold the name of your behavior class.
Behavior Class Library	This is the name of the class library or VCX file in which the behavior class can be found.

·Default Type	This holds the value for the default type to use when generating a default value. You cannot directly edit the file; you must use the Default Value Builder to set it unless you also change the DBC and AppIds table. The possible values are:
	   1—None
	   2—Expression
	   3—Incremental
	   4—GUID
	   5—Base62
	See the "Default Value Generation" section later in this chapter for more information.

Default Generation Value	This property ties in with the previous one. It needs to be populated if the above types are 2, 3 or 5.
Filterable	This is a logical property that indicates whether the field should be listed in the Filter Builder dialog that comes up when you use the Filter() method of a presentation object.
Search Index Tag	This indicates the index to use when this field is searched on in a grid. The properties window description indicates that it is used during Quick Find, but we don't think this is true at the time of this writing. It is only used when the field is in a searchable grid and you search for a value in the column populated by this property's field.
Searchable	This property controls whether or not the field will show up in the default VFE Search dialog.
Security Name	In Chapter 17, "VFE Security," you will learn about the VFE security system. This property allows you to put the security name here, and any control bound to this field will inherit this security name.

Interface page

Table 2 shows the properties and usage available on the Interface page.

Table 2. The Interface page properties and usage.

Property	Description
Caption Dialog Caption Form Caption Grid Caption Report Caption Status Bar Text ToolTip Text	These properties are fairly self-explanatory. The easiest way to set the captions is with the Caption Builder. Highlight any of the caption properties and press the Builder button to edit all the captions at the same time. A Synchronize button is provided to simplify using the same text for all caption properties. Here's a tip if you are using the List() method of the presentation object to build dynamic lists on the fly. Leaving "Grid Caption" blank will specify that that field will not be included in the list. You may want to do this for IDs or other fields that would show a foreign key.
Order	This indicates the order in which the field should be placed when displayed in a grid or list. The Field Display Builder gives you a simple drag-and-drop interface to order all the fields in the view.
Format Input Mask	These two properties hold the values you'll use for the control's format and input mask properties. The builder simplifies entering the data and codes for these fields.
Help Text	According to the properties tip, this field is to contain the Help text for the field. This Help text only shows up when you right-click on an object that's bound to a field and then choose Help.
Read Only	This property does what it says and will not allow this field to be edited. This property will flow from the field object to the control object on your user interface.
User Interface Class	In this property, you specify the user interface class you want to be used whenever this field is added to a presentation object or displayed in a grid. If you have created a special class to display this field, entering it here greatly simplifies building your screens and grids.
User Interface Class Library	This indicates the name of the VCX file in which your interface class is contained.

Structural page

We'll skip this page. None of these properties are editable, and this page seems to be available simply to provide some information to you should you need it. All the property descriptions are fairly straightforward.

Validation

Please see Chapter 12, "Data Validation," for a complete description of these properties.

Other

Once again, these properties are more informational than modifiable. There are two on this page you can edit:

- *Description*—It's not used anywhere; it's basically provided for people who may want to document miscellaneous items in the metadata and create VFP reports on it.

- *Note*—This is a property that you can type notes into. You really didn't expect anything more from it, did you?

Default value generation

There seem to be many questions about setting this up, so we'll explain how it works. VFE is utilizing the default property in the DBC to implement this function. Depending on the value generation method you select, a different method is used.

When you select the GUID method, VFE puts a call to the guid() function in the default value. You saw this earlier. The guid() function is provided in the framework in the KEYGEN.PRG file.

If you select the Expression method, you are prompted for the expression. This expression is placed into the default property of the DBC. You may use this to populate an order date field, in which case you would enter the expression "date()." You can also enter a static value here. If you want, you can create your own value generation function and put a function call to it here. Perhaps you number invoices by using the customer code, then adding the four digits of the year and finally adding an incremented number. Write a function to do this in the stored procedures of the DBC, and put the function call in the expression.

When you select either Incremental or Base62 value generation, VFE will ask you for two additional values (see **Figure 5**). First, we'll explain how VFE implements these functions, and it will become clear to you what these values are for. The first time either of these choices is selected, a table named APPIDS.DBF is created in your data directory. This file has a field to hold a key and a field to hold the last value.

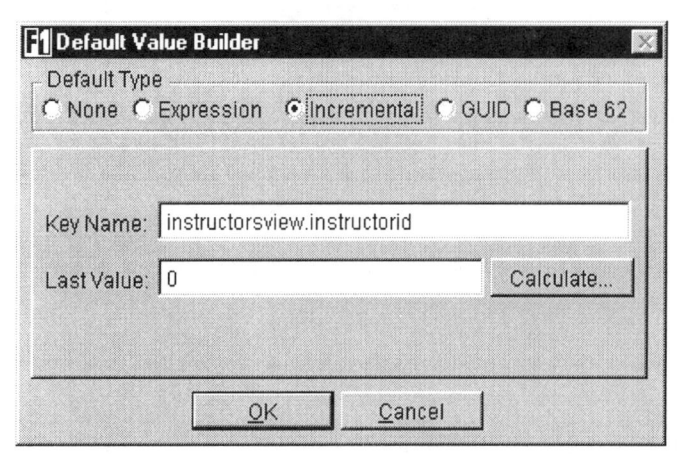

Figure 5. When Incremental or Base62 is selected in the Default Value Builder, you are prompted for Key Name and Last Value. The key name will be used to locate the correct record in the APPIDS.DBF file.

The function used to populate these default values is VFENewKey(). This function is passed the table and field name for which a generated value is required. From there, VFENewKey() looks up that table.field name in the metadata to retrieve the default value generation rules. One of these values is the key name, which you provided in the builder. The key name value is used to find the record in the APPIDS.DBF table with the matching key name. Once the record is found, the last value is retrieved and incremented accordingly, and the new last value is saved back. Finally, the function returns the value.

Some people confuse the value passed to VFENewKey() with the key value—they are not the same. Even if you set up a key value of "Invoice Number" to the Invoice.InvNo field, the call in the default would still look like this: VFENewKey('Invoice.InvNo'). In this case, if you are defining a default generation rule at the view level (which you may do for remote views), and more than one view adds records to the same table, be sure to use the same key name so that you don't try to duplicate values.

There is one final thing to remember. The default value defined for a table field is not used until the record is saved to the table. So, if you are using views and defining defaults at the table, you won't see your value in the view. If you do want to see the value in the view, you can define the default for the view field in the metadata. Of course, the one exception to this is your primary key when using lWritePrimaryKeyOnNew set to True in your cursor object.

Code examples

There may be times when you want to access information in the metadata tables programmatically in your application. Perhaps you are writing a report generator and need to list all the fields of a table. This is fairly simple to do using the MetaMgr class. This section will give you a few brief examples, and you can follow along in the command window. For more detailed information, you can't beat the DBCX2 manual.

First, run the Book Tutorial application and suspend using the Developers menu to obtain access to the command window. The first thing we need to do is get a reference to the MetaMgr object. Normally we will be coding in a class that has an oApplication property, and the MetaMgr is referenced in a property of the application class. (For more information about the application class, see Chapter 10, "How It Works.") So, in class code we would reference the application object using This.oApplication.

However, we don't have that luxury here, so we will use a function provided in the VFE utilities program, named FindApplication(), which will return a reference to the application object. Type the following in your command window:

```
oApp = findapplication()
```

This puts a reference to the application object into your oApp variable. The MetaMgr is referenced in the oMetaMgr property of the control object. So, to make sure we can access our MetaManager, let's ask it for its name:

```
? oApp.oMetaMgr.Name
```

You should get a return of "DBCXMGR," which is the name of the core MetaManager. First, you can use the manager to list certain types of entities. Let's populate an array with the caption of all the views in our database:

```
Dime MyArray1[1]
Open Database Tutorial
```

```
oApp.oMetaMgr.SetDatabase('Tutorial')
? oApp.oMetaMgr.DBCXGetAllObjects('View',@MyArray, 'Caption')
```

This last function should return a one (1), because there is currently one view in our database. If you check the value of the array property:

```
? MyArray[1]
```

you will get a return of "InstructorsView," the name of the single view currently in the database. Also remember that when you are coding in a class, you don't have to use "find application"—just use the oApplication property that all classes in the framework have:

```
This.oApplication.oMetaMgr ... etc
```

To find all of the other functions in DBCX2 and learn about how they work, consult the DBCX2 manual.

Summary

Well, the great mystery of metadata is solved. It's nothing more than several tables of data. That data happens to describe the tables and fields that make up your database, which is why we call it metadata. The DBCX Explorer gives you a simple way to edit the metadata tables, including several builders to simplify the job.

You've learned that the DBCX standard allows for simple methods to extend the metadata by subclassing the DBCXMgr class to provide new functionality and/or by adding fields to the meta tables to store more properties. In addition to this, you learned about the table that drives the DBCX Explorer, and you were given a homework assignment to look into it and figure out how it is used.

Finally, we covered some code examples to allow you to access metadata. As we mentioned earlier, most of the properties will be attached to the field; however, you may, for example, want to list all of the views for an export routine.

From here, we'll move on to the class where you will spend most of your time—the business object. See you there!

Chapter 6
Business Objects

The business object is the worker bee of your application. This is the class that models each entity in your application and encapsulates the rules and processes defined by or for that entity. Most of your processing and rules code will be placed into a business object class.

In the beginning of this book, you learned about Codebook 3.0 and how it introduced the business object to the Visual FoxPro programmer. Business objects were not a new concept in the object-oriented programming world, but they were new to FoxPro developers. After all, version 3 of VFP was the first FoxPro with object-oriented extensions, and even people with five or more years of FoxPro experience were suddenly wet-behind-the-ears OOP beginners.

The business object is the object that is modeled to match the real-world entity. For example, if you wanted to create a business object named "cat," you would start with some of a cat's attributes. First you would add whiskers, fur and color attributes. These attributes would become properties of the business object. Next you would model some of the responsibilities or functions of a cat. (Those of us who think a cat is the most useless animal in the world will have to set that thought aside for a moment.) A cat knows how to stretch, yawn, nap, eat and scratch. All of these would become methods of your cat business object.

Up until now, the classes you have looked at in the data layer are really generic and have nothing to do with a specific entity. Their entire purpose is to provide a means to persist or store the properties of a business object. The business object is the first class that becomes specific to your business domain. Your domain might be banking, finance or perhaps school registration. It is in the business object that you implement all the "responsibilities or functions" of the real-world entity.

Tutorial

So far, we have created the table that will physically store the Instructors information. Then, we created a cursor class to provide an object-based method to access the data. Finally, we created a data environment to hold the cursor. Now it is time to create a business object to encapsulate the attributes and actions of the real-world entity.

1. Open the Tutorial application in the Application Builder.

2. Switch to the Classes page and highlight the Business Objects node in the parent page. Press the New button. You will be presented with the wizard selection dialog.

3. As with the cursor wizard, the "Multiple..." wizard will create a bizobj for each data environment that you select without giving you many other options. Select the Single Object wizard and press OK. The Single Business Object wizard will open.

4. Step 1 asks you to select the data environment class for the bizobj. You're provided with a list of all data environment classes in the project. We only have one, so there is not much to do here except click the Next button.

5. Step 2 asks you to set three properties that exist in the business object. These can actually be changed programmatically as well. See the section on the Allow... methods later in this chapter for more information. For now, keep these all checked and press the Next button.

6. Step 3 wants to know the security names. See Chapter 17, "VFE Security," for more information on this. For now, just press the Next button.

7. Step 4 wants to know what to name the class and what library to put it into. The name is based on the DE class you chose. The word "Environment" is removed from it, and "BizObj" is added to that. You may change this if you like. As mentioned earlier, for this tutorial we are going to save all classes for a single entity in a single library. So, select the Instructor class lib from the pull-down menu.

8. At this point, you're done. Press the Finish button.

That was easy, wasn't it? And you thought creating business objects would be difficult. What the wizard did was subclass the framework business object class, iBizObj (which is the I-layer subclass of cBizObj). Because much of your time will be spent dealing with this class, we'll take a detailed look at it.

Business object class

The framework's business object class is designed to contain the common items that all business objects need. Technically, an Instructor can't save itself. In a perfect object-oriented world, a business object class would automatically persist (save) itself to the physical data layer without the programmer needing any knowledge of how that is done. Also, the properties of the object would include the properties of the entity being modeled, like Age, Name, SSN and so forth. But VFE delegates this information to the cursor class.

There are also times when a real-world entity will contain properties that require a separate bizobj in VFE. For example, each instructor may have an addresses property and a phones property. Each of these properties also contains attributes. There is also the possibility that there could be multiple addresses or phones. In a different environment, these types of properties would be defined as a collection.

However, there is no native collection data type in Visual FoxPro. In order to simulate this in VFE, you would create an additional business object for the addresses collection and one for the phones collection. Then, you would use a technique called "relating" the business objects.

Related business objects

Relating business objects in VFE is similar to the parent-child relationship you might find in a database design. The instructor business object would be the parent business object, and the addresses and phones business objects would each be a child business object. As in the database scheme, there would be a one-to-many relationship between these business objects.

While this is a bit removed from a purist approach to a business object, it is the implementation that we must use. In a purist approach, the instructor business object would have an addresses collection and a phones collection that belonged to the instructor. You wouldn't be able to access the addresses or phones outside the parent object. In reality, it takes three business objects to model the single "Instructor" real-world entity. These are what we call inter-object relationships. When representing this entity with multiple business objects, be sure to relate the business objects and files properly. In addition to the business objects, you would want to create referential integrity rules to create these inter-object relationships in the physical layer to mirror the relationships of the business objects that must be created.

This chapter specifically deals with the operation of the business object; for complete information on creating related entities and representative user interfaces, see Chapter 14, "Related Data and Forms," which covers related data.

Parent business object

The parent business object maintains a collection of child business objects. The parent business object cascades commands to all of its child business objects based on several property values. (Refer to the properties and methods sections of this chapter for information on those properties and methods.) The parent object also keeps its children synchronized with it by sending a Requery command to the child business objects when the parent record pointer is changed.

Child business object

In the VFE framework, the same base class is used whether your bizobj is a parent or a child. To indicate to a business object that it is a child, you can populate the cParentBizObj in the child business object. The child will find a reference to its parent and then notify the parent of its existence. VFE has other features that tell the child business object how to "register" with its parent when it is instantiated, but these aren't important right now.

The fact that object references can pass VFP data session boundaries allows you to create related forms that maintain private data sessions. This would not be possible if you wanted to relate two files in separate data sessions without the business objects.

For more information on some of these techniques, see Chapter 14, "Related Data and Forms."

Data Environment Loader

If you open the business object class in the class editor, you will see that it contains an object called the DELoader. This is the Data Environment Loader. You will find several loaders in VFE. The DELoader provides for two things in the case of the business object.

First, the DE that the business object uses can be modified to suit your business domain's purpose. Perhaps you have a different environment for the same business object in different circumstances.

The second reason to use the Data Environment Loader would be to instantiate a DE that resides in a separate physical layer from the business object. This allows the DE to exist in a COM or DCOM component.

The DELoader is a simple class that loads an instance of the DE class specified. The DELoader has a property named "cDataEnvironment" that holds the name of the DE to load. If loading from a COM object, there are other properties to specify the name of the object and the machine to load it from. The cDataEnvironment property is populated when you create the business object using the wizard.

Business rules collection
In addition to the DELoader object in the business object class, you will also find a business rules collection. This collection holds a reference to all the business rules objects that have been added to the business rules. When the business object is told to save a record, if there are any business rules objects in the business rules collection, they will be called one at a time.

Business rules class
The business rules class provides a method to implement rules that will be common across several business objects. This eliminates the duplication of source code. Instead of writing some code in a business class, you would create the code in the business rules class. When a business object is sent the Save() method, it will run the Execute() method of all the business rules objects in its business rules collection.

The Execute() method of the business rule can implement any domain rule or process required. If a True is returned, the business object will continue the save; if a False is returned, the business object will not continue the save.

The business rule provides a GetErrorMessage() method. This method will be called from the business object if a False is returned to display to the user. By default, GetErrorMessage() returns the value of the cErrorMessage property, or the cErrorMessageKey value is used to look up the error message in the MsgSvc table. It is up to the developer to populate the cErrorMessage property prior to returning False to the business object.

cBizObj of cBusiness.VCX
To implement your business objects, the VFE framework provides the cBizObj class. The cBizObj class is shipped in the cBizness library. The cBizObj class is a compound class that contains an oDELoader and an oBizRulesCollection object.

The following sections detail the properties and methods you will work with most often. As always, for the fullest understanding of the VFE framework you should read the code for the classes.

cForeignKeyExpression
Populate this property if the business object is a child business object. This property will hold the name of the field in the parent cursor that relates to the child cursor. This is a somewhat misnamed property. Think of it as the field you want to populate the child foreign key with.

Here's an example: In the typical overused example of Invoice and InvoiceDetail, the key file of the Invoice table, "InvoiceNo," is used as the foreign key in the InvoiceDetail file named "Invoice." In this case, you would populate the cForeignKeyExpress with the value "InvoiceNo." See the next section, "cKeyField," for the other half of this example.

The child business object will use the information in this field to populate the foreign key in the child cursor with the parent's key automatically. When using tables, the business object will use this information to set a relation between the two files.

cKeyField
Populate this property if the business object is a child business object. This property will hold the name of the foreign key field in the child cursor. This property is somewhat misnamed. The name implies that you enter the name of the key field of the child; don't make this mistake.

To continue with the aforementioned example of Invoice and InvoiceDetail, again the key file of the Invoice table, "InvoiceNo," is used as the foreign key in the InvoiceDetail file named "Invoice." In this case, you would populate the cKeyField with the value "Invoice." See the preceding section, "cForeignKeyExpression," for the first half of this example.

The child business object will use the information in this field to populate the foreign key in the child cursor with the parent's key automatically. When using tables, the business object will use this information to set a relation between the two files.

cParentBizObjName
This is the property that informs the business object that it is a child business object. Populate the property with the object instance name of the parent business object. The business object will look for the parent business object, and when it locates it, the parent business object is sent a message to register its new child. The parent business object will add its new child to its child business object collection.

cRelationTag
This property is used in a child business object. This property is only used when using VFP tables and is not needed when using views. This property holds the name of the tag for the child cursor that is used to relate the parent and child cursor.

lAllowDelete, lAllowEdit, lAllowNew
These properties provide a simple interface to disallow any of the specific actions. Recall that these properties were settable in the Business Object wizard. In the case that you want to allow or disallow one of these actions depending on certain values and criteria, leave this property set to True and use the similarly named methods to write code to make such a determination.

lConfirmOnDelete
This property is fairly self-explanatory, but you should be aware that there is no code in the business object class that looks at this property. The code that looks at the property is in the presentation object. So, if you are using a business object via COM and have set the property to True, it is up to your front end to request a confirmation from the user based on this property.

lNewOnParentNew
This property will only be used when the business object is a child business object. If this property is set to new, the parent business object will send a New() message to this, the child business object, when a new is performed at the parent level. (This is one of the big improvements over the Codebook business object. In Codebook, instead of this property there's an lNewChildOnNew, which is much more limited.)

lRequeryChildrenOnSave

This property indicates to the business object that after a save has been performed, a Requery() message will be sent to all of its children business objects. The default for this property is True.

lSaveAllRows

This property will force the business object to save all rows of a record buffered table when the business object is instructed to save. Be aware that this property is set to True by default.

lWriteForeignKeyOnNew, lWriteForeignKeyOnSave

These properties indicate to the business object when to write the foreign key value from the parent record to the child record. The lWriteForeignKeyOnNew property will be checked in the New_Perform() method, and the lWriteForeignKeyOnSave property will be checked in the Save_Perform() method. Be sure that you have coordinated these values with the lWritePrimaryKeyOnNew and lWritePrimaryKeyOnSave in the cursor object.

In other words, be sure that there is a value in the parent cursor's primary key field prior to trying to write it to the foreign key field in the child cursor.

oCursor

This property holds a reference to the primary cursor. The DE class sets this property when the cursors are instantiated. This property is the property the developer will use to access the data that is controlled by the business object.

For example, assume you were writing code in the instructor business object and you needed to check the value of the 'LastName' field. You would write code similar to this:

```
cLastName = This.oCursor.Fields.Item['LastName'].Value
```

oDataEnvironment

This property holds a reference to the DE object that was loaded for the business object. This allows you to use the services of the DE object, such as FindCursor().

oHost

This property holds a reference to the interface object that is hosting the business object. Generally this will be a reference to a presentation object. This reference allows you to send messages to the presentation object, perhaps to run a method in the presentation object that prompts the user for data or a yes/no response.

You will not want to write code in the business object that exposes a user interface in cases where your business object may be running as a COM object. This will violate your layered and n-tier design and make it more difficult to move to that environment. Therefore, use this property with caution and always check to make sure it holds an object reference before addressing it.

oParentBizObj
This property contains a reference to the parent business object. This property will be invaluable when creating related forms where each has a private data session.

oBizObjs
This property contains a reference to the child business object collection. The collection contains a reference to all of the child business objects. This property is added at run time when a child business object is registered with its parent. oBizObjs is actually a member object that gets added to a business object when a child is registered with it, but for all practical purposes it can be thought of as a property.

RecNo, RecordCount, VisibleRecordCount
These properties contain the value indicated by the name. Remember that the cursor object also contains these properties. Each of these properties in the business object has an access method associated with it. The access method actually requests the information from the cursor object and returns it to the business object property.

AllowNew(), AllowDelete(), AllowEdit(), AllowSave()
These methods determine whether the defined behavior is allowed. Here's the syntax:

```
Object.AllowXXXX()
```

Returns: Logical

Remarks
By default, each of these methods will check the value of its corresponding property, such as lAllowNew or lAllowDelete, and if those are True they will check security and the read-only property to determine whether to allow the function.

To maintain the default functionality and add your own, we recommend that you AND your result with the result of DoDefault(). For example, let's assume you only want to allow a user to delete a record if the termdate is not empty. An example of the code you'd put into the AllowDelete() method would be:

```
local lAllowIt
lAllowIt = .t.
if empty( This.oCursor.Fields.Item['termdate'].Value )
   lAllowIt = .f.
EndIf

Return lAllowIt AND DoDefault()
```

Calling DoDefault() will ensure not only that the record meets your business rules, but also that the user has security to delete a record in this business object, for example. If you want to totally override security, you would omit that call to DoDefault(), of course.

For example, suppose you want to allow anyone to delete a record that has a termdate even if they don't normally have security for this action. You would override AllowDelete() without calling the default behavior. This allows for extremely flexible business rules.

Cancel(), Cancel_Pre(), Cancel_Perform(), Cancel_Post()

The Cancel() method will "undo" any changes made to a record. It will also remove an added record that has not yet been saved. Here's the syntax:

```
Object.CancelXXXX( tlAllRows )
```

Returns: Constants:
   • FILE_OK
   • FILE_CANCEL
Argument: *tlAllRows*—Pass a True to indicate that all rows of a table buffered cursor should be canceled.

Remarks

Cancel() is the shell method that calls the _Pre, _Perform and _Post methods. The Cancel_Perform() actually calls the cursor object's Cancel() method to do the actual cancel.

The Cancel_Pre() and Cancel_Post() methods are hooks that allow you to perform some task or check prior to or after a cancel. Returning a FILE_CANCEL from Cancel_Pre() will actually cancel the cancel, as strange as that sounds. The Cancel_Post() method is only called after a successful cancel is performed. This allows you to add code that you want run after a successful cancel.

In the case of Cancel_Pre() and Cancel_Post(), if you want to return the default constant we recommend that you return DoDefault(). For example:

```
Local cSomeVariable
* You do some code here prior to a cancel
Return DoDefault()
```

By returning DoDefault(), you don't have to remember the valid return value for a successful completion of your function. If you look at the default methods of these hook properties, you will see that all they do is return FILE_OK.

Delete(), Delete_Pre(), Delete_Perform(), Delete_Post()

These methods delete the current record in the cursor. Here's the syntax:

```
Object.DeleteXXXX()
```

Returns: Constant FILE_OK or record number

Remarks

Delete() is the shell method that calls the _Pre, _Perform and _Post methods. The Delete_Perform() method calls the Delete() method of the cursor class in order to delete the record.

The Delete_Pre() and Delete_Post() methods are hooks that allow you to implement business rules, which are called before (_Pre) or after (_Post) a delete takes place. The delete will be canceled if you return FILE_CANCEL from the _Pre method. The _Post method will not be called unless the delete is successfully processed.

As indicated previously, be sure to return DoDefault() from your hook methods to assure you are returning the correct data type.

FindCursor()

This method returns a reference to the cursor based on the name you provided. Here's the syntax:

```
Object.FindCursor( tcCursor )
```

Returns: Object
Argument: *tcCursor*—Specifies the name of the cursor to find. If no cursor name is passed, the oCursor reference of the business object is returned.

Remarks

FindCursor() will search in the business object's DE object for the specified cursor. If the cursor is not located, the child business object's DE will be searched. If the cursor is not found, a null will be returned. If the cursor is not found and the business object has children, the child business objects will also be searched for a matching cursor.

FindField()

This method returns a reference to a field based on the name you provided. Here's the syntax:

```
Object.FindField( tcField )
```

Returns: Object
Argument: *tcField*—Specifies the name of the field to find.

Remarks

FindField() will search the primary cursor first, and then it will search the other DE cursors. If successful, it will return an object reference to the field object. If the business object is a child business object and tcField is not found in the business object's DE, the parent business object is also asked to find the field. If the field can't be found, a null value is returned.

FindViewParameter()

This method returns a reference to the specified view parameter object (see the "FindCursor()" section for more information).

GetValues(), SetValues()

GetValues() will return an object with the values of the current record in the object. SetValues() will take an object created by GetValues() and populate the current cursor with the values. This is an objectified SCATTER/GATHER and can be used to populate a cursor with values from a lookup table, for example.

GetRecordSet()

This method gets an ADO record set of all the data in the primary cursor of the business object. This will come in handy when creating Web pages or using non-VFP front-end user interfaces. Currently the framework does not provide a corresponding method to save a changed RecordSet, so unless you add this functionality yourself, this method is only useful for retrieving data. The designers will probably be adding more ADO support in future versions.

IsAdding(), IsChanged(), IsDeleted(), IsCursorEmpty()

These methods are self-explanatory. Each of these methods requests the information from the cursor object. A logical True or False will be returned as a result.

New(), New_Pre(), New_Perform(), New_Post()

These methods add a record to the primary cursor of the business object. Here's the syntax:

```
Object.NewXXXX( tcCursor )
```

Returns: FILE_OK or FILE_CANCEL

Remarks

The New() method is the shell method that calls New_Pre(), New_Perform() and New_Post(). New_Pre() is a hook where you can put code that will be run prior to adding a new record. You can also stop a new record from being added here by returning a FILE_CANCEL.

Be aware that New_Pre() is called from New() without checking AllowNew(). AllowNew() is called from New_Perform(). So, if you are using AllowNew() code and also putting code in New_Pre(), it is possible that you have run code and the record will not be added. We suggest that you check the AllowNew() method manually in your New_Pre() code to avoid potential problems.

After New_Perform() gets a True from AllowNew(), it will call on the cursor's AddNew() method to perform the physical add into the cursor. If the cursor returns a FILE_OK, the New_Perform() method will call WriteForeignKey() of the cursor if the business object is a child and if lWriteForeignKeyOnNew is set to True. Then, if the business object has children, it will call the Requery() of its child business objects. (Remember, the business object code supports the bizobj being either a parent or a child, and actually it can be both at the same time.)

Finally, New_Perform() will loop through its child bizobj collection calling the child's New() if its lNewOnParentNew property is True. If all this occurs without a problem, FILE_OK is returned to the New() method, which finally calls your New_Post() method. This is where you should do any additional operations, since you are assured that a record has been added. If a record was not added, the New_Post() will not be called.

OkToMove()

This method determines whether it is okay to move the record pointer. Basically, it is not okay to move if the current record has been edited and the cursor is record buffered, or if the business object is a parent business object and there are pending changes in any of its children.

Requery(), Requery_Pre(), Requery_Perform(), Requery_Post()

These methods pass a Requery() command to the cursor object to retrieve the data from the underlying tables of the cursor object. Here's the syntax:

```
Object.RequeryXXXX()
```

Returns: REQUERY_SUCCESS or REQUERY_ERROR

Remarks

Requery() is the shell method that calls Requery_Pre(), Requery_Perform() and Requery_Post(). As in the previous methods with hooks, if you return a REQUERY_ERROR from Requery_Pre(), the requery will not be performed.

Requery_Perform() will call the Requery() method of the primary cursor object to retrieve the data from the underlying table. If this is a success, Requery_Perform() will call the Requery() method of its child business objects.

If the Requery_Perform() is successful, the Requery() method will call the Requery_Post() method. The Requery_Post() is the ideal place to add code to Requery() other cursors in the DE to keep them in sync with the primary cursor. There is no need here to refresh controls; you will see in the next chapter, "Presentation Objects," that the Requery() method there will take care of refreshing the display.

Save(), Save_Pre(), Save_Perform(), Save_Post(), OnSaveNew()

These methods save the changes that have been made to the buffered cursors. Here's the syntax:

```
Object.SaveXXXX( tlAllRows, tlForce )
```

Returns: FILE_OK, FILE_ERRORHANDLED or FILE_CANCEL
Arguments: *tlAllRows*—Specifies that all edited rows will be saved in a table buffered cursor.
              tlForce—Specifies that the save should be forced even if VFP has sensed an update conflict.

Remarks

Save() is the shell method that calls Save_Pre(), Save_Perform() and Save_Post(). As in the previous methods with hooks, if you return a FILE_CANCEL from Save_Pre(), the save will not be performed.

It's a bit confusing why there is no code to call AllowSave(). It looks like the AllowSave() is only used to determine whether to display the Save button or not, which does make sense because if you allow an edit or a new, you must by default want to allow a save.

Save() will begin a transaction after calling Save_Pre() but prior to calling Save_Perform(). So, if you have to perform processing like Requery() or other things you can do under a transaction, do them in the Save_Pre(). However, if this is a child business object, be aware that the transaction will have been started in the parent business object.

Save_Perform() performs several steps:

1. If the lSaveChildrenFirst property is True, the SaveChildren() method is called. The SaveChildren() method loops through the oBizObjs collection calling each child business object's Save() method.

2. If this is a new record, and lWriteForeignKeyOnSave is True and this object is a child business object, then the WriteForeignKey() method is called.

3. The Validate() method of the oBizRules collection is called. As we discussed earlier, this method will loop through all the business rules objects that have been added to this business object, calling the Execute() method of each. If any of those fail, the save process will be done here and a FILE_CANCEL will be returned.

4. The Update() method of the primary cursor object is called to save the data to the underlying table. If this is a table buffered cursor and we are saving all rows, the UpdateBatch() method of the cursor is called.

5. At this point, if lSaveChildrenFirst is False, so we don't do this twice, the business object will call its SaveChildren() method.

If all of these steps are successful, the Save_Perform() will return a FILE_OK to the Save() method. The Save() method will then commit the transaction by calling the EndTransaction() method. If for some reason the Save_Perform() returned FILE_CANCEL, the Save() method will perform a rollback. At this point, if the lRequeryChildrenOnSave is True, the Save() method will call all the children business objects' Requery() methods.

At this point, Save_Post() is finally called. *Save_Post() is called after the transaction has been committed.* Save_Post() is not called, of course, if the save fails and the transaction is rolled back.

The Save() method has one more hook method called OnSaveNew(). This method is called after a successful save if the record saved was a new record—in other words, if we were saving a newly added record, OnSaveNew() is called after the successful save.

Once again, in the business layer you will see that there are no commands to refresh the user interface at all. That is all done in the presentation object.

SetField(), SetParameter()

These methods can be used to set the value of a field in the cursor object. Here's the syntax:

```
Object.SetField( tcField, tuValue )
Object.SetParameter( tcParameter, tuValue )
```

Returns: Logical
Arguments: *tcField*—The name of the field to populate with the specified value.
tcParameter—The name of the view parameter to populate with the specified value.
tuValue—The value with which to populate the specified field or view parameter.

Remarks

These methods can be used to replace the direct method of drilling down to the value of the field or view parameter object you want to populate, but in the end, they do the same thing.

However, using "setters" and "getters" is a more common programmatic interface for COM objects, and your code may be more readable if you use these methods.

Creating your business rules

Well, now that you are familiar with all of the default attributes and behaviors of the base business object class, you might ask, "Where do I put the code?" Remember that the business object is just an abstract class that gives you the mundane and common functionality.

It is up to you to add the properties and methods that are required for the entity you are modeling. In the example of the "Cat" entity, you would add the Scratch(), Yawn(), Sleep() and other methods to the business object. Also, keep in mind that if you have a rule or behavior that will be common to several objects, you should create it as a business rules class.

One example of a business rules class is an audit trail. Create a business rules class that writes all the changes of the cursor to an audit file of some kind. This file can have many different structures, depending on what you want to accomplish, from as simple as a time and user ID to as complex as saving the old and new value of every changed field.

Summary

The business object class is the worker bee of your application. This is the base class you will use to implement the entities of your business domain. The bulk of your code will be contained in the business objects. The framework has provided all of the infrastructures you need to persist or store the objects to the physical data layer.

You can also see the Chain of Responsibility pattern emerging here. Each layer is building upon the previous layer and using its services. The business object calls upon the cursor objects to do the physical work of adding records and saving edits. The cursor handles all the details and tells the business object it has completed successfully. The business object then performs value-added services specific to the business object. The business object coordinates with its parent and child business objects to be sure they are synchronized.

Finally, don't forget the little business rules class. Abstracting specific rules into their own class will allow you to share those rules with other business objects to maximize your code reuse. Each business rules class has the same interface, so you can add and remove the rules objects to the business objects and adapt to future needs of your business domain.

At this point you may want to go back and re-read the VFE documentation sections about the business object and business rules objects. If you can, read through the code of the Save(), New() and other methods as the book walked you through them.

You should now be starting to see the power of this framework. If you are designing a Web application with VFE, this is the point where you would stop. From here we'll go on to the user interface layer, which you may want to build as a Web front end or—say it isn't true—a VB front end. If you have created the data layer and the business layer, you have all the functionality in your application. Your Web page or your UI code is nothing more than a control panel that contains switches, dials and knobs so the user can control your application.

So, in the next chapter we will start creating a VFP/VFE-based user interface. The starting point is the presentation object. See you in Chapter 7.

Chapter 7
Presentation Objects

The presentation object is a container that holds user interface controls that display the data of a business object. The presentation object is the first class you will learn about that is in the user interface layer of the n-tier model.

Up to this point, all of the objects you have built have been non-visual objects. In other words, these objects are not displayed on the screen in any way. Essentially, what you have learned and created up to this point is the business domain aspect of the application. You have created your data layer and your business layer. In the business objects, you have created all the functionality that your program needs to perform within its business domain.

But to the user, your application is the user interface; the part of your application that the user can interact with is the program to the users. This would include the text boxes, combo boxes, forms, menus, list boxes, tree views and so forth.

It is possible to create this user interface in many environments. A Web browser-based interface has become very popular and is in vogue these days. For all practical purposes, you could attach several front ends to your application also. However, even though it's come a long way, the Web browser interface is still in its infancy. You have to write a lot of code—server-side and client-side—to provide functionality that FoxPro applications have had for many years. In addition, VFE gives you a rich set of user controls to build a VFP interface.

So, the first objects you will create to build your VFE application's user interface are presentation objects. Let's take a look at this powerful class.

Control panel

We have mentioned this before, but the analogy works, so we will use it again. The presentation object is the "control panel" or "dashboard" for your business object. It is through the presentation object that the user is able to access the data and processes of the business object to which it is connected.

The presentation object uses the services of the business object. The Chain of Responsibility pattern is continued to this layer of the application. Each method of the presentation object adds value to the business object methods controlling messaging and refreshing prior to and after requesting a service from its business object.

Each presentation object will represent a single business object. The presentation object has a property that contains a reference to its business object, through which it passes messages. The business object could in fact run on a remote machine as a DCOM object, or it could be compiled into the EXE where the user interface classes are deployed.

The presentation object is based on the VFP container class. This allows the interface controls that represent a business object to be encapsulated in a single class. You can use several presentation objects to create a single form. Or, you could place one presentation object on top of a second presentation object. You can also use the same presentation objects in many forms, providing the same interface for a business object in many different contexts.

Before we get into some of the details of the presentation object, we'll continue our Tutorial U application by creating an "instructor" presentation object.

Tutorial

In this section we will create a presentation object for the instructor business object. Previously we created the business object that models the "Instructor" real-world entity. Now the presentation object is the first step in providing a "control panel" to that business object.

1. Open the Book Tutorial application in the VFE Application Builder.

2. Select the Classes page and highlight the Presentation Object node.

3. Press the New button. VFE will display the wizard selection dialog. Select the Standard Presentation Object wizard at this point. We will discuss the other wizard in Chapter 14, "Related Data and Forms." Press the OK button, and the Standard Presentation Object wizard will be displayed.

4. Step 1 asks you to select the business object. Since a presentation is the control panel for a business object, this makes sense. Because we only have one business object created, that's all that is available to select. Press the Next button.

5. Step 2 requests that you specify the layout. The basic choices are Standard and Grid. Of course, Grid will create a single grid with all the fields that you select. The Standard interface will build a page with a separate control for each field you select. Notice that it also asks how many pages. If you select more than one, a page frame control will be added to the presentation object. For now, we will accept all of the defaults and move on to the next page. Press the Next button.

6. Step 3 lists all of the fields in the DE of the business object. VFE gets this information from the metadata. At this point you are specifying what data fields you would like controls for on the presentation object. Remember that in the metadata one of the properties on the Interface tab was the interface class. VFE will use that information to place the specified class on the presentation object for that data field. This is why it is advantageous to create your metadata prior to the presentation object. Also, VFE will retrieve the caption from the metadata to create a label for each control it adds.

7. Use the mover arrows to move the SSN, FirstName, MiddleName and LastName fields to the right side of the mover. These are the fields that controls will be created for and bound to on the presentation object. Do not put the InstructorID or AddressID on the presentation object; these are surrogate keys that the users have no knowledge of, and it would confuse them to view ID fields. Notice that the selected list box contains mover handles. The controls will be placed on the presentation object in the order listed in this list. Don't be overly concerned, because you will most likely edit the presentation object after it has been created. Press the Next button.

8. Step 4 requests that you set some properties of the presentation object. You will notice that these are similar to the properties you can set in the business object. We prefer to set these at the business object level unless it is specifically applicable to this user interface item only. This is generally not the case, but in your programming you may

find that you want to set these at the user interface level, and that's fine. Accept the defaults and press the Next button.

9. Step 5 asks for the method you want to use to bind controls to the data. We'll explain this in the "Data binding options" section later in this chapter. For now, accept the defaults and press the Next button.

10. Step 6 provides a list of "action" controls you can add to your presentation object. This is a matter of design selection. You can choose to put these types of controls directly on your presentation object, or to implement them with a VFP toolbar. In addition to these controls, most of these features are also implemented in the default menu provided in the framework, and also in the right-click menu of the presentation object. For the sake of completeness, let's select a few of these controls. Generally speaking, action controls should not be placed in a presentation object unless the presentation object is going to be used as a child. When action controls are placed in the presentation object directly, they call presentation object methods; when they are placed in a toolbar or directly on the form, they call form methods. Many of the form-level methods perform operations that should not be skipped, like the call to WriteBuffer in the form's Save() method.

11. Move the controls to the right list box in this order: iNewButton, iSaveButton, iDeleteButton, iSeparator, iPriorButton, iNextButton, iSeparator, iCloseButton. Press the Next button.

12. Step 7 is the Finish step, which requests the class name; we'll keep the default InstructorsViewPresObj (you can no doubt see how these names are constructed) and select the Instructors class library that we have been using so far.

13. Press the Finish button, and VFE will create the presentation object.

If you select the presentation object we just created and press the Open button, you should see something similar to **Figure 1**.

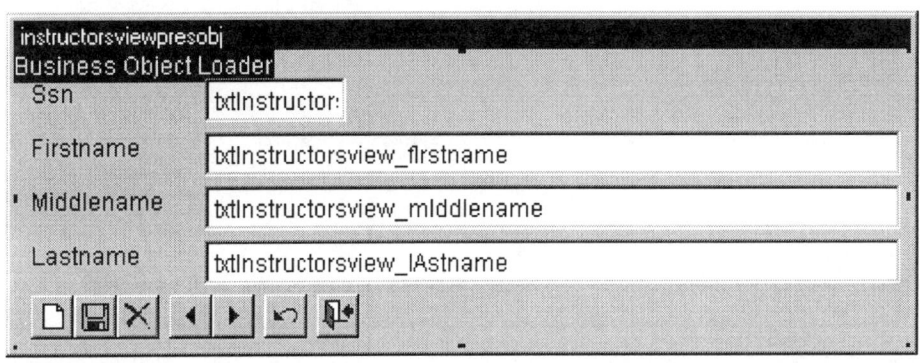

Figure 1. The presentation object we created using the Presentation Object wizard in the tutorial.

If you look at the presentation object, you will see that VFE added the fields in the order we specified. Because we didn't edit the caption properties, the field names were used for labels. This illustrates why it is advantageous to set up all of your metadata prior to creating the presentation object with the wizard.

Business Object Loader

If you look at Figure 1 again, you will notice that there is a "Business Object Loader" on your presentation object. This class exists on the presentation object base class. The purpose of the Business Object Loader is to load the business object.

The Business Object Loader is part of the class definition for a presentation object. Because it's built into the cPresentationObject class, Visual FoxPro instantiates it first whenever a presentation object is instantiated. A common mistake Visual FoxExpress developers often make is to use the "send to back" toolbar option when editing presentation objects, which causes other controls to be instantiated first. Because the Business Object Loader makes data available to the presentation object's controls, it is important that the Business Object Loader be instantiated first. If the send to back option is ever used on another control, it's important that the Business Object Loader be sent to back last, to make sure it is the first control.

Take a look at **Figure 2**. This is the builder for the Business Object Loader. To run this builder for yourself, open the InstructorsViewPresObj class from the VFE Classes page and right-click on the Business Object Loader. Then, select Builder... from the right-click menu.

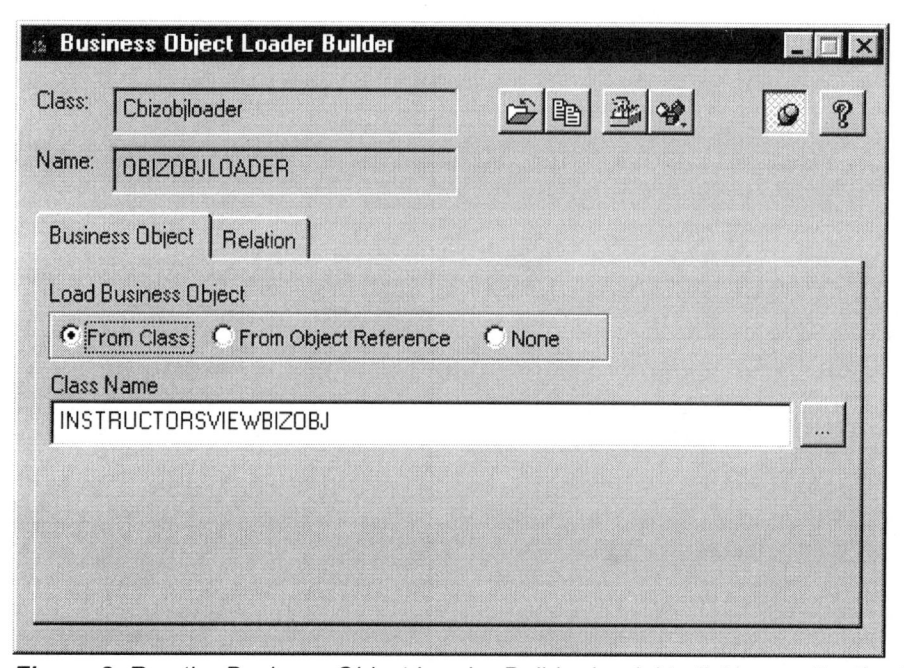

Figure 2. Run the Business Object Loader Builder by right-clicking on the Business Object Loader and selecting Builder... from the menu.

The builder shows the properties of the bizobj loader that were set by the Presentation Object wizard. Recall that we selected the bizobj to use for the presentation object. You can see that the bizobj we selected—InstructorsViewBizObj—has been used to populate the Class Name field, which is the cBizObj property of the loader.

When the presentation object is instantiated, the bizobj loader will also be instantiated because the presentation object contains it. When the bizobj loader is instantiated, it will create an instance of the specified cBizObj class. You can see where this happens in the SetBusinessObject() method of the loader, which is called by its Init() method.

```
.oBizObj = CREATEOBJECT(.cBizObj, This)
```

As you can see, the Business Object Loader passes a reference to itself to the business object as a parameter. The Init() of the business object will see that an object was passed, and it will populate its properties with the properties of the Business Object Loader.

Finally, the Business Object Loader will verify that the business object has been properly created, and it will set the presentation object's oBizObj property to reference the created business object.

```
.Parent.oBizObj = .oBizObj
```

This code works because the parent of the bizobj loader is the presentation object.

The Business Object Loader is not limited to loading the business object based on the class name. You can also specify a reference to the business object. You may do this if the object has already been created and you just need to reference it again. Do this by changing the radio button on the builder from "class" to "object reference." Just be sure that the object reference you specify is in scope of the bizobj loader.

You can also use the application's factory to create the object. Basically, the factory is an object that creates objects based on the "key name." The key name is looked up in a file to determine the name of the class to create. This allows the developer to change the class that is instantiated at run time rather than hard-coding the class at design time. This cannot be done from the builder, but it is as simple as populating the cFactoryName property with the key of the class you want to load.

Finally, the Business Object Loader can instantiate a bizobj from a COM or DCOM server. However, deploying a distributed VFE application is beyond the scope of this book, so we won't dive into this potentially powerful feature.

Once the presentation object has a reference to the business object, it doesn't matter how or where it was loaded; the presentation object is now able to make use of the business object's services and cursor class transparently.

cPresentationObj of cPresent.VCX

The cPresentationObj class is the base presentation object class. As we said, this class is the container for the controls you would need to control the business object you have created to model your real-world entity.

The properties and methods here are by no means all of those in the class, and you should browse the class properties and method code sometime to become familiar with how they work.

cEditForm
This property is used to put the name of a form you want to use to edit a record. This is generally used when you have a grid or a list view of records. When the user selects Add or double-clicks on a record in the grid, and you have populated the cEditForm with a form class name, that class will be instantiated to provide the user an edit type interface for the record.

See Chapter 14, "Related Data and Forms," for more information and an example of how to use this correctly.

cListFields
This property specifies a comma-delimited list of fields to display when the List() method is executed. The List() method is a method of the presentation object that lists all the current records in the cursor. The list is a grid in which the columns are added on the fly. If you have populated this property, the list grid will be built with the fields in this property in the order they are listed.

However, we prefer to use the display order and grid caption properties of the metadata to specify this information. Using the metadata allows you (or your user) to change the list grid at run time without modifying any source code.

cMenuPad
This property specifies the name of a custom menu pad object to create when this object is created on a form. The menu pad must already exist in the application and in the menu. The menu pad is actually not created but shown when the presentation object has focus, and hidden when the presentation object loses focus or the object is destroyed.

cSetFocusTo
This property holds the name of the object to set focus to when SetFocusToFirst() is called. This property should be used when you don't want the first tab order control to get focus on a new or delete. When you populate this property, include the full object path without the name of the presentation object.

For example, if you have a text box named "txtFirstName" directly on the presobj, you would populate this property with txtFirstName. But if this field were on the first page of a page frame, you would have to use pgfInstructors.Page1.txtFirstName, for instance.

lActivateOnUIEnable
This property indicates that the presentation object should become the form's active presentation object when its UIEnable event is passed True. This means that when the user clicks on this presentation object or tabs to it, the form's oPresentObj will be populated with a reference to the presentation object. By default this does not happen.

Why is this important? Well, getting ahead of ourselves here, toolbar controls work on the active presentation object. The active presentation object is not necessarily the one with focus; it is the one in the form's oPresentObj property.

First, this property is only used if there is more than one presobj on a page. Whether to set this to True depends on how you want your interface to work. Generally we advise that if the presobj is the only one on a page, you should set it to True. Also, keep in mind that if you set a presobj's lActivateOnUIEnable to True, you generally will set another one to True. This is necessary because when focus switches back to that other presobj on the form, you want it to become the active presobj again.

lAllowDelete, lAllowEdit, lAllowFilter, lAllowList, lAllowNavigate, lAllowNew, lAllowOrder, lAllowPrint

All of these properties are fairly self-explanatory. Also, you won't need to set lAllowDelete to False on the presentation object if you have already set lAllowDelete to False on the bizobj. You will also see that there is a corresponding method for each of these. The method looks at the value of the property, or you can override the method with your own code.

Just keep in mind that you should use these at the level they are placed. If you were working on an entity that you don't ever want records deleted in, you'd set the lAllowDelete at the bizobj level. However, if this is a presentation object that contains the customer address, and you are reusing it on the invoice presentation object, you may want to set lAllowEdit to False here, since you don't want someone to edit the customer's address in the invoice.

lConfirmDelete
This property indicates that the user should be asked for confirmation before deleting a record.

lDisplayNoRecordMessage
This property indicates that a message should be displayed when a requery doesn't retrieve any records.

lMain
This property indicates that the presentation object should become the main presentation object on the form that contains it when the form is instantiated. See the "lActivateOnUIEnable" section for a discussion on what being the active presobj means. This property is usually set to True by the presobj wizard appropriately.

oBizObj
This is an object reference to the business object associated with the presentation object. Most of the methods in the following sections will use the reference to send commands to the business object rather than implement them at the user interface level.

AllowEdit(), AllowFilter(), AllowCancel(), AllowNavigate(), AllowNew(), AllowOrder(), AllowSave()

These methods are called by the framework to determine whether the specified behavior is allowed. Here's the syntax:

```
Object.AllowXXXX()
```

Returns: Logical

Remarks
By default these methods first look at the value of the presentation object's same-named property. In other words, AllowEdit() looks at the lAllowEdit property, for instance. If lAllowEdit is False, that value is returned. However, if the value is True, the method calls the business object method of the same name. This allows you to disallow something in the presentation object that is allowed by the business object, but not the other way around. So, in the case that you have set the business object's lAllowEdit to False, setting it to True in the presentation object will not override that.

If you like, you can enter code in these methods to return a dynamic value; however, you may want to logically AND the result with the default method's return value. This code demonstrates how you might do that:

```
Local lResult
LResult = * Code here to determine whether edit is allowed

Return lResult AND DoDefault()
```

Cancel(), Cancel_Pre(), Cancel_Post()
The Cancel() method will "undo" any user edits and will also remove any new records that have not been saved. Here's the syntax:

```
Object.CancelXXXX( tlAllRows )
```

Returns: Constants:
             • FILE_OK
             • FILE_CANCEL
Argument: tlAllRows—Pass a True to indicate that all rows of a table buffered cursor should be canceled.

Remarks
Cancel() is the shell method that calls the _Pre and _Post methods. The Cancel() actually calls the business object's Cancel() method to do the actual cancel.

The Cancel_Pre() and Cancel_Post() methods are hooks that allow you to perform some task or check prior to or after a cancel. Returning a FILE_CANCEL from Cancel_Pre() will actually cancel the cancel, as strange as that sounds. The Cancel_Post() method is only called after a successful cancel is performed. This allows you to add code that you want run after a successful cancel.

The Cancel() method will also refresh the UI if needed.

Copy()
The Copy() method creates a new record with the same contents as the current record. Here's the syntax:

```
Object.Copy()
```

Returns: Constants:
             • FILE_OK
             • FILE_CANCEL

Remarks
Copy() is a simple but useful method. Copy() will add a new record to the cursor and populate the new cursor with the values that were in the record that was current when the copy command was run. Copy() will also skip populating fields that have defaulted or key values in them.

If you are using a grid-based presentation object and have the cEditForm property populated, that form will be created after the record is copied.

When the current record is an unsaved copy of a record, the lCopyInProgress property of the presentation object will be True.

Delete(), Delete_Pre(), Delete_Post()
The Delete() method will mark the current record for deletion. Here's the syntax:

```
Object.DeleteXXXX()
```

Returns: Constants:
             • FILE_OK
             • FILE_CANCEL

Remarks
Delete() is the shell method that calls the Delete_Pre() and Delete_Post() methods. The Delete() method actually calls the business object's Delete() method to do the actual delete. The Delete() method of the presentation object will also display a delete confirmation window if you have the lConfirmDelete property set to True.

The Delete_Pre() and Delete_Post() methods are hooks that allow you to perform some task or check prior to or after a delete. Keep in mind that these should be user interface level code, such as displaying a message box or enabling or disabling controls. Returning a FILE_CANCEL from Delete_Pre() will actually cancel the delete. The Delete_Post() method is only called after a successful delete is performed. This allows you to add code that you want run after a successful delete.

As an added bonus, the Delete() method will remove an item from a listobject that resides on the form, such as a list view or tree view, assuming that the PK value is the item index value. Finally, Delete() refreshes the presentation object.

New(), New_Pre(), New_Post()
The New() method will add a record to the cursor. Here's the syntax:

```
Object.NewXXXX()
```

Returns: Constants:
             • FILE_OK
             • FILE_CANCEL

Remarks

New() is the shell method that calls the _Pre and _Post methods. The New() method actually calls the business object's New() method to add the record.

The New_Pre() and New_Post() methods are hooks that allow you to perform some task or check prior to or after a new. Returning a FILE_CANCEL from New_Pre() will actually cancel the new. The New_Post() method is only called after a successful new is performed. This allows you to add code that you want run after a successful new.

In the event that the cEditForm is populated, the New() method will also call the cEditForm to allow editing of the new record. This method will also refresh the form and itself as needed.

IsAdding(), IsChanged(), IsDeleted(), IsCursorEmpty()

These methods are self-explanatory. These methods request the information from the business object, which requests the information from the cursor object. A logical True or False will be returned as a result.

It is probably worth noting that IsChanged() checks to see whether the presentation object's business object or any of its children has pending changes. To see whether there are changes pending only in the business object that is referenced by the presentation object's oBizObj property, IsChanged() should be passed .T.

Requery()

The Requery() method of the presentation object will call the Requery() method of its business object. If you want to Requery() a cursor from the user interface layer, it is best to call the Requery() of the presentation object and let the Chain of Responsibility design trickle down the layers. You should do this because when the user interface exists it is necessary to refresh the forms, and the presentation object layer will do this automatically if you have called its Requery() method.

Save(), Save_Pre(), Save_Post()

The Save() method will save any edits or new records to the underlying table. Here's the syntax:

```
Object.SaveXXXX( tlAllRows, tlForce )
```

Returns: Constants:
 • FILE_OK
 • FILE_CANCEL

Arguments: *tlAllRows*—Passing a True indicates that all rows of a table buffered cursor should be saved.
tlForce—Passing a True indicates that the save should be completed even if a conflict is detected.

Remarks

Save() is the method to call in the user interface level to save the current or all records. The Save() method will also call the Save_Pre() and Save_Post() methods. The Save() method calls the business object's Save() method. Any parameters received to this method will be passed to the cursor class. If a FILE_ERRORHANDLED message is returned from the business object, the presentation object will call its HandleError() method to display the error message.

The Save_Pre() and Save_Post() methods are hooks that allow you to perform some task or check prior to or after a save. Try to limit the code you put in these methods to user interface items only. Perhaps you want to prompt the user to create an e-mail reminder. The Save_Pre() would be where you would request the message, and then populate a property in the business object with the result. Returning a FILE_CANCEL from Save_Pre() will cancel the save. The Save_Post() method is only called after a successful save is performed. This allows you to add code that you want run after a successful save.

Search(), GetCriteria()
These methods are used to locate specific records in the underlying cursor. Here's the syntax:

```
Object.Search( tcSearchString )
```

Returns: Logical (results of search)
Argument: tcSearchString—A string that evaluates to an expression that will be used with a locate statement to find the requested record.

Remarks
Search() provides a method to pass a search string to the business object to locate a specific record in the main cursor. The string you provide will need to be an expression that evaluates to an argument for a locate. For example, you might set lcSearchString like this:

```
lcSearchString = "LastName='Smith'"
```

If you don't provide a search string, the Search() method will call the GetCriteria() method of the presentation object. This method will call the Query Criteria form, which is a form that provides a method for the end user to supply a value for each field in the cursor to search for.

Once GetCriteria() returns a string, it will be passed to the Search() method of the business object.

Presentation Object Builder
The Presentation Object Builder can help you set some of the more common properties of your presentation objects. To run the Presentation Object Builder, open any of your presentation objects in the Class Designer by selecting one from the Classes page of the Application Builder and choosing Open. Then, right-click on the presentation object and select Builder... from the shortcut menu (see **Figure 3**).

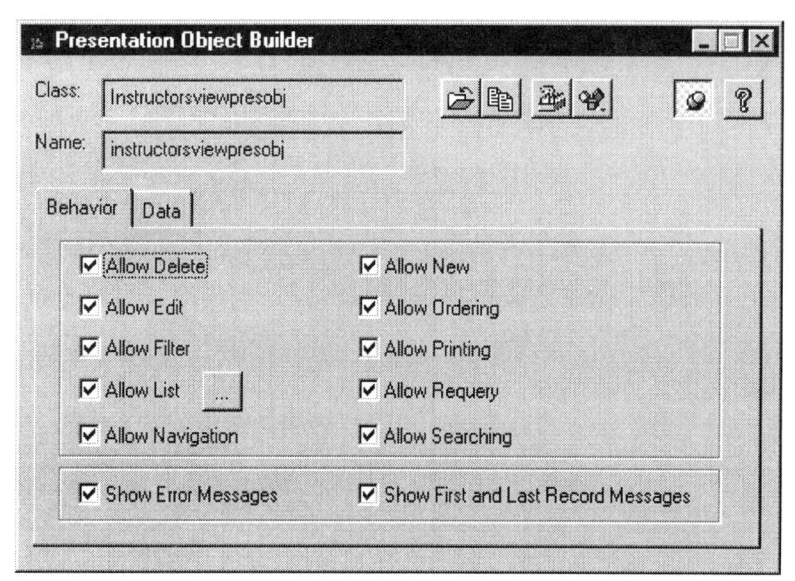

Figure 3. The Presentation Object Builder is run by editing a presentation object in the Class Designer and then right-clicking on the object and selecting Builder... from the shortcut menu.

The builder provides a quick interface to set most of the "allow" properties in addition to providing a pop-up dialog to edit the fields in the cList field. Pressing the command button next to the "Allow List" prompt accesses the list field selector dialog (see **Figure 4**). This mover interface simplifies the selection of fields that will be displayed when the List() method of the presentation object is called.

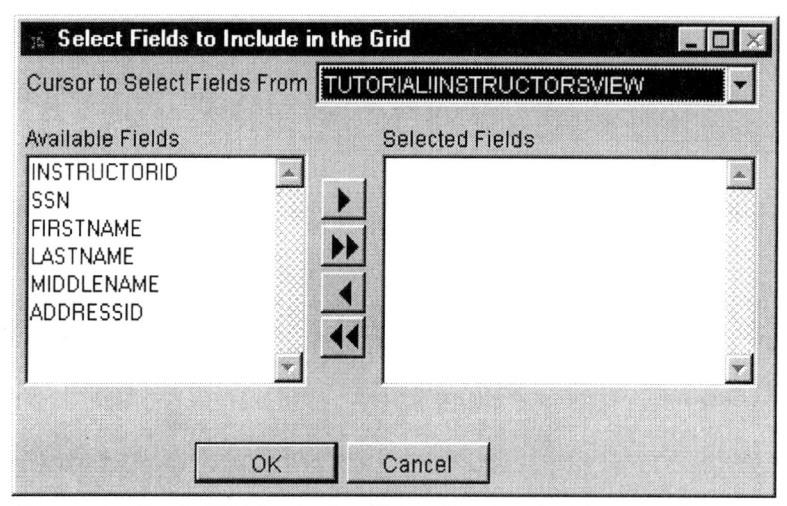

Figure 4. The list field selector dialog is accessed by pressing the command button next to the "Allow List" option on the Presentation Object Builder, as shown in Figure 3.

Data binding options

When building a presentation object, you have the option of selecting how the controls are bound to the data. Your choices are to bind to the field objects or to the fields directly. Both the Data page of the Presentation Object Builder (see **Figure 5**) and Step 5 of the Presentation Object wizard allow you to make this selection.

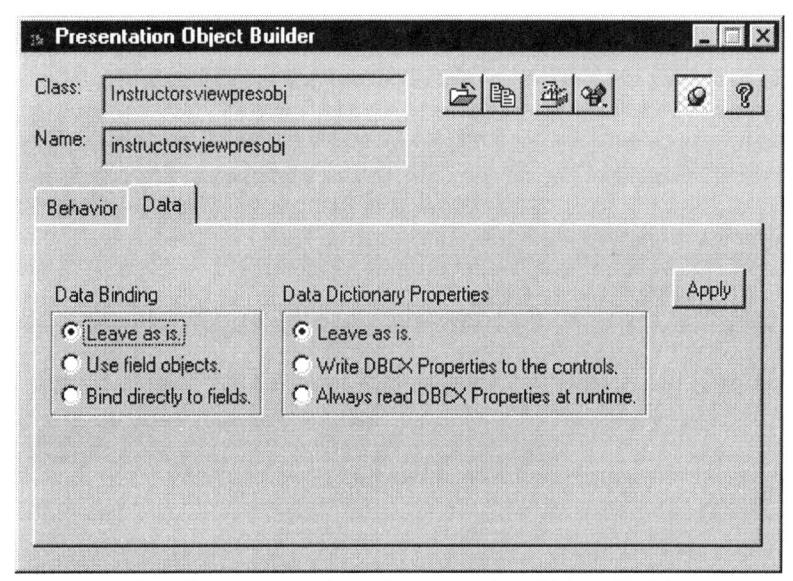

Figure 5. The Data page of the Presentation Object Builder allows you to set the method of data binding and decorating.

To modify the data binding method, select the method you prefer and press the Apply button. In addition, you can select when the field objects will be decorated. You can either write the properties to the controls at design time or have them read at run time.

The builder doesn't seem to indicate this, but if you bind directly to fields, the field object will not be decorated at run time. So be sure to select "Write DBCX Properties to the controls" if you are binding to fields.

Press the Apply button, and the builder will iterate through all the controls in your presentation object and make the appropriate property changes.

For a full explanation of the difference between binding to the field, which VFE calls "early binding," and binding to the field objects, which VFE calls "late binding," see Chapter 11, "Interface Controls."

Summary

The presentation object is a container in which you build a user interface to a business object. Its methods will generally use the services of the business object to manipulate the persistent data of that business object. Each presentation object will generally contain a single business object, which is loaded by the Business Object Loader. However, it is possible— and sometimes preferable—to place many business objects on a presentation object. The presentation object will also add value to those methods by ensuring that the interface is updated as needed.

The presentation object will also display prompts and message dialogs to the user based on the return values that it receives from the business object. These are generally error or warning messages such as "You can't select all records" or "This is the last record in the cursor."

Several hook methods are provided for the developer to provide a place for business domain and custom code. Keep in mind that you want to limit your code to user interface items. Ask yourself whether this code would need to run if you were interfacing the business object directly. Because you can't display messages from the business object, all of your interface code should be in the presentation objects.

Finally, the last piece of the puzzle is the form. The form is a container where you place your presentation object or objects. That's what we'll look at in the next chapter. Do get a paper cut turning the page.

Chapter 8
Forms

Most programmers are familiar with the VFP form class. It provides a container for the user interface controls and a place to put code to perform the processing of data. However, the VFE form class is a place where you will put very little, if any code.

The form is the object that is generally loaded when a menu option is selected. In the case of VFE, you do not use SCX-based forms but rather VCX-based form classes in your application. The main difference between the two is that the form class does not contain a data environment. However, because VFE provides a stand-alone data environment, this is not needed.

In form-based applications, you will find many methods added to the form to process data. If you look at the VFP class browser code, you will see this design method used. This is similar to the way you might create a FoxPro 2.6 application, as well—by placing many functions, specific to the screen, in the cleanup snippet.

In VFE, you have learned to implement the business domain functionality into the business object and the data handling into the cursor object. Furthermore, you have created a user interface for each business object in the presentation object. There is very little processing or code that needs to be written, so you are in the home stretch when you are creating forms.

Tutorial

Perhaps the first step would be to create a form for our Tutorial U school. We have provided all the functionality necessary to maintain the basic Instructor entity. But to complete the user interface, it is necessary to create a form class to host the presentation object. The following steps will guide you through this process.

1. Run Visual FoxExpress and open your project in the Application Builder.

2. From the Application Builder, select the Classes tab.

3. Expand the Forms node in the Classes tree view.

4. Select "Presentation Object Forms" and press the New button.

5. You will be presented with the wizard selection dialog. Select "Standard Presentation Object Form" and press the OK button. The Standard Presentation Object Form wizard will open.

6. Step 1 requests the name of the presentation object you would like to be placed on your form. Because there is only one presentation object, this step is simplified. Press the Next button.

7. Step 2 of the wizard will be different depending on whether the view is parameterized or not. If the view contains parameters, the wizard will present you with options for where to place the parameter fields. We all have our personal preferences; you may want to make several forms using the same presentation object and selecting different

settings here to learn how the wizard will build the form in each case. See the Note to learn about the list page.

> *Step 2 of the Presentation Object Form wizard has a check box titled "List Page." If you check this box, VFE will add a page to the page frame, and you will see it listed in the page order list box. A grid will be placed on the list page, and this grid will be bound to the view since you cannot bind a grid to the cursor object. In addition, the grid will be on the form, while the controls will be on the presentation object. Our preference is to create a list page on the presentation object, but you are free to use whichever method you are most comfortable with.*

8. For the purpose of this tutorial, set Step 2 of the wizard with the selections shown in **Figure 1**.

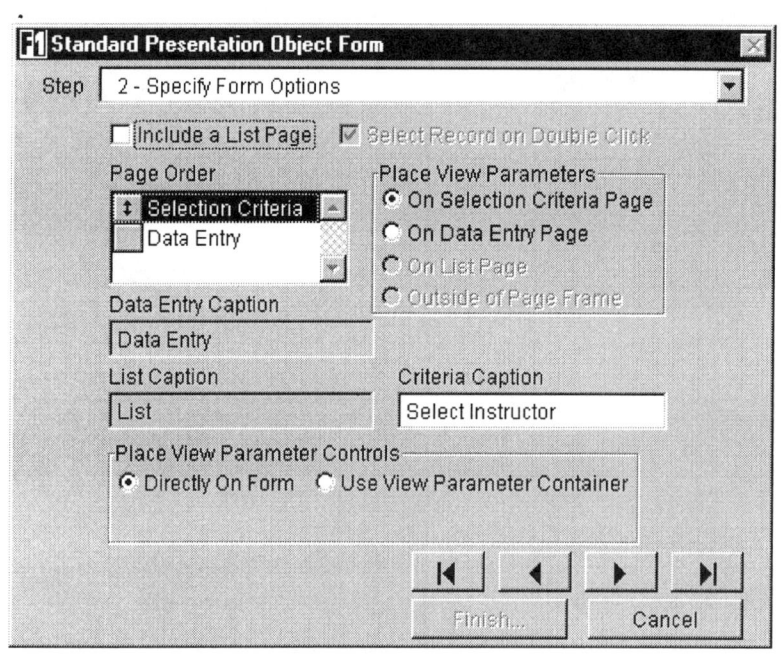

Figure 1. *Step 2 of the Presentation Object Form wizard shows the selections that were made for the Tutorial U application.*

9. Press the Next button to move to Step 3.

10. Step 3 has several of the form's property settings that you can set, including the form caption. Type a form caption of "Instructors," and then press the Next button.

11. Step 4 asks what toolbar you would like to be displayed when this form is in focus. Since we haven't created any specific toolbars, we will leave this set to the default. Remember that when we created the presentation object, we placed action buttons

providing an interface to allow for adding and saving records, record navigation and so forth. Press the Next button to continue.

12. Step 5 requests information it needs to create a menu item to launch this form. You are able to specify any current menu pad. By default the form caption is used as the menu caption, and the wizard adds the VFP special characters that make the first character a hot key. Also, the VFE default menu structure has you placing forms like this in the View menu. Once again, retain the defaults and press the Next button.

13. Step 6 asks for the name of the form class. (VFE doesn't use based forms by default.) Also, you are able to specify an existing class library in which to store your form class, or create a new one. Select the Instructor library, which we have been using to store our instructor entity classes.

14. At this point the wizard has all the information needed to create the form class, place the presentation object on it, and set the properties that you have specified. If you specified a list page, a grid will be placed on the list page and bound to the primary view in the data environment. (If you think backward through the layers, you will recall that when building the presentation object you selected a business object, and when building the business object you selected the data environment class. The wizard determines the alias of the primary cursor by looking at the primary cursor class in the data environment class.) Press the Finish button and let VFE build the class for you.

After you are returned to the Application Builder, you can press the Open button to view the class that was created. You will see that a page frame was placed on the form. Page one of the page frame contains a control for each view parameter of the cursor. The view parameter controls are bound to the view parameter fields of the cursor object. An Execute Query button was also provided. When the user clicks on Execute Query, the view parameters are populated with the entered value or values and the cursor is requeried.

All of this was done without writing a single line of code. As a matter of fact, don't be misled and think that the wizard generated any code, either. If you look through the form class, you will not see any code in any of the objects. This should dispel the common misconception that Visual FoxExpress is a code generator of some kind. All of the functionality is built into the framework classes; the wizards just exploit those classes.

Form class

You might be asking why you need a form if all of the functionality has been implemented. The VFE form class does provide some services—in addition to the basic VFP form class functionality, the ability to be added to the screen, to display controls, to provide a private data session and so forth. The VFE framework adds the following responsibilities to the form class:

- To add itself to the framework's form manager collection class.
- To provide resizing services via a "resizer object" or scroll bars.
- To set the session environment as desired.
- To display and maintain visibility of an attached toolbar.

- To add and remove itself from the Window menu pad.
- To store its last position to the registry and restore that position on loading.
- To maintain a collection of contained presentation objects.
- To provide access to the main presentation object's methods by passing messages to that object.

As you can see, VFE has provided a robust form class with all the functionality you will need to create a rich user interface for your application. While most of these features are easily understandable, let's look at a few of them in more detail before listing the properties and methods of the form classes.

Form manager

The form manager class is a system-level class. It is a collection class that maintains a reference to each form that is opened in your application. The form manager class works like any collection in VFE, providing a means to obtain a reference to a form through the item property of the collection.

The application object (see Chapter 10, "How It Works") contains the form manager class. It can be accessed programmatically from any object by using a reference such as This.oApplication.oForms. The methods and properties are the same as for the base collection class, which is what's instantiated to maintain the collection of forms.

Session environment

If you have been working with FoxPro for a while, you are very familiar with the large number of SET commands used to modify some of the aspects of the FoxPro environment. In Visual FoxPro, not only were some SET commands added, but they were also changed so that some settings were global and some were specific to the current data session. (For more information on data-session-specific settings, see the VFP manual.)

Because many of the commands are specific to the data session, and your application's forms will generally use private data sessions, VFE provides a simple method to set the environment settings to your preference. For example, you might want to SET CENTURY ON in all your private data session forms so that a four-digit century is displayed on all date fields.

The framework's base form class contains a Session Environment Loader. If you haven't guessed yet, the Session Environment Loader loads a session environment class. This class is nothing more than a list of properties, one for each SET command, and a method that issues every SET command with the value contained in its respective property. There are several ways to make changes to the commands that are issued when a form is instantiated.

First, at the global level you can change the properties of the "global" session environment class, which the loader uses by default—iSessionEnvironment.

If you want to make the changes to a single form, you have two choices. You can put the specific SET commands in the form's Init() method, or you can subclass the iSessionEnvironment class, make the changes to the properties you wish to change, and specify your new class in the Session Environment Loader's cSessionEnvironmentName property for each form that requires your custom environment. In the event you want to use your new class for all of your forms, it is possible to change the session loader base class to specify the session environment class to load by default. As you can see, there are several options for session settings.

At this time, the Session Environment Loader doesn't support the factory class as the Business Object Loader does. In addition, our recommendation is to have the form create a Session Environment Loader using the factory rather than coupling the session loader to the form. Even better, have the form load the session environment class directly using the factory class, eliminating the need for the session loader class. This would certainly simplify changing the settings or the class that is used. Although the changes listed here aren't very difficult, perhaps a future version of the framework will make this functionality a bit more flexible.

> *The session object is not based on the VFP session class.*

cPresentationObjForm of cForms.VCX

This form class is designed specifically to host presentation objects. The cPresentationObjForm class is not the only form class in the framework, but it is the one you will use most often. This class is a subclass of cBaseForm. cBaseForm encapsulates much of the functionality involved with displaying the form, displaying the toolbar, adding the form to the forms collection and so forth. The majority of the methods we will look at here are only included in the cPresentationObjForm.

If you follow the VFE n-tier layered design, it's likely that very little code will be put into your form classes, and this is as it should be. However, the form provides another layer that is just as important to understand as the cursor and presentation objects.

So, let's briefly look at some of the methods and properties of the form class that you should be aware of.

oPresentObj

This is arguably one of the most important properties on the form. This property holds an object reference to the currently active presentation object. This is used by the form's methods to pass messages received from the toolbar button on to the presentation object referenced in the property.

The presentation object referenced in this method is the one that will receive the toolbar commands, and it's known as the "active" presentation object. Recall from Chapter 7, "Presentation Objects," that the lActivateOnUIEnable property of the presentation object can be used to tell the presentation object to set itself as the form's active presentation object (oPresentObj) when it is activated. This is done so that any commands or messages will be passed to it.

oPresentObjs

This is an object reference to the form's presentation object collection. This collection provides the form with a reference to all of the presentation objects contained on the form. You can also use this collection in your code to obtain a reference to a specific presentation object, perhaps to get the value of a property or run a method.

AllowDelete(), AllowFilter(), AllowList(), AllowNavigate(), AllowNew(), AllowOrder(), AllowPrint(), AllowRequery(), AllowSave(), AllowSearch()

These methods return the result from the corresponding method of the active presentation object. Remember that the active presentation object is the one currently referenced in the oPresentObj property. The purpose of these methods at the form level is to allow for action buttons on a toolbar and corresponding menu items to determine whether they should be disabled.

For example, if you look at the Save toolbar/action button, the following refresh code is referring to the method of the form:

```
This.Enabled = _Screen.ActiveForm.AllowSave()
```

This button is able to send a message to the form, and the form will pass this message to the AllowSave() method of the presentation object, and then pass the returned value back to the button. This follows the object-oriented Chain of Responsibility pattern, which is a general design principal of objects passing messages along a specific chain, giving each object a chance to act on it and/or pass the message on.

FindBizObj(), GetBizObj()

We could not find a difference between these two methods, so we will list them together. This method provides the ability to get a reference to the business object opened in the form by one of the presentation objects. This may be useful if you need to have a business object in one form talk to the business object of another form.

Data methods

Most of the data handling methods in the presentation object are contained on the form. All of these methods work as the aforementioned Allow... methods work, by calling the same method in the presentation object and then returning on the result received from that message. This layer is provided to simplify the object referencing between forms and presentation objects.

Toolbars

We have not discussed the toolbars in depth, but we'll mention them here. A specific toolbar class can be attached to the form. The form class provides the methods necessary to handle the specified toolbar. Putting the class name of the toolbar into the cToolBarClass property of the form specifies the toolbar. Once the toolbar is tied to the form, the form will make sure it is made invisible or hidden if the form loses focus.

This functionality allows you to tie specific and different toolbars to your forms, or to reuse the same form over and over. The methods on the form also allow for toolbar reuse, since a certain programming interface is always expected on the form.

Summary

The form class is needed to provide a container to house your presentation objects. There are three basic form classes, including cBaseForm and cPresentationObjForm. The form creation wizards can add controls to the form that can simplify record retrieval and navigation for your users, such as with the list page and selection criteria page.

As you may suspect, we have now created all of the basic elements needed to run our application and view our handiwork. So let's move on to the next chapter and run our application and form.

Chapter 9
Your VFE Application

In this chapter we will finally run our Tutorial U application, and you'll see many of the features provided in the framework that may not be readily apparent.

While a VFE application is a standard application written with VFP code, the framework implements many features that do the work for you. As you know, the framework class handles the major functions of fetching and saving data, but it also handles many other small items that you would have to code yourself if you weren't using VFE.

At this point, you have a running application with a single maintenance form that is the visual representation of the instructor business object. You will be able to run your application and your form. In the form you will be able to add data, edit data, navigate through that data and delete those records if you like.

Your application contains a robust error handler and data utilities. When you close the form you created, the position it was in is stored into your computer's registry so that it can be opened in the same position the next time you run that form. The form allows for multiple instances, each with its own private data session, which provides you with a nice way to test multi-user access and conflict resolution.

Except for the business specifics of the Instructor form, the framework provides all of this common functionality for you. The classes are constructed to provide the things that are common in all general business applications. All of this exists without one line of code being written by you, or the wizards. Now, you will have to write code to build a full-blown application, but not for any of the stuff that already exists—that's the power of VFE.

Okay, let's take a look at how to build and run the application, and then we will show you some of the aforementioned features in a bit more detail.

Building your application

If you have worked with VFP at any point, you are aware that it is an interpreted language. What this means is that VFP or the "run time" evaluates your code line-by-line at the time it is executed. There is no need to build a binary executable to run your code. This allows you to run your application in development mode without creating an APP or EXE file.

However, there is still one aspect of VFP that is carried over from older versions. The menus that you create in the Menu Builder must be generated into a program. The program that creates your menu program is named GENMENU.PRG. Remember that when you first installed VFE, you set up VFP to use a replacement menu generator named GENMENUX.PRG. This program is a public domain replacement for the menu generator that allows "plug-in" modules to define and modify its behavior.

VFE takes advantage of this with the inclusion of a genmenux driver that creates menu classes using the information in the menu table. This menu program needs to be run whenever you have modified your application menu. The simplest way to run it is by building your application's project.

When you rebuild a project in VFP, FoxPro essentially verifies that all classes have been compiled. VFP also checks to see whether the menu file is newer than the menu program. If it is, the menu generator is called to generate the menu program.

Keep in mind that other than building an EXE for distribution, the *only* time you need to build your project is after you have modified the menu. Recall that when we built the Instructors form, we added an item to the View menu to call the form. Because this change to the menu took place, we need to build the project.

Building the project is simple. With your project opened in the VFE Application Builder, you will see a button labeled "Build" at the bottom of the Application Builder. If you press this button, you will be presented with the Build Project Options dialog (see **Figure 1**). At this point you would select the Rebuild Project action. If you wish, you can turn on any of the options.

Figure 1. The Build Project Options dialog is displayed when the Build button is pressed in the Application Builder.

If you press the OK button on the Build Project Options dialog, your project will be rebuilt. If you watch closely, you will see the genmenux program's dialog display as it informs you that it's generating the menu program.

That wasn't so difficult, was it?

Run your application

In a traditional VFP application, when the project is viewed, you will usually find the "main" file set to a program called MAIN.PRG or START.PRG. The VFP main program is the program that will run first when the application is launched as an APP (FoxPro application) or EXE (Windows executable). It is this program's responsibility to start the application and perhaps start the event handler.

Continuing with tradition and perhaps other frameworks, to get your application running in the VFP development environment, you would run the main program, which would start the application. This could be done in the command window or by highlighting the main program and pressing the Run button in the Project Manager.

However, if you've had a chance to look at your VFE application in the Project Manager, you've seen that a class is set as the "main" program. This class is the application class. To run your program, this class must be instantiated. We will discuss this process in Chapter 10, "How It Works," when we look in more detail at the application object.

Because it takes a small bit of code to accomplish this, VFE provides you with a much simpler way to launch your application in development mode. Look at the buttons on the bottom of the Application Builder. There is a button labeled "Run," which, believe it or not, will run your VFE application. Press the Run button—if you have built your project properly, the application will start.

Splash screen

Your application will start by displaying a splash screen, if specified. By default this screen is built with the information you provided when you created your application; however, it is fully modifiable to meet your tastes or aesthetic pleasures.

Options dialog

The first time you run the application, VFE presents you with the Options dialog (see **Figure 2**). This dialog allows the users to set some environmental settings to their own personal preferences. All of the settings made in this form will be saved to the machine's Windows registry. The registry is a database provided by the operating system, which allows the storage of configuration settings and other information.

This form can also be launched from the menu to allow the users to alter their settings at any time. Also, you may wish to subclass and modify this form to add settings that would be specific to your application's environment.

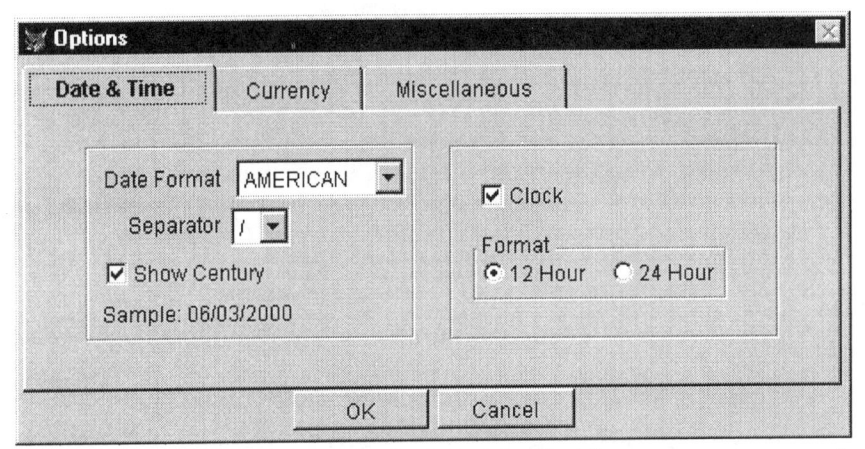

Figure 2. The Options dialog is displayed the first time you run your application. It allows for user-specific environmental settings used by your application.

Database utilities

If you select Database Utilities from the File menu, the Manage Tables dialog will appear (see **Figure 3**). From this dialog, the user can index and pack the VFP tables used in your application. Of course, this is only useful if you are using local tables, but it does save you time because you don't have to create it.

Notice that the names of the tables are the caption names that are in the metadata, as opposed to the table names. This allows for a much more user-friendly experience.

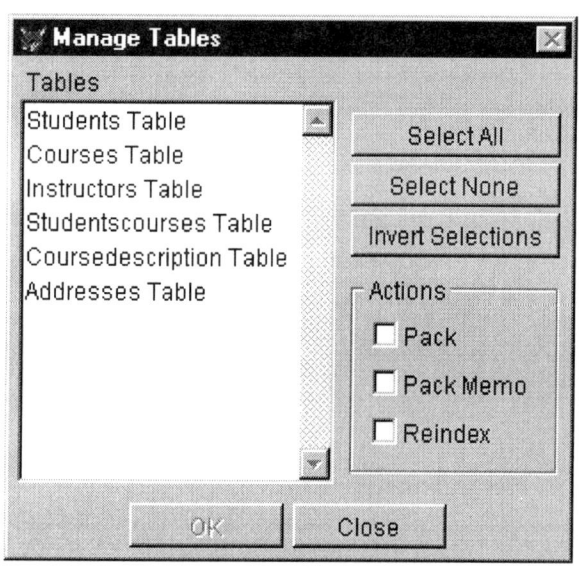

Figure 3. The Manage Tables dialog opens when Database Utilities is selected from the File menu. This is another example of framework-provided goodies.

Error log

If you select Error Log from the Utilities menu pad, you will see the VFE-provided error log (see **Figure 4**). The error log is populated when the program encounters any error. VFE does its best to recover from errors, based on what caused them and how the user responded; however, there may still be that occasional error that slips by. The error log captures as much environmental information as possible, making troubleshooting a bit easier for the developer.

Security

A full-featured security system is available to applications built with the VFE framework. The security system includes a login form and a security form for your application, which allow administrators to create user accounts and groups, and define the security levels of the items in your application. For more information of VFE security, see Chapter 17, "VFE Security."

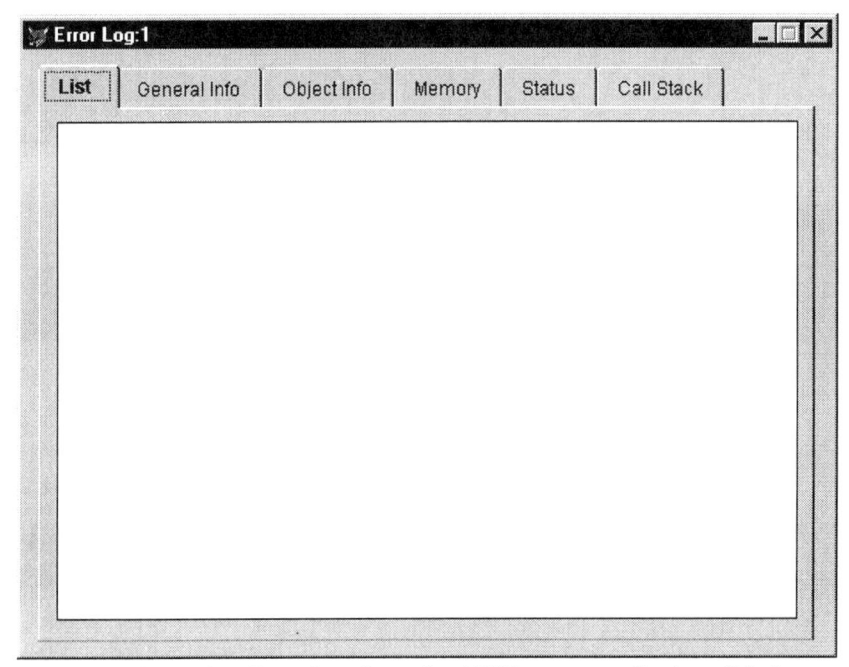

Figure 4. Selecting Error Log from the Utilities menu displays this form, which provides the developer with vital information.

Developers menu

A menu is provided to the developer that allows you to suspend the application or perhaps run the debugger (see **Figure 5**). This menu is displayed automatically if the system is running in debug mode. The application runs in debug mode if there is a file named DEBUG.TXT in the root directory of the application.

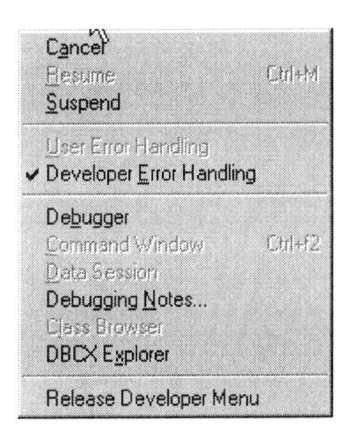

Figure 5. The Developers menu is available when the application is running in debug mode. This gives you quick access to your VFP tools.

Selecting Debugging Notes will open an edit window, allowing you to put text into the DEBUG.TXT file. You can use this not only for debugging; you can also use it while showing a prototype or training in order to put notes into this file based on user feedback. After the session, you will have all your notes in the text file on your PC, or you can copy the file to disk and take it back to your office.

Standard menus

In addition to the File menu pad, there are also Window and Help menus, which allow you to follow the Windows standards that are required if you want to use the "Designed for Windows" logo. The Window menu functions just as you would expect it to. While you have open forms in your application, the forms are added to the bottom of the Window menu, in addition to the New Window and Cascade commands.

Instructors form

Okay, it's time to check out your handiwork. From the View menu, select the Instructors form. The form will launch and be ready to do your bidding. Remember that this is a pretty basic form—we didn't include any code, but you will see that the framework provides all the "expected" functions. In other words, you will be able to add records, navigate through them and so forth.

Also, after you run the form, the Navigation and Tools menus will become available (see **Figure 6**). These menus provide one method to navigate through the records, if there were more than one record. Also, if you pull down the File menu, you will see that the New and Close items are available. If you made an edit or added a record, the Save item would also become available. The framework provides all of these features.

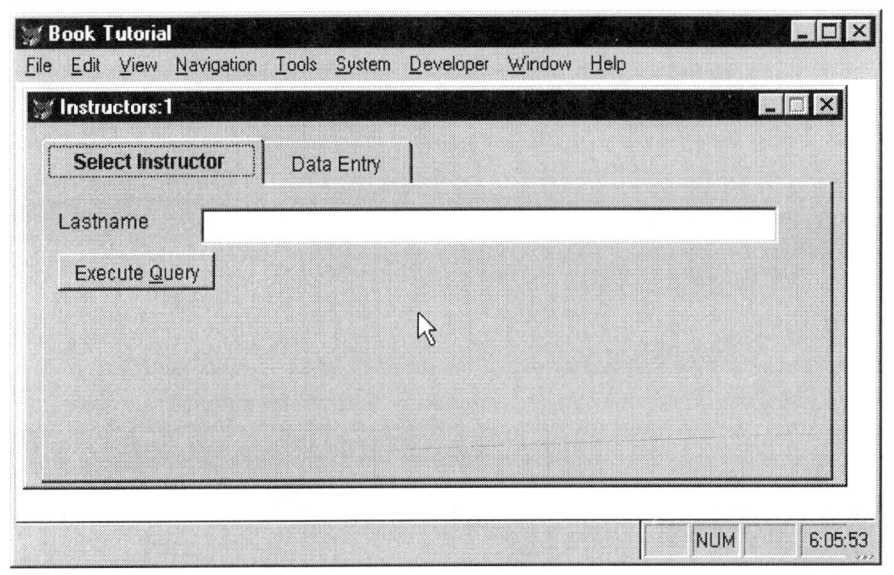

Figure 6. Your application running with the Instructors form you created. You can see that the Navigation and Tools menus became available for your use.

Navigation and Tools menus

The Navigation menu includes commands to navigate through the records in your view. Because this view is parameterized, we don't have any records on the client yet, so these menu options aren't yet available.

The Tools menu contains options to List, Filter and Query. Each of these tools brings up a VFE form that is built on the fly to allow for list, filter and query.

List tool

The list function provides a good reason not to put a list page on your forms. When you select List, a grid is built on the fly based on the metadata. Recall from earlier chapters that there are a few ways to control the list form.

One way is to specify the list fields in the presentation object. The Presentation Object Builder provides a simple way to create the list by giving you a mover interface. Another method is based on how you set up the metadata. The list will be built with every field in the view that has a "grid caption" set up in the metadata. Also, there is an order field that identifies in what order the fields are placed into the grid. (At this time, the order doesn't seem to work. This has been reported to F1 and they will certainly fix it. In the meantime, you can just change the order of the fields in your view.)

Add data

Now let's put some data into our form. To do this, you can go to the Detail page of the form and press the New button, or you can choose New from the File menu. The form will place you on the first field of the Detail page so you can start entering data. (Well, we've found our first bug—the full SSN is not being displayed on the form. Later you can go in and size that field on the presentation object.)

Enter the data as shown in **Figure 7**. Following along with the book will be easier if you enter the same data at this time. Don't press the Save button yet.

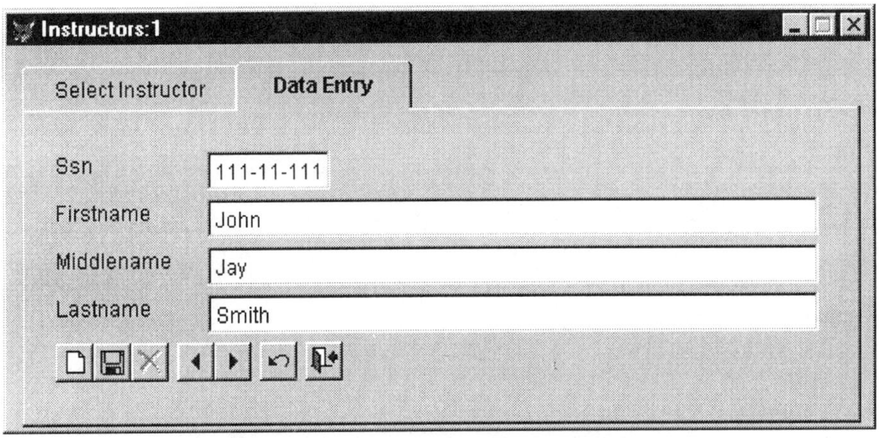

Figure 7. Insert your first record into the Instructors form.

You were asked not to save so that we can first demonstrate some of the features built into the framework. You get these without coding them, but they are commonly expected features. For example, try to close the form with the X in the upper right corner. You'll be prompted by the system because you have a new but unsaved record on the form. For now, press the Cancel button. Now try to exit the form by pressing the Escape key. Did you receive the same result? You'll also get the same prompt if you use the Close button that was placed on the form.

Okay, save the record now by pressing the Save button. You could also select Save in the File menu that should now be available. Great—if all is well, the record will now be saved to the table on the hard drive.

Add another record, this time using "Jones" as the last name, and save it. Try using the same SSN—you will see that you won't be allowed to. This is because we have SSN set up as a candidate key, meaning it must be a unique value table-wide.

Once you have your records saved, select List from the Tools menu. You will see both of your records in the list. This is because you added them at the same time. Because this is a view-based system, if you shut this window and then open it again, there will be no records. Let's give this a try—close the window and reopen it. If you try to list the records, you will see that the list is empty.

So in order to get a record to work with, you have to ask for it. This is a concept of client/server programming—don't get any data until you think it's what the user wants or needs. To retrieve the record you want, type "Smith" in the Select Instructor page. Press the Execute Query button, and the system will retrieve the record you requested. If there is more than one match, all of the records that match will be retrieved. At this point this is case-sensitive; there are steps you can take if you don't want it to be case-sensitive.

Summary

You have built a powerful application in very little time. The VFE framework provides the features you need, and the wizards help you quickly build the elements you need for your business domain.

Up to this point you have used all of the major building blocks to implement a real-life entity of an instructor into a business object. First, a table was created to persist the Instructors, and a cursor class was created to maintain that data. Then a presentation object was built, which is the control panel for the instructor business object. On this presentation object are user interface controls that display the attributes of the instructors and allow you to modify those attributes and save the modified instructor information to your persistent data store.

Finally, you ran your new application and tested all of these things. You found that all of the data handling, error checking and user interface code you needed already existed in the framework. You saw that there are several elements in the system that take care of the common items of an application so you can focus on the specifics. You ran a form that was created for your business domain and tested it.

All of this was accomplished using the wizards and tools provided with VFE. You didn't write any code to create your form, although you will need to create more business object code for more complex applications. While you've only scratched the surface of VFE at this point, you have used the majority of the classes and followed the necessary steps to implement most business entities in VFE.

Some of you might have expected this book to be full of examples of this and that. While we have included as much sample code as possible, it is more important for you to understand how the framework classes work together and what methods and properties are available to you. With this kind of knowledge under your belt, you won't waste time writing code to create a function or feature that's provided in the framework. The next chapter will give you a more detailed explanation of what's happening behind the scenes as you run your VFE application. See you there.

Chapter 10
How It Works

In this chapter, we will take a detailed look at the application object and walk you through the code that starts the application. After that, we'll examine the code that runs and the classes that are created during form instantiation.

If you have been following along throughout the book and building the tutorial application, you have seen that there are many classes that work together in the Visual FoxExpress framework to produce the end result—a powerful application that satisfies the needs of the users in your business domain. Up to this point you have learned about each of the major framework classes involved with implementing a business entity, and how to use the wizards to create the data, business and user interface layers. You've also discovered how those specific classes function.

What you haven't seen is much of what VFE provides in the way of system services. How is the application started, and what happens when you start the form you built? We believe that the best way to learn the Visual FoxPro framework is to trace through the code of most of the major system services. However, if you are new to Visual FoxPro, and object-oriented programming and Visual FoxExpress, this is a daunting task. Another aspect of VFE that makes it difficult to trace is the large number of access methods used. As you are running through the VFE code, you may enter three, four or five access methods before you actually get into the method you wanted to trace.

So, in this chapter we will start with the application object, and trace each method that is called and explain its function. From there we will look at what happens when you run a form. Finally, we will walk you through a few of the common processes of a typical business object form, such as the Instructors form of the tutorial.

System services

In discussions of the traditional n-tier application, you generally hear the terms "data services," "business services" and "user services." In previous chapters, you learned about the classes that are used to build functionality in each of these layers.

In VFE and most applications, there is an additional layer. This layer does not stand alone, nor is it necessary without the other layers. Of course, we mean the system services. The system services provide services to all the layers of an application, allowing them to perform common tasks without code duplication.

VFE has many system services classes, and we will discuss some of those in detail in this chapter. A few examples of system services are:

- Message system
- Menu system

- Forms manager
- Object factory
- Business object manager
- Error system
- Security system

Each of these systems is implemented as a class or set of classes in the VFE framework. However, in VFE there is a single class that is in charge of creating and managing most of the system services objects: the application class.

Application object

The application object is the foundation upon which the application runs. Your application starts by creating an instance of the application class. Just like the foundation of a house, the application object is important to your application because it provides a place to anchor or attach the many system services objects that are created upon application startup.

cApplication of cApp.VCX

The cApplication VFE application class is stored in the cApp.VCX class library. When you first created your VFE project with the Application Builder wizard, one of the items created for you was an application object. If you look in your Tutorial U project, you will see in the Other Objects node of the Classes tree view a class named "BookTutorialApplicationObject." The class is named after the project name you provided when running the New Application wizard from the Application Manager.

The application contains a number of properties that describe the behavior of your VFE application (see **Figure 1**). These properties hold the values you specified when you created the application. Each of these properties is used by a method in the application object during the startup and running of your application.

Application startup

At this point we will trace through the methods that are called as the application object is instantiated. Because the application class is set as the "main" file in the VFP project when the application or executable is loaded, the run time will instantiate that class.

When the class is instantiated, its Init() method is fired and the code inside will run. We will examine the methods that are fired as the application object instantiates, starting with the Init() method and then proceeding in order until we come to the READ EVENTS statement, which starts the VFP event handler that waits for the user to use your application.

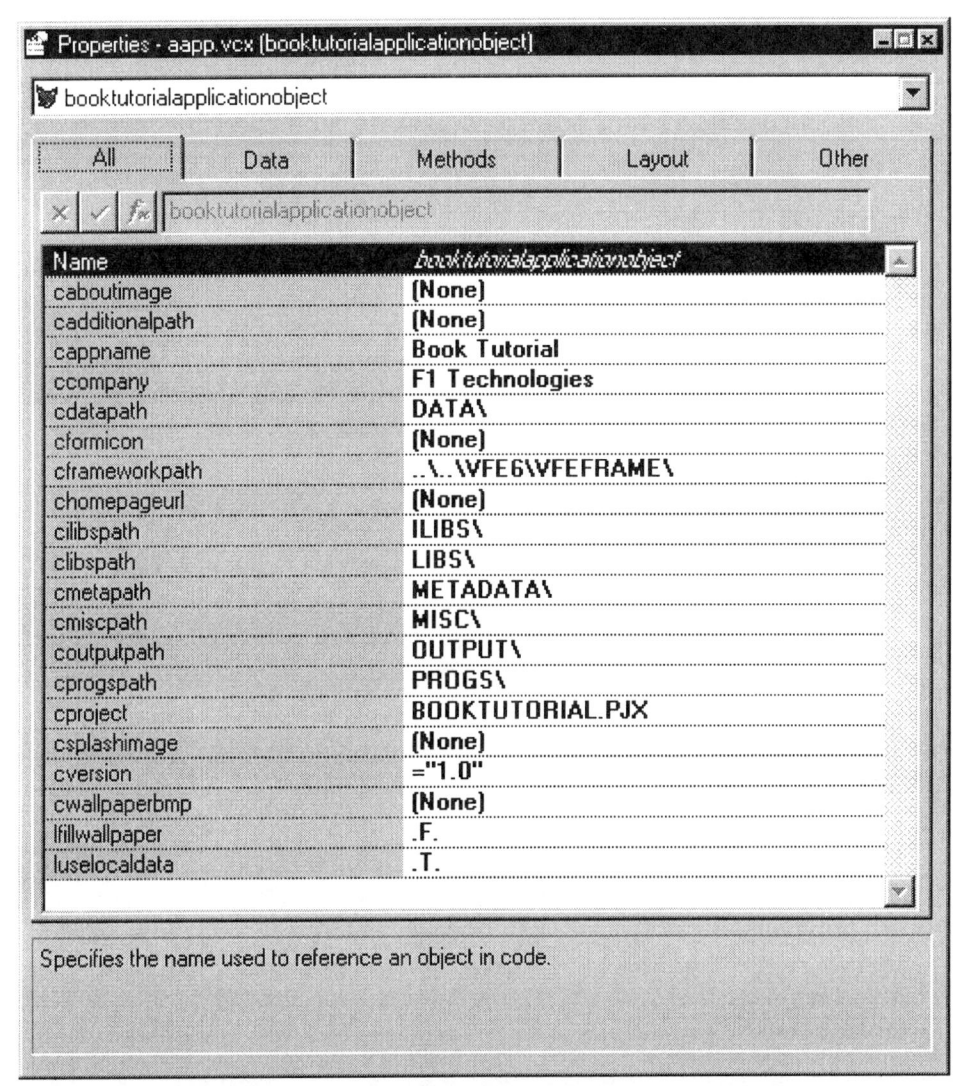

Figure 1. The Properties window of the application class shows many of the properties set by the New Application wizard. These properties are used during application startup and at run time to provide system services to the other objects.

Init()

It is in the Init() method of the application object that our journey begins. The Init() method has three fairly straightforward parameters, as shown in **Table 1**.

Table 1. Parameters of the Init() method.

Parameter	Description
tcUserID	Passes the ID of a user you want to log in as.
txPassword	Passes the password of a user who may not be able to support him or herself.
tlMode	Determines the mode in which to start the application. If False, it indicates not to run a user interface, while True points to running in debug mode.

If the tlMode parameter is passed, the method will call the SetMode() method of the application object. This method contains code that performs the following:

1. The Init_Pre() hook is called. If this hook returns False, the application object will return .f., stopping it from being instantiated.

2. The main screen is hidden for a cleaner application start.

3. If the lClearEnvironment property is True, a "clear all" and "close all" are issued.

4. The default directory is set to the application startup directory.

5. A reference to the application object is added to the SCREEN object as _SCREEN.oApplication.

6. The SetPath() method is called to set the FoxPro path to include the directories specified in the cMetaPath, cLibsPath, cProgsPath, cOutPutPath, cMiscPath, cDataPath, cAdditionalPath and cILibsPath properties of your application class.

7. The GetProjectData() method is called to create or open the project data file. If you are running in the development environment, the project is read to obtain a list of all class libraries and procedures in the project, and they are placed into the project data file.

8. The SetProcAndLib() method is called to SET CLASSLIB TO and SET PROCEDURE TO all of the class libraries and program files in your project data file. This is a nice feature; it means that if you add an outside class library, it is automatically added to the project data file and added to the SET CLASSLIB list by the framework.

9. The CreateFactory() method is called to instantiate the factory class stored in the cFactoryClass property. If this is successful, a reference to the factory object is stored in the oFactory property of the application object. (For more information about what the factory class does and how you can use it, see Chapter 16, "Extending the Framework.")

10. The EnableErrorHandling() method is called to instantiate the error class. If this is successful, a reference to the error object is stored in the goErrorHandler public variable. (This is the only public variable used in the framework.)

11. The CreateMembers() method is called. This method instantiates several objects that provide various system services to the application object and the application. The following methods are run from this method:

a. The CreateSystemSettingsManager() method is called to instantiate the system setting manager class and place its object reference into the oSettings property of the application object.

b. The CreateGlobalEnvironment() method is called to instantiate the global environment class and place its object reference into the oEnvironment property of the application object.

c. The CreateMetaManager() method is called to instantiate the meta manager class and place its object reference into the oMetaMgr property of the application object.

d. The CreateFormCollection() method is called to instantiate the forms manager class and place its object reference into the oForms property of the application object.

e. The CreateToolBarCollection() method is called to instantiate the toolbar manager class and place its object reference into the oToolBars property of the application object.

f. The CreateBizObjCollection() method is called to instantiate the business object collection class and place its object reference into the oBizObjs property of the application object.

12. The SetHelp() method is called to SET HELP to the Help file stored in the cHelpFile property of the application object.

13. If the lDisplayInterface property is True, the DisplayInterface() method is called to perform the following steps. (The framework sets the lDisplayInterface property when it determines how it was started. If the program was started as a COM object and not an executable or application, the lDisplayInterface property is set to False and none of the following steps take place.)

    a. ON SHUTDOWN is set to call the application object's OnShutDown() method.

    b. The SetScreenEffects() method is called to set up the interface for the main Visual FoxPro window. This includes setting the caption, main icon, wallpaper, status bar and so forth based on the settings of the matching properties in the application object. Also, this method calls a method that hides all of the standard VFP toolbars in the event that you are running in the VFP environment. Finally, this method calls the splash screen to display.

    c. The Login() method is called to instantiate the security class, which checks to see whether security has been turned on for this application. If it has been, a login screen is run and the security class is instantiated. A reference to the security class is placed in the oSecurity property of the application object.

    d. The CreateMenu() method is called to instantiate the menu class and place its reference into the oMenu property of the application object.

e. The GetUserPreferences() method is called to retrieve the user preferences from the registry and set them in the default data session in which the application object resides.

14. If everything has been loaded successfully, the Init() method will call the Init_Post() method. This method is a hook method that allows you to create any code you want to add to the Init() of your application object without having to modify the framework code. If Init_Post() returns True, the application will continue its startup; however, if it returns False, the application will call the cleanup routine and shut down. This is your final failsafe if for some reason you want to create code that stops the application from loading after all the preceding steps have been successful.

15. If Init_Post() hasn't returned False at this point, the application calls the Do() method. Also, the Do() method is only called if lDisplayUserInterface is True. If it is not, this means you are instantiating the application in COM and won't need for READ EVENTS to be called.

Do()

The Do() method basically gets the application running. It's the last method that is called by the Init() method, and it's only called if the application object is being run as a program and not as a COM object.

The Do() method gets your application going by performing the following steps:

1. The BeforeReadEvents() method is called. This is another hook method. This means that there is no code shipped in this method, and it is a place for you to put any code that you want perform at this time into your application object. You would use this method for code you want to run only when the application is run as a program and not as a COM object. If you want the code to run either way, you should use the Init_Pre() or Init_Post() method.

2. The CreateMainToolBar() method is called to instantiate the main toolbar class, which is stored in the cMainToolBar property. By default this property is empty, but if you have created a main toolbar class for your application, you would put that class's name into the cMainToolBar property. It will be instantiated and its reference put into the oToolBar property of the application object.

3. If the cStartForm property is not empty, the class named in this property will be run. This is used for a form you want to run every time you start your application—perhaps a Tip of the Day or some other type of launch pad form.

4. Finally, the READ EVENTS command is issued, which puts the application into a wait state to wait for your user to start using your application. Congratulations, your VFE application is running!

System classes

As you read through the trace of the Init() method, you learned that many classes are started and attached to the application object. Each of these classes is available to you as you write code for your application, so you should be aware of them and what they can do for you.

You can directly access these classes through the application object's properties, or in many cases the application object contains a method that will use the services of these classes. For example, the GetBizObj() method of the application object uses the oBizObjs collection class to return an object reference.

Table 2 lists the system classes and the properties of the application object you would use to access them.

Table 2. Application properties that hold a reference to a class that provides, or helps the application object provide, system services to the application.

Property name	Default class	Description
oFactory	cFactory	The factory class is built to create a concrete object from a nonconcrete class name. In the case of the VFE factory, the class name "tokens" are stored in a table that also stores the concrete class name to create. (For more information on the factory class, see Chapter 16, "Extending the Framework.")
oSettings	cRegistry	This class provides methods to store and retrieve data from the Windows registry.
oEnvironment	cGlobalEnvironment	This class issues all the SET commands that are global to your Visual FoxPro application. It also contains an instance of cSessionEnvironment that issues all the data-session-specific settings, including those stored in the registry.
oMetaMgr	DBCXMgr	This class encapsulates data access to the metadata for your application. For more information on this class, refer to Chapter 5, "Metadata."
oForms	cCollection	This class is a standard collection class. It will retain a reference to each form that is open in the application. Later, as we trace through the form instantiation, you will see that the form class is responsible for adding and removing itself from this collection.
oToolBars	cReferenceCollection	This class is a standard reference collection. As the forms create and destroy the toolbars, the toolbar class will add and remove them from this collection.
oBizObjs	cCollection	The standard collection class holds a reference to each business object instantiated. The oBizObjs collection is provided primarily for circumstances where the VFE application is being accessed as a COM object, but it is available in traditional desktop applications as well.
oSecurity	cSecurity	This class contains the properties and methods used by the framework to determine the access level assigned to each object for the current user. It also contains properties with information about the user.
oMenu	MainMenu (application-specific)	The menu classes provide the code to display the menu on the screen and methods to add and remove menu elements, in addition to synchronizing menu items with the toolbar and active forms.

Accessing the application object is simple, as every VFE object has a property named oApplication. You would use this property of the class in which you are writing code to access the application object, followed by the property of the application object that contains a reference of the class whose services you would like to use. For example, to access the metadata manager from a cursor object, you might write code like this:

```
LcReturn = This.oApplication.oMetaMgr.GetDBCXProperty('FirstName',;
  'Field','Caption')
```

We must confess that Table 2 is not fully correct: It lists the "C-layer" classes for each system class, when in fact the framework utilizes the "I-layer" classes. The C-layer classes are listed because those are the class libraries where all the code is implemented, and where you would do further research on your own to fully investigate the properties and methods of each class that is available to you.

Application object: Part 2

As they say in those all-too-familiar commercials, "Wait—that's not all!" There are still many properties and methods of the application object that you will find useful. As we've done previously, we will give you an overview of those you should be aware of. For a full list of properties and methods, check out the framework documentation or the cApplication class itself, which is the best and final reference.

cDataPath, cMetaPath, cLibsPath, cProgsPath, cOutPutPath, cMiscPath, cAdditionalPath, clLibsPath

These properties contain a path to the named item for the application. Each of these properties has an assign method that will call the SetPath() method after every assignment to this field. The SetPath() method will set the FoxPro path to all of the paths listed in each of these properties. So, in order to change any of these paths, all you must do is assign the new value; the assign method will make sure to set the path as needed.

Generally, all of these paths are needed when you are running from the library files as opposed to an APP or EXE file. If you are running from an APP or EXE file, Visual FoxPro will find the library and other files in the built application or executable file.

cFactoryClass

This property holds the name of the class to use as the application object factory class. This class is held in a property and not in the factory file "classes" because you cannot use the factory to create the factory.

For more information on the factory, see Chapter 16, "Extending the Framework."

cStartForm

This property holds the class name of the form that you would like to be started automatically when the application is started. This could be used for a Tip of the Day or some type of navigation form. If this property is empty, no form is started automatically.

IDisplayInterface

This property holds a True or False value and is populated by the application object at startup if it is initially True. You can set the IDisplayInterface property to False if you want to instantiate the application object without any interface in native VFP. This can be very useful if you want to work in VFP to debug your application before attempting to use it as a COM object. If the application is started as a COM object of some type, this property is automatically set to False. If this property is False, none of the visual items of the application are created, and no READ EVENTS handler is used or needed.

IMaximizeOnStartUp

This property indicates whether the application's _SCREEN should be maximized on startup. We recommend leaving this at its default setting to allow the user to control the startup state of the window in the shortcut properties.

> *Developers who are new to VFE are often confused by this property because it can cause the screen to "jump around" when the application is started. When you distribute a VFE application, the CONFIG.FPW file should contain the line SCREEN = OFF so that all of the "jumping around" takes place before the screen is visible.*

IUseSecurity

If this is True, it indicates to the framework that it should instantiate the security system. You may want to turn this off once you have set up your security and you are still testing other items to be sure the security doesn't interfere. You can change this property via the Security check box on the Application Builder dialog.

GetClass(), Make()

These methods use the factory object to retrieve a concrete class name based on a class "token" name passed to the method. However, if you call the Make() method, the factory will actually instantiate the object and return a reference to it. (Be careful if you are using Make(), because the object will be created in the default data session where the application object resides and not in the specific data session you may be calling the method from.)

GetMetaManager()

This method will return a reference to the metadata manager that was instantiated by the application object. This will, of course, return the reference stored in the oMeta property of the application object.

Init_Post(), Init_Pre()

These are empty hook methods that allow you to add code to your application object to customize or extend what happens when the application object is instantiated. For information about when these are called, refer to the "Init()" section earlier in this chapter, which traces the object instantiation process.

SetSecurity()
This method will set security of the passed object. This method will pass the object reference you passed to it on to the security class's SetSecurity() method.

Form instantiation
In addition to application startup, one of the most important processes to understand is what happens when one of your forms is run. This is necessary in order to understand how the user interface controls are tied to the field objects, when the data environment is established and how the various collections are populated.

Understanding the process is important when you want your code to be involved in it in some way. Let's take a look at what happens when you run your form from the menu. The menu item will call the DoForm() method of the application object, passing the name of the form class.

In addition to the form class name, it is possible to pass a parameter to the form as well. Generally, if you want to pass more than one value to a form, you should create a parameter object and populate each property of the object for each parameter value.

So, without further ado we find ourselves at the beginning of the DoForm() method.

DoForm()
DoForm() is a method of the application object. As we said before, it is responsible for instantiating the form and passing parameters on to that form. Let's look at the steps it takes:

1. Accept the class name to run, and also an object reference to be passed to the form as parameters.

2. Instantiate the form class name passed with the Create Object function.

3. Verify that the form was created successfully and, if so, run the Show() method of the form. As you know, all visual classes are instantiated with the Visible property set to False, so you must set it to True or call the Show() method.

At this point, assuming the form is nonmodal, the DoForm() method has performed its task; if you are tracing the code, the current line of code would now be sitting on the READ EVENTS command. If the form is modal, execution stops until the form is closed, and if the form has a uRetVal property, its value is returned by the DoForm() method. Next we will look at what happens during Step 2 while the form object is being created.

Form startup
When a VFP object is created, its Init event is fired, which runs the code in the Init() method. However, when the class is a form class, the Load event actually fires before the Init event. In addition to this, if the class contains other classes, those classes are instantiated prior to the container's Init running.

So we will trace through the code as the presentation object form loads. The base form super class performs some of this implementation; however, it is not necessary to separate out the code in each class at this time, as the majority of forms you will be running will be based on the presentation object form class.

We will be using the Instructors form, which is a basic form with a single presentation object and some controls. We will list the class and the method that is running, as it runs, so you can understand which code is in each class.

Form load
As we've mentioned, the first thing that will fire when you instantiate a form is the Load() method. The following steps show what is performed in the Load() method of the presentation object form:

1. SET TALK is set off.
2. The _SCREEN.Mousepointer property is set to an hourglass.
3. SET MESSAGE is set to "Loading Form."

Before the form's Init() will run, all of the classes contained must be instantiated. Let's quickly look at the classes that are loaded and what each does to set itself up to run in the form environment.

oSessionEnvironmentLoader
Before the form's Init() will run, all of the classes contained in the form class will be created first. The oSessionEnvironmentLoader is an object that resides on the form class by default. If the property cSessionEnvironmentName is not empty, the class named in this property is added to the form as an object named oSessionEnvironment. (At this point, because we are instantiating a new object, the code will jump to its Init() method while it is being created.)

Because this is the last code that executes here, we won't return to this method. But if you were tracing the code, you would see the pointer return to this method and execute its return statement.

oSessionEnvironment
The session environment class will issue all of the sets to the value stored in each of its properties. Here are the steps the code takes:

1. It calls the default code of the parent class. The parent class is cEnvironment.
2. The cEnvironment class calls the Set() method.
3. The Set() method issues all of the SET commands using the values stored in the property of the class.
4. The Set() method calls the SetUserPreferences() method to set all of the settings to the values stored for the specific user in the registry.

Using the Session Environment Loader and subclassing the cSessionEnvironment class, you can define any environment you want for your forms. They could each use the same environment, or you could define a specific class for each form.

oResizer

The next object on the form is the resizer class. This class is responsible for responding to the Resize event of the form and resizing all the controls on the form proportionately to the form's size change. Here are the steps involved:

1. The Init() method of the object class calls its SetUp() method.

2. The SetUp() method sets some of its properties to the current values of the form, such as height, width and others.

3. The LoadExcludedArray() method is called. This method calls the mExcludeFormResize() and mExcludeFormReposition() methods. Each of these methods is a user hook method where you are able to populate an array with the controls you want to exclude from the resizer's antics.

4. The BuildFormsControlsArray() method is called to loop through all the controls on the form and create an array that will be used for resizing functions.

As you can see, if you have a form with many controls, using the resizer could cause some overhead at form instantiation. If you want a form to load faster, you might want to try it with the resizer turned off, by setting the lAllowResize property of the form to False, and see if you can improve your load time.

Controls

At this time all of the labels and text box controls will be instantiated. We won't trace through each one, because they all work in the same way. However, we will step through one so you can see the process. Keep in mind that this will happen for every control you have placed on the form.

1. The Init() method will call the SetUp() method.

2. The SetSecurityName() method is called to set the security name of the object. If security is enabled and no security name is specified for the control, and if the control is bound to a data object, the framework will get the security name for the data object and apply it to the control.

3. The SetCaption() method is called to populate the caption of a label control. This will only happen if the label is bound to a data item. (If you want to speed up your form load time and don't want the caption to be loaded from DBCX data, your best bet is to not bind the labels to data items.)

4. A reference of the cGlobalHook class is attached to the control, and its reference is put into the oGlobalHook property of the control. There is one instance of the global hook class that is shared by all controls. If it hasn't been created yet, it will be created on the instantiation of the first control class.

5. A reference to the control is passed to the global hook's Initialize() method. This method performs the following steps:

    a.   If the object has a cSecurityName, an object reference of the control being initialized is passed to the security class's SetSecurity() method. The SetSecurity() method will set the access level of the control.

    b.   If the lAlwaysDisable property of the control is set to True, the control's Enable property is set to False.

    c.   If the lAlwaysReadOnly property of the control is set to True, the control's ReadOnly property is set to True.

6. If the control is not a label, and it is bound to data (that is, it has a value in its cField or cViewParameter property), a reference to the control is added to the cGlobalHook class's oControls collection property.

As we said, these steps are duplicated for all of the controls that are on the form. Keep in mind that the form is instantiating controls from the inside out, so at this point the data is not yet available.

BizObjLoader

At some point after the controls are instantiated, the Business Object Loader is going to fall into line. This should occur after all of the controls have been instantiated because the BizObjLoader class is placed on the presentation object class, where the controls are placed on the instance of the presentation object that exists on the form.

Remember, the Business Object Loader is responsible for instantiating the business object. At this point we could be going to another tier, because the business object could be a COM object. However, in our example the business object is an internal VFP class.

The Init() method fires, and the following code is run:

1. The Init() method calls the SetBusinessObject() method.

2. The SetBusinessObject() method will instantiate the business object class, or obtain a reference to a business object based on the Business Object Loader's properties.

Unless the business object is being loaded by reference, the business object will instantiate at this point. While the code trace pointer will return to this code, it will just be to exit it. So we will not return to this code.

BizObj

The loader has instantiated this object. However, it is possible that you have directly placed the business object on the form, or perhaps you instantiated the business object in code. However it is created, it will conform to the following steps to load and instantiate. Once again, the classes contained by the business object will be created first. Let's trace through the objects that are created and the code that runs as they are instantiated.

oDELoader

The Data Environment Loader will load a data environment class. It exists so that the same business object can use several environments. Perhaps you have live data and archived data; this could be a case where you would use the same business object with two different data environments.

We will start tracing what happens here in the Init() method:

1. Based on the properties set in the loader, the Init() method instantiates the data environment class specified.

2. The oDataEnvironment.oBizObj property is populated with a reference to the parent class, which in this case would be the business object.

3. The Init() method will return True if the DE was loaded successfully, or False if it was not.

Of course, if you are tracing the code, the tracer would move to the Init() method of the data environment class at Step 2. Let's take a look at what happens when the data environment class is instantiated.

oDataEnvironment

We've mentioned this several times already, but we'll say it again. The data environment class is mainly a container that holds your cursor objects. Also, since VFP instantiates classes from the inside out, even though the last line of code we traced said, "Create this data environment class," we find ourselves in the Init() code of the first cursor class contained by the data environment class.

oCursor

In this case, your code pointer will be in the class named "InstructorCursor1," which is the name of the instance of the cursor class in the Instructors data environment. There could be one or 10 cursor objects in the data environment; we will follow just one cursor object through its startup code.

The Init() method of the cursor class accepts three parameters. If you wish to specify the cursor that is opened by this class, at this time you can pass these parameters. However, because we have set up this cursor specifically for our view, nothing is passed. In the case that parameters were passed, they would be used to set the corresponding properties of the cursor object.

Once all of the cursors are instantiated, the code will return to the data environment class and run its Init() code.

oDataEnvironment Init()

After all of the cursor objects contained by the data environment class are loaded, control is returned to the data environment class and the code in its Init() method is run. Here's what happens as this code runs:

1. If lPrivateDataSession is True, the code will create a private data session using the session class of Visual FoxPro. This functionality is primarily to be used when you are running your application as a COM object.

2. The oBizObj property of the data environment object is populated with a reference to the business object.

3. The Init_Pre() method is called. This is a hook method that allows you to place code you would like to execute at this point in the processing. However, in this class the code does not check the return value of the Init_Post(), so any return value will be ignored.

4. The LoadCollections() method is called to create two collections that are attached to the relations and cursors properties of the object. Once these collections are created, they are populated with references to the cursor and relation objects, which reside in the data environment.

5. The OpenTables() method is called. At this point, the OpenTables_Pre() method is called. This is a hook method that provides you with a place to put custom code that you would like to run at this point. If False is returned from this method, the next method won't be called.

6. The OpenTables_Perform() method is called if True was returned from the OpenTables_Pre() hook. This method calls the Open() method of each of the cursors in the cursors collection of the data environment object.

We will now follow the code into the Open() method of the cursor. Once those return, we will come back to the data environment object and continue with its instantiation.

oCursor Open()

The Open() method of the cursor object has been called by the data environment object to open the underlying view or table that the cursor is designed to control. Keep in mind that this process is repeated for every cursor object; however, we will only trace it once. We will pick up the code trace at the top of the Open() method for the first cursor:

1. The Open_Pre() method is called first. If this method returns False, the Open() method will return with a False and won't continue.

2. If the preceding method returned True, the Open_Perform() method is called to continue the process.

3. The Open_Database() method is called next to verify that the correct database is opened. If it is not, this method will open it. If the database is opened, a SET DATABASE TO command will be issued.

4. Next, the method verifies that the alias specified is not already in use.

5. The GetUseCommand() method is called to create the USE statement, which will open the table or view. The statement is built based on the properties of the cursor object. Attributes like ALIAS, NOUPDATE, SHARED and others are added to the USE command as needed.

6. A new work area is selected, and the command returned from the previous method is issued as a macro to open the view/table.

7. If the USE was successful, CreateIndexes() is called. This method will create the indexes defined in the metadata for views.

8. The buffer mode for the view is set based on the value of the nDefaultBufferMode property of the cursor object.

9. At this point the fields collection is created. This is done by creating the class cFieldCollection. The fields collection class populates itself, creating a field object for each field defined in the metadata using the class defined in the metadata.

10. A view parameter collection is created as in the previous step, by creating the cViewParameterCollection class, which also populates itself.

11. If appropriate—meaning you didn't select NODATONLOAD, and other parameters are met—the view is requeried to retrieve the data from the underlying table.

12. The order is set to the order specified by the order property of the cursor object, and the record pointer is set to the top, as the view was actually opened in this method.

13. Finally, the Open_Post() method is called. This method is a hook method that allows you to create custom code that you would like to run at this point in the process.

We haven't seen what happens if something here fails. The error handling of each object is designed to capture the specific errors that may be caused by opening a table, and it tries to handle the error as effectively possible.

oDataEnvironment, continued

After the Open() method of each cursor is called and the cursor goes through all the preceding code, control is returned to the OpenTables_Perform() method of the data environment object. We will pick up our trace at that point:

1. The SaveCursors() method is called, which will place all of the opened cursors into the cursors array property of the data environment.

2. The OpenTables_Post() method is called. This is an empty hook method that provides you with a place to put custom code you would like to run at this point. We are now returned to the Init() method.

3. The SetRelations() method is called to set the relation for each relation class that is contained in the data environment object.

4. The Init_Post() hook method is called, allowing you to create custom code that will be run at this point in the processing.

The full data environment has now been created. Each of the cursor classes has been created, all of the views/tables are opened and indexed, and the relations are set up, if there were any.

oBizRules

The next object to instantiate is oBizRules. This instance is contained by the business object class and will instantiate before the business object Init() runs. The oBizRules object is based on the cBizRuleCollection class, which is a subclass of the cCollection class. When this object loads, the AddItems() method is called. This is an empty method that you can use to create instances of the business rules that apply to this business object.

That's all there is to this class, and this is the final class that is contained by the business class. If you are following along with the debugger, you will see that the business object Init() is the code that will run next.

oBizObj Init()

Well, now that the objects contained by the business object are loaded, and they have performed their functions and provided their services, the business object Init() method will be run. So we'll pick up our story at the beginning of the business object's Init() code:

1. The Init() method of the bizobj accepts a parameter. Recall that the Business Object Loader passed a reference to itself on to the business object.

2. If the passed parameter is an object, the following properties are populated from the properties of the same name of the passed object: cParentBizObjName, cForeignKeyExpr, cKeyField, cRelationTag and oHost (set to the parent object reference of the passed object).

3. The oDataEnvironment property of the bizobj is populated with the oDataEnvironment property of the oDELoader. Then, the oDELoader class is removed.

4. The Register() method is called and passed the name of the parent bizobj. (For more information on parent and child bizobjs, see Chapter 14, "Related Data and Forms.") The Register() method populates the cParentBizObj and/or the oParentBizObj property of the object. Then, the application object's AddBizObj() method is called, passing a reference of itself—this will add this business object to the application-level business object collection.

5. The SetRelation() method is called to perform the following:

    a. If this bizobj has a parent bizobj, see whether it can be located. If the parent bizobj can be located, call the RegisterChild() method of the parent bizobj passing a reference to itself. This will inform the parent bizobj that is has a child bizobj here.

    b. Populate the relational properties to the parameters passed to this method, if they were passed. These are the same properties as in Step 2.

    c. Set a relation between the parent and child cursors of the business objects if there is a cRelationTag property defined. This is only used if you are using tables in your application. No relationships are set between views; however, they could be if you wished.

d. SetRelationFilter() will be called to set the relation filter if the tlSetFilter parameter was passed as True.

6. The Init_Post() hook method of the business object is called.

This completes the instantiation of the business object. Each of the contained classes has done its job to provide the various services and data layer for the business object, which is the business layer for this entity.

Presentation object Init()

If you think back to the building blocks we used to create the Instructors form, you will remember the presentation object you created that contained the business object and the controls. Also, recall that when we started this trip, it was to trace form instantiation, and we still haven't run the form methods.

So let's take a look at what the presentation object does to get ready to be used. Keep in mind that all of the classes contained by the presentation object have been loaded, and all of their Init() code has fired. Also, up to this point there have been no errors, which is a real treat.

Let's pick up our map and start following the code in the Init() method of the InstructorsPresObj class:

1. First, the form's lockscreen is set to True. (Lockscreen keeps the screen picture from updating as interface objects are manipulated.)

2. The Register() method is called to register the presentation object with the form. The form has a presentation object collection that keeps track of any presentation objects on the form. The Register() method calls the RegisterPresentationObject() of the form passing a reference to itself.

3. If the presentation object is set to be read-only, or if its AllowEdit() method evaluates to False, then all of the contained controls' enabled properties are set to False.

4. The form's lockscreen property is set back to what it was when this method entered the form. Because this is the only presentation object, this means it was False.

That's it for the presentation object. Basically it is registering itself with the form.

Form Init()

Earlier in this chapter, we started tracing what happens when a form is loaded. We watched as all of the classes contained on the form started, and all of the layers of the framework started coming into play and meshing into a functional whole. Finally, we have come to the Init() code of the form. At this point the business objects are in place, the data environments have been established, the views are open and the controls are ready.

However, we have a bit more to do, because those controls aren't talking to the data yet. Also, the form needs to do some work, putting up a toolbar and registering itself with the application's forms manager class.

We've finally reached the form's Init():

1. The UnrecoverableError() method is called to ask the presentation object, if it exists, whether there were any errors when it was starting up. Checking for error messages, this will essentially travel through the layers to see whether any of the objects contain an error message. (Since the framework is n-tier, we couldn't display a message if loading a view failed because there is no user interface at this layer.)

2. If the previous method returns True, the Destroy() method of the form is called and the form is not loaded.

3. The SetPresentObj() method is called to find the primary presentation object. This is the presentation object with the lMain property set to True. The oPresentObj property is set with a reference to the object determined to be the primary.

4. The BindControls() method is called. This method will loop through the controls collection of the oGlobalHook object and set the ControlSource property of each control to the value in cField or cViewParameter. In other words, the data is bound to the controls.

5. SET MESSAGE is set to the caption of the form.

6. A reference to the form is passed to the oGlobalHook.Initilize() method. (The properties that this sets were covered earlier.)

7. The CreateToolBar() method is called to instantiate the class stored in the cToolBar property. If cToolBar is empty, the value from the application object's cDefaultToolBar is used.

8. HideToolBars() will hide any toolbars in the toolbar collection that are not associated with the form, except the main application toolbar.

9. If the lSavePosition property is True, the RestorePosition() method is called to restore the form to the position values stored in the registry the last time the form was closed.

10. The Decorate() method is called to set the Icon and Picture values to the application object defaults. WindowState is set to normal, and BorderStyle is set based on whether the form is resizable.

11. Next the form adds a reference to itself to the forms manager of the application object. (Modal forms are not added to the collection.)

12. The form calls the AddToMenu() method to add itself to the bottom of the Window menu.

That's all there is to it! The form has been loaded, all of the contained classes have started up, and the form is now displayed on the desktop, waiting for the user to interact with it. As you become more familiar with the framework, you should trace the code through this sequence and see for yourself all the code that is executed. We did omit a few trivial items that you may or may not want to know about.

BindControls()
Yes, you are probably asking how that BindControls() step works. And yes, there is a lot more to it than what was presented here. For more information on what happens during the BindControls() method, consult Chapter 11, "Interface Controls."

Summary
You should now have a good understanding of how all the classes in all the layers work together to help you build a solid application. As we've said, nothing beats taking the debugger for a drive and tracing the framework code as it does its work. As you get started, you may want to make good use of the "step over" button so that you won't go into all of the access and assign methods.

What you saw in this chapter was a good overview of the system services that are in the framework. You were exposed to several examples of how some of those services were used as we traced through the form load. Don't forget that the application object and other system classes are there—they can save you a lot of time and code duplication.

From here we'll build upon the basics that you have learned so far—how to advance the interfaces, validation, business rules and so forth. But if you are still a little stumped, you should perhaps go back and review what has been covered up to this point in the book. As there are really no new classes to learn, we will just look a bit more closely at each class as we continue.

Chapter 11
Interface Controls

The framework contains a class library of controls that all have a consistent interface and function. In this chapter, we will take a look at the controls that you bind to data and the global hook class that provides much of the controls' common functionality. We'll also explore how toolbar controls work and take a look at the menu classes.

Well, so far you have seen the advantages provided by this well-designed framework. Much of the common code you would normally write to open files, access data and perform other functions is encapsulated in the business objects and cursor objects.

You can expect just as much help with the control classes. The classes are designed to simplify your job and include most if not all of the common functionality you would expect or want in your application.

Data edit controls

For the purpose of this book, we will divide the controls into two types. The first type is data edit controls. These are the controls that you drop on the form and bind to a data field or variable. These controls are generally in the tab order and provide a method for the user to edit their values, by typing in characters, selecting from a list or the like.

These controls, by the VFP base class name, are the text box, list box, drop-down combo, check box, tree view and so on. In the framework, each of these controls has been subclassed to provide you with some enhanced functionality and also to couple them somewhat to the VFE framework.

In this chapter we will take a look at some of the common properties and methods you will find on the data edit controls, and then we will explore some of the specific features of a few of the data edit controls.

cRightClickMenu

Yes, it is that easy to add a right-click menu to your controls. Actually, there is already one there by default. By default, when you right-click on your (data edit) control, you will load the cFieldRightClickMenu, which has the appropriate actions you would want to take.

In the property you can specify a class name, or, if you want to do it the old-fashioned way, you can create a shortcut menu with the menu editor and specify the name of the MPR (menu program) in this property. Make sure you specify it with the MPR extension, which is what tells the control that you are specifying a menu program as opposed to a menu class.

If you want to use a menu class, you can subclass the cFieldRightClickMenu and modify it, or you can subclass cRightClickMenu and start from scratch. Look at these classes for the method of building a shortcut menu class.

There's one more thing: If you leave this property empty, the framework will attempt to run the control's parent's right-click menu. Remember, the parent is not the parent class but rather the class in which this control is contained, such as the form.

cField, cViewParameter

If the control is being bound to a data item, one of these properties will be populated. The control will be bound to the data item named in one of these properties. Of course, if the data item is a field, the cField will be populated with its name. The name will be in the format Alias.FIELDNAME.

If you are using the control to display or prompt for a view parameter, the cViewParameter property should hold the name of the view parameter. This property will also take the format Alias.PARAMETERNAME.

If you use the Presentation Object Builder, you will find that these properties have already been populated correctly. If you add a control yourself, be sure to populate one of these properties. They tie the control into the framework, so to speak. You will gain a better understanding of this when you read about binding the controls later in this chapter.

lNoValidate

This property is False by default. Setting this property to True will disable the validation as focus leaves the control. However, this will not change the fact that the value is verified. Upon a save, the business object will run the validation of all the field objects in the cursor to verify that no incorrect data has been entered.

lAlwaysDisable

This property is provided so that the disabling of the control will work more smoothly with the framework and the metadata. Recall that you can also specify that a data item be read-only. The framework looks at several items such as security, the data item and lAlwaysDisable to determine how the enabled property should be set, and then it sets the control accordingly.

Of course, if it is set to True, it will override security and also the setting on the metadata and disable the control. However, you may prefer to set it at this level because you have other screens that display the same data item in a context where it can be edited.

lAlwaysReadOnly

This is similar in function to lAlwaysDisable. Setting this to True will make the control read-only regardless of the security and metadata settings for the field. However, for some controls the framework will set enabled to True to implement read-only rather than setting the read-only property to True. This option might be coded because the control has a different visible look, and also the user will not be able to give the control focus.

oApplication

This property contains a reference to the application object. In the Chapter 10, "How It Works," we discussed the application object and how many useful services it provides. Each control has this property, which means that when you are coding in your controls' methods to access the application object, you would use This.oApplication to reference it.

oField

This property holds a reference to the field object for the data item the control is bound to. This might be one of the items you refer to many times in your code. In Chapter 4, "Data Storage and Classes," you read about all the methods and properties of the field object. Thus you should be able to see that if you type This.oField in the control's method, you will gain access to each of those properties and methods.

Using these object references is how you will keep your program tiers separate and distributable. If you referred to the view and/or fields in a user interface control, and then later separated the user interface layer from the business layer, the field would not be open in the user tier. Keep this in mind while you are writing code.

oGlobalHook
This is a reference to the global hook class. You will find many useful methods in the global hook object that you may need while writing code in the user interface layer.

For more information on the global hook object, see the next section.

Global hook class
You've seen references to the global hook object in previous chapters of this book. The global hook class is designed to provide common functions to similar classes without duplicating code. Its most prevalent use in the VFE framework is to extend the user interface control classes. If you were to look at the code in the controls, you would see that most of the methods call a method of the class referenced in the oGlobalHook property.

The global hook property provides these methods, since the functionality of each of the controls is common, and the global hook provides a place to implement the method without duplicating it in each control class.

If you look closely at one of the data edit controls, you'll see that the oGlobalHook property has an access method that is fired whenever code tries to access the global hook class. This access method first checks to see whether a reference is already stored in the property. If not, the method will get a reference to the global hook class from the oGlobalHook property of the application object.

cGlobalHook of Utils.VCX
This class contains methods that are called by the controls when various methods fire. Let's take a look at some of the functions that are implemented in the global hook class.

Initialize()
In Chapter 10, "How It Works," we traced the form startup; recall that each interface control called the Initialize() method of the global hook, passing a reference of itself to the hook object.

The Initialize() method will set the read-only and enabled status of the control, and then it will set the security level. Finally, the control will be added to the controls collection of the global hook object for later binding.

ValidateControl()
This method is well named, because it speaks its function, as all well-documented code should. However, the validation does not take place in this method. Recall from Chapter 4, "Data Storage and Classes," that the field and view parameter objects contain the functions

that validate the data entered into the field. So this method calls upon the bound object's Validate() method.

Depending on the result returned by the object's Validate() method, this method will show a lookup form, display an error message or simply return True if the control passes all validation tests.

LostFocusHook()

This method is called by the control's LostFocus() method to handle the LostFocus event, which is common to all interface controls. This method is cleverly coded to determine how the LostFocus event was fired. If it is determined that the control lost focus because the user was trying to close the form, that is allowed. However, if the user exited the control with purpose, and validation is set up for this field, then validation takes place by calling the ValidateControl() method.

The method also activates a very popular feature, found in many applications, that VFE has provided without much work. If the user has entered a value and it is not in the lookup table, a form is provided to add a record to the lookup table. Of course, this is only done if you have specified an "addlookupform" in the validation section of the metadata.

We will take a closer look at using the lookup add form in Chapter 12, "Data Validation."

GetController()

This method is used much more often with "action controls" (command buttons). However, it may still be useful in a data edit control as well. The controller is basically the significant container in which a control is placed. GetController() will find either the presentation object or form that the control is in or, in the case of an action control, the presentation object or form that it controls. (See the "Toolbars" section later in this chapter for more information about controllers.)

RightClickHook()

This was discussed earlier in this chapter, in the "cRightClickMenu" section. This method contains the code that will determine what to run based on the information in the property.

BindControls()

Earlier we instructed you to place the field name into the cField property of the control. But as a VFP programmer, you know that in the method used to bind a control to a variable or field, you set its ControlSource property. The problem is, if the control is instantiated and the field or variable you bound the control to doesn't exist, you will receive an error.

In order to solve this problem, VFE waits until all of the objects in the form are created, and then it runs the BindControls() method. In Chapter 10, "How It Works," you learned that this method binds the controls to the data, but this is oversimplified. The BindControls() method performs several task to prepare the controls for the framework.

Let's take a look at the full process of BindControls(). This process calls several methods that are contained in the global hook class, so we will list the class along with the method to ensure that you'll understand in what class the method being explained resides.

Recall that in our previous story, all of the objects in the form had been created and properly added to the collections. Finally, control was given to the Init() method of the form. At one point in the form's Init(), the BindControls() method was called.

This method is basically a loop that calls the SetCritical() method of the global hook class for each object in the controls collection of the global hook object. Each control that contained a value in cField or cParameter (except for labels) was added to this collection. Let's start by tracing the code in the SetCritical() of the global hook object:

1. The SetObjectName() method is called to add and set the cObjectName property of the control. This name is determined from the cField or cViewParameter value, but basically it will be the same as the cField value, with the database name removed if it was there.

2. The SetControlSource() method is call to set the ControlSource property of the control. This is the actual data binding. The property is generally set to this.oField.Value. This is the value property of the field object for the data object of the field named in cField.

3. The oField.DecorateObject() method is called. This method of the field object is called to perform the following:

   a. First, the oProperties (of the field object) property is checked for null. This is done because oProperties has an access method that, if null, calls the GetProperties() method. (Recall from Chapter 4, "Data Storage and Classes," that oProperties contains an object that contains all of the DBCX properties. This is done to limit the number of times data must be accessed when a property value is needed from the metadata.)

   b. oField.SetSecurity() is called to populate the cSecurityName property of the control to the security name of the data item. Then, the control object reference is sent to the SetSecurity() method of the system security class. If you are using security, this will set the security level of the control based on the security name and user information. (See Chapter 17, "VFE Security," for more information.)

   c. SetCaption() is called to set the caption to the value stored in the metadata for controls with captions. This method also checks to see whether the control is hosted in a grid, and, if so, the column header of the grid will be set to the stored caption value.

   d. SetInputMask() is called to set the InputMask property of the control. This will only set the property if it is empty, so if you want to set this in the control, it will not be overridden. If you have set an input mask in the metadata for this data item, it will be used for the control. Finally, if the property is empty and the metadata property is empty, a default input mask will be derived based on the data type and length of the field. This method will also populate the format property using the same sequence described previously to determine how to populate it.

   e. The SetToolTip() method will set the ToolTipText property of the control from the value in the metadata for the data item the control is bound to.

f. The SetStatusBarText() method will set the StatusBarText property of the control from the value in the metadata for the data item the control is bound to.

g. The SetReadOnly() method will set the read-only or enabled property of the control based on the value of read-only for the data item in the metadata. The setting of read-only or enabled depends on the base class. In addition, if the control is to be read-only and it is hosted in a grid, the grid column will be set to read-only also. Of course, this method takes security into account accordingly.

h. The LookUpSetUp() method will prepare the properties and data environment for field validation. (For more information on validation and lookups, see Chapter 12, "Data Validation.")

i. The AddInList() method will add the listed values in metadata to the combo or list box, or set up an @M picture code in a text box.

j. The SetHiLowValues() method will set the high and low range values for a spinner control.

As stated earlier, the SetCritical() method will be called for each control in the global hook object. After the loop has completed, the ClearAllReferences() method of the global hook object is called. This will clear out the controls collection to prepare it for the next form's use.

Early vs. late binding

In Chapter 7, "Presentation Objects," we discussed binding to fields or field objects. By default the controls are bound to field objects to maintain the n-tier separation of data layer and interface layer. This default is known as "late binding." Late binding refers to the fact that the controls are bound to their data after they are created by a separate process (BindObjects(), in this case).

Initially there were some complaints about form load time, so the framework was modified to support "early binding." This means that at design time you would populate the ControlSource property rather than the cField property. cField being empty also means that the control is not decorated from metadata, which is why the Presentation Object Builder has a selection to write the metadata properties directly to the controls at design time. These modifications will save time when starting the form.

Because Service Pack 2 was released with many performance enhancements, early binding has a very small speed advantage over late binding. However, the choice is yours. You may try a hybrid method of specifying the ControlSource and the cField property. This should allow you to bind to the field and also have the control decorated at run time. We have not experimented with this method here; we'll leave that to you as homework.

Builders

Another nice touch provided by VFE is that each control class has a builder specific to it. These builders allow you to specify whether the control is bound to a field or view parameter. A combo box is provided to select the data source.

You can access the class builders while you are in the Class Designer. To access the builder of any control, place the mouse on the control and right-click. A shortcut menu will be displayed (see **Figure 1**) that will have a Builder… selection. Selecting Builder… will run the specified builder.

```
Undo
Cut
Copy
Properties...
Builder...
Code...
Help...
```

Figure 1. Display the object shortcut menu by placing the mouse over a control and right-clicking. This gives you a selection to run the builder.

If you examine the control builders (see **Figure 2**), you will observe some differences on each one. This is because the builder is written specifically for the class you are working with. In the background, the builder is setting properties of the object.

Textbox Builder

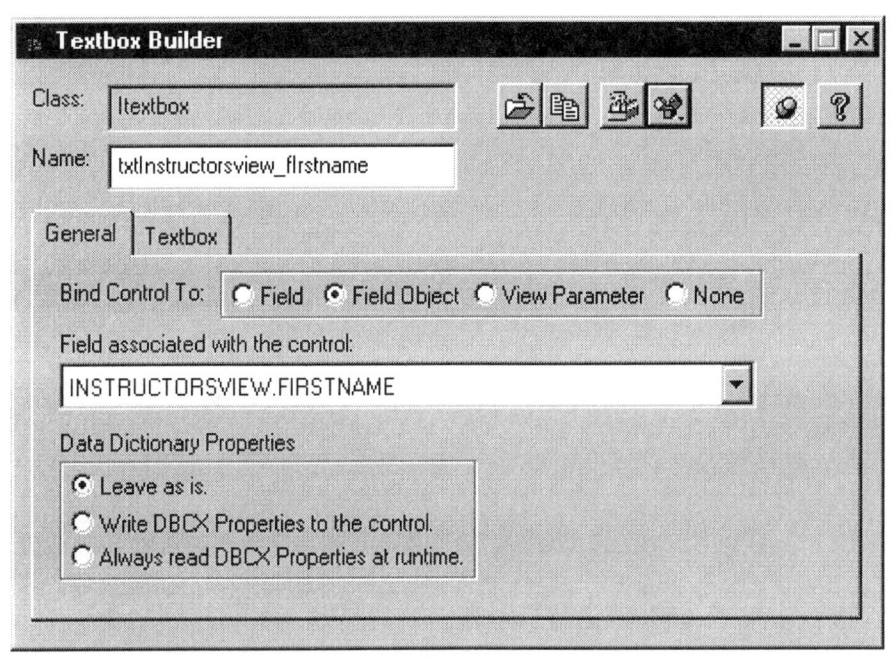

Class: ltextbox
Name: txtInstructorsview_firstname

General | Textbox

Bind Control To: ○ Field ● Field Object ○ View Parameter ○ None

Field associated with the control:
INSTRUCTORSVIEW.FIRSTNAME

Data Dictionary Properties
● Leave as is.
○ Write DBCX Properties to the control.
○ Always read DBCX Properties at runtime.

Figure 2. Selecting the Builder… item on the object shortcut menu launches the Textbox Builder.

Each builder is based on a public domain class library called "Builder-B." Builder-B provides a set of classes to simplify creating builders. Normally, when you select Builder... from the object shortcut menu, the program or application defined in the _BUILDER variable of VFE is run. This program looks at the builder property of the class and runs the specified builder.

In order to use Builder-B, you must add a property named "builderx" to each of your class libraries. The builderx property is used to specify the builder you have created for your class using Builder-B classes.

Prior to VFP 6.0, it was also necessary to modify the program stored in the _BUILDER variable to a program named BUILDERX.PRG. This program was designed to check whether builderx was populated. If not, this program called the VFP default BUILDER.APP program to perform the "out-of-the-box" builder menu. However, since the author of Builder-B was a member of the Visual FoxPro 6.0 development team for a time, the default builder program in VFP now recognizes the builderx property also.

The code for all the builders is also included with the framework. This will allow you to subclass them and modify them if you modify and create your own controls for which you want to create builders. You will find the code in the \VFE6\Tools\BuilderB\VBUILDER.VCX class library. The Builder-B class libraries and documentation can also be found in this folder. We will leave it to you to investigate this further.

Quick-fill text box

One feature of a text box control that solves one of the most commonly asked questions is what we call the quick-fill text box. The problem is how to display the business code or a description that the user understands when you have stored the foreign key in the file. If you are following the recommended rules of normalization, you are storing the key in your table; this key is a meaningless (to the user) value that was generated by your system, rather than being user-defined.

For example, in an invoice you have the user select a part number. The part number comes from a Parts table. When you designed your Parts table, you listened to all the experts and created a surrogate primary key that holds a GUID to uniquely identify this part record. Of course, you also stored the GUID in the Invoice table rather than the part number that is familiar to the user.

Some folks would use a combo box to solve this problem. A combo box natively allows you to bind the control to one field and specify a "recordsource" that contains the values to display. This works well when you don't have many items, but more than 50 or 100 items really pushes the limits of a combo control. Not only is it difficult to find an item in a list of thousands in a combo, but it also takes quite a while for the combo box to load all of these values.

To solve this, the cTextBox class has a property named "lQuickFill." Setting this property to True activates some code that emulates a combo box, in that the text box will be "bound" to a different field than it displays. It will also "quick-fill," meaning that as you type in values, it will locate the closest match and fill in the rest, still highlighted, so you won't need to type the entire value. This is similar to the behavior of the URL entry box of Internet Explorer.

In order for this to work, you must set up a validation for the field that you are binding to. Since we haven't discussed validation yet, you may need to come back to this after you have read Chapter 12, "Data Validation." What the quick-fill text box does is use the first "display" field you select in your validation to display.

If you did not want to use the first field, you would place code in the GetDisplayField() method, overriding the default behavior, and return an alternative field name. As an example, consider an application that has a foreign key that's related to a table, which has an entity with a "code" that the user enters and a "description" that the user enters. On the form that edits that field, there are two text boxes with lQuickFill set to True. The first text box uses the default behavior and displays the first field specified in the validation's display field list. The second text box displays the description. Even though the description text box is bound to the same field, the following code is included in the GetDisplayValue() method:

```
Return 'Description'
```

This method is called when a quick-fill text box refreshes to determine what field to display. The advantage of using two text boxes is that the user is provided with the choice to enter the code or the description of the entity that they are specifying. When the user enters the value in one, the text box will populate the foreign key field with the key value. This will cause the second text box to show the description when the user tabs off the text box.

One other item you should be aware of is the input mask of the text box. By default it will be set to the length and type of the field you bind to the control, not the field you are displaying. It will be necessary to set the input mask on the control if the default will not be sufficient.

Date text box

If you bind your text box to a date field, certain behaviors are activated that simplify data entry for your user. These items don't seem to be documented, and they are quite useful.

Table 1 describes what happens when the specified key is pressed when a text box bound to a data field or variable has focus.

Table 1. Shortcut keys that are available when entering data into a date field.

Keystroke	Behavior
+ or =	One day is added to the current date value. If the control is empty, one day is added to today's date.
- or _	One day is subtracted from the current date value. If the control is empty, one day is subtracted from today's date.
T or t	The value is changed to or populated with today's date.
M or m	The value is set to the first of the current month if empty. If there is a date value, the day value is changed to 1.
H or h	A month is added to the current value. If empty, a month is added to today's date.
Y or y	The first date of the date's year is entered. If empty, the first day of the year of today's date is entered.
R or r	The last date of the date's year is entered. If empty, the last day of the year of today's date is entered.

Grids

The grid class in VFE has built-in behavior to sort and search within the grid. We will work with the list of our Instructors as an example, but the following setup can be used on any grid you create in your application.

There are three basic steps you need to follow to provide searching and sorting in your grids:

1. Set the grid's lAlwaysReadOnly to True. By default, the grids built on the fly from the List() method will be set this way. If you are putting a grid on a presentation object, you would set this property manually. If you are using the builder, you would check the Searchable Grid check box.

2. Create an index in the view for each column you want to be sortable/searchable.

3. Populate the Search Tag metadata property of the field in the view.

Although it's not discernible in the printed version of **Figure 3**, the Last Name column header of the Instructors list is green. The green header indicates that the grid is sorted by the values in this column and that they are ascending. If the user were to click on the column, it would change to blue, which indicates a descending sort on that column.

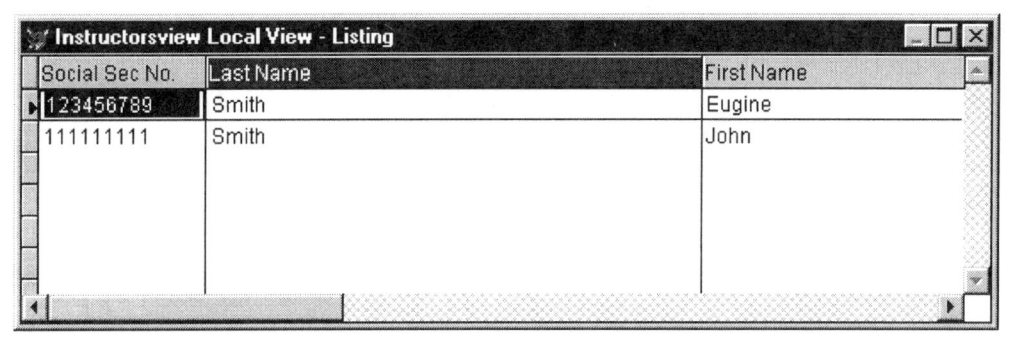

Social Sec No.	Last Name	First Name
123456789	Smith	Eugine
111111111	Smith	John

Figure 3. The listing of the Instructors has been sorted by last name, which can also be searched.

The user is also able to type in letters that will be concatenated and searched for in the highlighted column. The search string is displayed in a wait window. Setting the lShowSearchString property to False will disable the wait window.

Let's follow the previous three steps to implement searching and sorting for this grid by last name and Social Security number:

1. Bcause this grid is a list grid built on the fly, the lAlwaysReadOnly property is already set to False, so we don't need to do anything here.

2. Open the DBCX Explorer by clicking on the Data Dictionary button on the Project tab of the Application Builder.

3. In the DBCX Explorer, navigate to the INSTRUCTORSVIEW and expand it. Select the Indexes node, and then press the Add button. This will bring up the Create Index dialog (see **Figure 4**).

Chapter 11: Interface Controls 141

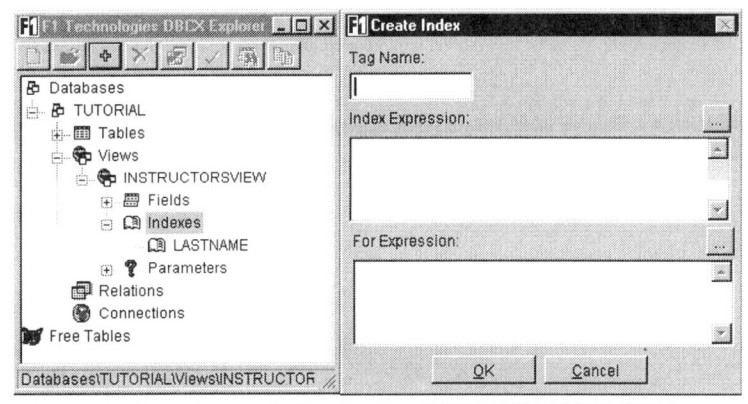

Figure 4. Creating an index for the INSTRUCTORSVIEW.

4. Create a tag named "LASTNAME" with an expression of "lastname," and then repeat Step 3 and create a tag named "SSN" with an expression of "ssn." After creating each index, you will see them listed in the Indexes node of the Explorer.

5. In the DBCX Explorer, expand the Fields node for the INSTRUCTORSVIEW. Highlight the field you would like to make searchable/sortable. In the Behavior page, highlight the Search Index Tag property. Press the Builder button, and then select the appropriate tag name (see **Figure 5**).

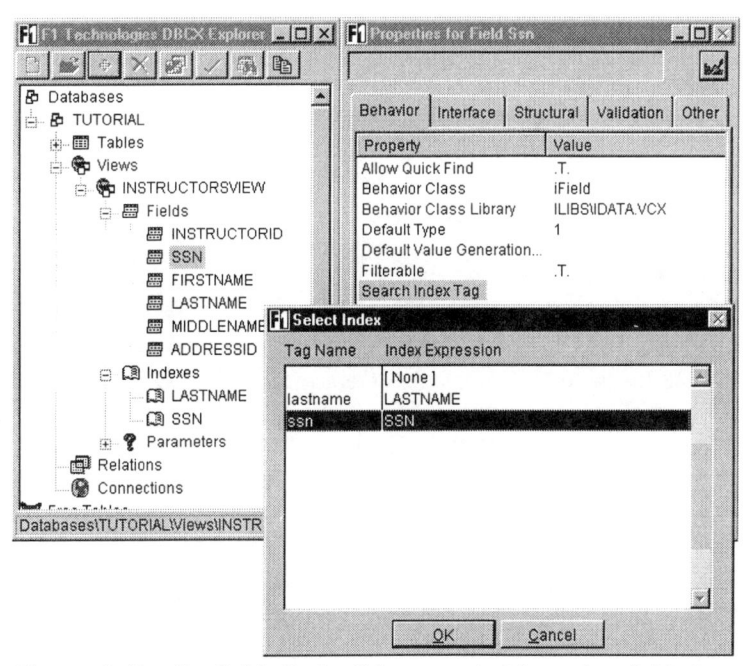

Figure 5. For the fields that will be searchable and sortable in a grid, populate the Search Index Tag property with the appropriate tag name.

Many people on various VFP support forums ask how to implement this feature, and that's really all there is to it. VFE has done all the work for you; all you have to do is set a few properties, and it works.

There are a few other properties on the grid you should be aware of, to save you from writing code to do something that could also be accomplished just by setting a single property to True.

lGetHeaderCaptions

This property defaults to True and instructs the code to populate the header captions with the caption value of the field object used for that column. This will use the grid caption property of the field to populate the header. If you don't need data-driven headers, turning off this setting will speed up instantiation just a bit.

lPopulateOnInit

This property defaults to False. If it is set to True, the Populate() method will be called. This method builds the columns for the grid based on the information in the metadata. This allows for data-driven grids; this property is True for the list grid that we used earlier.

lRefreshParentOnRowChange

This property defaults to False. If it is set to True, the presentation object will be refreshed. You would use this when you have a grid and controls on the same presentation object and you want the records to stay synchronized. This is needed because the presentation object doesn't know that the record being pointed to has been changed if it was changed in the grid.

This is only necessary if you have controls in the same presentation object as the grid. If the grid is the only control in the presentation object, there is no need to set this to True. This is why the default is False, so as not to waste time refreshing when it isn't needed.

lRequeryChildrenOnRowChange

This property defaults to False. If it is set to True, the children business objects of the grid's presentation object's business object will be requeried. This may not make sense now, but we will revisit this property when we discuss related interfaces and when it is needed.

lSelectRecordOnDoubleClick

This property defaults to False. If it is set to True, it instructs the grid to run its SelectRecord() method when the user selects a record by double-clicking or by pressing Enter. There is default code in SelectRecord(), which we will discuss Chapter 14, "Related Data and Forms." You can also override the default behavior by placing code in this method.

Action controls

The second category of controls we'll discus are the action controls. For the most part, these are command buttons. All of the command buttons can be found in the CTOOLBAR.VCX class library. Each of these command buttons has been coded to work whether you drop them on the presentation object or in a toolbar.

A concept called the "controller" is what makes it possible for the same code to work in both containers. Another function of the global hook class is the GetController() method. This method is used to determine what object is the controller of another object.

Okay, then, what is a controller? The controller is the controlling container of the action control. Or, more appropriately, it is the container to which the button should send its message. Essentially there are two classes that could be the button's controller: a form or a presentation object. What GetController() does is drill up the container hierarchy until it finds a presentation object, a form or a toolbar. If a toolbar is found, the active screen becomes the controller.

Heed this note from the VFE documentation: *Toolbar/action controls should never be placed in a presentation object unless the presentation object is a child presentation object. Toolbar/action controls that are intended to work on the primary presentation object in a form should be placed directly in the form or on a toolbar used by the form.*

So an action control is basically a command button that sends a control to its controller. For example, the Save button will call the Save() method of its controller when it is pressed.

Toolbars

It is a rare occurrence these days when a Windows application does not have a toolbar (or 50). VFE provides you with a couple of ways to easily hook your toolbars to the application.

The first toolbar is considered an application toolbar. The application toolbar is loaded at application startup and exists for the life of the application. This toolbar may have an Exit button on it, or it may have a button to launch a recently used form. Perhaps it launches a calculator or other tool the user may need.

The second toolbar is one that you would attach to your forms. You know from Chapter 10, "How It Works," that the form will automatically display the toolbar when it is launched or given focus, and it will hide the toolbar when it is moved to the background. Remember also that there are two ways to specify the toolbar to the form. You can place the class name of the toolbar in the form's cToolBar property, or you can populate the application object's cDefaultFormToolBar, which will then be used with all forms that don't have the cToolBar property populated.

Because we broke the rule from the VFE documentation when we created our Instructors presentation object, let's move the action buttons we placed there into a toolbar class. This is a fairly generic toolbar, so we will also make it the default toolbar.

1. Open the Tutorial application from the Application Manager.
2. Select the Classes tab.
3. Highlight the Toolbar node on the Classes tab.
4. Press the New button.
5. In Step 1 of the Toolbar wizard, select the classes in the order shown in **Figure 6**. Notice that the space (iSeparator) is used several times. (The one selection you can't see in the figure is iCloseButton.)

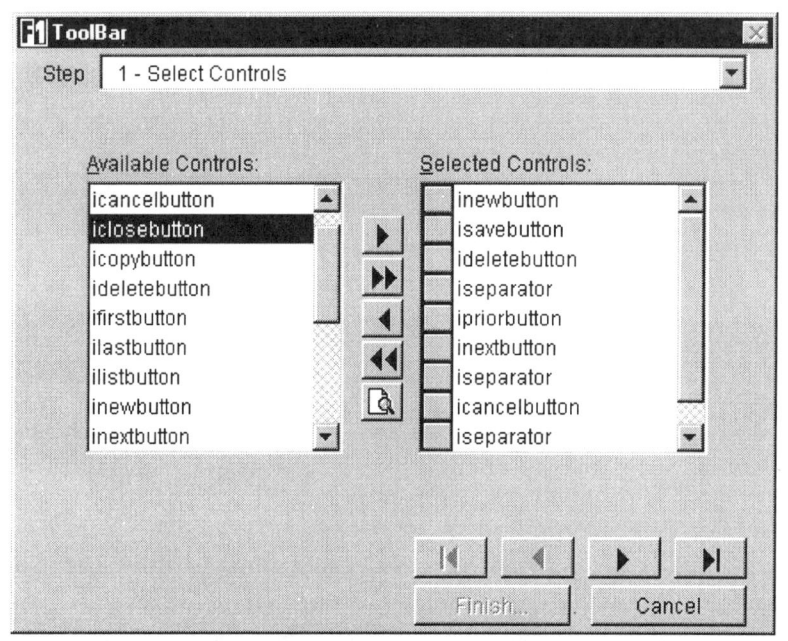

Figure 6. Select the items on the right to create the toolbar for our forms.

6. Press the Next button on the wizard.

7. In Step 2 of the wizard, you will see three settings that need no explanation. Press the Next button.

8. In Step 3, you are asked to provide a class name for the toolbar and a library to place it in. Use a class name of DefaultToolbar, and save it in the default class library ATOOLBAR.VCX. (The reason we don't save it in the Instructors library is because this is a common class that will be used for all forms.)

9. Press the Finish button, and the wizard will create the toolbar class, adding the button objects specified. You may then want to edit this class and expand the toolbar so it looks like **Figure 7**.

Figure 7. The DefaultToolbar class we built with the Toolbar wizard.

10. Close and save your toolbar class, if you haven't already.

11. On the Classes tab of the Application Builder, open the Presentation Object node and edit the InstructorsViewPresObj.

12. Delete the action buttons from the class.

13. Close the Class Designer and save your changes.

We have created the toolbar, but we haven't connected it to the form of the application. Because this is a basic toolbar and we called it "default toolbar," we will specify it as the default toolbar for all forms.

14. On the Classes page of the Application Builder, expand the Other Classes node.
15. Select BookTutorialApplicationObject or, if you used a different name, WhateverYouCalledItApplicationObject. Press the Open button.
16. Set the cDefaultToolBar property of the application object to DefaultToolBar, as shown in **Figure 8**.
17. Close the Class Designer and save your changes.

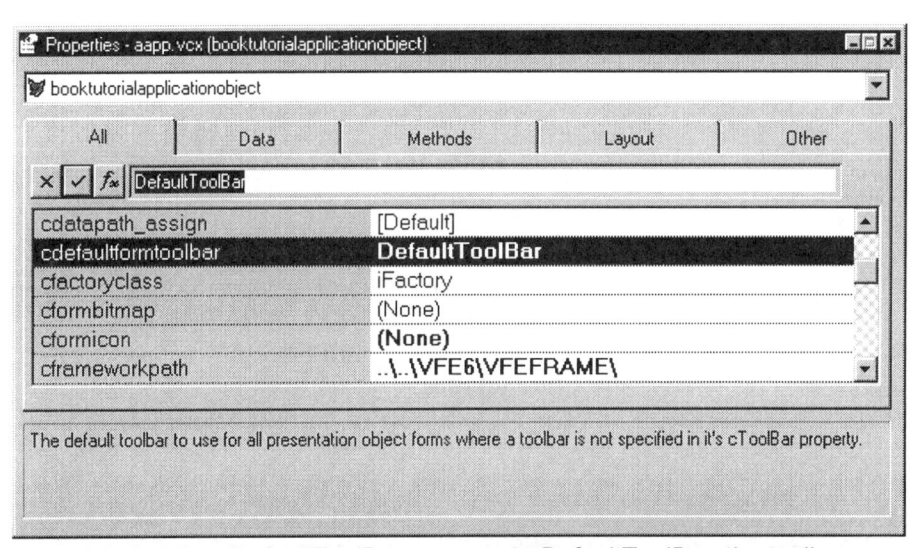

Figure 8. Set the cDefaultToolBar property to DefaultToolBar, the toolbar we created in the previous step.

At this point, you can press the Run button to test your changes. Remember, there is no need to build at this point because we didn't make any menu changes, and that is the only type of change that requires a build in order to work. If you did everything correctly, the toolbar will be created when you run the Instructors form. You'll also see that it acts like a standard VFP toolbar—you can undock it, move it around or dock it somewhere else. It will also remember its position and position itself the next time you load the form.

Menus

The Visual FoxExpress menus are a combination of menu objects and VFP menu commands. The VFE menu classes are wrappers around the VFP menu commands, so you can access your menus as objects if you like. However, it is not necessary for you to build the menu classes yourself.

The menu system in VFP is based on a menu program that is generated by program GENMENU.PRG. This program comes with VFP and uses the menu file as input to create a program that builds the menus for you. A menu editor is provided to create the menu file. Using the menu editor, you visually build your menu by filling out properties and snippets.

In VFE you also build your menus by using the built-in menu editor. The difference here is that VFE uses a program named GENMENUX.PRG to generate the menu program; genmenux provides enhanced features to your menus by adding specific comments to the comments section of the menu field in the editor.

Another feature of genmenux is the idea of drivers. A driver is an external program to genmenux that it calls for a specific purpose. In the case of VFE, a driver program called CBMENUS.PRG is called to generate the VFE menu program. This program will create class definitions for each of your menu items. If you look at the generated menu program after doing a build, you will see all of your menus defined as a subclass of various VFE classes.

The VFE menu classes cBar, cPad, cMenu and cPopUp are the classes that your menus will be created as. Each of these objects has code to generate itself as a VFP menu by issuing commands to create the menus. Once the menus are created, the menu objects exist as system services that you can use in your code as needed. We will leave it to readers who are interested to investigate the menu classes further.

Unfortunately, there does not seem to be any documentation for genmenux included with the framework. If you read the GENMENUX.PRG file, you will see some information in the comments about the extension keywords you can use to create various features of your menu; however, all of these might not be available with the cbmenu driver in place. (You can download genmenux documentation from www.stevenblack.com/SBCPublicDomain.asp.)

The upside is that you can run the menu editor from the Classes page of the Application Builder, and pop-ups, pads and the classes are all generated for you in the background; the menus function as you would want and expect.

Summary

VFE controls are designed to provide a consistent interface for the developer. The use of the global hook class provides a place to implement the common code for all of the control classes, which simplifies using and understanding this code.

VFE has also provided a builder for each class. This includes the page frame and presentation object and other interface classes, controls not bound to data, like shapes, and containers that were not discussed in this chapter. Once you've learned the common properties of each control, you should then investigate the individual properties. If you are looking for a specific behavior, look through the properties. Most of the properties are named to describe their function.

Also, don't think that you're limited to what the wizard creates for you. Be aware that you can change how the wizard sets up the controls and forms to create your own look and style. Keep in mind that you should also be creating your own controls. Subclass the controls to provide specialized controls for your own purposes.

In the next chapter, we will discuss an issue that is closely related to data controls and the user: validations and lookups. Don't miss it.

Chapter 12
Data Validation

In this chapter, we will look at what the framework provides for us to validate our data. In addition to simply validating the values entered by the user, we will also look at how to build pick lists and lookups and how they are handled.

Data validation is an important topic of any book that discusses building business applications. There are several aspects of data validation, and many consider data integrity to be part of this general topic as well.

We are lucky that Visual FoxPro, for the most part, automatically deals with the issue of data types. The product will take care of ensuring that the correct data type is entered into a field. For this to work, you must just select the correct data type. VFP will validate that the user enters a valid date. Of course, a valid date in VFP includes dates up to the year 9999, which makes you wonder who will write the first Y10K-ready application.

The focus of this chapter is more along the lines of domain data testing. You have to deal with the issue of values and ranges. Many times the value entered must exist in another field, or sometimes the validation depends on the value of a different field.

First we will look at the various validation methods and how to set up and define these validations. Then we'll discuss when and where the validation occurs. Finally, we will walk through the validation code so you'll understand how everything coordinates to validate the data.

After we finish with the standard design, we will discuss the limitations of the VFE lookup type validation and offer some alternative methods you might wish to evaluate. Luckily, the default lookups are implemented in classes, and it's relatively easy to customize these to suit your needs.

Lookups

The most common validation you will define is a lookup. Lookups are provided to ensure that the value entered in a field is contained in a field in another table or view. In other words, does the value that was entered exist in another table, the lookup table? If it does, we will consider the value valid. This type of validation is fully supported by the framework. As the developer, all you have to do is create a view and populate some metadata.

The first step in setting up lookup validation for a field is to create the lookup view. It's possible that you have a view to use for this already; however, you may still want to consider creating a new view specifically for validation. Why would you do this?

Suppose, for example, you are creating an application for a car dealership. One of the tables you create is to store the inventory data. In the Inventory table, you have 70 fields that include all the information about that specific automobile. In another table—Sales—you want to link to a specific automobile in the Inventory table. If you use the full inventory view that you created for your inventory business object, doing a lookup will require pulling all of that data into the views. So you would create a lookup view with just the fields needed to validate the data and provide a pick list to the user—perhaps field, auto_id, inventorynumber, model and description.

After you create the view you will use to validate a field, the next step is to set up the validation information in the metadata. To edit the metadata, you will use the DBCX Explorer. Each field has a set of extended properties maintained in the metadata. The Validation page of the metadata has several properties to define validation (see **Figure 1**).

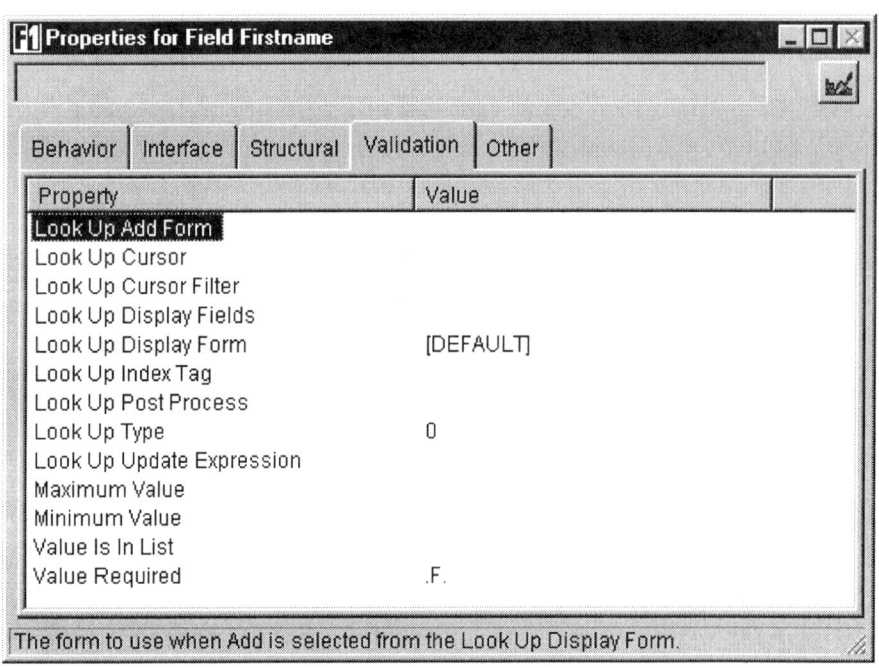

Figure 1. The Validation page contains the properties of the field where you define its lookup information.

To simplify setting up a lookup, validation uses the Look Up Setup Builder (see **Figure 2**). To launch the builder, click the Builder button in the DBCX Explorer property sheet when any of the properties associated with a lookup is highlighted. Figure 2 shows a validation that is set up in VFE's sample application.

There are several sections in the builder. In most cases, you are provided with a list of selections that would be valid based on the selections you have made. This validation is for the cproduct_id field of the lv_orderitems view in the sample application's data. Simply stated, only allow the user to enter a product ID that exists in the Products table. Now, let's take a look at each section of the builder.

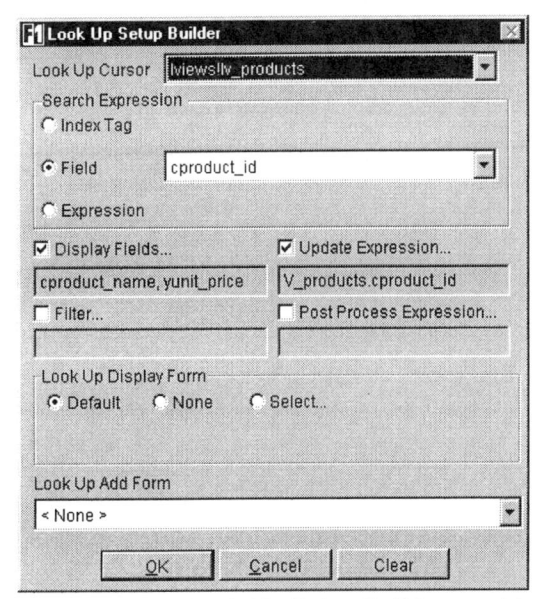

Figure 2. The Look Up Setup Builder provides a simple interface to define the lookup.

Look Up Cursor
The essential question here is, "Where will I look up the valid value?" The control provides a combo box of all the cursors in the system. In this context, cursors are views or tables, not cursor classes that you may have created. However, when the lookup cursor is opened, the framework does so by instantiating a cursor class. By default an instance of iCursor is used, but you can use a custom cursor class by setting the Default Cursor Class property for the lookup cursor in the DBCX Explorer. Select the view you have created to validate the data for this field. In the case of the sample application, the lv_products view has been specified. As we mentioned earlier, in a real-world application you would most likely create a view specifically for this validation because it will retrieve fewer fields of data. It is also possible to do table-based validation; however, views tend to be easier to implement.

Search Expression
The system needs to know where in this cursor it should look for the value. You are given three choices by the framework. Each method will attempt to locate the value in the lookup view a little differently.

Index Tag
The index you specify here will be used to locate the value. The framework sets the order of the lookup table to the tag you specified and then does a "seek" to see whether the value exists. If you have specified an index for your lookup view, you can use this method. Keep in mind that there is overhead involved with adding an index to a view that must be created every time the view is opened or queried. This may be a good choice if you are using tables and the index already exists.

Field

The field you specify here will be searched to locate the value. This is by far the most common choice if you use view-based lookups. The system will use the "locate" command to find the value. Some may consider locate slow, but it is actually quite fast if you are following the rules of keeping your views as small as possible.

If your lookup view contains many records and is used often to validate values, you may want to create an index and move to that method. You should test both cases to see which yields better performance for you.

Expression

The expression option gives you the flexibility to perhaps search on compounded fields. Or you may use this if the value you are seeking would have a year prepended to it—for example, if you put the year in front of an invoice number, you may prepend the current date in front of the field and use an expression such as year(date())+v_invoice.

Display Fields

In the framework, the lookup validation not only defines what to validate the value against, it also defines how to display a pick list to the user. Display fields are where you will define what columns in the validation are displayed in the pick list and in what order.

When you select the Display Fields check box in the Look Up Setup Builder, a Mover dialog is displayed that allows you to select the fields that will be displayed in the pick list (see **Figure 3**). The fields will be displayed in the order selected in the right-hand list. Notice that there are no handles on the right-hand list to order your fields, so you will have to select them in the order you require.

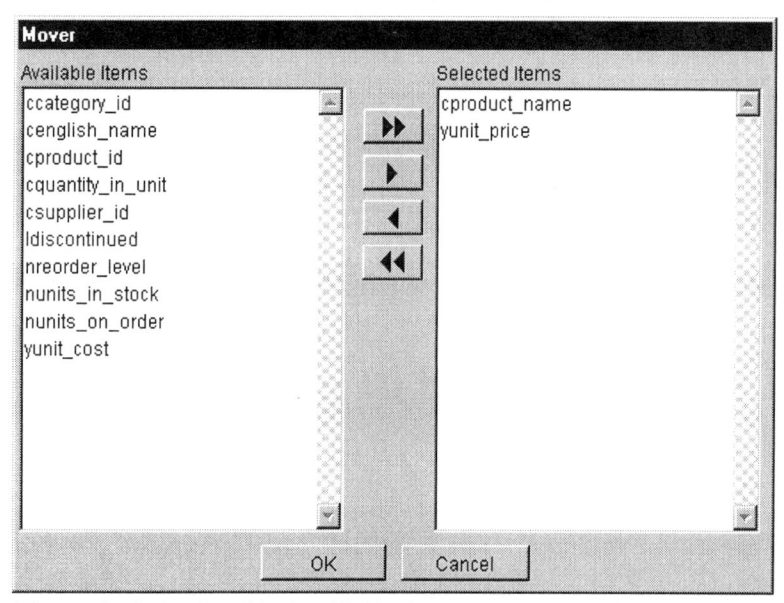

Figure 3. Selecting Display Fields from the Look Up Setup Builder dialog provides a Mover interface to select the display fields.

If the field for which you are setting your validation uses a combo box or a quick-fill text box (see Chapter 11, "Interface Controls"), the first field in this list is the field that will be displayed. In the case of the combo box, the first field will be displayed when the combo is closed; all the other fields will be displayed, in the selected order, in the drop-down list.

Update Expression

This property is also used only for lookup, not validation. When you select this pick list, you will be presented with the VFP Expression Builder. In effect, VFE wants to know what value to populate into the field being validated once the user makes a selection from the pick list. If you are using the field method of validation, this property will generally match that property.

For the other selections, specify what you want to be placed in the field being validated. For instance, you may want to update the field with product_id when your display field is productcode. This is generally done when using a combo box or a quick-fill text box.

Filter

This is an expression that will be used to set a filter on the lookup view. This filter will be applied to the view after it has been fully populated. It cannot be a dynamic value. In other words, a SET FILTER TO is issued once there is data in the view, and it is not issued again.

If possible, you should try to filter the data as it is brought into a view rather than filtering it after the view has retrieved the entire table. This is done by creating a WHERE clause on the view when it is created in the View Designer or when you manually create the SELECT statement.

Post Process Expression

This option allows you to enter a function name or method call to be made after the lookup is performed. This option is generally used to carry additional fields over from the lookup cursor into the table or view on which the lookup is being performed. F1 left this property in to help people who were migrating applications from previous versions of VFE to VFE 6.0; it is generally not recommended.

Look Up Display Form

This option allows you to specify the form you would like the framework to display when a pick list is requested or the lookup fails. You can also specify "none," which indicates not to display a pick list. The default form is a grid that is built on the fly. A column is created for each display field you selected in your metadata.

This form will also have an Add button on it if you specified a "lookup add form."

Look Up Add Form

This option is where you specify a form to be called to add a record to the lookup view or table. This form can be called in two ways. The first way is to use the Add button of the lookup display form. The second way is from a quick-fill combo or text box control in which the user enters a value that does not exist in the validation set.

Creating a lookup add form is fairly simple. If you do not already have a standard presentation object created for the lookup table, you will need to create it. Once it is created, you will add a form to your project. In this case, you will select the Single Record Modal Add Form wizard. Go through the steps and let the wizard create the form. For more information on creating a lookup add form, see the topic "Adding to the lookup cursor on the fly" in the VFE Help.

Defined range

A second method of validating data is to specify the maximum and minimum range within which the value must fall. This is used mostly with dates and numbers; however, it can also be used with character data. Once again, we will turn to the metadata to define the high and low range for a data item.

There are two properties on the Validation page of the metadata: Maximum Value and Minimum Value. Populate these properties with the upper and lower ranges of values that would be valid.

For example, we know that no one will have a birth date that is later than the current date. We can also assume that no one is older than 150 years old. So in the sample application, you'd find the dbirth_date field. On the Validation page, enter date() in the maximum value. In the minimum value, enter gomonth(date(),-1800) (there are 1,800 months in 150 years). If you now run the sample application and try to edit an employee's birth date outside of these ranges, you will see a validation error message.

Value Is In List

In the event that the list of values is static and only contains a few items, it seems like overkill to create an entire table and view to hold a few values. You can handle situations like this by using this property. Enter the items in a comma-delimited list. For example, suppose one of the fields in your file is "gender." As far as we know, there are only two relevant responses to this field. To enforce this list, you would enter: 'Male', 'Female'.

The data will be limited to this data. Also, if you are using a text box, the values will be used with the correct format mask to create a pseudo-quick-fill functionality. Pressing M will display Male, and pressing F will display Female.

Value Required

This is a pretty self-explanatory field. If you want to require the user to enter data here, set this property to True. Because the value is required, the user will not be able to save the record without entering a value here.

Mix and match

None of the preceding validations are mutually exclusive. You can mix and match validations as you wish. Of course, some combinations don't make sense—if you specify a list, there is no need to specify a maximum or minimum. Remember too that a lookup validation doesn't require the user to make an entry, so if the user doesn't enter anything into the field, it won't be validated.

Table and field rules

One of the great new features of Visual FoxPro was the addition of the database container. This file not only allowed us to define captions and defaults to database entities, but it also gave us the ability to create field rules, table rules, stored procedures and triggers.

The advantage of creating rules at the database level is that they are enforced no matter who or what is accessing that database. You may have two applications sharing the same database that will enforce the rules defined in it. This makes the database a bit more self-contained and a bit more powerful, like its big brother SQL Server.

Using VFE doesn't eliminate this feature; you can still use table and field rules in your VFE applications, and the framework will combine the rules you have defined in the database with those you have defined in the metadata. Creating rules is beyond the scope of this book; if you are interested in this topic, you should refer to the Visual FoxPro documentation.

When is data validated?

There are two occasions when data is validated. This may seem like more than necessary, but you will soon see that it is not. The first time data is validated is after the user enters it. When the user moves off the field, it is validated. This provides instant feedback to the user if an incorrect value has been entered.

The second time validation is performed is when the user tries to save data. You might wonder how it could be wrong now if it was already validated when the user entered it. There are some instances when the value of one field relies on the value of another. So if only one of those fields is changed, the mismatch will not be found unless the validation is checked on all fields when the record is saved. In addition, you may have specified that a field value is required. If the user never entered and exited the control associated with that field, validation at save will notice that there is no value and require data entry.

If you prefer, you can turn off the validation that occurs when the user exits the field. If you set the lNoValidate property to True, validation won't be performed on the LostFocus event. (See Chapter 11, "Interface Controls," for more information about the lNoValidate property.)

Validation trace

Whether the validation is called from the LostFocus of the control or the save, it is performed in the data object. In the case of the LostFocus, the Validate() method of the field object is called. If the record is being saved, the Validate() method of each field object is called until it's completed or one of the validations fails.

Let's take a look at the Validate() method of the field object. This method calls the default code of the abstract data item. This code in turn calls the Validate_Perform() method. We will step through the Validate_Perform() method.

1. The CheckFieldRule() method is called to run the field rule. The field rule is evaluated, and if it is True the system continues the validation rule. If the rule is False, the rule failure message is retrieved from the DBC. If this text exists, it is used to display an error message; if not, a default message is created.

2. The CheckRequired() method is called to determine whether the field is required. If a value is required and the value is empty or null, the validation stops and a message is displayed.

3. The CheckMinimum() method is called to verify that the value of the field is not lower than the specified minimum. If there is no minimum value, this validation passes.

4. The CheckMaximum() method is called to verify that the value of the field is not higher than the specified maximum. If there is no maximum value, this validation passes.

5. The CheckLookUp() method is called. This method will verify that the value meets the defined lookup validation as described in the metadata. If the value is not found, the field object will return the constant FIELD_LOOKUP. In the event that this validation was called from the LostFocus of the control, the lookup display form will run so the user can pick a valid value. If "none" was defined, a message that the value is not in the lookup will be displayed.

6. Finally, the CheckInList() method is called to determine whether there is a list in the metadata. If there is, the value is compared with the values in the list. If there is no list, this validation passes.

As each of these steps is performed, a success or failure code is returned to the Validate_Perform() method. If one of the steps fails, none of the subsequent steps will be called.

If the validation is called from the LostFocus of the control, control will be returned to the user. As stated previously, either a pick list, message or nothing is displayed to the user, based on the return code.

In the case of the validation being called from the Save() method, the framework discontinues the save if any validations fail. If the validation is successful, the system continues to save the record. At this point, if there is a table-level rule, VFP will run it. If the table-level rule fails, an error will be raised. VFE will check the error number, and if it indicates that the table rule was violated, the table rule text from the DBC will be retrieved and displayed to the user.

The trouble with lookups

The problem with the default VFE lookups is that there is too much data being put into the views. Recall that in the beginning of the book we discussed writing your application with a client/server mentality. One of the guidelines was to limit the amount of data you bring into your views to what is needed at the time.

Here's a secret that we left out when we traced the form instantiation previously. Remember that we told you each object was "decorated." Well, part of this decoration is the LookUpSetup() method. This method checks the metadata of the data item, and if there is a lookup defined, the following events take place:

1. The OpenLookUpCursor() method is called. This method will create the lookup cursor's cursor object.

2. If the cursor object is created without error, the oLookUpCursor property of the field object is populated with a reference to the cursor object.

3. The Open() method of the lookup cursor object is called.

What does the Open() method do? Well, if you have been following along since Chapter 1, you know that this uses the view. Also, because a lookup view is not normally parameterized, all the records for the view are retrieved at this time. This certainly adds to the overhead of creating forms, and it also adds to the amount of data brought over the network wire.

The other issue here is that of volume. The preceding lookup scheme works fine when the number of lookup records is reasonably small. We use the default lookups for a field such as "states" because we know that there are only 50 records with two fields. But what happens when we have a partnumber field on an invoice? Well, if we are a large automobile manufacturer, there may be 40,000 parts in our file. We would be bringing all those records over just to open the invoice screen.

So why are we retrieving data we don't need yet, and why are all of the records being retrieved? Currently, this is the way VFE lookups work. However, there are a few alternative methods you can use to avoid all of this extra data taking up bandwidth and time.

Hand-code the validation

"Hand-code the validation?" you might be asking. The reason you are using a framework is to avoid writing code to perform common operations! But you know from the previous section that there are some drawbacks to the default lookup validation.

You know how to write the code: Create it in the validation of the control, just as you did back in FoxPro 2.6. Use a SELECT statement that will pull one record if the value is valid and none if the value isn't valid.

A drawback to this is that when the business object is saved, the validation will not be called because you wrote the code in the business layer. Another problem is that if you separate your tiers, the interface layer will not have access to the data. The solution is to code the validation in a data behavior object. We will discuss how to set up and use these objects later in the book.

Another problem with this method is that there is no automated means to provide a pick list. When you use the VFE validation, the view is there, with all the records that show up in the pick list. If you don't create a lookup view that is fully populated, the automated lookup form provided by the framework will not work either.

Parameterize the view

This may be the best compromise; however, it will require creating a custom cursor object and custom lookup display form for each lookup view that you create. Actually, this isn't much of a hardship because the benefits outweigh the costs.

The first step is to create a view parameter variable. The filter of the view should be set up so that if the value the user entered is used to populate the view parameter variable, a record will be returned. Use this view as the validation view, and set the validation up as you normally would if the view were fully populated.

Create a cursor class for the lookup view, following the same steps as when you created your cursor classes for your CRUD views. The next step is to define to the framework that it should use this cursor class when it creates a cursor for this lookup. To do this, open the DBCX Explorer and select a view. In the right-hand frame, select the Behavior page (see **Figure 4**); you will see that you can specify the cursor class to use when opening this view. If you press the Builder button, you will be able to select the cursor class to use for this view. Choose the cursor class you created.

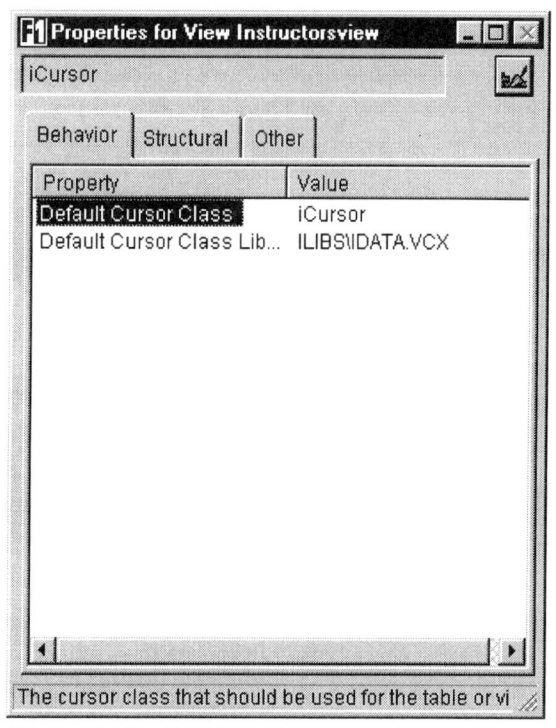

Figure 4. On the Behavior page of a view's properties, you can specify the cursor class to be used.

Okay, the reason we created a custom cursor is so that we can populate the view parameter with the value of the field that we will be looking to validate with this view. So you should edit your cursor class and, in the Requery_Pre() method, populate the view parameter with the value entered.

We'll use a fairly popular example—a ZIP code database. This is certainly a good example of a table that you don't want to bring all of the records into just to validate your field. Earlier we told you to create a parameterized view—in this case, you'll create v_zipcodes. On the Filter tab (the Filter tab builds the WHERE of your SELECT), set it up so the WHERE will look like this:

```
v_zipcodes.zipcode = ?vp_zipcode
```

As you know, the "?" tells the View Designer not to expect to evaluate the variable now, but that it will be there at run time. Don't forget to add this parameter to the view's parameter list. You need to do this so a view parameter object will be created in the cursor. (You'll learn more about this in Chapter 13, "Working with Views.")

Now we need to put code in the cursor's Requery_Pre() method, which populates the view parameter with the ZIP code you want to check. Let's say that the field you are validating is zipcode in the v_customers view. Here's the code you would use:

```
This.Parameters.Items['vp_zipcode'].Value = v_customers.zipcode
```

Now, when the cursor is queried, the single record that matches this value will be retrieved. But the default behavior of the lookup code does not Requery() the cursor, so we'll modify the behavior of the framework with the I-layer. Don't worry, you will learn a lot more about how to do this in Chapter 16, "Extending the Framework."

Earlier you learned that the field object is where the validation code takes place—specifically, the CheckLookUp() method performs this type of validation. This method is called from the Validate_Perform() method. However, the CheckLookUp_Pre() method is called right before that. This provides the ideal place for us to Requery() the lookup cursor. We will put code in the _Pre() hook to perform this task. Put the following code in the I-layer class iField's CheckLookUp_Pre() method:

```
IF VARTYPE(This.oLookupCursor) = T_OBJECT AND ;
    TXNLEVEL() = 0 AND ;
    This.oLookupCursor.Parameters.Count > 0
    This.oLookUpCursor.Requery()
ENDIF
```

Once you have done this, you won't need to do it again. You put this behavior in a class from which all field objects inherit, so they will all have this code. It is possible that you won't want this to happen if you don't use this method for all of your lookups. If this is the case, you can create a field class that contains this code and specify it for any fields in which you will use parameterized view lookups.

Let's summarize what we have done here:

1. Create a parameterized view for the framework to use for validation.

2. Create a custom cursor class specifically for the preceding lookup view.

3. Add code to the custom class to populate the view's parameter with the value that was entered.

4. Add a call to requery the lookup cursor of a field just prior to the lookup validation being checked.

5. The lookup code will work as usual, seeking or locating the value in the view, but there will either be one or no records, and the value will still be found or not.

6. Because this method is based on a slight modification of the framework, the validation will work if called from the control's LostFocus or the cursor's Save() method.

> *This method will only work for fields that are marked as required. VFE checks required first, and if the field is empty, it will pass validation and the lookup won't be performed. If the user enters a value, the lookup will take place when the control is validated. This is important because the view cannot be requeried while a save is in progress, as VFP doesn't allow Requery() to be issued during a transaction. Note the code changes we made to accommodate this. We also added a check to see whether the view has parameters before requerying it.*
>
> *Also, with a local view, the suggested syntax may retrieve more than one record. For example, in the updated sample, all of the employee IDs are character 6 padded with leading zeros, so there are IDs such as 000010, 000011, 000012 and so on. Because of the way VFP does string comparisons, entering 00001 for the view parameter will retrieve records with IDs of 000010 – 000019. Your method still works well here because if you include a few extra fields, like first and last name, a total of 10 records are retrieved and the default pick list can be used, but with fewer records. You could add some additional code here to force the user to enter a string greater than n characters before doing the default validation as well. If you want to force the view to only retrieve a single record, you can use ==, or if you want to limit the view to a certain number of records, you can use top n. Top n would work really well in this scenario because if the user just entered 00, they'd still only get n records and have to enter more information to get the desired employee.*

Here we have eliminated most of the drawbacks of the framework's default validation. No records are being brought over at form load, so the form will load faster. When we do need to validate, we are only bringing the single record that we need, so network traffic has been reduced. (If we are using remote data, server resources are being saved.)

If you have been following along, you realize that while this solves the problem of the validation, it doesn't help with the pick list. In the event that the value is not found, the lookup cursor will be empty when the default lookup display form is loaded. This is why you will need to create a custom lookup display form. This also gives you the advantage of creating a parameterized view for the pick list and putting view parameters on the lookup display form. Even though we need to display this form, that doesn't mean we want the user to have to wade through those 40,000 part numbers.

The default lookup display form is cLookupSelectionForm. There are no wizards for creating custom lookup display forms. When you create the custom lookup display form, keep in mind that it must accept the same parameters as the default form. The custom form must set a property named uRetVal to a logical value when it is closed. You should begin developing your custom lookup display form by subclassing the default lookup display form.

> This chapter has covered some complex topics, but hopefully you've been able to follow along and grasp the material we presented. Unfortunately, we were unable to provide a sample of this in the first release of the Developer Download files available at www.hentzenwerke.com, but we hope to create a sample and update the files shortly after the book is released to print.

Summary

Validating data is probably one of the most important features that you can build into your application. If your application is to process properly, the data must be as accurate as possible.

You learned in this chapter that VFE supports several ways to verify that the data is being entered correctly. The lookup validation built into VFE is simple to set up and simple to use. In addition, any field that is populated from this lookup, such as a combo, will be set up to use the defined lookup. Finally, the framework displays a pick list that is built on the fly from the display fields you specified in the Look Up Setup Builder.

We don't live in a perfect world, and you have to take the good with the bad. We have been asking for more robust, client/server-friendly lookup validations since beta. However, instead of crying over spilled milk, we came up with a few methods to either work around the built-in functionality or slightly modify how it does work so as to produce satisfactory results. The reality is that the framework designers can't really determine what lookups are going to be parameterized on and when the lookup cursors should be requeried. If you take responsibility for filtering the lookup cursor before the default framework lookup features kick in, the native functionality should work well for you in most scenarios. Hopefully you can use some of these ideas also, not just for validation but also to realize that you are not bound to the default behavior—you can work with it or around it to get the results you want. But that's another chapter.

This book has been preaching and praising views to you, so the next chapter will present a bit of information about working with views. See you there.

Chapter 13
Working with Views

Views play an important role in a VFE application. You should know how to work with them and understand the tools that are available to create and maintain them. In this chapter, we will examine several methods to create and maintain a view and the properties associated with them. In addition, you will learn what makes a view parameterized and what needs to be done to allow VFE to recognize those parameters.

A view is a combination of a SQL statement and field properties stored in the VFP database container. The current version of VFE is designed with views in mind. This is true whether you are using a local or a remote data source.

There are two methods to create views. This first method is to use the View Designer. The View Designer is provided by VFP and is a visual tool you can use to create a view. The second method uses the CREATE SQL VIEW command of the Visual FoxPro language. In this chapter, we will also discuss some third-party tools that make dealing with views a little more manageable.

The View Designer

The VFP View Designer is a visual tool that's provided to create a SQL statement and set the properties of the fields in the view. A view is opened in VFP just as a table is, by using the USE command. The view's stored SQL statement will be executed when this command is issued at the command window or in your code. When the view is opened, a results cursor is created in the data session. The difference between using a view and using the SELECT INTO CURSOR command is that the cursor created with a view is not read-only. The cursor that results is a buffered cursor.

If you are familiar with using buffered tables, it is simple enough to adjust to using views, because by definition a view is buffered. In this case, the TableUpdate() command will find the "dirty" records—records that have been modified—in the view and issue UPDATE statements for them. These statements will be run to update the underlying table. In the event of an updatable remote view, the SQL statements are sent to the database server, where they will be executed and the results converted into a read-write cursor for you by VFP. VFP will use the field property information to determine how to build the SELECT statement knowing which fields are updatable and which make up the primary key.

The View Designer has seven pages that allow the user to visually create the SQL statement. Basically, each page is equivalent to one of the parts of the standard SQL SELECT statement. In addition to the pages to define the SQL are pages that allow you to set general information about which fields are updatable and which make up the primary key or uniquely identify a record, as well as how the WHERE statement will be constructed when an update is issued.

Filter tab

The Filter tab of the View Designer is equivalent to the WHERE portion of the SQL. This page can contain information to limit the records selected based on hard-coded values such as WHERE MyView.State = 'TX', or you can use more dynamic information on this page such as WHERE MyView.State = ?vp_state. When coding a view in this manner, the view is known to be "parameterized." The vp_state memory variable is called a "view parameter." The question mark preceding the parameter indicates to VFP that the value is a parameter and that it is to be evaluated before running the SQL. For example, ?alias.field means to evaluate the field instead of using it as an old-style join in the WHERE clause.

Using parameters allows you to limit the number of records (rows) that are retrieved to match a value that will not be known until run time. In addition to placing the view parameters on the Filter tab, there is a parameter list that is used to define the view parameter variables and their data types. The parameter list is accessed from the Query menu that is available when you are working in the View Designer.

Creating parameters

When building a filter (parameters) for a view, placing a question mark in front of an expression will indicate to the View Designer that this expression, while not available at design time, will be there at run time. If the value or expression is not there at run time, VFP will prompt the user for the value of the parameter.

Parameter uses

View parameters are designed for one thing—to limit the number of records that are retrieved when a cursor is queried. During application run time, your code will be able to change the value of the parameter variable and requery the view. Subsequently, the view will retrieve a different result set, which matches the parameter's new value.

For example, let's assume you have a "students" file. You want to be able to work with all of the students who are a certain age, so you create a "studentview." You know this is how you will always be retrieving the records, but you don't know what the age will be ahead of time. In this case, you would substitute a variable to hold the age at the time the query is processed. So in the Filter tab of your view, you would create a parameter variable such as the one shown in **Figure 1**.

The value of the variable vp_studentage is replaced in the SELECT statement that's created by VFP prior to retrieving the data. If you have not populated the variable prior to requerying the view, VFP will prompt the user for this value. You certainly don't want VFP dialogs popping up in your well-crafted application, so be sure not to skip this step.

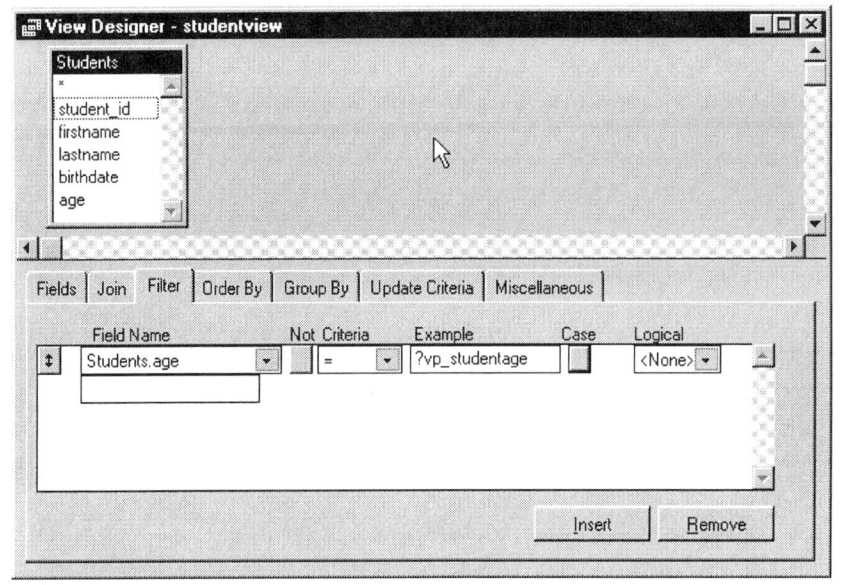

Figure 1. The Filter tab of the studentview creates a parameter variable, vp_studentage, that will be used to build the SELECT for this query.

Parameter list

While the view as defined previously is adequate for VFP to run, in order for VFE to use this view you will need to put the parameter variable in the parameter list. The parameter list is accessed by selecting View Parameters... from the Query menu (see **Figure 2**). The parameter list (see **Figure 3**) must be populated in order for VFE to be aware of the parameter's existence.

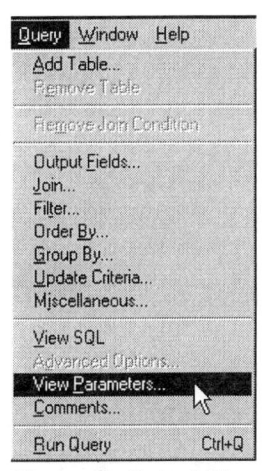

Figure 2. Select View Parameters... from the Query menu to define view parameter variables that VFE will be aware of.

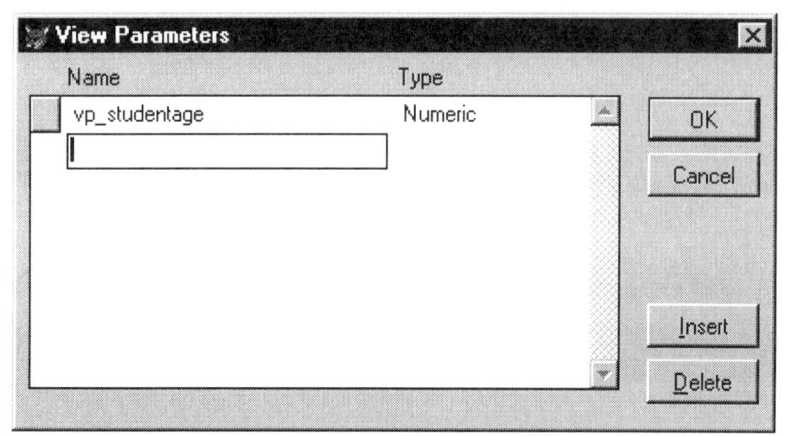

Figure 3. Add all the view parameters you want VFE to be aware of into the View Parameters dialog.

For more information about what we mean by "VFE to be aware of," see Chapter 4, "Data Storage and Classes," for a discussion of the cursor class and its view parameter collection. Here's a basic guideline: If the view parameter (that is, the expression with the "?" in front of it in the Filter tab of your view) already exists, do not add it to the parameter list. For example, this would include a parameterized view based on a form or business object property, or a field in another view. These items already exist in the environment and don't need to be populated by a control or code.

As we can expect from the great Microsoft, there is a bug that will not allow you to remove a view parameter from the view parameter list. It will look as if it has been removed, but the next time you open the view it will still be there. To remove your view parameters without deleting the entire view, use this code in the command window with your database file open:

```
dbsetprop('YourViewName','View','ParameterList','')
```

Of course, replace 'YourViewName' with the actual name of the view for which you want to delete the parameter list. This will delete all of the view parameters for the view, so you'll then have to add back the view parameters you want to keep. Although this technique requires that you delete the entire list, it is better than deleting the view and starting from scratch. You can also specify the correct parameter list here using the DBSETPROP() function.

Relating views

There are two ways in which you can relate the views in your application. The first is to use a field from the parent view as the parameter in the child view. The second is to create a view parameter on the child file to the foreign key, and populate it with the value from the parent view in your bizobj's Requery_Pre() method or in the GetRequeryValue() method of a custom view parameter class.

The second method allows the view to be more reusable and can also lower the number of views you need in your finished application. However, both techniques work, and you can choose whichever one you are more comfortable with. Here's a brief example of what each might look like. Assume you have a parent view named "Parent" with a primary key field named "PK," and a child view with a foreign key to the parent view named "ParentPK." Here's what your filter would look like if you were directly relating the views:

```
CHILD.PARENTPK == ?PARENT.PK
```

Here's what your filter would look like if you used a variable:

```
CHILD.PARENTPK == ?VP_PARENTPK
```

As you can see, with the first filter you'll get a syntax error if the parent view doesn't exist. In other words, you can only use this view when the "Parent" alias exists. In the second instance, you would populate the view parameter with the value of the parent primary key. You're no longer limited to using the parent view/alias as the parent view. You could even use this view on an ASP page where a user enters their ID, and you only need to open the child, populate the view parameter, requery the child view and return the result set.

In Chapter 14, "Related Data and Forms," we will show you how to populate the view parameter object of the cursor object with the value from the parent view. In addition to reusing views, this works great when you want to use child forms that aren't tied to the parent's data session.

Complex views

As you will soon see, the View Designer will not work well with multiple joins or tables with many unrelated children. Developers struggle to create five-page SELECT statements to solve all their needs in a single swipe. There are some alternatives to using such a complex single view.

We suggest that you not use such complex views in your application. Limit your views to two tables. If you need more than this, it may be possible to create multiple views and relate them with business objects (see Chapter 14).

For example, let's say you have a Customer table, with an Address table and a Phone Number table. The Address table uses a ZIP Code table to verify the city, and the Phone Number table has an Area Code table to make sure that at least the area code is valid. Don't try to build one view that joins all these tables to maintain a customer; rather, break it up into a customer view, customer address view and customer phone view. You will not only find it easier to write less complicated views, but you will also find that the three views may actually run faster than your five-table join.

Views are not able to update multiple tables in general. It's okay to include fields from other tables in a view for display purposes, but in all cases a view can never update more than one table.

View Designer tip

On occasion you will see a red X through the view icon for a view in the DBCX Explorer. The DBCX Explorer attempts to open views when their nodes are expanded in its tree view. If the DBCX Explorer can't open the view, the view's icon is changed to a view icon with a red X through it. There are many possible reasons why a view cannot be opened, but most often it is due to changing the underlying table of a view, which contains all fields. If you view the SQL of the view and it contains a SELECT * command, this is where the problem occurs. Every time you open the view in the View Designer, the information in the DBC is reconciled with the information in the SELECT statement when VFP parses the SQL.

If you originally used the asterisk, and you added or removed a field from the underlying table and then opened the view again, the list of fields in the DBC for the view will not match the list of fields that are actually in this table. To avoid this problem, simply change the order of the fields in the list by dragging one field to a different order. When you view your SQL again, all the fields will be listed. While this doesn't solve all of the problems with the View Designer, it does solve one of the more common problems.

Remote view tip

If you are creating client/server applications, there are a few settings that you should watch out for on your remote views. When you have the View Designer open and select Advanced Parameters…, the Advanced Options dialog will appear (see **Figure 4**).

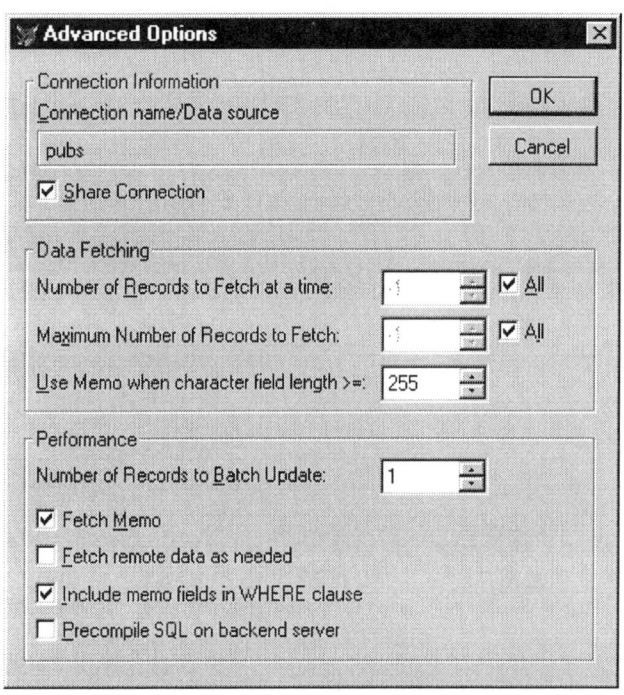

Figure 4. The Advanced Options dialog of a remote view is available when you are using the View Designer.

You should set the options of your view as shown in Figure 4 for VFE. First, you should make sure that Share Connection is turned on. If you don't do this, your application will create a new connection to the server every time a new view is opened.

Second, you should set Number of Records to Fetch to "All." If this is not set to All, you will encounter "Connection Busy" errors because VFE will not clear the shared connection prior to using a remote view. Of course, you can turn off Shared Connection, but your DBA would undoubtedly have a problem with this.

Finally, be sure that Number of Records to Batch Update is set to 1. This is especially important for views you are using with standard data maintenance screens. If you don't have this set to 1, when the user saves a modified record the edit will be queued and not sent to the server until the batch number is reached. In this case, if there is an error there will be no immediate feedback, and VFE will assume the update happened successfully. Of course, if you are doing a batch process in your business object, you may want to modify this number using the CURSORSETPROP() function to reduce network traffic and better utilize transactions. See Chapter 19, "Client/Server," for more information on VFE and SQL databases.

We also suggest that you use the Tools | Options | Remote Page menu option to set these as your default settings.

View parameter containers

VFE provides a class to set up controls that are bound to the parameters of a view in a container separate from the presentation object. This allows you to reuse the view parameter layout you have created when necessary. The class that you create is called a view parameter container. It is also useful if you have several that use the same parameters—for example, Customer, Employee and Vendor tables may all use Number, FirstName and LastName as parameters.

For an example of a view parameter container, open the VFE sample application from the Application Manager. Once the sample application is open, select the Classes tab in the Application Builder, and then open the View Parameters Container node of the tree view. Double-click on V_CUSTOMERPARAMETERCONTAINER, and you should see a screen similar to **Figure 5**.

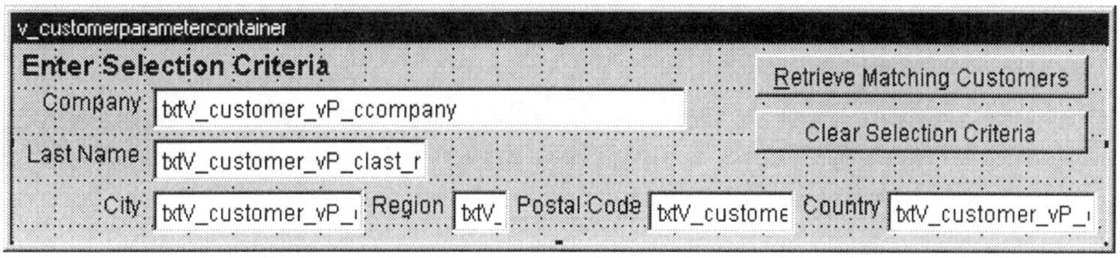

Figure 5. The v_customerparametercontainer of the VFE sample application.

If you open the builder of the first text box, you'll see that it is set to bind to a view parameter named V_CUSTOMER.VP_CCOMPANY (see **Figure 6**). This view parameter container can now be used on any form where the customer view is used. This is a great example of reuse and will simplify building your user interface if you use your view in several forms or presentation objects. VFE also provides an option that will automatically integrate your custom view parameter container into the wizard used to run reports and queries at the appropriate step.

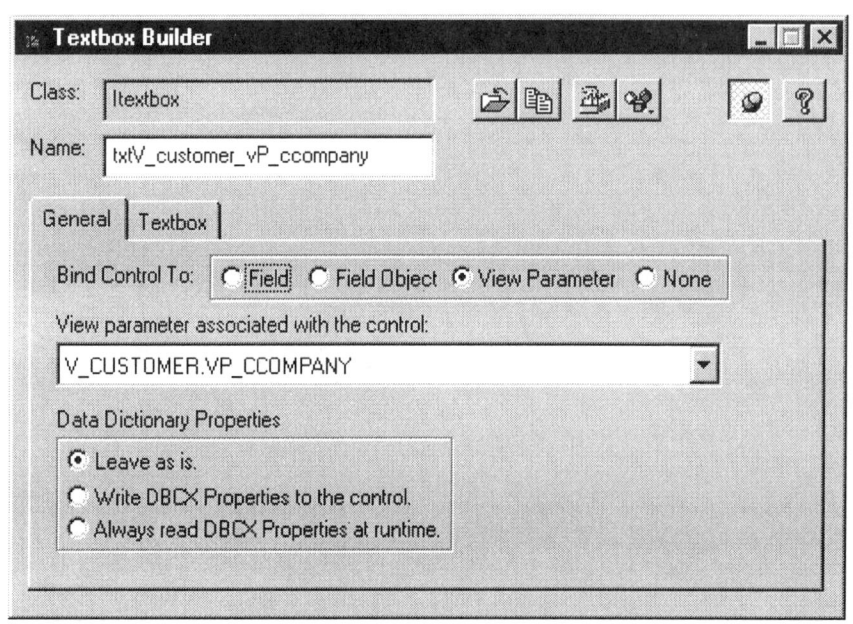

Figure 6. *The Texbox Builder for a text box in a view parameter container. The text box is bound to a view parameter in the view, to allow limiting the number of records retrieved to the smallest number necessary.*

Hand-code your views

As many of you know, the View Designer is a little dimwitted. The *Hacker's Guide to Visual FoxPro 6.0* by Tamar E. Granor and Ted Roche has this to say about the View Designer:

> *"It's much easier to create views with the VD than in code, but you have to accept the serious limitations of working within the VD. In Visual FoxPro 5, in a move to make VFP more ANSI-SQL compatible by supporting the new JOIN clause, Microsoft broke the View Designer badly. Because of the way join clauses form intermediate results between tables, multiple joins to the same tables (such as a parent with two sibling children) often cannot be expressed properly by the Designer. It complains while saving a view that it will not be editable again, or gripes that columns cannot be found."*

With that said, what is the alternative? Create the views programmatically. This is a fine solution, but there's one warning you must heed when you do this for a VFE application: Make sure, after you run the code that creates the views, that you validate your metadata (see Chapter 5, "Metadata").

One of the best ways to hand-code a view is to start with a simple view in the View Designer. The advantage here is that you can generate the code needed to create this view with a program called GenDBC. This program is shipped with VFP, and you can use it for this purpose if you wish. However, there is an enhanced version of this program, written by Steve Arnott, named GenDBCX. This program is in the public domain, and we have included a copy of it in the Developer Download files available at www.hentzenwerke.com.

Here's an example of the code produced by GenDBCX for the InstructorsView of our sample application:

```
PROCEDURE vwINSTRUCTORSVIEW
       LOCAL vp_lastname
       vp_lastname = "A"

       CREATE SQL VIEW "INSTRUCTORSVIEW" ;
          AS SELECT Instructors.instructorid, Instructors.ssn,;
            Instructors.firstname, Instructors.lastname,;
            Instructors.middlename FROM;
            tutorial!instructors WHERE Instructors.lastname = ?vp_lastname

       =DBSetProp('INSTRUCTORSVIEW', 'View', 'UpdateType', 1)
       =DBSetProp('INSTRUCTORSVIEW', 'View', 'WhereType', 1)
       =DBSetProp('INSTRUCTORSVIEW', 'View', 'FetchMemo', .T.)
       =DBSetProp('INSTRUCTORSVIEW', 'View', 'SendUpdates', .T.)
       =DBSetProp('INSTRUCTORSVIEW', 'View', 'UseMemoSize', 255)
       =DBSetProp('INSTRUCTORSVIEW', 'View', 'FetchSize', 100)
       =DBSetProp('INSTRUCTORSVIEW', 'View', 'MaxRecords', -1)
       =DBSetProp('INSTRUCTORSVIEW', 'View', 'Tables', 'tutorial!instructors')
       =DBSetProp('INSTRUCTORSVIEW', 'View', 'FetchSize', 100)
       =DBSetProp('INSTRUCTORSVIEW', 'View', 'ParameterList',;
          "vp_lastname,'C'")
       =DBSetProp('INSTRUCTORSVIEW', 'View', 'Comment', "")
       =DBSetProp('INSTRUCTORSVIEW', 'View', 'BatchUpdateCount', 1)
       =DBSetProp('INSTRUCTORSVIEW', 'View', 'ShareConnection', .F.)
       =DBSetProp('INSTRUCTORSVIEW', 'View', 'Prepared', .F.)
       =DBSetProp('INSTRUCTORSVIEW', 'View', 'CompareMemo', .T.)
       =DBSetProp('INSTRUCTORSVIEW', 'View', 'FetchAsNeeded', .F.)

       *!* Field Level Properties for INSTRUCTORSVIEW
       * Props for the INSTRUCTORSVIEW.instructorid field.
       =DBSetProp('INSTRUCTORSVIEW.instructorid', 'Field', 'KeyField', .T.)
       =DBSetProp('INSTRUCTORSVIEW.instructorid', 'Field', 'Updatable', .T.)
       =DBSetProp('INSTRUCTORSVIEW.instructorid', 'Field', 'UpdateName',;
          'tutorial!instructors.instructorid')
       =DBSetProp('INSTRUCTORSVIEW.instructorid', 'Field', 'DataType', "C(16);
          NOCPTRANS")
       * Props for the INSTRUCTORSVIEW.ssn field.
       =DBSetProp('INSTRUCTORSVIEW.ssn', 'Field', 'KeyField', .F.)
       =DBSetProp('INSTRUCTORSVIEW.ssn', 'Field', 'Updatable', .T.)
       =DBSetProp('INSTRUCTORSVIEW.ssn', 'Field', 'UpdateName',;
          'tutorial!instructors.ssn')
       =DBSetProp('INSTRUCTORSVIEW.ssn', 'Field', 'DataType', "C(9)")
       * Props for the INSTRUCTORSVIEW.firstname field.
       =DBSetProp('INSTRUCTORSVIEW.firstname', 'Field', 'KeyField', .F.)
       =DBSetProp('INSTRUCTORSVIEW.firstname', 'Field', 'Updatable', .T.)
       =DBSetProp('INSTRUCTORSVIEW.firstname', 'Field', 'UpdateName',;
          'tutorial!instructors.firstname')
```

```
        =DBSetProp('INSTRUCTORSVIEW.firstname', 'Field', 'DataType', "C(50)")
        * Props for the INSTRUCTORSVIEW.lastname field.
        =DBSetProp('INSTRUCTORSVIEW.lastname', 'Field', 'KeyField', .F.)
        =DBSetProp('INSTRUCTORSVIEW.lastname', 'Field', 'Updatable', .T.)
        =DBSetProp('INSTRUCTORSVIEW.lastname', 'Field', 'UpdateName',;
            'tutorial!instructors.lastname')
        =DBSetProp('INSTRUCTORSVIEW.lastname', 'Field', 'DataType', "C(50)")
        * Props for the INSTRUCTORSVIEW.middlename field.
        =DBSetProp('INSTRUCTORSVIEW.middlename', 'Field', 'KeyField', .F.)
        =DBSetProp('INSTRUCTORSVIEW.middlename', 'Field', 'Updatable', .T.)
        =DBSetProp('INSTRUCTORSVIEW.middlename', 'Field', 'UpdateName',;
            'tutorial!instructors.middlename')
        =DBSetProp('INSTRUCTORSVIEW.middlename', 'Field', 'DataType', "C(50)")
ENDPROC
```

As you can see, the code starts with the CREATE SQL VIEW AS statement, which stores the SQL to the DBC. When the view is stored, VFP will also create a record in the DBC for each field in the view. So it is now necessary to create some properties of the view and also set the properties of each field. If the fields are not made updatable and the primary keys defined, this view will not update anything.

Once you have this starting point, you can modify the SQL and the property statements to create the view you want. As long as the SQL is correct, VFP will accept the view.

After you create this view by running the code, make sure that the first thing you do when you get back into VFE is validate the metadata. This is very important, because the metadata is so heavily relied upon at run time.

Version control

Even if you don't hand-code your views, you may consider generating the program. This is a good way to manage version control with the DBC, although it's admittedly simpler if you only have views in your DBC because then there is no data in local tables to deal with.

The general idea is that the DBC generating program, which is generated by GenDBCX, is added to the project and excluded. The file is checked into version control. This allows a developer to check out the program with a lock. This developer can modify the program, or he or she can modify the DBC with the View Designer and then regenerate the DBC program and check it back in.

Having this program in version control allows users to "get the latest version" of the program and run it, knowing that they have the latest view definitions. Developers must remember to generate a new DBC before editing it if they are going to use a visual tool, rather than manually editing the generation program.

eView

This is another tool that combines hand-coding views and using a visual tool. Basically, you are given access to edit the SQL by hand, combined with a visual interface to all the properties of the view and the fields (see **Figure 7**). We have also included a copy of this tool in the Developer Download files available at www.hentzenwerke.com. This tool is written by Eric Moore, who can be found on the usual VFP forums such as Universal Thread and Wiki.

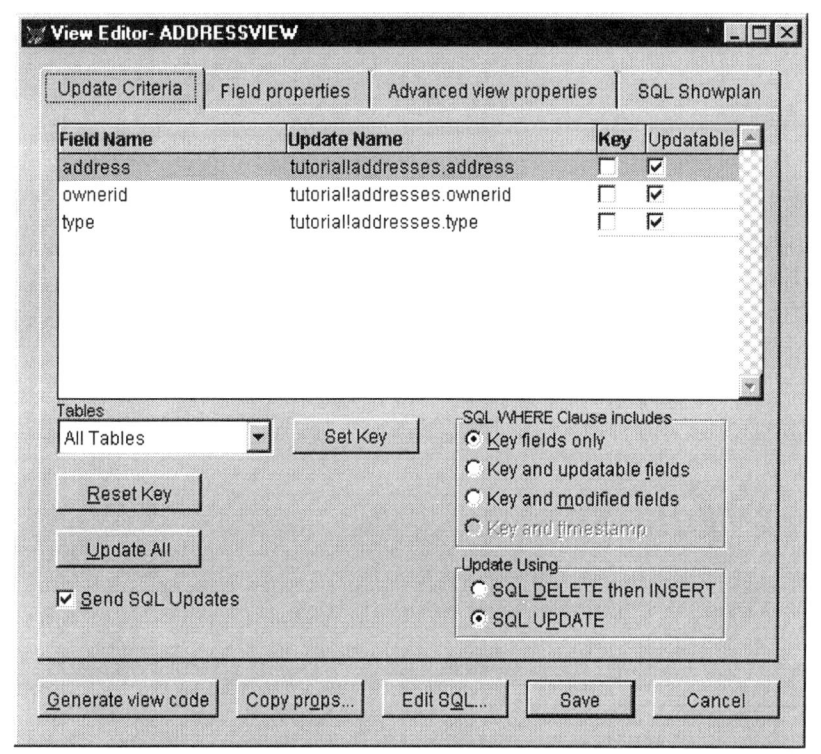

Figure 7. eView is a free tool you can use to maintain and hand-code views while still having access to visually edit view and field properties.

Summary

We can't say it often enough: VFE shines with views. Know how to properly relate and parameterize them to limit the number of records you are retrieving. Use all of the tools available to you to create them—start with the View Designer, and then move on to eView or hand-coding to refine them. Also, use GenDBCX to simplify version control of the DBC among multiple developers. This will ensure that your application is simple to maintain. Your application will also perform much better, especially in a remote data situation.

Chapter 14
Related Data and Forms

In this chapter, we will look at several methods of creating related data interfaces using the framework's tools to work with related data. Because the majority of screens in your system will come from more than one table, it is necessary to be able to provide an interface that seamlessly works with this related data.

When working with the VFE framework, you are provided with many methods to display and work with related data. Each of these methods requires a different setup. The VFE wizards create many of these interfaces for you, but if you don't understand how it works, it will be difficult to work with and modify those classes.

SET RELATION TO
The SET RELATION command was commonly used in the FoxPro 2.6 days. This command related two tables and kept the record pointers synchronized for the developer. As you moved the pointer in the parent table, the system would seek to the related records in the child table based on the relation you set up.

If you are using tables with VFE, this method is still valid. However, there are drawbacks. The first problem arises if you want to provide a different display order for the child file than the index that is needed for the relationship. An example of this would be displaying a list of a customer's invoices by invoice date descending. Well, in order to relate the customer and the invoice file, it is necessary to use the index order of the customer number or ID on the invoice file. What this means is that your interface suffers in order to simplify your implementation.

If you needed to accomplish this, it would be necessary to either populate the child records into an array to display them in the order you prefer in your list, or use the index you preferred on the child and set a filter on the child file. Finally, you could also create a compound index on customer ID + invoice date. With the advent of the SELECT command, most developers moved to selecting the invoice records that belonged to the customer and ordering them by the invoice date. This is actually what you are doing when relating views, but it is a bit more automated for you.

Related views
If you are one of the developers who learned to SELECT the specific child records that belonged to a parent so you'd have fewer records to deal with, then you understand the use of related views. The difference is that when you relate views, you do not have to issue the SELECT every time. This is because you will create your child view and parameterize it based on a value in the parent view.

Setting up a parameterized view is not difficult. It's just a fancy way of saying that the WHERE clause of the view has a parameter value that is dynamic. This dynamic parameter effectively changes the WHERE clause of the child view, so when you requery it you will get a different record set. To define a parameter in a view, you would precede one of the values in the Filter tab with a question mark. This indicates to VFP that this is a dynamic value, and also that it will not be able to find this item in the current view.

There are methods you can use to create a parameter. The parameter can be a memory variable, or it can be a field from the parent table. What we will do here is create an address view for our Tutorial U application. This is a view that contains all of the fields from the Addresses table. (The Addresses table should be in your database if you copied it in from the Developer Download files available at www.hentzenwerke.com.) If you take a look at the Filter tab shown in **Figure 1**, you will see an example of a parameter that is a field name from the parent view.

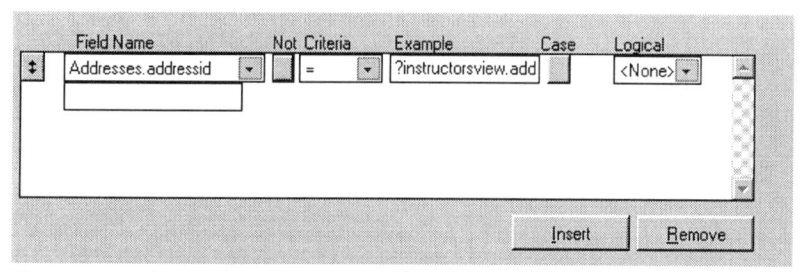

Figure 1. The Filter tab of the AddressView demonstrates using a field name from the parent view as the parameter.

This is rather difficult to see in Figure 1, so we will take a look at the SQL for the view:

```
SELECT *;
 FROM tutorial!addresses;
 WHERE Addresses.addressid = ?instructorsview.addressid
```

As you can see in the WHERE section, the view is selecting the records in the Addresses table WHERE the addressid is equal to the addressid of the current record of the InstructorsView. This, of course, will require that the InstructorsView be open and available when this view is queried.

The second method is to use a variable for the parameter. **Figure 2** demonstrates the use of this method.

Figure 2. The Filter tab of the AddressView demonstrates using a memory variable as the parameter.

Take a look at the SQL for this view:

```
SELECT *;
 FROM tutorial!addresses;
 WHERE Addresses.addressid = ?vp_addressid
```

In this case, in the WHERE clause the addressid field in the table is compared to the value of the memory variable vp_addressid. You can also assume that it's necessary for the variable to be populated. We will take a look at how to do that shortly.

You may be thinking that the first method is less work than the second, and this would be true if this view were always used as a child of the Instructors table. However, in our database design we're using the same table for the Students also. So if you prefer the first method, you will find yourself creating a second view of the Addresses table for the students. There is actually nothing wrong with this, and we will show you both methods and let you decide which to use in your applications.

The key to using either of these parameterized views is that they must be requeried each time the parent record pointer changes. This may seem like a bit of work, but the framework will take care of this for you if you relate your business objects.

Related business objects

The business object class is designed so that when it is an object it can be a parent or a child business object. The parent/child relationship of the business objects is directly related to the entities (tables) that they represent. As we continue with our Tutorial U application, you will see that the instructors business object becomes the parent object, and the address business object becomes the child.

The related business objects carry out the tasks needed for the underlying related views or tables.

1. If you are using tables, the business objects will create a relation between the tables by issuing a SET RELATION TO command. As we said in the beginning of this chapter, if you do this you will not be able to reorder the child. If you were to reorder the child, you would lose the relationship. By the way, this is standard VFP behavior, not a VFE limitation.

2. If you are using views, the parent business object will instruct the child business object (or objects) to requery whenever the parent's record pointer moves.

3. The child business object will also populate the foreign key field in its table with the parent table's key field value when you add a record to your child table.

4. There are also several behaviors that will occur based on how you set the properties, such as the parent saving its children when the parent is saved, a new record being added to the child automatically when a new parent is created, and so forth.

At the risk of being repetitious, let's go over the properties of the business object that are used to specify the business object relationships.

cForeignKeyExpression

Populate this property if the business object is a child business object. This property will hold the name of the field in the parent cursor that relates to the child cursor. This is a somewhat misnamed property. Think of it as the name of the field with whose value you want to populate the child's foreign key.

Here's an example: In the case of an Invoice and InvoiceDetail business object relationship, the key field of the Invoice table, "InvoiceNo," is used as the foreign key in the InvoiceDetail file named "Invoice." In this case, you would populate the cForeignKeyExpression with the value "InvoiceNo." See the next section, "cKeyField," for the other half of this example.

The child business object will use the information in this field to populate the foreign key in the child cursor with the parent's key automatically. When using tables, the business object will use this information to set a relation between two files.

cKeyField

Populate this property if the business object is a child business object. This property will hold the name of the foreign key field in the child cursor. This property is somewhat misnamed. The name implies that you enter the name of the key field of the child—don't make this mistake.

To continue with the previous example, in the case of an Invoice and InvoiceDetail business object relationship, the key field of the Invoice table, "InvoiceNo," is used as the foreign key in the InvoiceDetail file named "Invoice." In this case, you would populate the cKeyField with the value "Invoice." See the preceding section, "cForeignKeyExpression," for the other half of this example.

The child business object will use the information in this field to populate the foreign key in the child cursor with the parent's key automatically. When using tables, the business object will use this information to set a relation between two files.

cParentBizObjName

If this property is populated, the business object is a child business object. Populate the property with the object instance name of the parent business object; this name is not necessarily the class name. The business object looks for the parent business object, and when it locates it, the child business object sends a message to its parent that it exists. The method of the parent object RegisterChild is called, and the child object's reference is passed. The parent business object will add its new child to its child business object collection.

cRelationTag

This property is used in a child business object. This property is only used when you're using VFP tables and is not needed when you're using views. This property holds the name of the tag for the child cursor that is to be used to relate the parent and child cursor.

Related interfaces

Now we'll create each of the related interfaces you will commonly build. Initially we will use the VFE wizards, and then we'll take a look under the hood at the properties that were set by the wizard so you'll understand what is going on. Here are the types of interfaces we are going to look at:

- Parent/child presentation object
- Single record modal add form (cEditForm implementation)
- Multiple presentation object form
- Parent-child forms

These names are the names used by the VFE wizards; we will stick with them so you will recognize them when you run the wizards.

> *In all of the examples that follow, it is possible to use a grid type presentation object as the parent. If you do this, it is necessary to set the lRequeryChildrenOnRowChange property of the grid to True. The wizards will not do this for you. This is necessary with a grid because in the grid, it is possible for the record pointer to be moved without using the navigate methods of the business object if the grid has focus and the user moves the record with the arrow button. Setting this property to True instructs the grid to call its host business object's RequeryChildren() method to keep the child view populated with the matching records. Keep this in mind.*

Parent/child presentation object

Placing the child presentation object (or objects) onto the parent presentation object creates what VFE calls a parent/child presentation object. This is a nice technique because it encapsulates the entity into a single object. We like to contain child objects in parents that actually own the child objects. Recall from the earlier discussion of entity relationships that this is called an intra-entity relationship. This is an excellent method to add the address object to the instructors object because the instructor owns the addresses, and without the instructor there would be no address entity.

The first step is to create both the parent and child presentation objects. We have already created the instructors presentation object, but we still need to create the child—an addresses presentation object. Prior to this we will need a cursor, data environment and bizobj. Create these classes following the same basic steps you used previously, and store them in a class library named ADDRESSES. (The steps needed to create these classes were covered in previous chapters.)

> *Due to a glitch in the system, before you follow these steps you will need to delete the InstructorsViewForm. Do this in the Classes page of the Application Builder. Select the form in the tree view and press the Delete button. Once you have created the classes, we will use the Standard Presentation Object wizard (see **Figure 3**).*

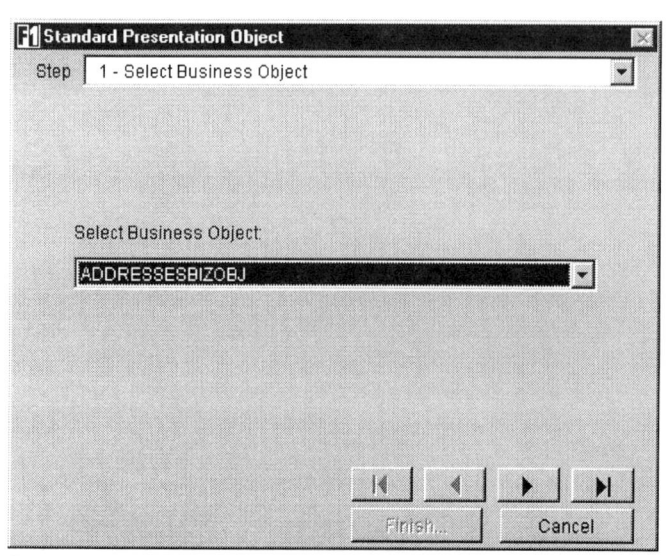

Figure 3. Select the ADDRESSESBIZOBJ to use with the presentation object.

1. In the Standard Presentation Object wizard, press the Next button twice, skipping the Layout page and accepting the defaults to move to Step 3 (see **Figure 4**).
2. Select the fields you want to display, and then press the Next button to move to Step 4.
3. In Step 4 we will accept the defaults. Press the Next button and move to Step 5.

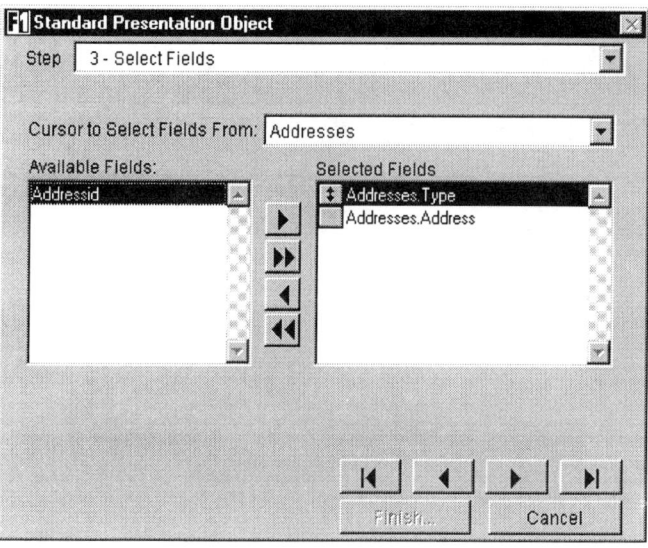

Figure 4. Select the fields you wish to display on the presentation object.

4. Accept the default values in Step 5 and move to Step 6.

5. In Step 6 (see **Figure 5**), select the buttons you would like to add to the presentation object. Because this will be a child presentation object, you should place buttons to manipulate the child business object. Press the Next button.

6. In Step 7, select the ADDRESSES class library and press the Finish button to create the class.

7. Open your presentation object, and organize the objects so they are arranged as you prefer (see **Figure 6**).

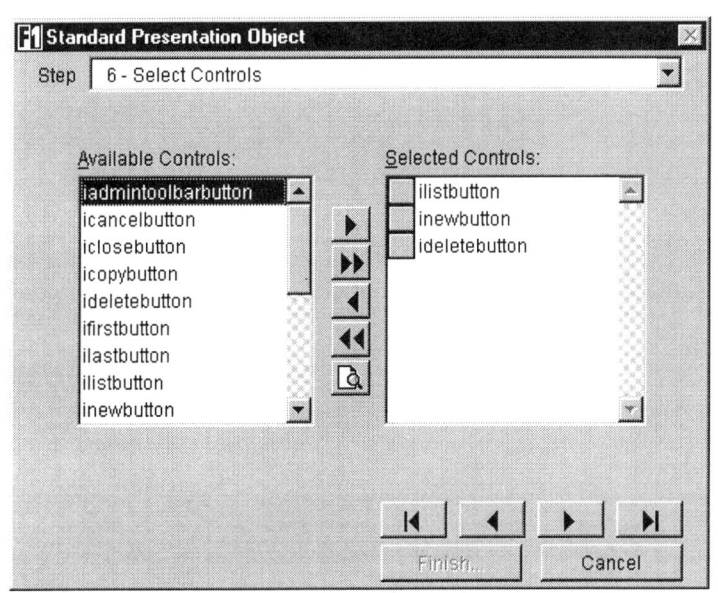

Figure 5. Select the buttons to be added to the presentation object.

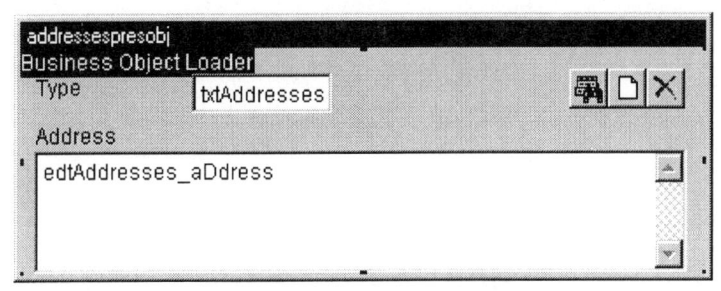

Figure 6. The completed addresses presentation object.

Create the parent/child presentation object

Okay, now that we have the parent and the child presentation objects, it is time to create the related presentation object. We will use the Parent and Child Presentation Object wizard to do this, and then we'll take a look at the properties that were set to relate the business objects.

1. Select the Presentation Object node of the Classes page and press the New button. Select the Parent and Child Presentation Object wizard from the list.

2. In Step 1 of the wizard, select the presentation object that will be the parent entity in your final parent/child relationship. Select INSTRUCTORSVIEWPRESOBJ (see **Figure 7**), and then press the Next button.

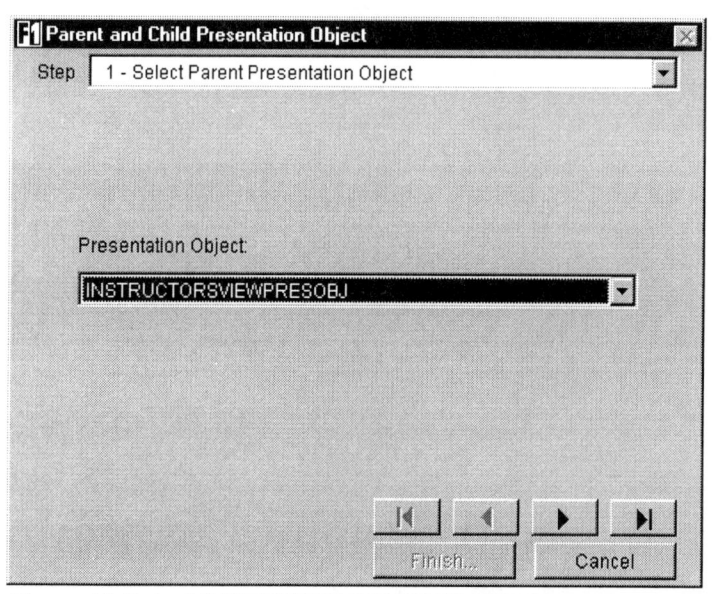

Figure 7. Select INSTRUCTORSVIEWPRESOBJ to be the parent object.

3. In Step 2 of the wizard, select the presentation objects whose business object entities have a child relation to the parent object. Select the ADDRESSESPRESOBJ here (see **Figure 8**). If you select Add Children in a Page Frame, the wizard will put each of the children presentation objects in its own page of a page frame that is added to the parent presentation object. Because we only have one child in this case, the page frame is not necessary, so turn this option off. Press the Next button.

4. In Step 3, set the parent/child relationship information for each child presentation object that you have selected (see **Figure 9**). This is a bit of misdirection, because you are actually defining how the business objects will be related. So press the Relation Properties button.

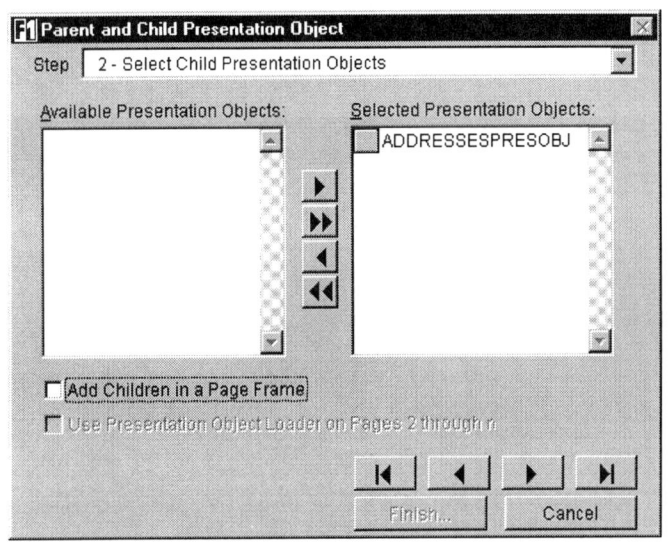

Figure 8. Select the child presentation objects to add to relate to the parent.

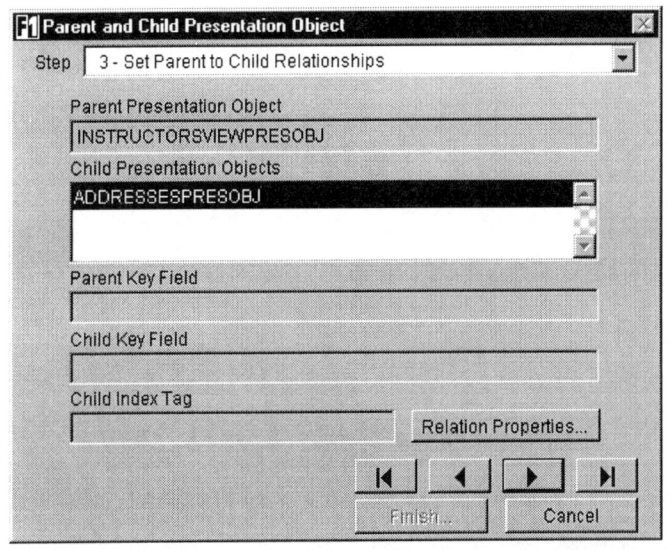

Figure 9. Set the relation information for each child object.

5. In the Relation Information screen, set the Parent Key Field and Child Key Field values. The Child Key Field is not labeled properly in our opinion, because this is looking for the foreign key field in the child that relates back to the parent. Set the form as shown in **Figure 10**. Also, the documentation states that this information is only needed when using tables, not when using views, but that is not really correct. If you are using tables, this information is used for the SET RELATION TO

command. However, if you are using views, the business object still needs to know this so it can populate the foreign key field for you when you add a record. (The information is not necessarily needed with views because many people use the Default expression option on their foreign keys to specify the PK from the parent.) When using views, though, the Child Index Tag is not needed; pressing Ctrl-0 will clear it.

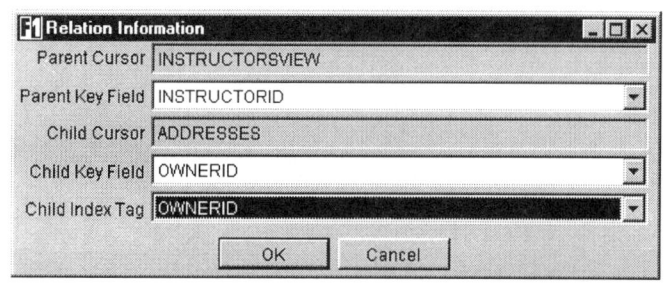

Figure 10. Set the relation information that will be used to relate the business objects.

6. Once you have set the relation information for this child, press the OK button to return to the wizard, and then press the Next button of the wizard to move to the next step.

7. In Step 4 of the wizard, name the new presentation object "InstructorAddressPresObj" and store it in a class library named "RELATED." After you have made these entries, press the Finish button.

The new class will be created and added to the Presentation Object node of the Classes page. We will now modify the class and investigate what the wizard has done for us. At this point, your class should look like **Figure 11**.

Figure 11. The resulting parent/child presentation object built by the wizard.

If you look at the properties of the presentation object, you will see that it is a subclass of the InstructorsView presentation object. This allows you to modify the parent class, and the changes will be inherited to this class. The child presentation object, however, is not a subclass of the AddressesView presentation object but an instance of it. The wizard performed the equivalent of dragging the AddressesView presentation object from the project to the Class Designer, creating this instance. (If you don't understand this, read the sections on pseudo-subclassing in Markus Egger's book, *Object Oriented Programming with Visual FoxPro 6.0*.)

Now let's see how the business objects are related. The prior discussion about the Business Object Loader explained how the properties set on the loader are copied to the business object when it is loaded. Take a look at the properties of the child presentation object's bizobj loader; you'll see that the wizard set the relation properties based on the relational information you provided (see **Figure 12**).

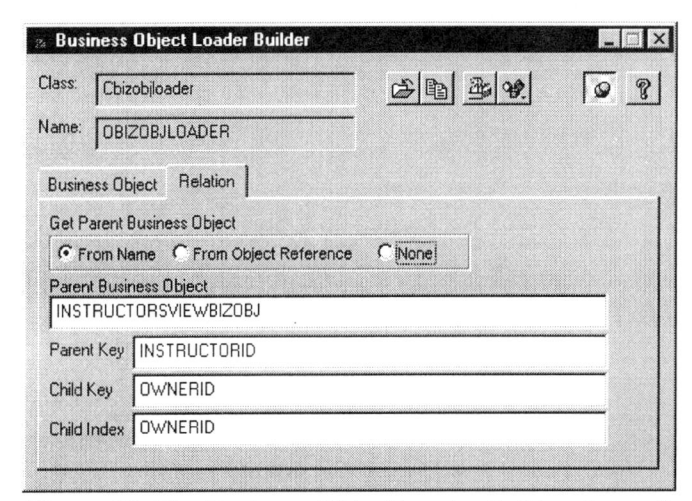

Figure 12. The Business Object Loader Builder shows the relational properties that will be set in the child business object.

If you look at the Relation page, you will see Get Parent Business Object selections. Because this is set to From Name, the business object will look for that named business object in its own form to get a reference to it. This child business object needs a reference to its parent so it can register itself with the parent. The parent business object doesn't know it has a child until the child registers with it, which is a little different from real life.

Once the parent object knows it has children, it will pass messages to the children as necessary, such as to save, delete or requery.

The child business object uses the Parent Key and Child [foreign] Key information when its New() method is called. The business object's New() method will call the WriteForeignKey() method, which will populate the foreign key field in the child cursor with the value of the parent primary key. This is what relates the data in the underlying tables. While you have this builder displayed, you should remove the Child Index value because this isn't used when you are using a child view.

Create a form
To test the parent/child presentation object, we need to create a form for it. Use the Standard Presentation Object Form wizard and select the presentation object we just created for it.

Follow the same steps and selections you used when we created the form that just contained the instructors presentation object. Use a form caption and menu prompt such as "Instructor-Address PC Form"—because we will be making more samples similar to this, you will be able to access each of them. Finally, store your form in the RELATED class library.

Test the form

After you create the form, you will need to build the project. This is necessary because we added an item to the menu, and it is necessary to build the project in order to generate new menu classes. So press the Build button, select to build the project and then press OK. After the project is built, press the Run button to run your application.

If you select the form from the View menu, your form should run. If you've followed the tutorial, you should have some data in the Instructors table. If so, type "Smith" in the Last Name view parameter text box and press the Query button. When you select the Data Entry page, your form should look similar to **Figure 13**.

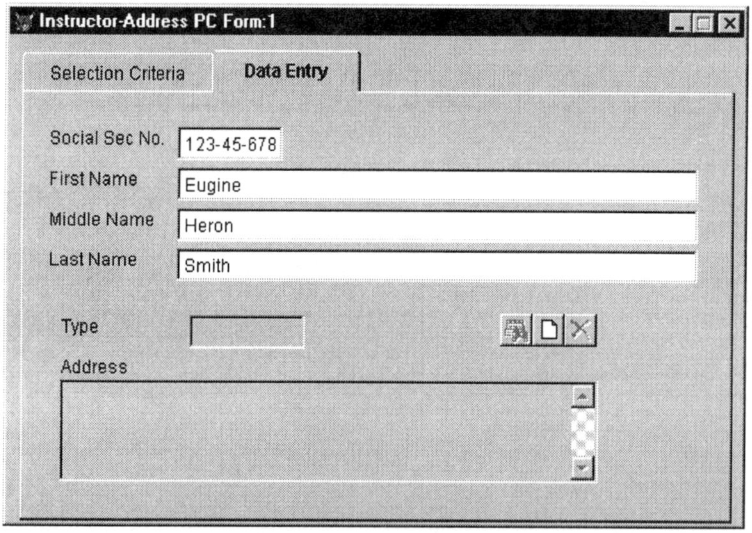

Figure 13. Your first form with a parent/child presentation object.

Notice that there is no address for Eugine yet. Press the New button for the addresses to add an address (see **Figure 14**).

To save the address, just press the Save button on the toolbar. This will send a message to the form, which will pass it to the primary presentation object, which will pass it to its business object, which, in turn, will pass it to its children business objects, which of course the address object is. The address is saved. Look at the record that was created and you'll see that the ownerid field was populated with Eugine's instructorid. This was done by the child business object using the parent key field and child foreign key field properties (see **Figure 15**).

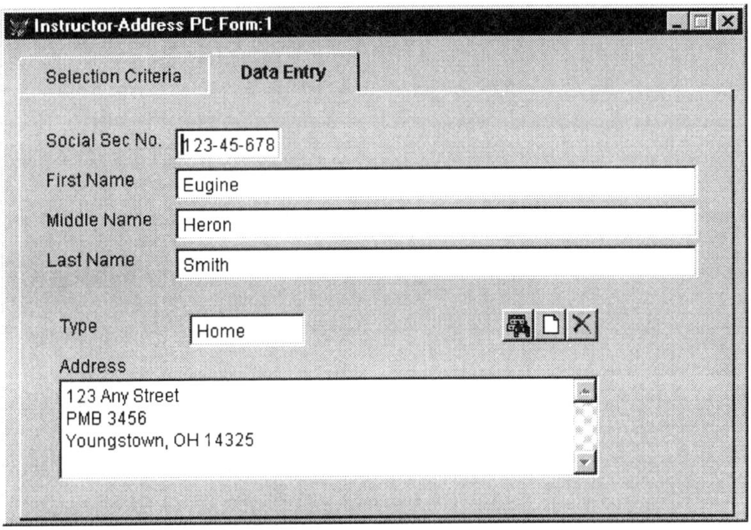

Figure 14. Adding an address to Eugine's record.

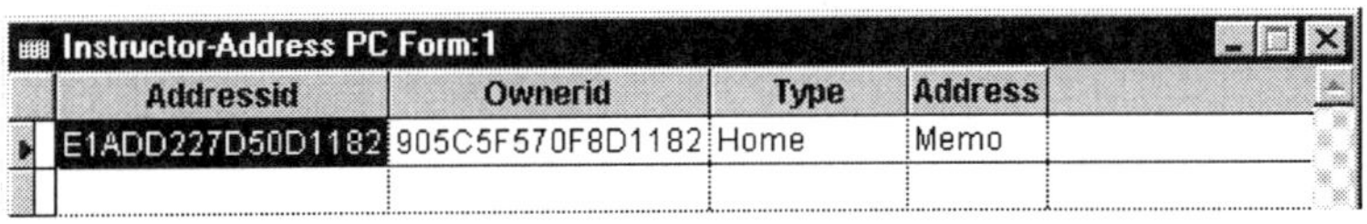

Figure 15. The ownderid foreign key was populated by the business object.

As you move through or add different instructors, you will see that the correct address for each person is displayed in the address presentation object. Even though you didn't write code to do this, the parent business object is calling the Requery() method of its child.

Single record modal add form

This form is used for two purposes. The first purpose is to add a record to a lookup view. The second is to create a cEditForm. cEditForm is a property of the presentation object. If cEditForm is populated, this form will be called when you edit or add a record. This is generally implemented when the records are displayed in a grid or list.

To demonstrate this interface, we will create a list-based presentation object of course descriptions. This list will be available from the View menu. The view will not be parameterized, so all courses descriptions will be in the list. Then we will create a standard presentation object that will be used in a single record modal add form to edit and add course descriptions.

1. First, create a view named CourseDescriptionsView. This view should include all of the fields in the CourseDescription table. On the Update tab, be sure to set Send Updates to on and set the primary key field to editable. Also, change the where type to "key fields" only. Do not set a filter; this view will show all of the course descriptions available at Tutorial U.

2. Set the metadata for the coursedescriptionid field in your new view to default to a guid. This is the primary field.

3. Create a cursor class for the view named CourseDescriptionCursor, and save it in a library named COURSEDESCRIPTION.VCX.

4. Create a data environment with the CourseDescriptionCursor class in it, and save the data environment as CourseDescriptionEnvironment in the CourseDescription cursor.

5. Create a business object using the newly created data environment, name it appropriately and store it in the correct class library.

6. Create a standard presentation object using the Standard Presentation Object wizard. In Step 1 of the wizard, select the bizobj you created in the previous step. In Step 2, change the Style of the presentation object to Grid. In Step 3, select all the fields except for the primary key. There is no need to display this surrogate key in the grid. Step through to the last page, accepting the defaults. On the final page, name your object and select the correct library in which to save the class.

7. Open the new presentation object in the class editor. We expanded our class to make it a bit bigger, and then expanded the grid to the same size.

8. Run the Grid Builder by right-clicking on the grid and choosing Builder... from the shortcut menu. You may have to set the grid as the current object using the combo box at the top of the property page.

9. On the builder, check on Searchable Grid and then Select Record On Double Click. The first selection sets the grid's lAlwaysReadOnly property to True. This sets up the grid so the user cannot edit the values directly in the grid. The second selection sets the lSelectRecordOnDblClick property to True. This tells the grid to call the SelectRecord() method when you double-click on one of the records. (For all of this to work, you must not have made any of the fields, the cursor, the business object or the presentation object read-only. If any of these are set to read-only, the controls will be disabled and the double-click event will not be fired.)

10. Close the builder and the class editor, and save your changes.

11. Finally, create a presentation object form using the Standard Presentation Object builder. You should know the steps: Use the <default> toolbar, accept the default name and save the class to the COURSEDESCRIPTION library.

At this point, you can build your project and run it. Run your new form. Notice that you can add a new record, but there is no way to edit it. So let's create a single record form that will pop up when you want to add or edit a course description.

1. Create a presentation object using the Standard Presentation Object wizard as you did before. But this time, create a Standard rather than a Grid style. Once again, don't put the primary key field on the form. Call the class CourseDescriptionsSinglePresObj, and store it in our library. Edit the new class (see **Figure 16**).

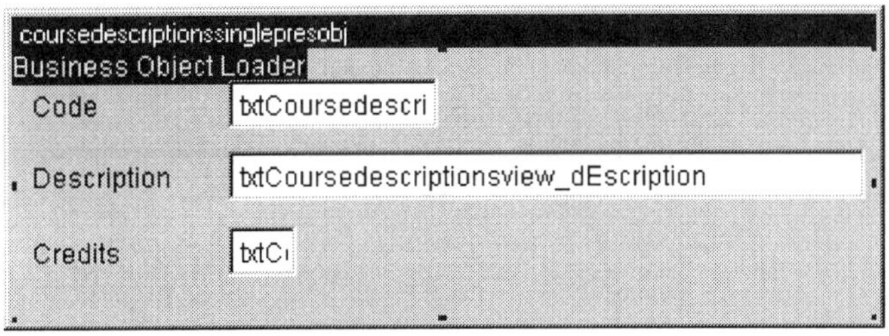

Figure 16. Editing the new CourseDescriptionsSinglePresObj class.

Now that we have the presentation object, we'll put it on a modal form and then tie it to the grid presentation object as the cEditForm. Close the Class Designer after you're finished viewing the presentation object, and then continue on:

2. Create a new form. This time, select the single record modal add form.

3. In Step 1 of the wizard, select the CourseDescriptionsSinglePresObj class. Press the Next button.

4. In Step 2, type the form caption. We used "Edit Course Description." Press the Next button.

5. In Step 3, accept the default name and select the COURSEDESCRIPTION.VCX library to save it to. Finally, press the Finish button.

If you edit this class, you will notice that Save and Close button were added to the form. The form is also set to use the default data session. What this means is that it will be created in whatever data session existed when it was created. Notice that the grid form we created has a private data session. Finally, the form is modal. This means that nothing can be done until this form is closed.

To link this form to the previous one, there is one more step you must perform. Edit the CourseDescriptionPresObj—this is the class that has a grid on it. The presentation object has a property named cEditForm. Populate the property with the class name of the form you just created. In our case, this is CourseDescriptionsSingleForm.

At this point you can run the application and the form. If you press the New button on the toolbar, the form will pop up, waiting for you to add a record. If you double-click on a form or press Enter, the single record form will also pop up, allowing you to edit the data. (There was a bug with this functionality in SP2, and if you haven't applied SP3 of VFE, you may not be able to double-click on the records.)

Here the New() method of the form is called. This method calls the New() method of the primary presentation object. The primary presentation object passes the new message to its business object, which adds the new record, populates default values and so forth. Once program control returns to the New() method of the presentation object, it checks to see whether the presentation object's cEditForm property is populated. If this property is populated, the form is called with the DoChildForm() method. The DoChildForm() method is used so that the modal form will be instantiated in the same data session as the parent form. If the DoForm() method of the application object was called, VFP would have switched to the data session that the application object was created in, and the child form would not have worked correctly.

In the case of editing a record, the double-click method of the grid checks to see whether the presentation object in which it is hosted has a cEditForm property that is populated. If it does, once again the edit form is called with the DoChildForm() method. Because the form is modal, it doesn't require any other synchronization of record pointers. The child form is opened, and the fields are bound to the existing view; therefore, the existing record is displayed in the edit form.

There is one modification that we recommend to this functionality. If you think about it, you will realize that the business object is being instantiated a second time when you run the single record add form. Of course, the views aren't opened twice because the cursor objects are smart enough to check and see whether they are already open. However, between loading the business object, data environment, cursor classes and so on, there are several hundred lines of code running here.

If you want to optimize your applications for speed as much as possible, you may want to follow these extra steps:

1. Edit the ChildDescriptionsSingleForm class by opening it in the class editor.
2. Run the builder for the Business Object Loader.
3. Populate the Business Object Loader as shown in **Figure 17**.

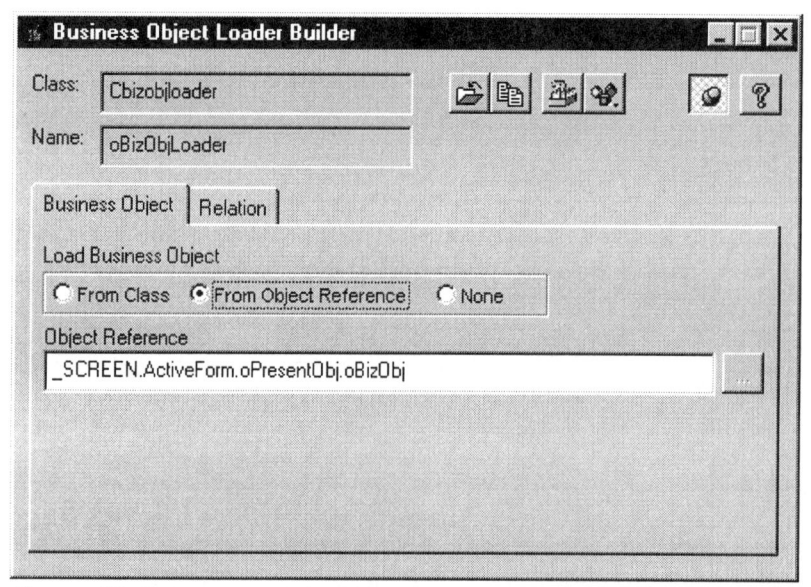

Figure 17. Set your modal add form to use the existing business object.

As you can see, you are instructing the Business Object Loader to use an existing business object. The existing business object is, of course, in the parent form. Why does ActiveForm work? Because when the Business Object Loader is doing its thing, the child form has not completed instantiating so the parent form is still reported as the active form. Setting the loader this way instructs it to just place the reference into the oBizObj property of the presentation object rather than instantiating a business object. In our opinion, there is no need to create that second instance.

If you make this change and test it, you will notice that it functions the same as previously. If you had the ability to time it, you would see that you are saving time by not running all that code. Of course, the more code, cursors and so forth, the more time you will save. The sample application available in the Developer Download files at www.hentzenwerke.com uses this method.

Multiple presentation object form

This form is similar to the parent/child presentation object. The difference is that instead of the parent presentation object being subclassed, the form class is used as the base container. The parent and the selected presentation objects are selected and placed on the form.

Why is this different from or better than the parent/child presentation object? We use this method when the entities are related but neither actually owns the other. In the previous example, the address belongs to the instructor, yes, but without the instructor the address record is meaningless—this is an intra-object relationship. Now consider the relation between an instructor and a class he is teaching. The class is related to the instructor, but it would still exist without the instructor. This is also similar to a customer and invoice relationship. While an invoice is created for a specific customer, it also stands alone as an entity, perhaps with sales information on it. These types of related objects are considered to have an inter-object relationship. We recommend that you use this type of relationship for the multiple presentation object form.

We have established that a parent presentation object and one or more children are selected. You establish the relationships as you did previously; however, the wizard will create a form class and place each presentation object on the form. For the parent object, you could select a single presentation object, or you could select a parent/child presentation object. We will create a parent-child form using the instructor and his classes. This form will not be to assign courses to the instructor, but only display which courses are assigned. Assigning the instructor to the course would be done on the course form.

1. Create a view named InstructorsClasses that is a view of the table Courses joined to CourseDescriptions to obtain the description. Select the fields as shown in **Figure 18**.

2. Set the filter (parameterize the view) to only retrieve the courses with the current instructorsid, as shown in **Figure 19**. Because this view will only be used to display information, there is no need to fill in the Update page of the View Designer.

3. Next, create a cursor and data environment and business object class for this view. You should be able to do this by now without step-by-step instructions. We'll store this in the RELATEDPOFORM library.

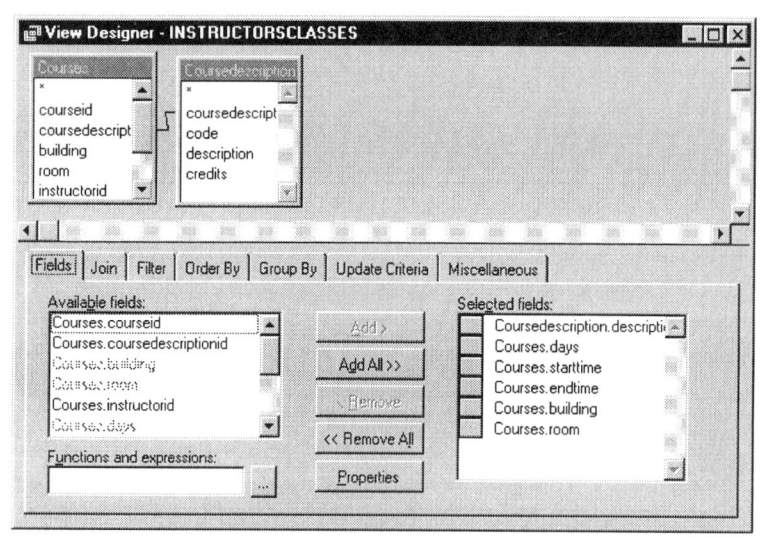

Figure 18. Select the fields for the InstructorsClasses.

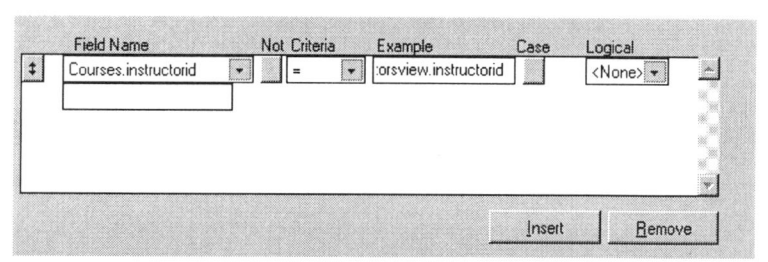

Figure 19. Parameterize the InstructorsClasses view to show only the current instructor's courses.

4. Create a presentation object using the Standard Presentation Object wizard. We're going to show you an interface technique here that you may want to use with your child objects. We'll create a grid type presentation object that displays the course description, and then, after the wizard has created it, we'll edit it and put standard controls on it to display the rest of the fields.

5. Using the wizard, create a grid style presentation object, select the description field only and set it to read-only; you won't need any controls on it. Stick with the default name, and store the class in your RELATEDPOFORM library.

6. Now you'll edit your new presentation object. Expand the presobj a bit and resize the grid so it is on the left edge of the form. Change the header caption to Courses. Also, set the lGetHeaderCaptions property to False—this tells the grid not to get header captions for your metadata. Set the scrollbars property so that only the vertical bar is used. Finally, set Gridlines to None.

7. Now we are going to add some controls to the presobj and bind them to the view. If you followed the directions in Chapter 4, "Data Storage and Classes," on setting up your environment, you should have the iControls library added to your Tools toolbar. If not, press the View Classes button on the toolbar—this is the icon that looks like books—and select the iControls library. If it is not there, select the Add... option and add ICONTROLS.VCX. Make sure you select it from your project directory and not from the VFE6 directory.

8. Now put five text boxes on your presobj, and five labels. The ToolTip should show the controls as iTextBox—we'll explain this a bit more in Chapter 16, "Extending the Framework."

9. The five labels you put on your presobj label each text control. If you're lucky, you will end up with something that looks like **Figure 20**.

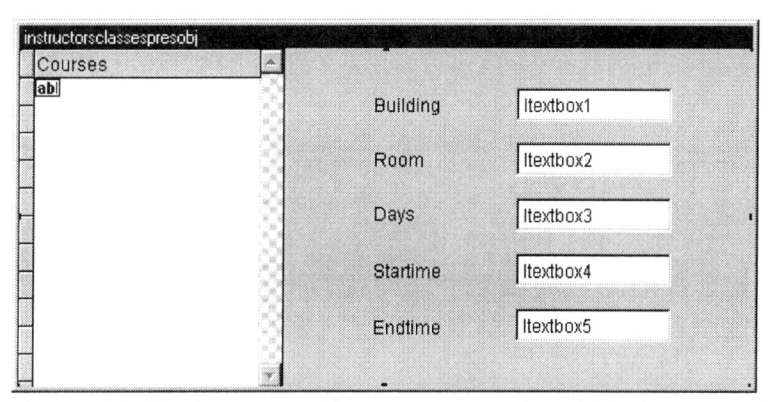

Figure 20. The InstructorsClasses presentation object is shaping up.

10. Now you need to bind the controls to the field objects. The easiest way to do this is to use the builders. Run the builder and select the appropriate field for each control—this, of course, sets the cField property. You can also set the cField property of the labels if you want them to get captions from metadata and participate in security. See **Figure 21** for an example of how to set the building text box. Notice that we haven't changed the object names of these controls. It's generally best not to do that unless you're going to put code into them, or refer to a control in code.

11. Finally, close and save your child presentation object.

12. Now is the time to create the parent/child presentation object form. Select the presentation object form's node on the Classes tree view and press the New button. In this case, you will select the Multiple Presentation Object Form wizard.

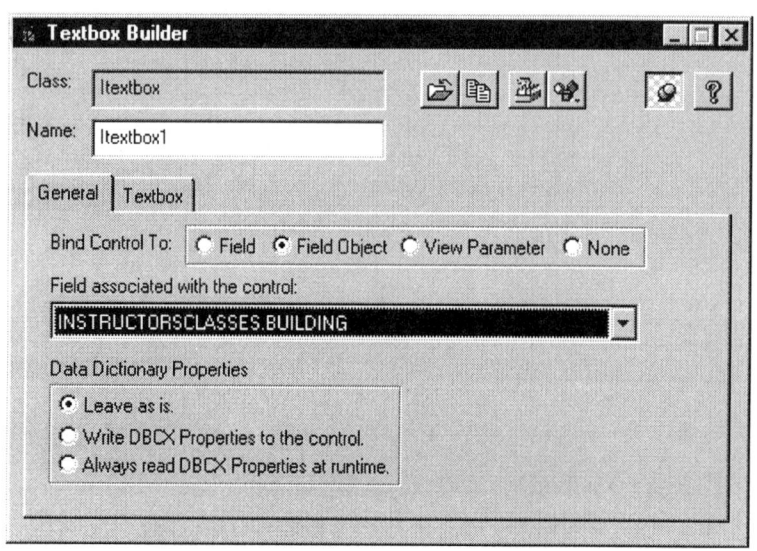

Figure 21. Bind the controls to the appropriate field object.

13. Select the InstructorAddressPresObj and InstructorClassesPresObj for this form. Notice that the parent object we are selecting is actually a parent/child presobj itself. Deselect the check box at the bottom of this page. (The Use Presentation Object Loader will put a Presentation Object Loader in place of the presentation object on page two and up. This can speed up your form load if you have a lot of presentation objects.) Move on to the next step.

14. Enter the form's caption for this step—we've used "Instructor and Classes." Move on to the next step.

15. Accept the defaults for the remaining steps. In the last step, be sure to change the name of the form class, because we already created one with the default name. We've used the name "InstructorAddressClassesForm." Also, store the class in the RELATEDPOFORM library.

The truth of the matter is that this wizard is not specifically designed to create related interfaces. It can also be used to create multiple-page forms of multiple presentation objects that all use the same bizobj and data environment. This is a good wizard to use if you have this type of multi-page form, because you can take advantage of the Presentation Object Loaders. The wizard will put a Presentation Object Loader in the place of each presentation object on page two and up of your page frame.

Using the Presentation Object Loader is a good way to speed up your form by delaying instantiation of the controls and lookups on the forms of the hidden pages. When the user selects the page, the presentation object will be loaded and the controls will be decorated and bound to the field objects.

Therefore, the wizard doesn't relate the business objects for us. Recall that when you ran the wizard, it didn't prompt for this information. Also, the wizard put each presentation object on a page frame, and we want both presentation objects to be on the form. So to get this form to work properly, we will need to do a bit of work. As you can see, using the wizard in this case was actually more work than just dropping the presentation object into the form in the first place. But most people prefer to use the wizards, which is why we're presenting it in this way.

The first thing to do is remove the page frame from the form. You do this by cutting your presentation objects from the page frame and pasting them on the form. If you have been working with VFP for a while, you should know how to do this; if you haven't, it will be an interesting challenge for you. Once this is done, we will manually relate the business objects so our form will work correctly.

1. Edit your newly created form and move the presentation objects onto the form, and then delete the page from the control. You should have a form that looks something like **Figure 22**. Of course, we cheated a bit and sized down the InstructorClasses presentation object a bit. If you are working in 640x480, you may not be able to lay out this full form.

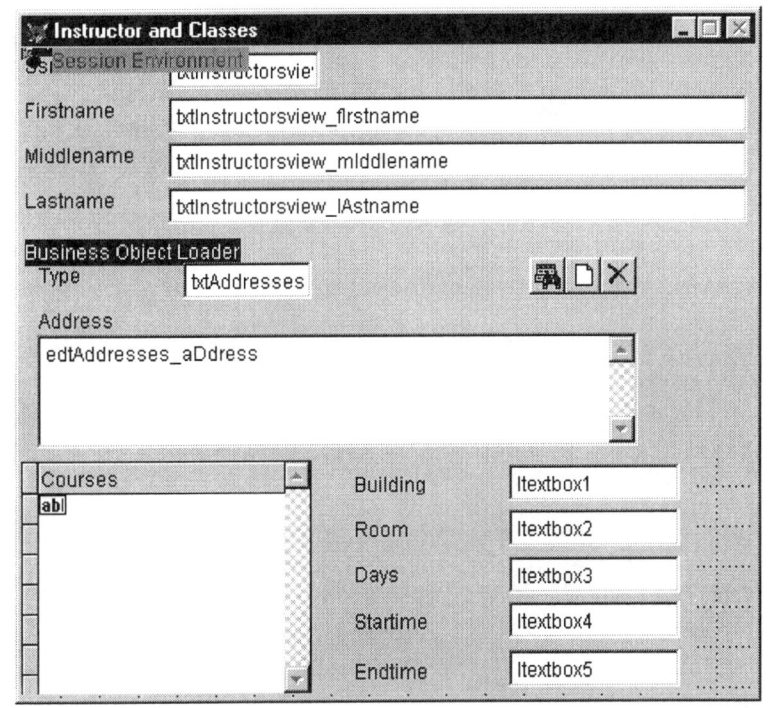

Figure 22. Final layout changes to the parent/child presentation object form.

2. Next, you want to relate the InstructorClasses business object to the parent business object. You accomplish this by setting properties of the InstructorClasses Business Object Loader. The Business Object Loader you want to edit is hidden behind the course grid. The best way to run its builder is to select the InstructorClasses presentation object with the mouse. Then the Business Object Loader will be the

first object contained in the properties object combo. If you select this in the combo, it will be highlighted on the form. Select the class editor by clicking on its title bar; you can then use the right-click mouse button on your keyboard to bring up the shortcut menu. Select the builder from the shortcut menu.

3. Once you have the correct Business Object Loader's builder running, set the Relation tab with the name of the parent business object. The parent business object will be on the same form, so you can use the name directly. Doing this will set the cParentBizObjName property of the loader, which will be propagated to the business object (see **Figure 23**).

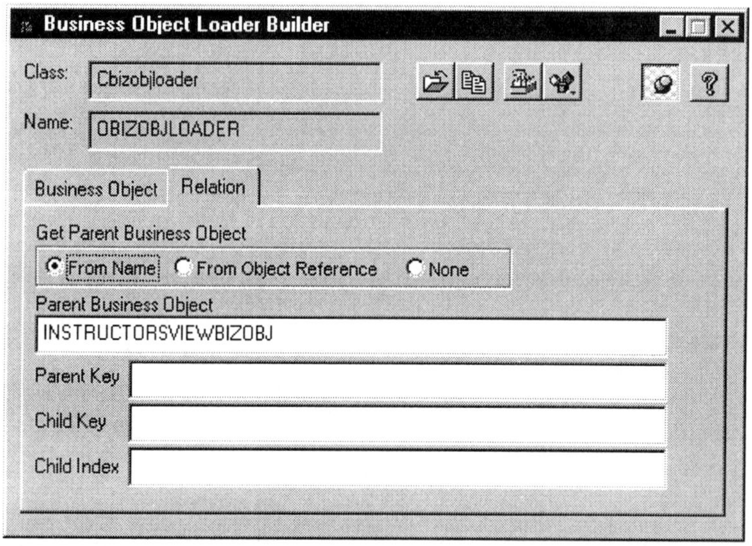

Figure 23. Relate your child object to its parent to complete the interface.

Having done all of this, we now have a few problems. The first is that the instructors view, which is the primary view, is parameterized. Notice though that this wizard did not ask whether you wanted a selection criteria page built. For the sake of simplicity, you can just choose Refresh from the File menu when you run the form. But then you'll run into another problem—the business object is set to not allow you to retrieve all the records in the view. To fix this little problem, edit the instructors bizobj, run the builder and set Allow Select All on.

Now you can finally test your form. Be sure to build the project—because you used a form wizard that adds an item to the menu, it is necessary to allow the menu to rebuild. After you build the application, you can run the form to see how it works. You may not see any data here unless you have populated the data files. You can manually create a few records if you need to see this work, or you can copy the data directory from the completed samples available in the Developer Download files at www.hentzenwerke.com (see **Figure 24**).

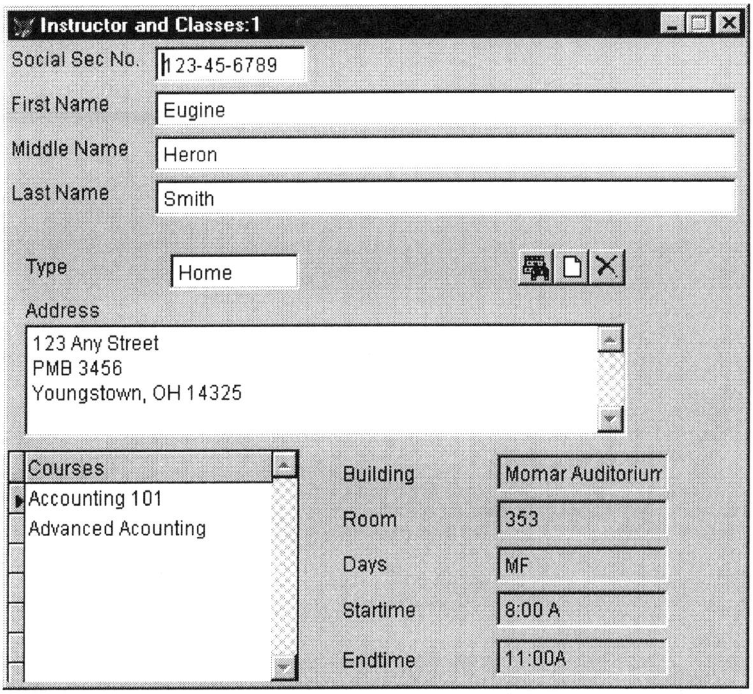

Figure 24. The multi-related presentation object form running with data.

You can also see the little interface technique at work here. By using a grid to simulate a list, we have eliminated the problems of using a list, such as populating it and moving the record pointer to match the item in the list. This is a nice interface that allows the user to select the identifiable item from the list, and see the details in the standard controls. Once again, this interface is read-only, but it could be made read-write as well.

Nits and gnats

This demonstration was not as smooth as the previous ones. This is due to the fact that this wizard wasn't really designed to create related presentation objects within a form interface; however, it is a fairly popular interface. You don't have to build them this way, and you could always use the Parent and Child Presentation Object Builder; however, this method keeps the parent and child presentation objects separate, which is preferable when working with inter-object relationships.

However, you might want to build this type of form by hand. As you've seen, this wizard doesn't do the following:

- Allow for the creation of a nonpaged form
- Set the relationships for parent-child entities within the form
- Create a selection criteria page or parameter container for parameterized objects

So why would you use this wizard? Well, that's up to you. It does add the form to the menu for you, which can be a chore to do manually, so that's a plus. As long as you understand how to relate business objects and set those properties on the child object or loader, you will be able to make any related interface you need.

Parent-child forms

This is a great type of interface to use when you're dealing with inter-related entities. These types of forms have also been called "related forms" and seem to be difficult for many VFP programmers to put together. You're in luck, because VFE makes this difficult task rather simple. The way this interface works is that a button is placed on the parent form that calls the child form. The child form is linked to the parent while containing its own business object and environment. The child business object is related to the parent business object in the same way as on a parent/child presentation object.

Creating this type of interface is fairly simple with VFE. First you will create two forms. You can use more than one child form, and you can actually have a child form call another form that will be its child. After you have created the parent and child form, you will use the Parent and Child Form wizard, which will put a button on the parent form that calls the child form.

To save some time, we have created two forms (see the sample application in the Developer Download files available at www.hentzenwerke.com): a form to edit the student data (StudentsForm) and one to edit the student address data (StudentsAddressForm). The child form uses a parameterized view. You can also use the parent view's field directly as the parameter, or you can use a variable. We have chosen to use a variable in this case—the reason will become clear shortly. Create each of these forms with the Standard Form wizard. When you create the child form, because it is based on a parameterized view the wizard will want to put a parameter and perhaps a page frame on the form. If this is the case, just let it do this and then edit the finished result as needed. **Figure 25** shows the Students form, and **Figure 26** shows the Student Addresses form.

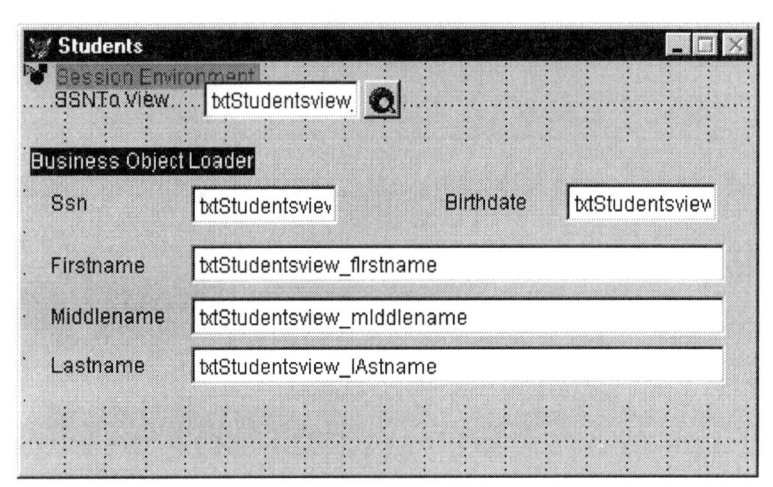

Figure 25. The Students form will be the parent of the parent–child relationship.

Chapter 14: Related Data and Forms 197

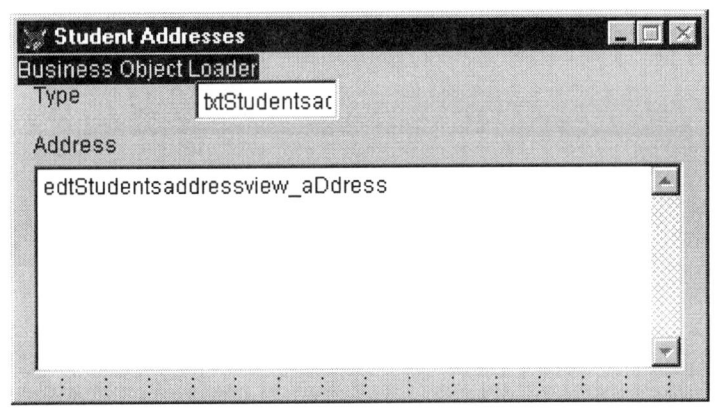

Figure 26. The Student Addresses form will be the child of the parent–child relationship.

Now that you have created the two forms, relating them is actually quite simple using the Parent and Child Form wizard.

1. Select the presentation object form's node and press the New button.

2. Select the Parent and Child Form wizard.

3. Step 1 of the wizard requests that you select the parent form. Select StudentsForm and press the Next button.

4. Step 2 asks for the presentation object that is the parent object. Remember, it is actually the business objects that will be related in the end, so VFE determines which business object is the parent by asking you to indicate which presentation object and then using that object's business object as the parent. Select the students presobj and press the Next button.

5. Step 3 requests the name of the child form. Select StudentsAddressForm here, and than press the Next button.

> This form gives you a nice informative message about requiring the child form to use the default data session. As you know, the default data session actually tells VFP to use whatever data session is active when this form is created. The framework assumes that you have related the views by having the child reference the parent view in its parameter. However, we used a variable as the view parameter. Because this is an n-tier framework, we're going to assume that the business objects were loaded as COM objects and the user interface has no access to the views at all. Because this is the case, you will only have access to the data objects. So we will show you how to use private data sessions with a view parameter value and still have the relation work properly.

6. Step 4 asks for the presentation object on the form, which will be the child of the presentation object you specified as the parent. Once again, VFE will get the name of

the business object being loaded for this form to set up the business object relationship. Press the Next button.

7. Step 5 asks for the relationship information. You should be familiar with this wizard step, because it is the same as the relationship step in the Parent and Child Presentation Object wizard. Press the Relation Properties button and set the relationship as shown in **Figure 27**. By now this should be old hat for you.

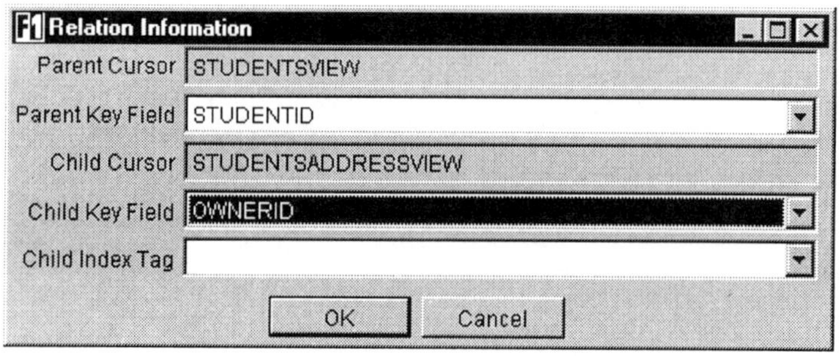

Figure 27. The relation properties for the parent and child form objects.

8. Press the OK button, and then press the Next button.
9. Step 6 asks for the caption of the button that will load this child form. You can use "Addresses" for this, as we have.
10. Press the Finish button. The wizard will now add a button to the parent form to call the child form.

Normally this is all you would need to do in order to use this as designed from VFE, and if you related the views using the parent view field as the parameter view in the child. However, because we used a variable as a view parameter, we must add code to populate that variable with the value from the primary key of the parent so the child fields can be found.

To do this, we will add code to the Requery_Pre() method of the child business object. Recall that this hook method is called before the requery takes place and is the perfect place for your code to manually populate parameters. In the StudentsAddress business object, put the following code in that method:

```
WITH This
   .SetParameter('vp_ownerid', .oParentBizObj.GetPKValue() )
ENDWITH

Return DoDefault()
```

This code populates the view parameter of the child cursor using the cursor object. To do this, there is a method in the business object named SetParameter() that takes as its arguments the name of the parameter and the value to populate it. The oParentBizObj property holds a reference to the parent bizobj, so we can call its GetPKValue() method to get the current primary key value. We will use this value to populate our view parameter. *Voilà*—when the child is requeried, the parameter will be populated with the value of the parent's key field, and the correct child records will be retrieved.

Now, you are probably wondering what purpose is served by this button that's placed on the parent form. Actually, the magic happens with the DoChildForm() method of the parent form. This method is passed the information from the button, including the child form name, parent bizobj, child bizobj and so forth. This method then calls the child form and sends information to the child business object. You should now be able to trace through this method and understand it, because you are practically a VFE expert at this point.

Is it n-tier?

You may have noticed that if you relate the views, this will not be n-tier. Because the business objects and the views would be in a COM object somewhere, they wouldn't be able to be related to each other. This is the reason we told you to use a memory variable as a parameter. As we demonstrated earlier, you can populate the view parameter of the child with the value of the parent's primary key without writing code that uses the views of their fields.

This change does what's necessary to make this relationship more "n-tierish," if you will. To prove this, the sample application is shipped with the child form set to use a private data session. You will see that this works just fine and simulates that fact that the child view can't talk to or see the values of the parent view.

There is one chink in the armor, and hopefully the VFE folks will straighten this out. We told you to set the relationship data even when you are using views because the framework needs this information to populate the foreign key field in the child cursor when you add a record. However, when you do this, the Parent and Child wizard assumes that you are using tables. It therefore sets the lFilterChild property of the button, which calls the child form, to True. You must set this property to False for the form to work with a private data session. If you don't, the framework will try to relate the parent and child views, thinking that it's working with tables.

Summary

It's all about data. No, it's all about the interface. No, it's all about design. Er, it all depends. What you can be certain of is that you will need to display related data in any one of many ways. Also, don't feel limited by what you think the wizards can and can't do. As you've seen, sometimes you have to help the wizards a bit to get the end result you were hoping for. Other times, you can't use the wizards at all. However, you should have enough information now to understand how the framework deals with these relations, what needs to be set up in your views and how to manage the data sessions when your business objects are accessed as COM objects.

Chapter 15
Data Behavior Classes

The data behavior class is nothing new to you. A data object is created for each field and view parameter in the cursor. These objects generally use the cField or cViewParameter class definitions. It is possible for you to create a custom data class and instruct it to be used instead.

In Chapter 4, "Data Storage and Classes," you learned about the cursor object. Recall that the cursor object contains two collections. One collection, the *fields* collection, contains references to the field objects. The second collection, the *parameters* collection, contains references to the view parameter objects.

The data objects are contained in these collections. Each of these objects is created by instantiating either the cField class or the cViewParameter class. Both of these classes are subclasses of the cAbstractDataItem class. These objects encapsulate the behavior necessary to manipulate the underlying data item. These behaviors include accessing and assigning values of the underlying data item, validating the value based on the data items' validation rules that are stored in the metadata, and providing lookup information.

At times you may wish to modify the default behavior of the data object for a specific data item. You can do this by creating what VFE calls a "data behavior class." Once again, don't read too much into this. In reality, what you are doing is subclassing the default data object classes and putting code in to meet your needs.

Creating a behavior class
The VFE wizards make creating a data behavior class very simple. In the Application Builder, expand the Data Classes node and highlight the Data Behavior Classes node. Press the New button, and the wizard selection dialog will be displayed. From here, select whether you want to create a field or view parameter behavior class. From this point, the wizard only requires the name of your class and the library to which it should be saved.

Specifying the behavior class
Once you have created the behavior class, it is necessary to bind it to a data item. If you don't bind the behavior class to an item, it will not be used. You perform this step on the Behavior page of the DBCX Explorer. One of the attributes is used to specify the class that is to be used. This metadata is read at run time, and the class that's specified here is used to create the field or view parameter data object.

To specify that the class you created is to be used, highlight a data item in the Explorer (see **Figure 1**) and move to the Behavior page. Select the Data Behavior Class attribute, and then press the Builder button. Here you will be prompted to select the class to use. Hopefully in the future VFE will provide a simple combo that lists all of the data behavior classes you have created.

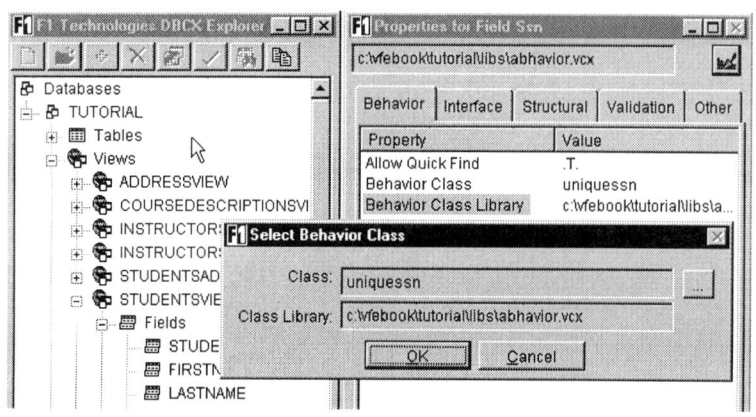

Figure 1. Associate your behavior class with a field in the DBCX Explorer.

Custom validation

One reason to create a data behavior class would be to define custom validation, which requires rules that are not supported by default in the framework. One of the validations that comes to mind is requiring a unique value.

Custom validation should be added to the Validate_Post() or Validate_Pre() method of a field or view parameter class. If the field passes whatever checks have been coded in these methods, the method should return the constant FIELD_OK. If the field does not pass whatever checks have been coded in these methods, FIELD_POSTVALID or FIELD_PREVALID should be returned. To display an error message when a field does not pass custom validation rules, the cErrorMessage property of the field should be set to the appropriate error message.

Let's consider the example of a field having a unique value and see what type of code you might use. One method you might use here is to just set a unique constraint or index on the database. The problem with this is that the user must save the record before receiving feedback that the value is not unique. But perhaps you want to provide instant feedback—in this case, you can write code in the Validate_Pre() method.

The first question you want to ask is how you will determine whether the value is unique. The answer depends on whether you are using local data or remote data. If you are using one or the other exclusively, you can use a SELECT statement for the local data or a SELECT statement with SQL pass-through with remote data. If you have an application where you are writing for both data sources, you may want to use a parameterized view. With the view, your code would populate the view parameter with the value of the field.

After you have decided, it is a simple matter to code your method. If your code determines that the data is not valid (not unique), you would return the constant FIELD_PREVALID; if the value is unique, return FIELD_OK. Before doing that, populate the cErrorMessage property with an error message to display to the user. The following is an example of code you might use with a parameterized view. Suppose you have created a cursor named uniquessn, which is created for a parameterized view that you created to verify that the Social Security number being entered is unique. Make sure the cursor's NoDataOnLoad property is set to True. Finally, add your cursor to the data environment of your form. (For an example of this, look at the students presentation object and the uniquessn behavior class.)

```
Local ;
   OCursor, ;
   lnMax

If TXNLEVEL() = 0
   With This
      lnMax = IIF(.IsAdding(), 0, 1)

      oCursor = This.oBizObj.oDataEnvironment.FindCursor('uniquessn')

      If type('oCursor.Name') <> T_CHARACTER
        .cErrorMessage = ;
           "Uniqueness of Social Security number could not be verified."
        Debugout PROGRAM() + " UniqueSSN is missing from data environment."
        Return FIELD_OKPREVALID
      Endif

      oCursor.Parameters.Item('vp_ssn').Value = .Value

      oCursor.Requery()

      If oCursor.RecordCount > lnMax
        .cErrorMessage = 'Social Security number already exists!'
        Return FIELD_PREVALID
      Else
        Return FIELD_OK
      Endif

   Endwith
Else
   Return FIELD_OK
Endif
```

The code is placed in the Validate_Pre() method of the data behavior class that we created called uniquessn. We then bound this class to the ssn field of the students view. Finally, we added the cursor class to the students data environment. Okay, let's take a quick look at what this code does.

The first line determines whether the current record is being added or edited, and then it locates the cursor object. Because we placed the object in the data environment, we can use the FindCursor() method of the business object to obtain a reference to the cursor object. Next, we verify that we have obtained this reference; if not, we return an error code and set the error message to indicate that the SSN couldn't be verified. We've also included a DEBUGOUT statement, so when we go to figure out the problem we'll be able to see that we forgot to put the cursor in the data environment.

The next thing the code does is populate the cursor's view parameter variable with the value of our field object. Then we requery the cursor. If the data contains this value already, a record will be returned to the cursor. For this reason, check to see what the record count of the cursor is—if the record count is 0 and we're adding, or 1 and we're editing, everything is okay.

If the SSN is not unique, we populate the cErrorMessage property with an appropriate error message and return the constant FIELD_PREVALID, which will indicate to the validation routine that the validation failed. This code will be returned to the UI layer, which will display the error message we stored in the field objects property. Of course, if there are no records in the cursor, we have verified that the current value doesn't yet exist in the table and will return FIELD_OK, indicating to the validation method that our code has passed the value.

Keep in mind that you should still set up a unique constraint or rule at the database level. With this method, if two users are entering the same value at the same time, the client will verify to both of them that the value is good. Therefore, the database must verify this again on a save. Also remember that you cannot perform a requery during a save, because this is not allowed in the midst of a transaction. In this scenario, the SSN has already been verified as unique at the time it was entered, so we don't need to run the check again. If another user has saved a record with the same SSN, it was validated, so the database constraint will catch it.

Lookup_Post()

This method is called after a lookup is performed and the user has selected the value. Many times it is necessary for your program to populate fields other than the one being validated based on the lookup value selected. This is the perfect place to do this. We can't explain the method to do this any better than the F1 documentation does:

Often it is necessary to save the values of fields in a lookup cursor into fields in the cursor that contains the field being looked up. Using a custom field class for the field the lookup is performed on and adding the necessary code to the CheckLookup_Post() method is the easiest way to accomplish this. After a lookup is complete, the CheckLookup_Post() method is called immediately, while the record pointer in the lookup cursor is still positioned on the record that was looked up. At this point a number of methods can be used to update the cursor that contains the field that was looked up. The following code uses the GetValues() method of the lookup cursor and the SetValues() method of the cursor containing the field being looked up to carry over all of the values from the lookup cursor that have matching field names in the cursor containing the field that was looked up.

```
LOCAL ;
    loValues

IF This.IsChanged()
   loValues = This.oLookupCursor.GetValues()
   This.oCursor.SetValues(loValues)
ENDIF
```

Lookups may be performed as the user tabs between the fields in the interface. You should always check to see whether the field has actually been changed before carrying over the other fields from the lookup cursor. This avoids dirtying data when the user is simply viewing a record.

Value_Access()
As you know, the value property of the field object is used to store the value of the underlying table. Well, the truth is that the value property has an access method. The access method retrieves the current value from the underlying table and returns that information to the value property.

You may want to manipulate what is returned based on certain values. One example is when you are using date fields in SQL Server. SQL Server doesn't allow date fields to have an empty date as FoxPro does. You basically have two choices. The first is to allow nulls in your database for these date fields. Some purists don't like this solution. The SQL Server solution is to put a date of 12/31/1980 into all date fields where you send no data to them.

If you don't want to use nulls for your dates, you can set up a behavior class to return an empty date from the Value_Access() method whenever the date is equal to 12/31/1980.

There may be other uses you can think of for this as well. We will leave that up to you. If you think of any clever (or not so clever but useful) ideas, please let us know.

Raise an event
Have you ever needed to run a method whenever the user changes the value of a field? Using the data behavior class as a way to trigger this event is much cleaner than using the lost focus or value of the control. One main advantage is that the trigger is pulled in the data layer as opposed to the UI layer. This can be very useful if you are using an HTML front end to your application, or even if you are using a VFE front end, and you are just using the same cursor in several forms. If that is the case, putting the code to trigger your method in the data behavior class will save code in the UI controls.

Here's an example that demonstrates this technique in action. Consider a project where the "job" business object has several attributes (or properties) that are calculated using employee salary, salary mode and pay frequency. The data is denormalized (values that can be calculated are stored) to optimize the speed at which the payroll processing engine calculates earnings. Precalculating the hourly rate and storing it in the table is advantageous for this reason. The point of the example is that the business object has code to recalculate these three fields. This code needs to be called when any of those other three fields change. So, instead of putting a call to the business object method in the lost focus of each of those controls, we'd create a data behavior class that calls the method from the Validate_Post() method. We'd then bind the three fields to this behavior class.

The Validate_Post() method of the behavior class is a single line of code:

```
This.oBizObj.RecalculateRates()
```

The RecalculateRates() responsibility (method) of the job object is called on whenever the user edits one of the values on which this calculation is based.

Using the data behavior object in this way provides you with the ability to "raise an event" that tells the job object to recalculate the rate values, and you only need to write the code once. Because this trigger is installed at the data layer, if you move this form to a Web front end, the recalculation will still take place when those new values are saved.

To raise the event, you could also call your method from the Value_Assign event of the data object. You may want to do this if you are not validating your controls on a lose focus.

Because the Value_Assign is called every time the user changes the value, you can be sure that your method will be triggered.

Summary

The data item behavior class is rather ubiquitous when it comes to the framework. You could write several whole applications and never create a custom behavior class. However, there are times when you can simplify what you are doing or eliminate putting the same code in several places by using one of these classes.

So, when you are doing validation on a specific field, populating fields after a field lookup, or triggering a calculation or method from the lost focus of several user controls, consider whether you could get the same results with less code and confusion by using a custom data behavior class.

Chapter 16
Extending the Framework

In this chapter, we will take a look at the techniques you can use to customize the framework to meet your needs. We will also look at the factory class that will allow you to modify the behavior of your application without even needing to recompile.

It seems that if you ask 100 people how to accomplish a programming task, you will receive 100 different answers. With this in mind, it is possible that the framework doesn't operate or perform some function quite the way you would like it to. This is to be expected, and the framework's design anticipates and allows for these changes.

In addition to customizing the existing framework class, you may also have your own class libraries or third-party class libraries that you would like to use in your applications. Because we are still dealing with a VFP application, this is certainly possible.

Finally, you may want to replace a class with an entirely new one. You can do this by using the factory class. We will take a look at each of these methods in this chapter. There are many methods you can use to customize the framework. As a last resort, you can modify the code in the C-layer by moving it to the I-layer and modifying it.

The I-layer

The I-layer, or intermediate layer of the framework's class hierarchy is a set of classes that are subclassed from each of the C-layer classes. So, where there is a cBusiness class, it is subclassed to iBusiness.

This isn't the first time that the I-layer has been mentioned in this book, but now it's time to take a closer look and see exactly what we're talking about. In previous chapters where we've discussed a class library, we used the C-layer name of its class. We did this because the C-layer of the framework is where all of the classes are implemented. In other words, this is where all the code is.

In reality, when the wizards are creating classes they are using the I-layer classes. In addition, when you are dropping classes onto your form classes, you should also use the classes in the I-layer.

All of the classes in the I-layer can be found in the iLibs directory of the framework. When you first created your application, you specified which iLibs directory to use. If you specified one other than the default, a new iLibs directory was created and all of the I-layer files were copied to this location. This allows for each application to have its own set of I-layer classes.

It is up to you whether you want to create a separate I-layer for each application, or use the same I-layer for all of them. It is also possible to use the same I-layer for more than one application. For example, you could have an iLibs directory for each client, or for common groups of applications, such as one for financials, one for sales and so forth.

What's it for?

The I-layer provides a place for you to customize the framework's behavior without modifying the C-layer classes. Generally, you would have to edit the delivered code directly, and then write down all of your changes so that when an upgrade was shipped you could redo your modifications. So, the I-layer provides you with a place to change the framework without editing the delivered code.

However, we must warn you that the iLibs are still shipped with the service packs, so you should back up your I-layer before applying a service pack. New I-layers are shipped because new classes are added to the framework that may require a new class to be placed into one of the I-layer classes. Also, only the iLibs directory in the VFE6 directory will be updated, so you will have to update any other iLibs directories from there. In other words, you still need to pay attention to what you are doing when you apply a service pack.

Making modifications

There are generally two methods you would use to modify a framework class in the I-layer. First, you may just add code that you want to run before or after the C-layer's method. Second, you may want to replace the code in its entirety.

If you are adding something and still want the delivered method, you would use the DoDefault() function in your code to run the C-layer code. This function can be placed anywhere in your code. When you call it, the delivered code will be run, and then control will return to your method.

Be sure to avoid the two most common mistakes that occur when using DoDefault(). The first mistake is neglecting to pass the parameters. If the method accepts parameters, you need to pass them to the default method with the DoDefault() function. In VFP 6, we are fairly spoiled because the parameters of the parent class method are duplicated for you in the editor. All you need to do is cut and paste those parameters into your DoDefault(). The code may look something like this:

```
LPARAMETERS tlAllRows, tlForce
DoDefault( tlAllRows, tlForce )
```

The second common mistake is to ignore the return value of the method. When a method is called in the framework, the calling method is usually relying on the return value to determine how to proceed. The previous code makes the mistake of ignoring the parent class return value. So, we would rewrite this code to something a bit better:

```
LPARAMETERS tlAllRows, tlForce

Local luReturnValue

luReturnValue = DoDefault( tlAllRows, tlForce )

*** Your code goes here

Return luReturnValue
```

In this code, we are capturing the return value of the parent method, and we also need to return that same value to the calling method. Now, there may be times when you want to modify your code's behavior based on that return value, or change the return value, which is fine. Be sure you know what value and type to return. Many of the framework's methods return various integer values indicated by constants located in the VFE.H file.

The preceding code demonstrates how you may write code where you want to add some behavior after the delivered code runs. Sometimes you want your code to run before the delivered behavior, so you might write code similar to this:

```
LPARAMETERS tlAllRows, tlForce

*** Your code goes here

Return DoDefault( tlAllRows, tlForce )
```

This code calls the parent class method after it has performed its tricks, and in addition the return value of that call is directly returned to the calling method. Of course, you could also modify the first example so as to write some code, and then call the default code, then some more code. The important points to remember are to pass the parameters to the parent and to return the correct return value to the calling method.

Replacing code

At times you may come across a situation where you want to modify a large portion of the code as opposed to adding some behavior to it. In this case, you could copy the code from the parent method and paste it into the I-layer class. After that, you can modify it as needed. If you do not use the DoDefault() method, the parent code will not be called at all, which is what you were looking for.

Just keep in mind the same two rules: Accept the same parameters, and return the appropriate values and types to the calling method.

Don't use hooks

You have a well-designed framework with all of these hook methods. Previously we told you that a hook method was the place to put your business or domain code. However, in our opinion you shouldn't put customization code in the hook methods in the I-layer. The reason for this is that even though it is convenient, if someone is using your modified version of the framework, they don't expect to have to call the default method in a hook.

Hook methods are delivered without implementation code in them, so when you use them in your application classes you know there is no default behavior. If you put implementation code in a hook method in the I-layer, and another developer puts application-level code in the same hook method, your customization will be overridden.

You can, of course, do it whichever way you prefer; this is just a bit of advice that will work well when you are a member of a team of developers.

Subclassing

There are many times where you want to create a specialization of a framework class. This is exactly what subclassing was designed for. You don't want to modify the behavior of the framework's text box if you are happy with it, but you might want to create a text box that will know how to deal with your shop's part numbers.

In this case, you would subclass the iTextBox class and create a new class. We recommend putting any new classes you create into a separate class library that you create. This will simplify installing updates. If the subclasses you are creating are very application-specific, you'll probably want to put them into an application-specific class library. For example, if you're going to create a subclass of iTextBox as described previously, you might choose to place this subclass in the aContrls.VCX library in your application's LIBS directory.

There are two ways to specify that your class be used. If you are creating a user interface class that will only be used for some fields, you can specify the class in the metadata. There is a place to select the class to use on the Interface page of the field properties (see **Figure 1**). If you highlight this property and press the Builder button, you will be able to select the specialized class you created (see **Figure 2**).

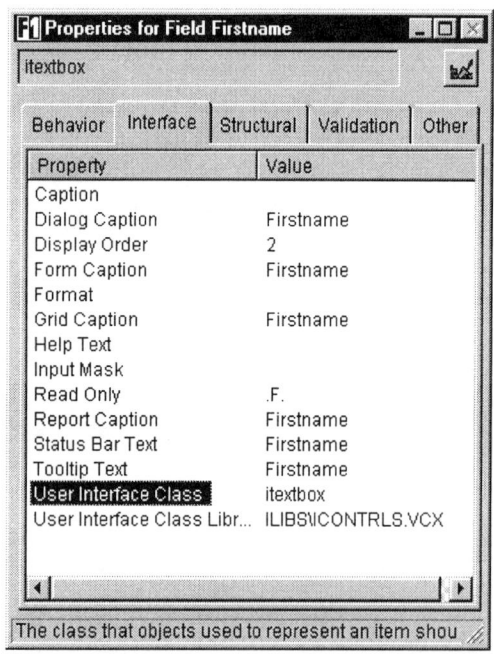

Figure 1. The interface properties of a field let you specify the interface class to use.

Figure 2. Select the interface class you wish to use for this data item.

Once you have made this specification in the DBCX Explorer, the wizard will use this class when creating presentation objects. The class will also be used in grids that are built on the fly and specified to use the metadata class.

If you have created a class that you want to be used for all occurrences of a certain data type, you can modify the Objects list in the Preferences dialog. We discussed this dialog in Chapter 3, "VFE's IDE," where we described the various parts of the IDE.

If the subclass you have created is not a user interface class, you can use the factory class to specify your new class.

Factory class

The factory class returns a concrete class name from a passed token. The class can return the class name, or it can actually instantiate the class and return the reference. The class does this by looking up the token in a data file to retrieve the concrete class name. If you use the factory class, you can modify the data file that will change the way your application works or looks. Of course, you must have the Classes table(s) in the EXE for this to work.

The factory class is instantiated automatically on application startup. A reference is stored in a property of the application class named oFactory. This application class contains a property named cFactoryClass. By default this is populated with iFactory.

Each factory class is tied to a data file. The iFactory class is tied to iClasses.DBF, and the cFactory class is tied to Classes.DBF. The factory subclasses work a little differently than you might expect. The class is designed to call its parent if the token that you passed cannot be found in its data file. This allows you the flexibility of not having to change the shipped Classes file. To override an item in Classes.DBF, all you need to do is add an entry with the same token to the iClasses.DBF file.

You can even extend this to your application if you wish. You can subclass iFactory to aFactory, for example. To do this, you would also have to copy the Classes.DBF file structure to aClasses.DBF. In your aFactory class, set the cTable property to aClasses. Finally, open your application object and change the cFactoryClass value to aFactory, and set the cNextFactory property of your aFactory class to iFactory. There is a more detailed article on this subject available on Steven Black's Wiki Web site at http://fox.wikis.com/wc.dll?Wiki~VFEExtendingTheAbstractFactory~VFP.

Making changes

If you take a look at the Classes table, you'll see some of the classes that are instantiated in this data-driven method. Most of the classes are for system-type issues such as the error handler, the query form and so forth. You can replace any of these classes with one of your own, or with a third-party class.

However, you must be sure that your class is polymorphic to the class that it replaces. This means that it must have all the same PUBLIC properties and methods, and all the same parameters and return values. In other words, the framework should not notice a difference between the original class and the new class. This is generally why subclassing the original class is the best method.

If you take a look at the Classes table (see **Figure 3**), you'll see that the cDescript field holds the token. The token is a tag or name given to the class. That token is passed to the factory class, which will either return the class name from the cClass field or instantiate the class and return the object reference.

Cdescript	Cclass
Meta Data Manager	dbcxmgr
Global Environment	iglobalenvironment
Global Hook	iGlobalHook
System Settings Manager	iRegistry
Form Collection	iCollection
Preference Form	iUserPreferenceForm
Set Preference Iterator	cSetPreferenceIterator
Write Preference Iterator	cWritePreferenceIterator
Print Reports Form	iRunQueryForm
Change Password Form	iChangePasswordForm
Database Utilities Form	iDatabaseMaintenanceForm
Error Log Form	iErrorLogForm
About Form	iDefaultAboutForm

Figure 3. *The Classes table is used by the factory class to instantiate a concrete class from a token value.*

For example, if you wanted to change the class that was used to print reports, you would create a record in the iClasses.DBF table with a cDescript of Print Reports Form and then the cClass name of your class. Because you put this in the iClasses table, and iFactory is the class you specified to your application, the entry in the iClasses table will override (be found first) the entry in the Classes table.

You can also make use of the factory class for your own purposes. Rather than hard-coding class names, use the factory to return the class names. This way, you can change the behavior of your application by shipping or modifying the iClasses table. For instance, if you have created all of your forms in English and Spanish, you could install the correct iClasses table for the language you want to use.

Using the factory

To use the factory in your code, you can access it via the application object, which contains a method that calls the current factory.

To return the concrete class name from a class token, use the following code:

```
LcClassName = This.oApplication.GetClass( 'Error Log Form' )
```

To have the factory instantiate the class and return an object reference, use this code:

```
LoClass = This.oApplication.Make( 'Error Log Form' )
```

Why would you use one method over the other? The application object is instantiated in the default data session, so when its methods are called VFP changes the data session to the default data session. If the object you're going to instantiate can live in this default data session, calling the make method is fine. If you need your object to be created in the current data session, you should call GetClass() and use CREATEOBJECT or ADDOBJECT with the class name that is returned. You may do something like this:

```
ThisForm.AddObject( 'SSN', This.oApplication.GetClass( 'SSN TextBox') )
```

In the preceding code, the GetClass() method will return the class name that will be used by the AddObject() method of the form.

Implementation class

As we said earlier, using a class in place of a framework class requires that the class have the same programmatic interface or be polymorphic to the class it replaces. If you are using a third-party class or an ActiveX control, this may not be possible.

Perhaps you want to replace the pick list grid with an ActiveX list box control from ABC Tech. This list box isn't polymorphic to the grid. In addition to this, because you didn't create it and don't have the source code, you can't change the class.

In this case you can create an implementation class, or a wrapper class for your new control. First you would subclass the original control. Set it to be invisible, and then override all of the methods. In this Init() of your subclass you would instantiate your ActiveX object, or perhaps it is a form onto which you placed the ActiveX control. Either way is fine.

Once you have done this, you should override each method so that it calls a corresponding method in the class you want. You may need to write some code to get this to work. This is best demonstrated by Stonefield Technologies. With each of the tools they sell, they provide an implementation wrapper class for use with VFE. The best example is the Query tool. They have created a wrapper class that calls the Query tool and returns values as the framework would expect from the original class. Once the implementation class is created, it is a simple matter to make an entry into the factory table.

Third-party classes

The VFP add-on market includes hundreds, if not thousands of classes that you can add to your applications. Even VFP 6.0 comes with a large collection called the Fox Foundation Class. But can you use these with the framework? The simple answer is, if you can use it with VFP you can use it in a VFE application. The difficult answer is, how would you implement that class?

As shown previously, you may need to write a wrapper class for the new class. If the classes are user interface controls like data pickers and others, you may need to subclass it and create the fields VFE expects to see there, such as cField. VFP is powerful in that you can subclass an ActiveX control to customize it to your needs.

The main issue you have to consider with ActiveX controls that bind to data is that they may not bind to the field objects. You may still be able to use the control. Most of the ActiveX controls that we have seen have an event that fires when the value changes. In this event, you can take the value of the control and populate it to the field object to which it is related.

Another thing to keep in mind is tying the control to the security. The best place to do this may be in the Refresh of the OleContainer. You have access to the security class via the application object. Because these controls will not have the oApplication property, you can use the FindApplication() function to get a reference to the application object.

User interface classes often do not need to communicate with other controls directly; it can be very easy to simply drop a user interface class (or ActiveX control) into an instance of VFE's iContainer class, which has the interface that the framework expects for a control. Then you simply have to add code to the user interface class to communicate with its container in order to change the value of its container's field object.

Adding files to your project

VFE makes it very simple to add a class library or other file to your project. On the Files page of the Application Builder (see **Figure 4**), highlight the node of the type of file you wish to add. Press the Add button (the button with the plus icon). This will bring up a file selector dialog. The selected file will be added to your project and will also now be listed on the Files page.

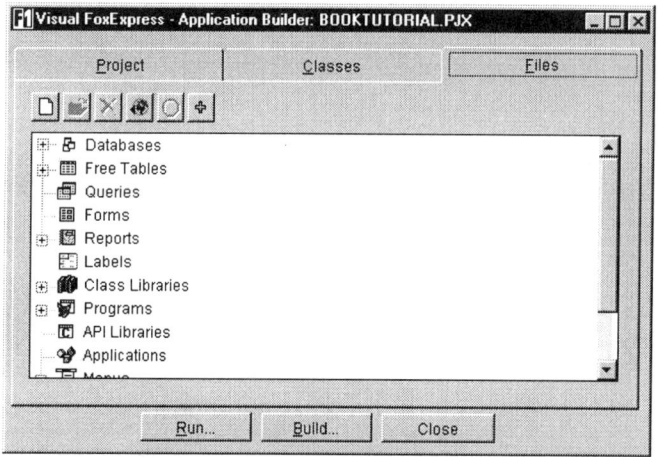

Figure 4. You can add files to your project by using the Files page of the Application Builder.

Summary

While the VFE framework is loaded with power and flexibility, there are times when it doesn't behave just the way you want it to, or when you want to add an ActiveX control or your own class library. To modify the existing classes, use the I-layer. Remember to pass parameters and return values from the default method. If you are overriding the default method, do the same.

If you are creating user interface classes, you can use the metadata or the Preferences dialogs to inform VFE about your class. When replacing other classes, it may be that a simple change to the factory will eliminate the need for a code change when creating the objects.

When you want to replace a class, consider writing an implementation or wrapper class. Doing this will make using the new class as plug-and-play as using framework classes.

The key to getting those outsider classes to work in your application is patience. However, the result at times makes it well worth it to give your application functionality that it would take you much longer to duplicate using native FoxPro code. Both you and your users will be happier.

Chapter 17
VFE Security

Professional business applications should contain some level of security. This can be as simple as an initial login screen to gain access to the application, or as complex as allowing only certain people access to particular features of the application. There also may be sensitive data fields that some users should not be allowed to see. Applications that are developed using Visual FoxExpress can have any level of security the client or user requests. This chapter introduces VFE's security system and shows how to configure it to meet your client's needs.

There are several levels of security that you can implement in a VFE application. The simplest is login security. The user is presented with a login screen where they must enter a user ID and password. Once this data is verified, they have full access to all features of the application.

Security can also be a very complete access control system. Using the security features provided by the VFE framework, you can control access to particular menu options or forms. You can also control which users may add, edit or delete records from business objects. You can even control which users can have access to certain fields or controls on the forms. The VFE framework makes all of these security features easy to use, once you understand how it all works.

You can lay the groundwork for security while developing the application or at any time afterward. However, it is much easier to start laying this groundwork at the very beginning and continue as you develop the application. You'll better understand the reasons for this as you read through this chapter.

There are five parts, or steps, to implementing security in a VFE application:

1. Define security names.

2. Assign these security names to classes you create while building the application—these include business classes, presentation object form classes and so forth.

3. Create user groups. This allows you to easily assign permissions or privileges to users assigned to a group.

4. Assign security names to the user groups, and then assign privileges to each security name.

5. Set up the users of the application and assign them to user groups.

This may sound like a complicated and laborious job, but after you read the rest of this chapter and become more familiar with how these different security components are related, you will see that it is not very difficult.

Implementing security from the beginning

It is easier to use the security features if you begin designing the application with security in mind. You turn on the security option, and then build the security names and assign them to the objects as they are created. The VFE wizards and builders make it easy.

Turning on security

To turn on security, click on the Security... check box on the Project tab of the VFE Application Builder. This will launch the Security Setup wizard. This wizard has two steps: First you must select the location of the System Security tables, and then you define the security behavior.

The first step of the Security Setup wizard is shown in **Figure 1**. You have two choices for the location of the System Security tables. You can place the tables in the application data directory or in the metadata directory. Place the tables in the data directory if your application will use multiple data directories and the security access will differ depending on which data directory is being used. Place the tables in the metadata directory if your application will only use one data directory or the security access will not differ when the data directory changes.

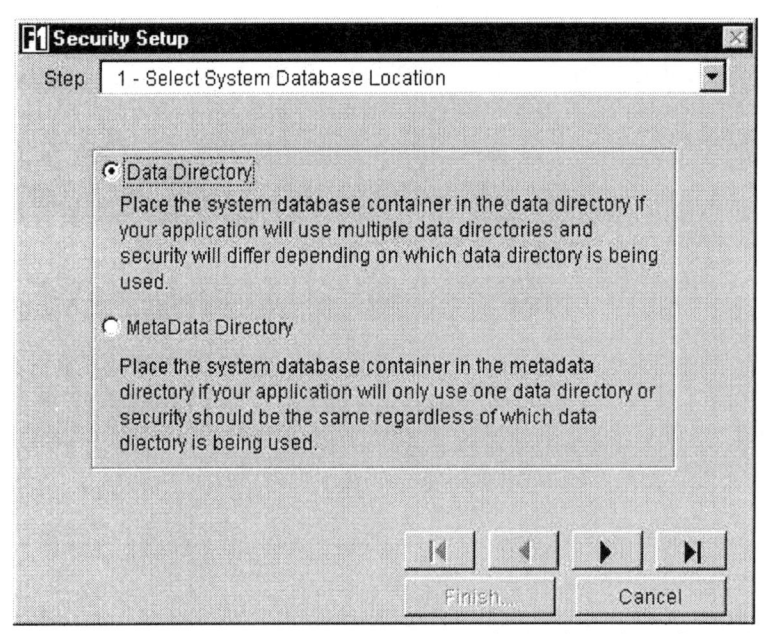

Figure 1. The first step in setting up security is choosing where the system database will be located.

In most cases the System Security tables should be in the metadata directory. This is the default choice for the first step in the Security Setup wizard.

The second step of the wizard is shown in **Figure 2**. The purpose of this step is to define the security behavior. **Table 1** describes each option and shows the default values.

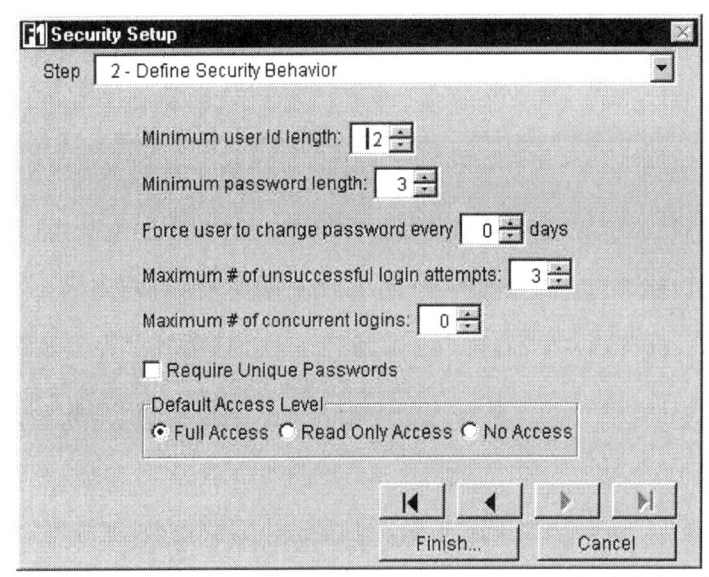

Figure 2. The second step in setting up security is defining the security behavior.

Table 1. Descriptions and default values for defining security behavior.

Option	Description	Default value
Minimum user ID length	Defines the minimum length of the user ID.	2
Minimum password length	Defines the minimum length of user passwords.	3
Force user to change password every ? days	Defines how often users will be prompted to change their passwords. A zero here means that users are never prompted to change their passwords.	0
Maximum number of unsuccessful login attempts	Defines how many times a user is allowed to try to enter a valid user ID and password before the application terminates.	3
Maximum number of concurrent logins	Defines how many concurrent logins the user is allowed. A zero here means that users may log in once, but a second (concurrent) login is not allowed.	1
Require unique passwords	Indicates whether two or more users may have the same password. If this box is checked, each user must use a unique password.	False
Default access level	The default security level determines what the access level should be for groups that don't have an explicit security level established for them that corresponds to the security name assigned to a particular item. In other words, if an item has a security name assigned to it and the current user's group does not have an access level established for the item's security name, the default security level is used.	Full Access

Once these settings are finalized, click on the Finish button and you will be returned to the Application Builder.

Adding security names

Once security is set up in your project, you can begin adding security names. It is a good idea to add security names before using VFE's wizards to build the application objects, because in the business object and form wizards you are prompted for security names in one of the wizard steps. If you already have the appropriate names entered in the Security Name tables, you can assign the names at the proper step in the wizard. For each business object, we create three security names: one for add permission, one for edit permission and one for delete permission. For example, if you have a business object for customers, you would add these security names to the Security Name table: Customers – Add, Customers – Edit and Customers – Delete.

In addition to the business object security names, if there is going to be a form object for the business object, you'd add an additional security name so you could control permissions to the form. Again, for the customers example, there is going to be a form object, so you would add a fourth security name: Customers.

Even if you don't think you will need security for a business or form object, we recommend that you create security names for them and assign them at the appropriate steps in the wizards. It is much easier to do this now than to add it after the objects are created.

To add security names, click on the Security... check box in the Project tab of the Application Builder. If security is already configured, a form similar to **Figure 3** will be displayed, allowing you to add/edit/delete security names.

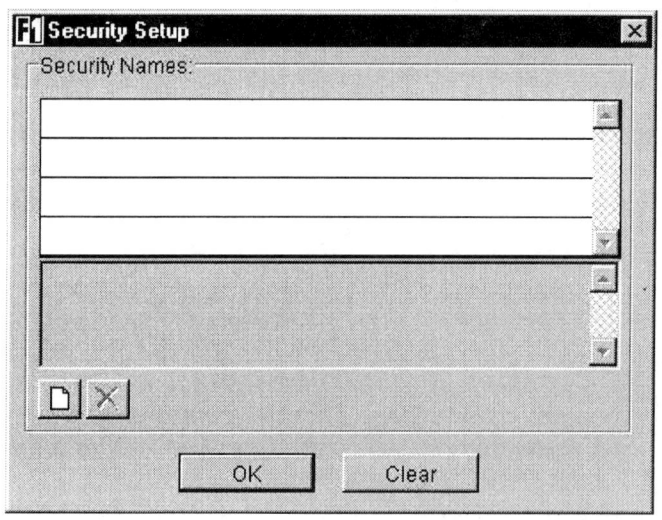

Figure 3. This form is used to add/edit/delete security names.

It is not necessary to add all of your security names at this point. You can always come back to this screen by clicking on the Security... check box on the Project tab of the Application Builder. You should, however, add the appropriate security names before creating business objects and form objects. **Figure 4** shows the Security Names screen with our four security names filled in.

Now that we have security names, we can start creating business objects.

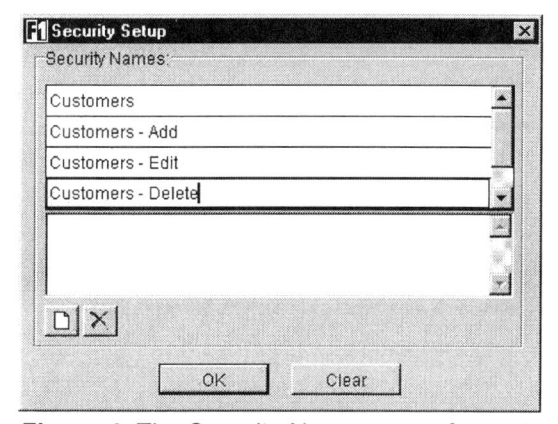

Figure 4. The Security Names setup form with some security names added.

Security in business objects

Using security names in your business objects allows you to control which users are allowed to add, edit and delete records. As we stated earlier, even if you don't think you will need this level of security, we recommend that you add the names and assign them to the business object properties anyway. If your security requirements change, you will not have to recompile the application.

You cannot use the Multiple Business Object wizard if you want to assign security names. The third step of the Single Business Object wizard is where the security names are assigned; this step is shown in **Figure 5**. Notice that there are four combo boxes available, one for each of our security names.

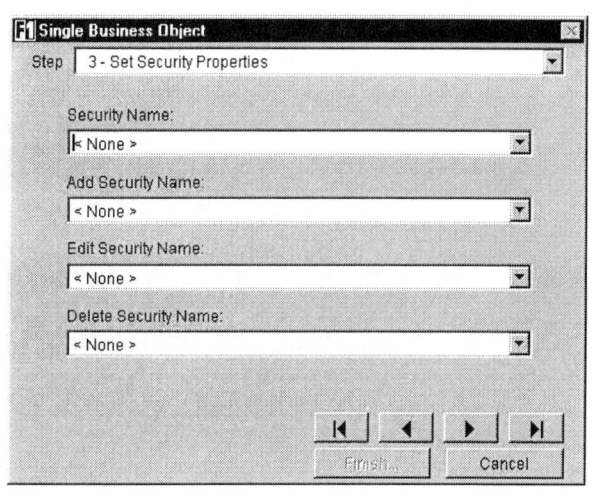

Figure 5. Step 3 of the Single Business Object wizard, where security names are specified.

Fill in each of the combo boxes with the appropriate security name so that the form looks similar to **Figure 6**.

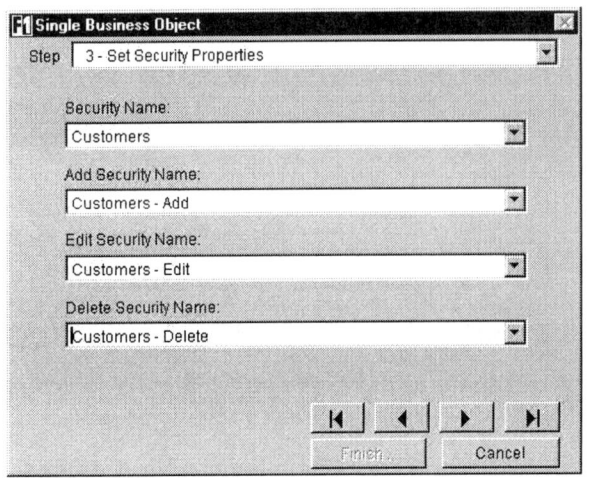

Figure 6. Step 3 of the Single Business Object wizard with security names filled in.

As you will see in a later section, this wizard places these security names in the appropriate properties of the business object. In a later step of the security setup process, you will create group names, assign these security names to groups, and then assign an access level to the security names. It may seem complicated now, but it really isn't that difficult.

> At this time, the Security Name property (the first combo box in Step 3 of the wizard) is not used by the framework. This property may be used by the developer for custom security features, if desired.

Menu items security

Menu security names are specified when you create the form objects. They are used to control which users can gain access to the forms. For example, with our customer's form we may not want a particular group of users to see any of the data in the form. You can assign *No Access* rights to the security name, and the menu option for the form will not display on the menu.

Make sure you have the appropriate security name added to the Security Name table before running the Standard Presentation Object Form wizard. Again, if you want to assign security names, you cannot use the Multiple Presentation Object Form wizard.

The third step of the Standard Presentation Object Form wizard is where the security name is assigned. **Figure 7** shows this step of the wizard.

Assign the appropriate security name in the Security Name combo box. This will assign the security name in the appropriate locations of the menu object. We will look at this in more detail in a later section.

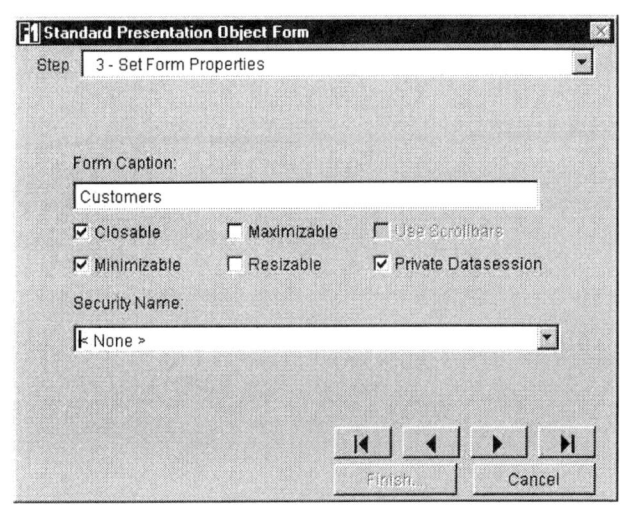

Figure 7. Step 3 of the Standard Presentation Object Form wizard, where the security name is specified.

Child form security

If you will be using child forms, you can control which users will have access to these forms as well. The Parent and Child Form wizard allows you to assign a security name to the form. Step 6 of the wizard, shown in **Figure 8**, shows where the security name is assigned to the child form.

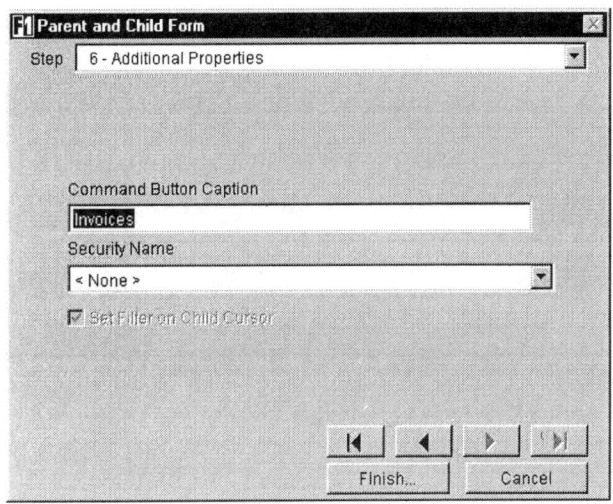

Figure 8. Step 6 of the Parent and Child Form wizard, where the security name is specified.

Assign the appropriate security name in the Security Name combo box. This will assign the security name to the appropriate property of the child button object. We will look at this in more detail in a later section.

Implementing security after creating the objects

It is possible to add security to an application that is completed or partially completed. For the business and form objects that have already been created, you must manually fill in the appropriate class properties with security names. In the case of menu security, you must add some code to the appropriate menu items.

Turning on security

You will need to turn on the security features for the project. This process is the same as described in "Turning on security" in the "Implementing security from the beginning" section earlier in this chapter.

Adding security names

Security names must be added to the Security Name table. This process is the same as described in "Adding security names" in the "Implementing security from the beginning" section earlier in this chapter.

Business objects security properties

Business objects have four properties that are used to control security. You will need to fill in these properties manually to implement security at the business object level. **Table 2** describes these properties.

Table 2. Security properties of the business object.

Property name	Purpose
cAddSecurity	Controls who is allowed to add records via the business object.
cDeleteSecurity	Controls who is allowed to delete records via the business object.
cEditSecurity	Controls who is allowed to edit records via the business object.
cSecurityName	The framework does not use this property. The developer may use it for custom security features.

Menu security

The VFE framework has the capability to treat menu options as objects. You do this by adding code to the menu option's procedure code, which can be accessed via VFP's Menu Designer. If you have a menu option that launches a form without security, the option's procedure code will look similar to this:

```
This.oApplication.DoForm("CustomersForm")
```

If you want to add security to this menu option, you will have to add the following code:

```
PROCEDURE Init
  LPARAMETERS ;
      tnBarNumber, ;
      tcPopupName

  This.cSecurityName = "Customers"
  DODEFAULT(tnBarNumber, tcPopupName)
ENDPROC
PROCEDURE Click
  This.oApplication.DoForm("CustomersForm")
ENDPROC
```

Obviously, you will substitute your security name for the security name property and your form class name for the parameter in the DoForm() method call.

Child form security

The Parent and Child Form wizard places a button on the parent form that is used to gain access to the child form. This button has a security property that is used to control access to the child form. You will have to modify the button and add the appropriate security name to the cSecurityName property.

Field-level security

The framework allows you to control access at the field level as well. If you have some fields in a table that contain sensitive data that some people should not be allowed to change or even see, you can use field-level security to control this.

Let's say, for example, you have a Credit Limit field in your Customers table. This field should be read-only for everyone except members of the Credit department. To implement this security, you would first add a security name (Credit Limit) to the Security Name table. Then you must specify that security name in the Security Name property of the field definition in the DBCX Explorer. **Figure 9** shows this property.

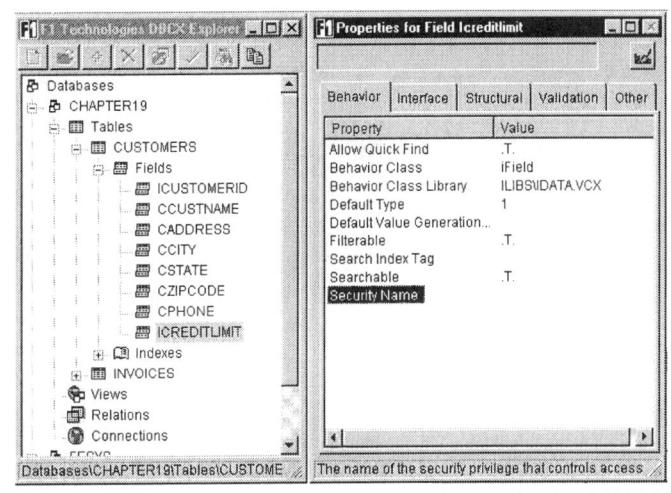

Figure 9. The field Security Name property in the DBCX Explorer.

To fill in this property, click on the Builder button in the upper right-hand corner of the properties window. In the form that appears, shown in **Figure 10**, enter the security name in the Security Name combo box.

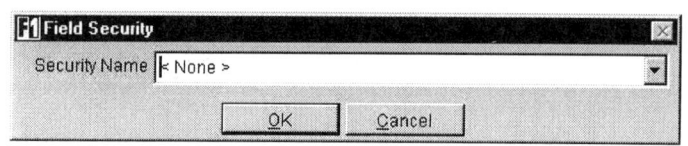

Figure 10. The Field Security builder form for specifying the field's Security Name property.

Creating security groups

The next step in the security setup process is to create the security groups. Security groups are the logical grouping of users of the application. The grouping of users should be determined by what they will be allowed to do and see. For example, members of the Customer Service department should be able to see and look up invoice information, but not add new invoices or change the Credit Limit field in the Customers table. Members of the Credit department should not be able to add or delete customers, but they should be allowed to modify the Credit Limit field. You would create a different group name for each group of users.

Creating group names

To create group names, you must run the application. The first time you run the application after turning on security, you will be prompted with a message similar to the one shown in **Figure 11**.

Figure 11. The message box that's displayed the first time an application is run after turning on security.

Click Yes here to allow the application to create the Security tables in the locations specified in the Security Setup options that were defined when you configured security for the application. You will then be presented with the Security form that will be used to manage and maintain the security features for the application. This form is shown in **Figure 12**.

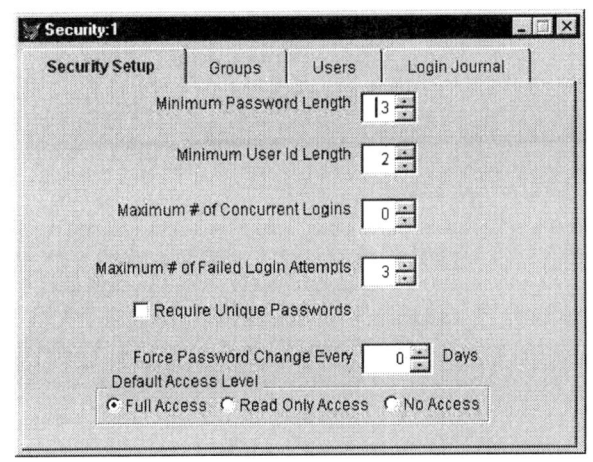

Figure 12. The Security Setup tab of the Security form, which is displayed when running an application for the first time after turning on security.

The first tab of the Security form allows you to change the security setup options that were set when security was first configured. The second tab is used for creating user groups and assigning security names and access rights. The third tab is used for creating new users, and the fourth tab displays the login journal.

The first thing you will need to do at this point is set yourself up as a user. We will discuss all of the options for setting up users in a later section of this chapter. For now, click on the Users tab and enter your name for the user ID. Enter and confirm your password, and make sure the System Administrator check box is checked. Be sure to save this record by clicking on the Save button on the toolbar.

Now you are ready to set up user groups. Click on the Groups tab of the Security form; the screen will look like **Figure 13**.

Figure 13. The Groups tab of the Security form.

Now you can add your group names and an optional description for each. Once you've added your group names, you're ready to assign security names and access rights to the groups.

Assigning security names and access rights to groups

The next step in the security setup process is to assign security names to your user groups and assign access rights. Continuing with our example, we will assign security names and access rights to our Customer Service group. Members of this group will be allowed to view invoices but not add, edit or delete. They also will be able to see the Credit Limit field but won't be allowed to change its value.

To accomplish this, first locate the Customer Service group on the Groups tab of the Security form, and then click on the Select Rights button. A form similar to **Figure 14** will be displayed.

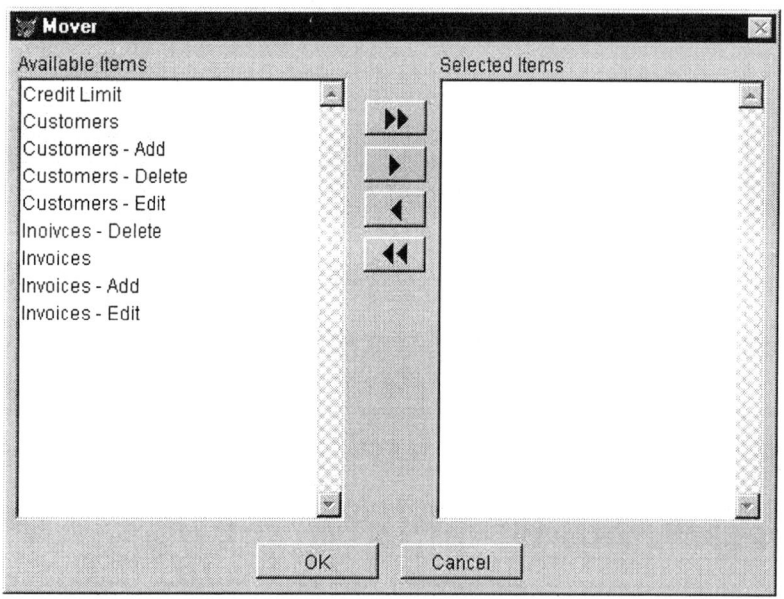

Figure 14. The Mover form used to assign security names to a security group.

This Mover form allows you to assign or remove security names for the current group. Move the security names to the Selected Items list by clicking on the double right arrow button. Then click on the OK button to save this list of assignments.

It is not necessary to assign all security names to the group. Any security name that is not assigned to the group will inherit the default access level defined on the Security Setup tab. We prefer to add all names to the groups and specify access to each name for each group.

After you've assigned security names, the Groups tab of the form will look similar to **Figure 15**.

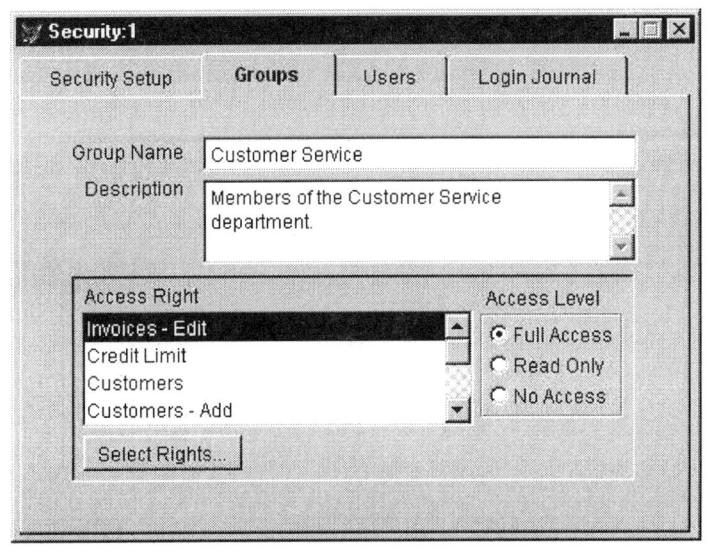

Figure 15. The Groups tab after assigning security names.

Now we need to scroll through this list of security names and assign the appropriate access level for each. The access level will default to the default access level defined in the Security Setup tab of this form. In our example, we want to assign the access levels shown in **Table 3**.

Table 3. Security name access levels for the Customer Service department.

Security name	Access level
Credit Limit	Read Only
Customers	Full Access
Customers – Add	Full Access
Customers – Delete	Full Access
Customers – Edit	Full Access
Invoices	Full Access (This will allow the users access to the form.)
Invoices – Add	No Access (This will disable the New toolbar button.)
Invoices – Delete	No Access (This will disable the Delete toolbar button.)
Invoices – Edit	No Access (This will disable all controls on the Invoices form.)

If you assign the Read Only access level to security names that are used in menu options, the menu will be displayed but not selectable. If you assign No Access to these security names, the menu options will not display.

After assigning these access levels to the appropriate security names, you must click the Save button to save these assignments. We will also assign access rights to our Credit department. Members of this group are not allowed to add or delete customers. They are allowed to edit all customer fields, including the Credit Limit field. They also are allowed to add, edit and delete invoices. **Table 4** shows the appropriate access levels to accomplish this.

Table 4. Access levels assigned for the Credit department.

Security name	Access level
Credit Limit	Full Access
Customers	Full Access
Customers – Add	No Access
Customers – Delete	No Access
Customers – Edit	No Access
Invoices	Full Access
Invoices – Add	Full Access
Invoices – Delete	Full Access
Invoices – Edit	Full Access

Creating users

Now you need to add the users to the Users table and assign them to a security group. It is not necessary to create security names and user groups and then assign each user to a security group. If all you want is a login screen to control who can run the program, turning on security and setting up users is all that is required. The security names and user groups are there to give you more security control if desired.

Figure 16 shows the Users tab of the Security form. This is where you add the users of the application and optionally assign them to a group.

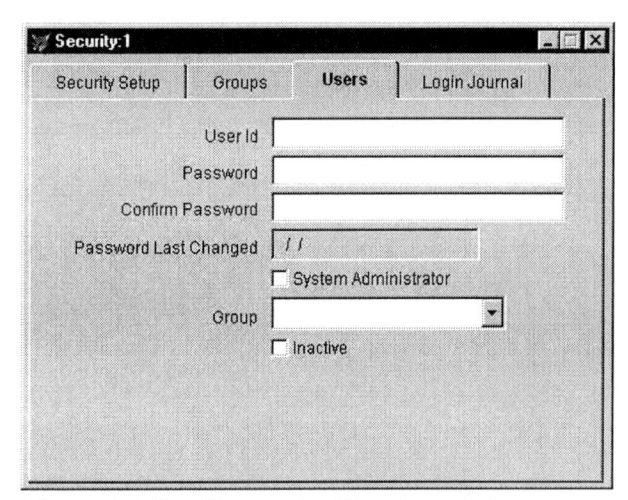

Figure 16. The Users tab of the Security form.

Fill in the User ID and Password fields, and then confirm the password (both are case-sensitive). The application should have at least one person labeled as System Administrator. System administrators can log into the application multiple times regardless of the Maximum Concurrent Login setting on the Security Setup page. Also, system administrators are the only people who can access the Security screen.

If the user is going to be a member of a user group, select the group from the Group combo box. Click on the Inactive check box if you want to disallow this user access to the system without deleting the user record.

There are a few other things you should know about user IDs. VFE's security system, by default, will use the WNetGetUser API call to get the network user name. This user name will be forced to uppercase and automatically displayed in the User ID text box on the login form. With this in mind, you should use the network user IDs for the users of the application. You should also enter them in uppercase. This way, the security system will automatically fill in the user ID, and the user will just need to enter a password.

If you do not want the user ID to be automatically filled in, there is a property of the security object that controls this. The property name is lGetUserNameFromOS; its default value is True. You can change it in the oSecurity object found in ISECURE.VCX if you want all of your applications to behave in this way, or you can make an application-level subclass of the security object and change this property for the current application.

Security maintenance

In addition to modifying Security Setup options, adding and editing groups, security name assignments and access levels, and editing/adding users, you will also need to use the Login Journal tab. The security system will automatically record when each user logs into the application and when they exit the system. One purpose of this is to manage the concurrent logins for the user. However, there will be times when a user will not exit the application normally—this may be due to a power failure, system lockup or (heaven forbid) an error in the application.

When this happens, the login record for the user will not be cleared from the login journal. Once the user reaches the maximum number of concurrent logins, he or she will not be allowed to log into the application. If this happens, a system administrator will have to log in and go to the Login Journal tab of the Security form and manually clear the logins. The Login Journal tab is shown in **Figure 17**.

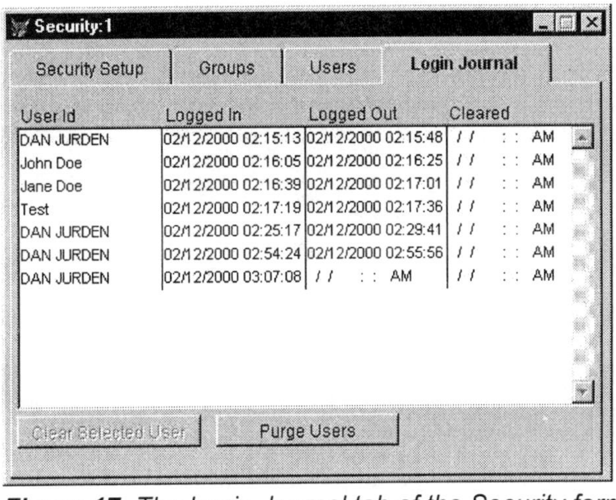

Figure 17. The Login Journal tab of the Security form.

If the user exits the program normally, there will be an entry in the Logged Out column. If the user is currently logged in or did not exit the program in the normal manner, the Logged Out column will be empty, as in the last row of Figure 17. If that login record needs to be cleared, select that row and click on the Clear Selected User button. This will place the date and time the record was cleared in the Cleared column. That user will no longer be considered logged into the application.

If you want to delete all records in the login journal that were successfully logged out or manually cleared, click on the Purge Users button. All login records, except for the ones currently logged in, will be deleted from the list.

Summary

The security system in a VFE application can range from a simple login screen to a complex system that grants different access rights to different users. Once the developer understands how to set up the security features in the framework and configure the security options, it is not that difficult to do.

It is much easier to plan your security as you are building the application, because VFE's wizards prompt you for the security names and place them in the appropriate properties or add the required code. However, security can also be added during or after development of the application. It is a bit more difficult and time-consuming to do it this way, but it's not impossible.

Now that you have a better understanding of the features and implementations of VFE's security, give it a try!

Chapter 18
Outputting Data

The main purpose of most business applications is to collect data and produce information. The most common way of returning the information is in the form of reports. The data might also need to be inserted into a spreadsheet or other format, which would allow further analysis by the user to produce the required information. In this chapter, we'll take a look at how to accomplish all of this.

Visual FoxExpress allows developers to produce information via its output objects. Output objects can be used to develop reports or export data into several different file formats. Output objects are a very powerful component of VFE and are very easy to implement. VFE provides wizards to guide the developer through the process of creating report output and export output classes. This chapter will give you an introduction to creating and using the output objects in VFE.

In this chapter we assume that you already know how to manipulate report files using VFP's Report Designer; this includes grouping, subtotals and so forth. We also assume that you know how to create views and VFE cursor, data environment and business object classes.

It is worth noting here that the VFE report output class and the wizards included are not intended to be an end-user report creation tool.

Report output class

The Report Output Class wizard consists of 10 steps. After completing the 10 steps of the wizard, you will have a report output class and a VFP report file (FRX/FRT). The output object wizards only work with a single cursor; the actual output object classes can work with multiple tables or views, but you have to add the code to create the join conditions by hand in the GetFrom() method. The classes also support returning a UNION clause from the GetUnion() method, as well as other additional SQL options not exposed by the wizard. Even though these features are available in virtually all cases, the easiest way to create reports for a VFE application is to design a view that includes the data you want before creating the report. If the view is not a view for which you have already created cursor, data environment and business object classes, you will also need to create these classes before creating a report. Also, if you want to apply security to the report—only certain people can run it—you will need to add the appropriate security name to the Security Name table (see Chapter 17, "VFE Security").

We're going to use VFE's sample application to create a report. This process will show the 10 steps of the wizard and the resulting output. The report will print a list of products grouped by category and provide a count of the number of products per category. To do this, we first need to create a view to join the Products table and the Category table and select the desired fields. **Figure 1** shows the view in the View Designer. *Note that the view is sorted by Category Name, then Product Name.*

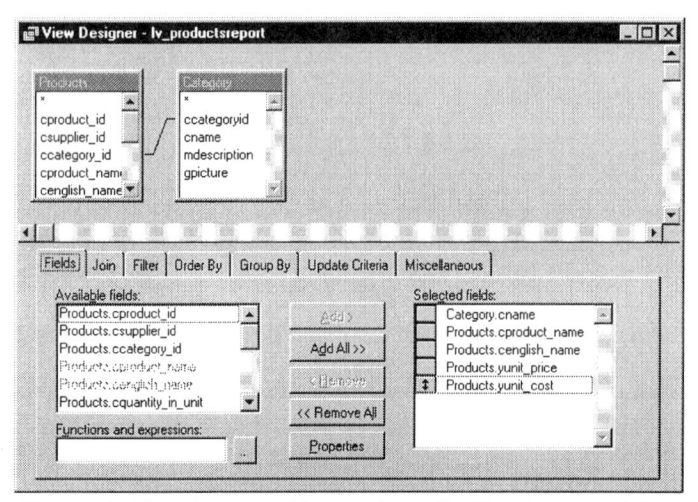

Figure 1. The view used to combine the Products and Category tables for the report.

If you are going to have grouping in your report, it is best to have the fields that are being grouped selected first in the view, and also to sort the view on those fields. After creating the view, create a cursor, data environment and business object based on the view. Now we are ready to create the report class.

In VFE's Application Builder, select the Classes tab then the Output Objects group. Then click on the New Object button. We are creating a report here, so select the Report Output Class wizard. This launches VFE's Report Output Class wizard, which will guide us through the 10 steps of creating the class. The first step is to select the business object the report is to use to get its data. This step is shown in **Figure 2**.

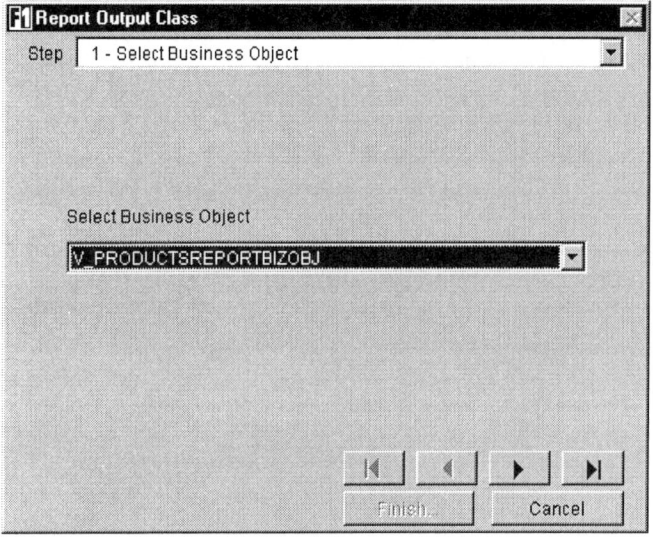

Figure 2. Step 1 of the Report Output Class wizard—selecting the business object.

Select the appropriate business object, and then click the Next button. The second step is to select the fields you want to include in the report. In this case, we want all of them. **Figure 3** shows this step.

Select all of the available fields so that they all appear in the Selected Fields list, and then click on the Next button. The third step is to specify the order for the report; this is shown in **Figure 4**.

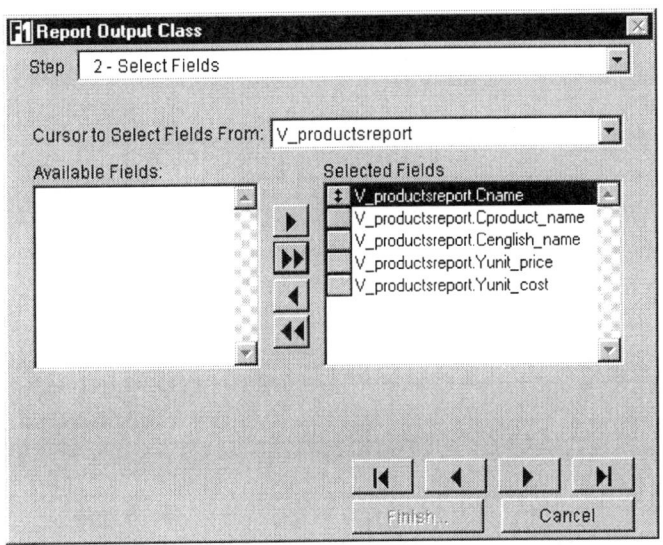

Figure 3. Step 2 of the Report Output Class wizard—selecting the fields.

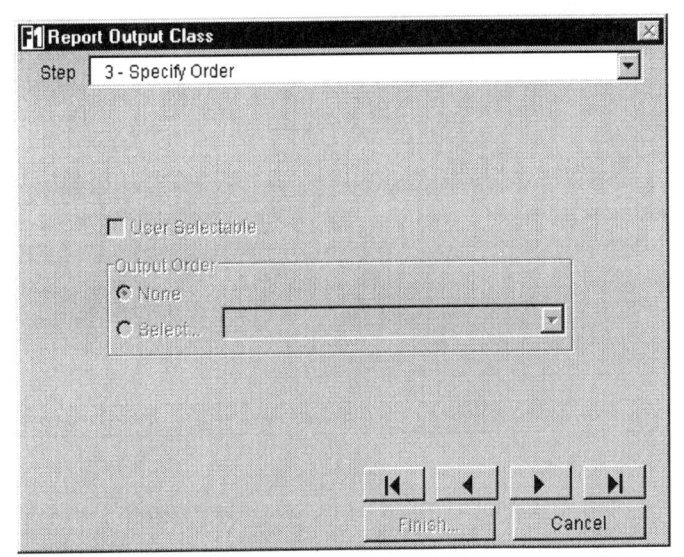

Figure 4. Step 3 of the Report Output Class wizard—specifying the order.

The controls on this step are not available because we have no indexes built on the view. If we had one or more indexes built, we would use this step to select the order and, using the User Selectable check box, specify whether the user will be allowed to select an order when they print the report. Be careful here. If you are grouping the report on a field or fields, the data must be sorted on those fields. If the user is allowed to change the sorting order on this type of report, it could give very different results!

Because we have no indexes in this view, click on the Next button. The fourth step in the wizard is to set your grouping options and summary options; this is shown in **Figure 5**.

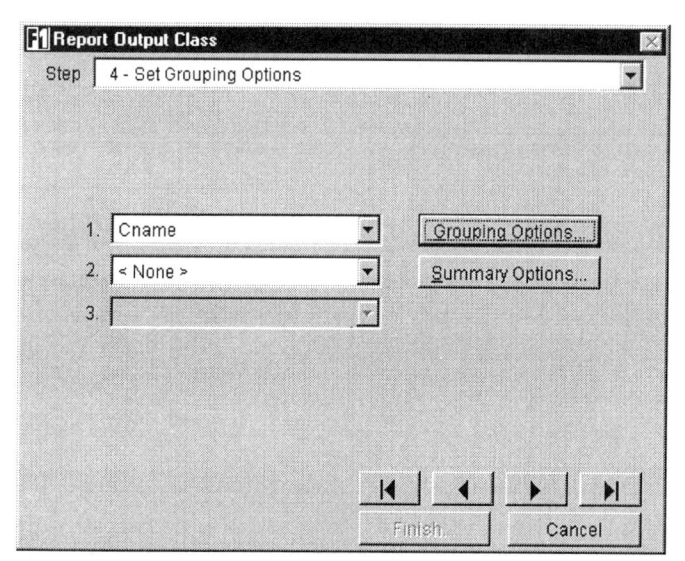

Figure 5. Step 4 of the Report Output Class wizard—setting grouping and summary options.

For our report, we want the products to be grouped by category name. In this step we need to select the cName field for the first field. This step of the wizard has two buttons: Grouping Options and Summary Options. The Grouping Options button allows us to specify the grouping intervals for the group. This tells the report how to break the records into groups. The options are to use the entire field value, the first character, the first two characters and so on, up to the first five characters of the field. If you choose the first two characters option, the report will start a new group anytime the characters in the first two positions of the field change. In our case we want to use the entire field. The Grouping Intervals dialog is shown in **Figure 6**.

Figure 7 shows the Summary Options dialog box. This dialog allows us to provide summary calculations for the items in the group. Because our report requirements want a count of products per category, we need to place a check mark in the Count column for one of the fields in the report. Because we are just counting and not summing or averaging, it does not make any difference which field is selected.

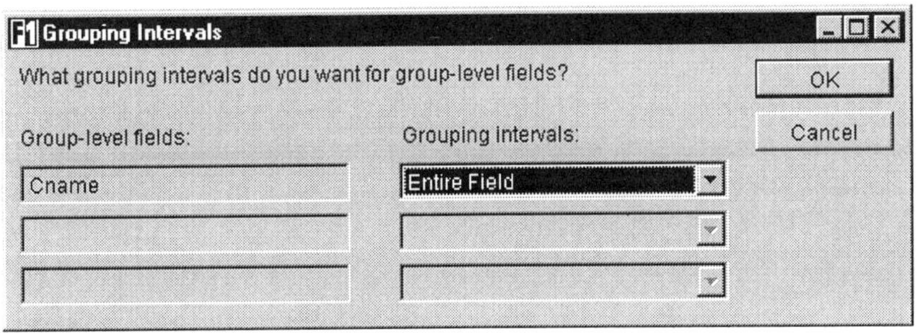

Figure 6. The Grouping Intervals dialog box.

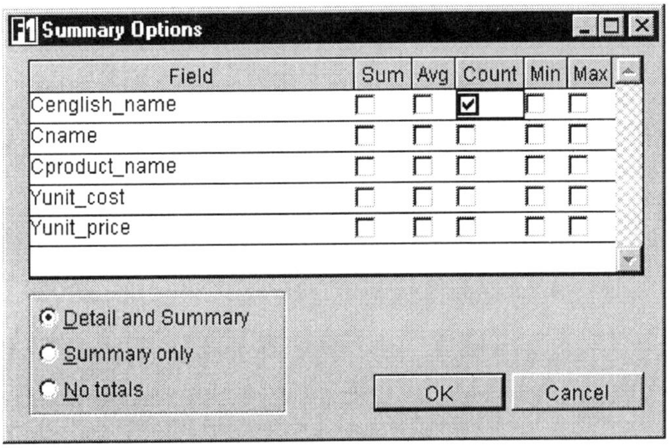

Figure 7. The Summary Options dialog box.

At the bottom of the Summary Options dialog box, we have more options to control the summary calculations. These are Detail and Summary, Summary only and No totals. The Detail and Summary option will cause the wizard to put fields in the group footer band and in the report footer band showing group totals and report totals. The Summary only option will put fields only in the report footer band to show report totals. The No totals option will not display the summary calculations on the report.

At this point you might be asking, "Why wouldn't I want to display the summary calculations?" You may need the value to do some other calculations on the report but not necessarily need to display the value. The wizard will create the report variable that holds the values. You can then modify the report in the Report Designer to use the values as needed.

For our report we want Detail and Summary. Make sure it is selected, and then click the OK button. Click on the Next button to move on to Step 5 of the wizard.

This step, shown in **Figure 8**, allows you to set output options for the report. This includes setting the report title, the category and the query form, specifying search options, and assigning a security name to the report class.

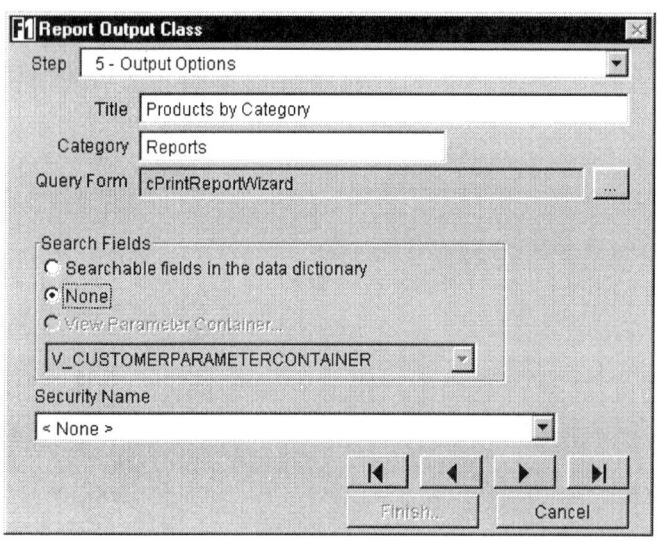

Figure 8. Step 5 of the Report Output Class wizard—setting the output options.

The first option to set here is the report title. This is used in two different places: It is placed on the report as the report title, and it is displayed in the report list in the application where the user selects the reports. This will be discussed in more detail in a later section. The title for our report is "Products by Category."

The second text box is where you specify the category. The report list that is presented to the user for report selection uses the tree view control. The report titles are placed into groups or nodes in the tree view. This option allows you to specify in which category VFE should place this report title.

The next option allows you to indicate which query form you want to use to allow users to set report options at run time. You can create a custom class for this or use the one provided by VFE. In this case we are using the default wizard from VFE.

The fourth option allows you to specify how the user is going to select records to print. There are three choices here. The first is to allow the user to set filter conditions on any field that is marked as searchable in the data dictionary—the VFE wizard will display a form allowing the user to set the filter criteria if this option is selected. The second option is to prevent the user from setting any filter conditions. The third option is to use a view parameter container—this is used if the report is based on a parameterized view. VFE will display a view parameter container, created by you, to allow the user to enter the criteria for selecting records. For our report we do not want the user to set any filter criteria, so select None.

The last option is to select a security name. This allows you to control who has access to print the report. If the user is not assigned to a group that has the appropriate access to the security name assigned to the report, the report name will not be displayed in the tree view control for selecting reports. For this report we have no security, so leave this set to <None>.

After setting these options, click on the Next button to move on to Step 6 of the wizard, which is shown in **Figure 9**. This step lets us select which style we want our report to use. The wizard is going to use VFP's Report Wizard to actually create the report files. VFP's Report

Wizard has several styles to choose from; if you're not familiar with these styles, run VFP's Report Wizard and investigate the differences among them. For our report we are going to use the Executive style.

After selecting the desired report style, click on the Next button to move on to Step 7. This step allows you to select the report layout; again, this information is going to be passed on to VFP's wizard to be used in creating the report file. **Figure 10** shows this step.

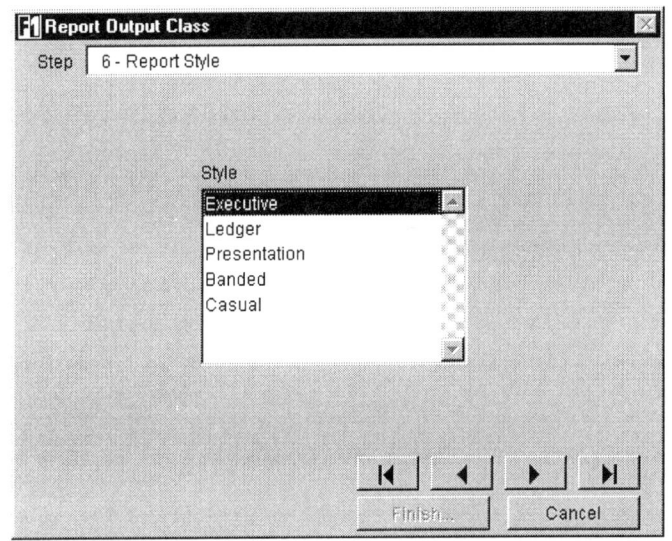

Figure 9. Step 6 of the Report Output Class wizard—selecting the report style.

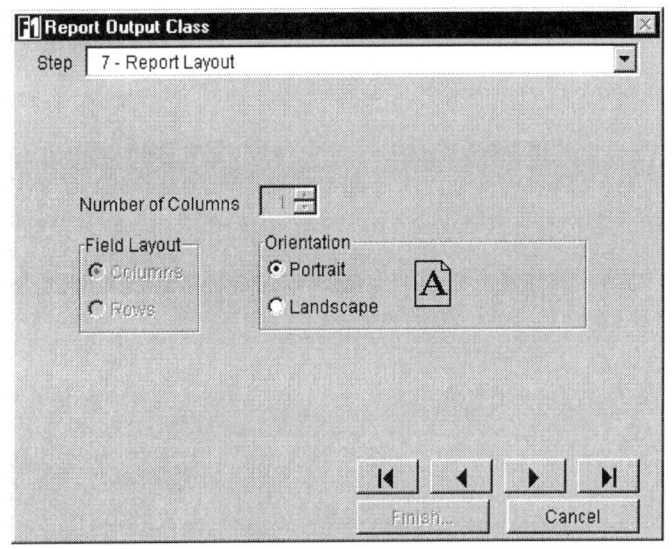

Figure 10. Step 7 of the Report Output Class wizard—selecting the report layout.

In this step we can select the number of columns, the field layout (columns or rows) and the orientation (portrait or landscape). For our report we are going to accept the defaults. Now click on the Next button to move on to Step 8.

This step, shown in **Figure 11**, allows you to specify where VFE should place the table that holds the report entries. This table is used to build the tree view that is displayed to the users for report selection.

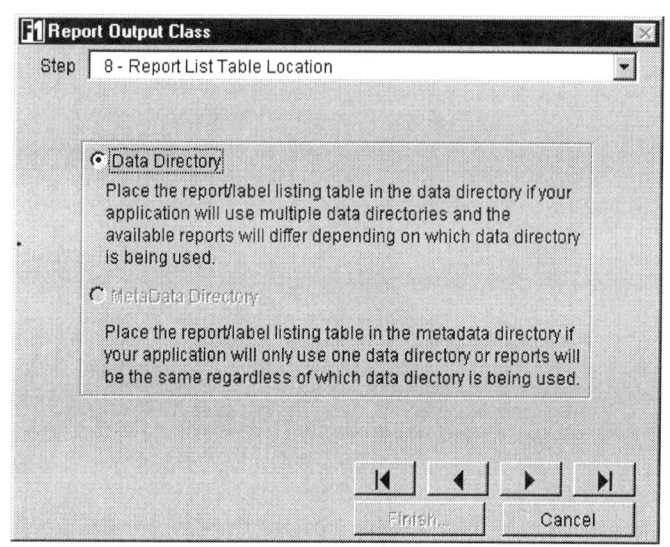

Figure 11. Step 8 of the Report Output Class wizard—selecting the report list table location.

Here our only choice is the data directory because the table already exists. If this were the first report, we would be able to choose the location. Click on the Next button to move on to Step 9. This step, shown in **Figure 12**, allows you to name the report file that the wizard is going to create. It also allows you to specify whether you want the report file to be excluded from the project. If you exclude the report from the project, you will need to distribute the report files. If you include the report, it will be compiled into the EXE or APP, so the report files will not need to be distributed.

Our preference is to exclude the report from the project. This way, if the user wants the report to be modified, you do not have to recompile the EXE or APP in order to send them the updated report. You can just modify the report and send them the updated FRX/FRT files.

After specifying the file name, click on the Next button to move on to the tenth, and last, step in the wizard. This step allows you to name the class and specify the visual class library where it should be stored; it's shown in **Figure 13**.

Select the default values here and click on the Finish button. Now we are ready to test our report.

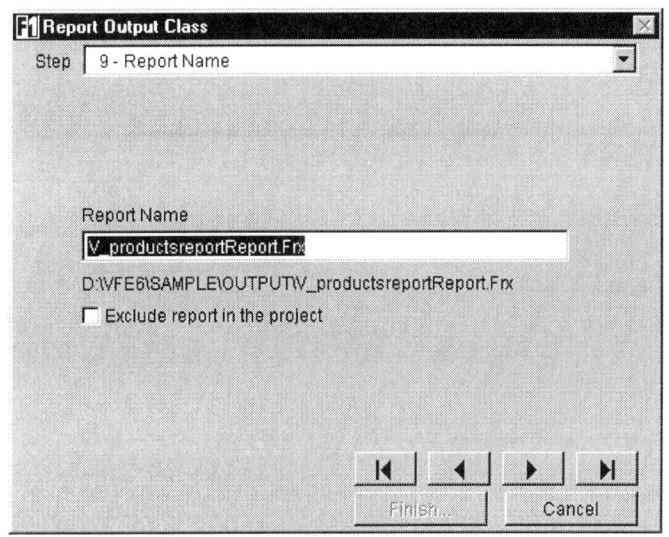

Figure 12. Step 9 of the Report Output Class wizard—selecting a report file name.

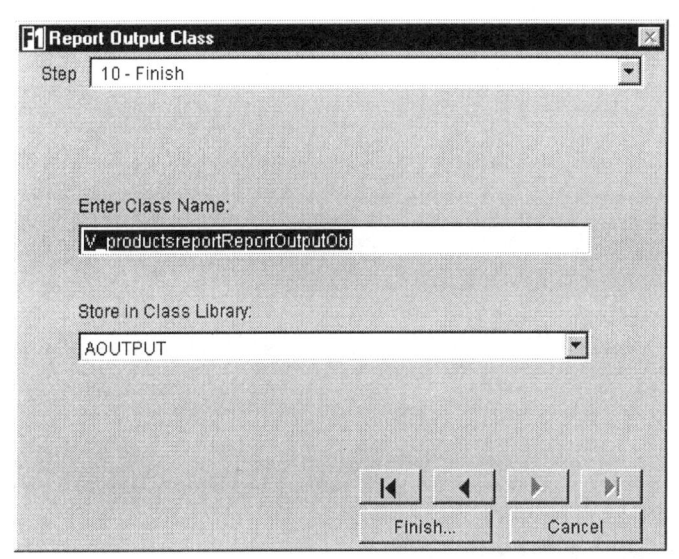

Figure 13. Step 10 of the Report Output Class wizard—specifying the class name and library.

Testing and modifying reports

To test our report and see what the wizard created, we need to run the application. After starting the app and entering the user name and password, go to the File menu and select Reports & Queries, or click on the Reports button on the application switchboard form. This

240 *Creating Visual FoxPro Applications with Visual FoxExpress*

will display a form that contains the tree view control with all of the reports in the application. The form is shown in **Figure 14**.

Because we put our report title in the Reports group, click on the plus sign next to Reports to expand that node. You will then see our Products by Categories report; click on it, and then click on the Run button. VFE's end-user Report Wizard will display (see **Figure 15**).

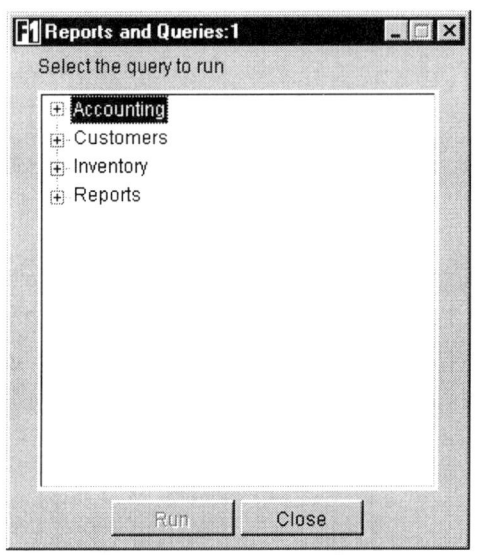

Figure 14. VFE's Reports and Queries selection form.

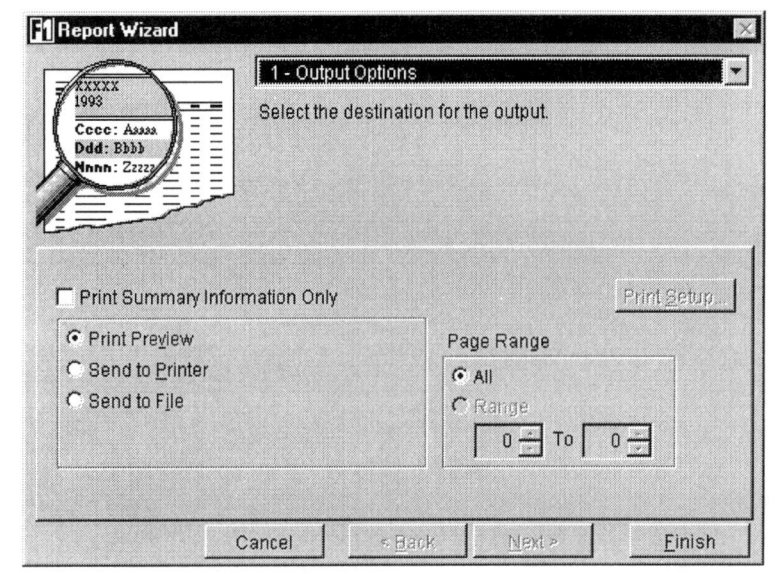

Figure 15. VFE's end-user Report Wizard.

The number of steps in the wizard will depend on what options were selected while running the 10-step Report Output Object wizard; in this case, there's only one step. Click on the Finish button to see our report—a partial view of the report is shown in **Figure 16**.

As you can see, the report needs a little polishing. We want the items and costs to appear all on one line. To accomplish this, exit the application and open the report file. Modify it in the Report Designer so it looks similar to **Figure 17**.

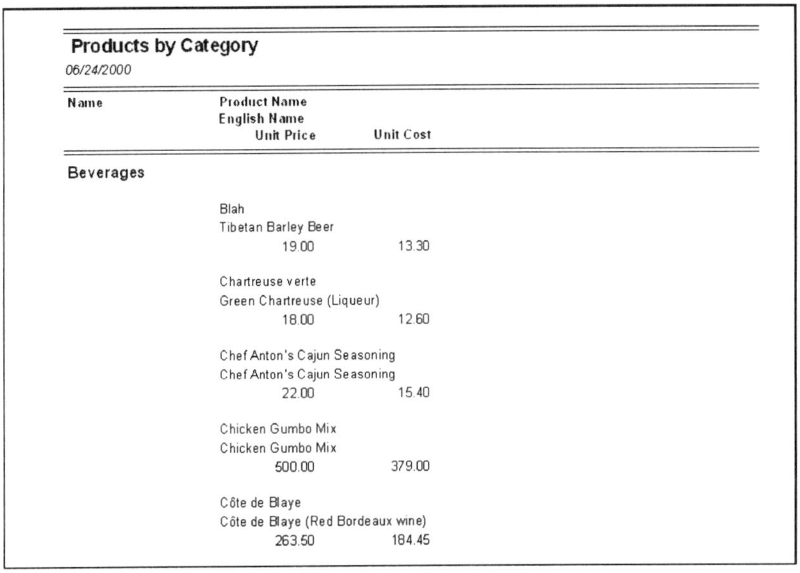

Figure 16. A partial view of the output from the Products by Category report.

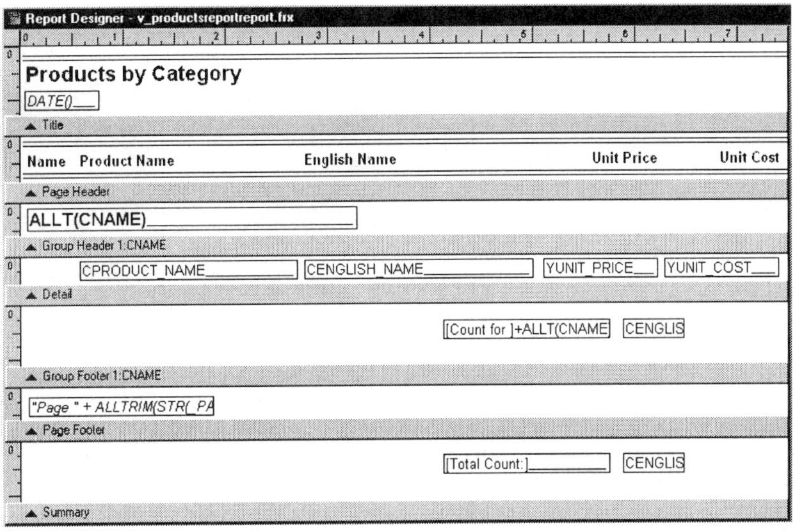

Figure 17. The modified Products by Category report in VFP's Report Designer.

Save this report and run the application again. When you run the report again, the output should look similar to what is shown in **Figure 18**.

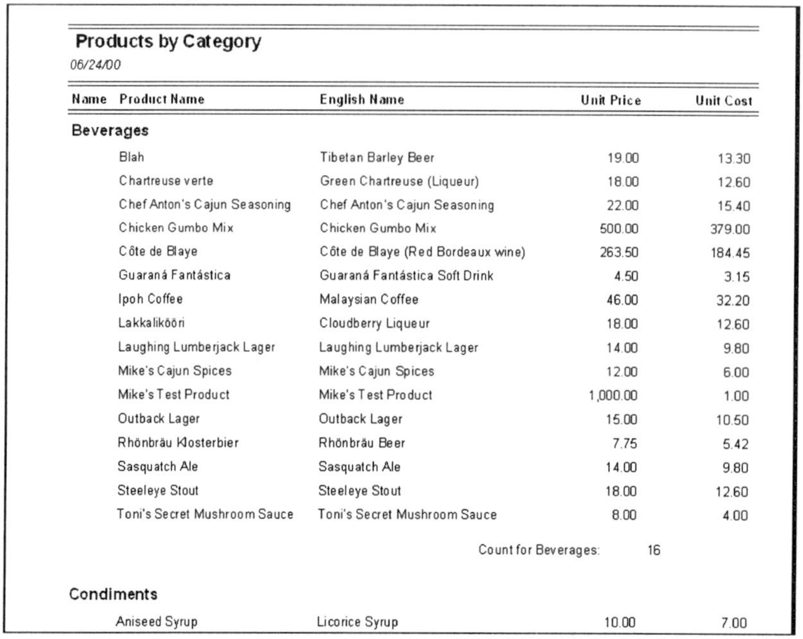

Name	Product Name	English Name	Unit Price	Unit Cost
Beverages				
	Blah	Tibetan Barley Beer	19.00	13.30
	Chartreuse verte	Green Chartreuse (Liqueur)	18.00	12.60
	Chef Anton's Cajun Seasoning	Chef Anton's Cajun Seasoning	22.00	15.40
	Chicken Gumbo Mix	Chicken Gumbo Mix	500.00	379.00
	Côte de Blaye	Côte de Blaye (Red Bordeaux wine)	263.50	184.45
	Guaraná Fantástica	Guaraná Fantástica Soft Drink	4.50	3.15
	Ipoh Coffee	Malaysian Coffee	46.00	32.20
	Lakkalikööri	Cloudberry Liqueur	18.00	12.60
	Laughing Lumberjack Lager	Laughing Lumberjack Lager	14.00	9.80
	Mike's Cajun Spices	Mike's Cajun Spices	12.00	6.00
	Mike's Test Product	Mike's Test Product	1,000.00	1.00
	Outback Lager	Outback Lager	15.00	10.50
	Rhönbräu Klosterbier	Rhönbräu Beer	7.75	5.42
	Sasquatch Ale	Sasquatch Ale	14.00	9.80
	Steeleye Stout	Steeleye Stout	18.00	12.60
	Toni's Secret Mushroom Sauce	Toni's Secret Mushroom Sauce	8.00	4.00
		Count for Beverages:	16	
Condiments				
	Aniseed Syrup	Licorice Syrup	10.00	7.00

Figure 18. The output from the modified Products by Category report.

> If you want to interactively preview your report with data while editing it in the Report Designer, you will need to do this outside of VFE's Application Manager. Issue the following commands in the command window:

```
set default to c:\vfe6\sample\data
oP = newobject('v_productsreportcursor', 'c:\vfe6\sample\libs\acursor.vcx')
oP.Open()
```

Then open the project file and edit the report. You can now preview while editing the report.

Export output class

The export output class allows you to create an output object that will export the data into one of many different file formats. With only seven steps, this wizard is a little shorter than the Report Output Class wizard. Once again, you should create a view that joins the tables and includes the fields containing the data you want to be exported. Then create VFE cursor, data environment and business objects based on the view. To demonstrate the export output class, we will use the same classes we created for the report output class.

Select the Classes tab on the Application Builder, click on the Output Classes node, and then click on the New Class button. This time we will select the Export Output Class option. This launches the Export Output Class wizard. The first step of the wizard is shown in **Figure 19**.

Select v_productsreportbizobj and click on the Next button. The second step, shown in **Figure 20**, allows you to select which fields to export.

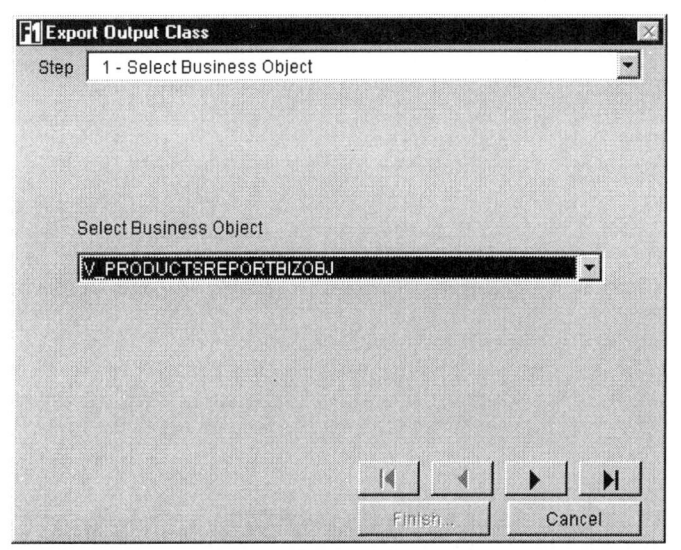

Figure 19. Step 1 of the Export Output Class wizard—selecting the business object.

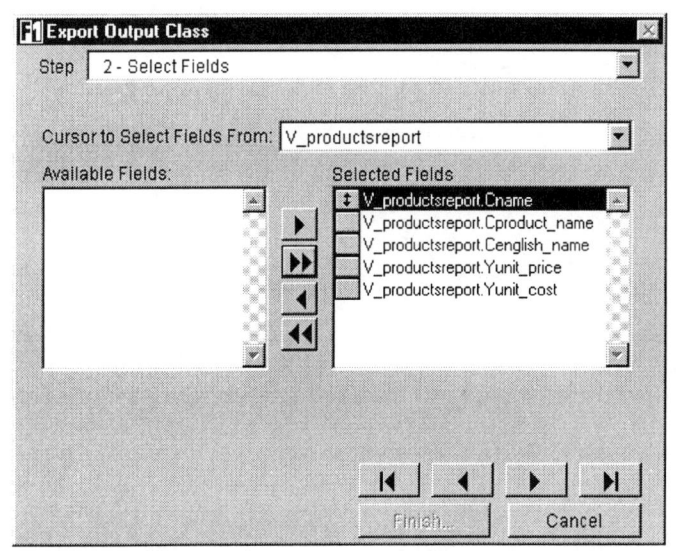

Figure 20. Step 2 of the Export Output Class wizard—selecting the fields to export.

For this export, we want all fields. Move all of the fields to the Selected Fields list, and then click on the Next button. The third step, shown in **Figure 21**, allows you to select how the records will be ordered. Because we have no indexes on our view, the options in this step are not available.

If we had one or more indexes created, we could select a default order and specify whether the user will be allowed to change the order when they actually export the data. We cannot change anything here, so click on the Next button.

The fourth step of the wizard allows us to set the output options; it's shown in **Figure 22**.

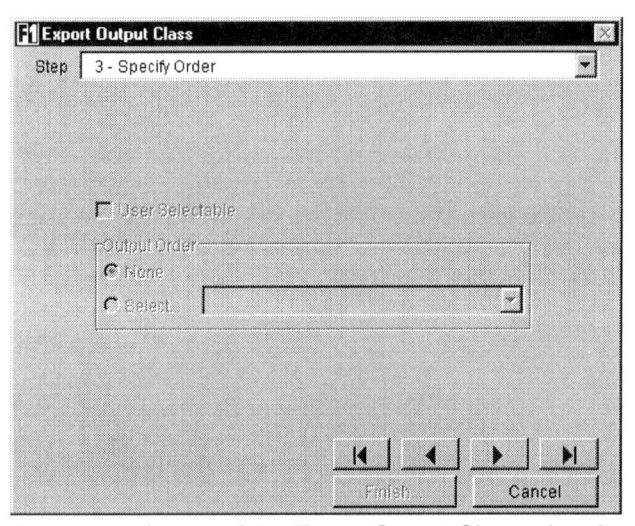

Figure 21. Step 3 of the Export Output Class wizard—specifying the order.

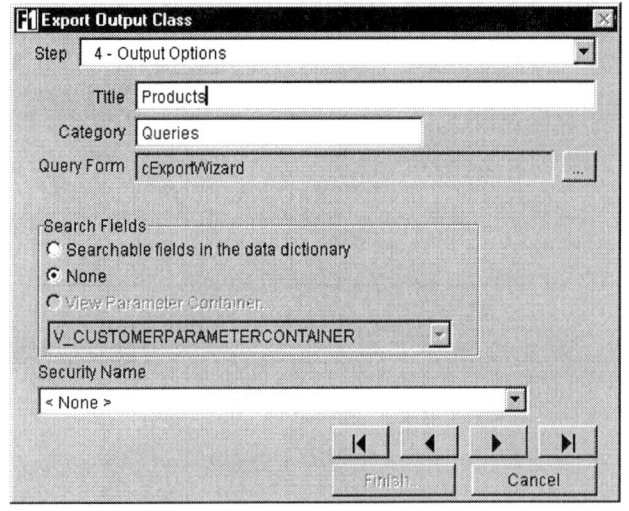

Figure 22. Step 4 of the Export Output Class wizard—setting output options.

The first option to set here is the title to be displayed in the Reports & Queries tree view control. The title for our query is "Products."

The second text box is where you specify the category. The list that is presented to the user for report selection uses the tree view control. The query titles are placed into groups or nodes in the tree view. This option allows you to specify in which category VFE should place this query title.

The next option allows you to indicate which query form you want to use to allow users to set report options. You can create a custom class for this or use the one provided by VFE. In this case we are using the default wizard from VFE.

The fourth option allows you to specify how the user is going to select records to export. There are three choices here. The first is to allow the user to set filter conditions on any field that is marked as searchable in the data dictionary—the VFE wizard will display a form allowing the user to set the filter criteria if this option is selected. The second option is to prevent the user from setting any filter conditions. The third option is to use a view parameter container—this is used if the query is based on a parameterized view. VFE will display a view parameter container, created by you, to allow the user to enter the criteria for selecting records. For our export we do not want the user to set any filter criteria, so select None.

The last option is to select a security name. This allows you to control who has access to export the data. If the user is not assigned to a group that has the appropriate access to the security name assigned to this export class, the query name will not be displayed in the tree view control for selecting queries. For this export we have no security, so leave this set to <None>.

After setting these options, click on the Next button to move on to Step 5 of the wizard, which is displayed in **Figure 23**. This step allows us to select the type of file we want to create to hold the exported data.

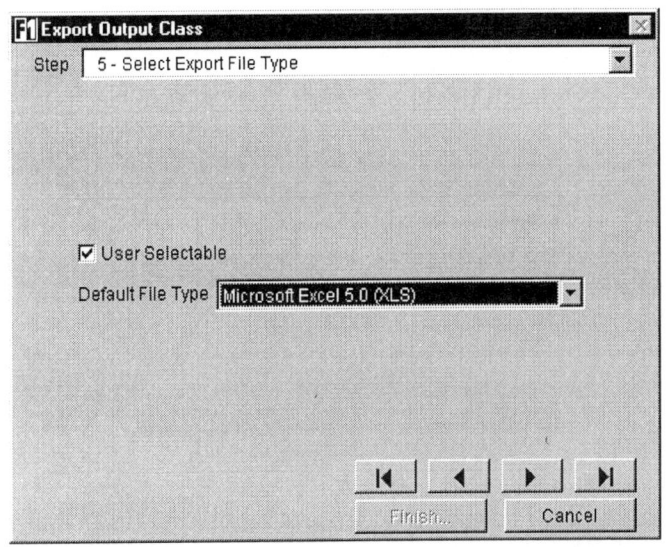

Figure 23. Step 5 of the Export Object Class wizard—selecting the export file type.

Here we want the default file type to be an Excel worksheet, but we will allow the user to select a different file type if necessary. Select Microsoft Excel 5.0 (XLS) from the combo box, and then click on the Next button to move on to Step 6 of the wizard

This step, shown in **Figure 24**, allows you to specify where VFE should place the table that holds the export/query entries. This table is used to build the tree view that is displayed to the users for report selection. This is the same table that is used for the report objects. We will discuss this table in more detail in a later section.

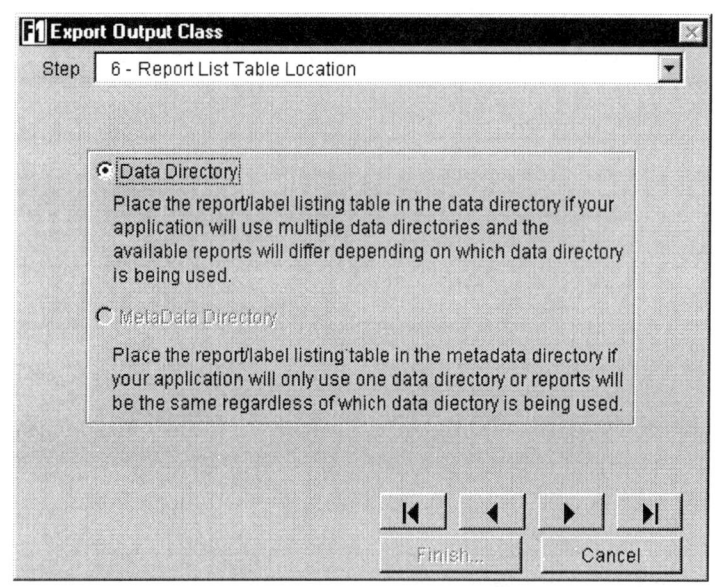

Figure 24. Step 6 of the Export Output Class wizard—selecting the report list table location.

Here our only choice is the data directory because the table already exists. If this were the first query/report object created, we would be able to choose the location. Click on the Next button to move on to the seventh, and final step. This step, shown in **Figure 25**, allows you to name the class and specify the visual class library where it should be stored. Accept the defaults here and click the Finish button.

After finishing the wizard, run the application. Go to the File menu and select Reports & Queries; you will notice a new node named Queries in the tree view. Click on the plus sign next to that node and you will see the Products option (see **Figure 26**).

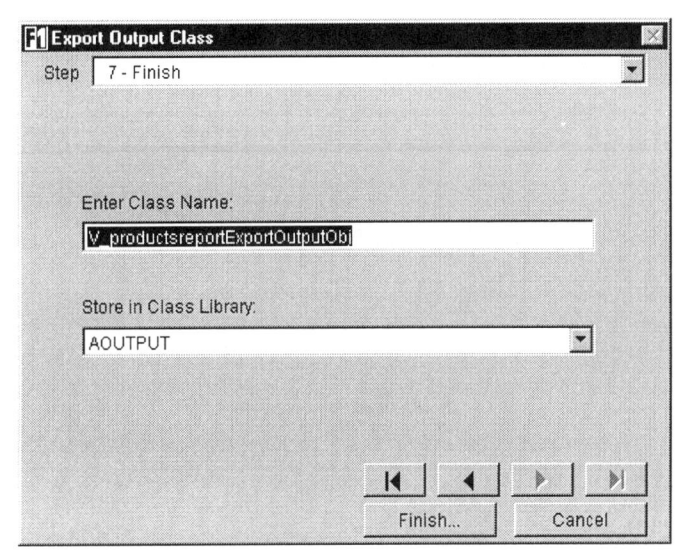

Figure 25. Step 7 of the Export Output Class wizard—specifying a class name and library.

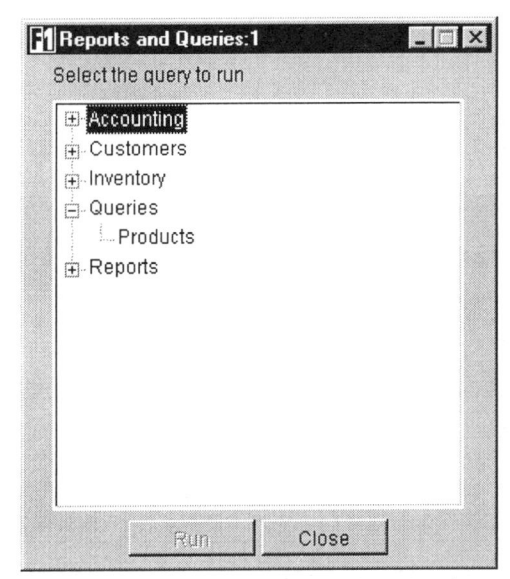

Figure 26. The Reports and Queries form showing our Export Class object in the tree view.

Select the Products entry and click on the Run button. VFE's end-user Export Query Wizard will run (see **Figure 27**).

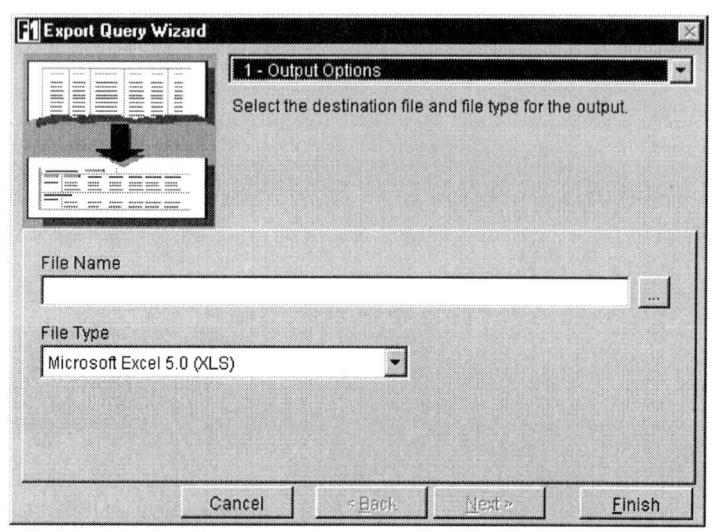

Figure 27. *VFE's end-user Export Query Wizard.*

The number of steps in this wizard will depend on the options that were selected while creating the export output class; in our case, there is only one step. The end user can select a file name and change the file type if they choose. To test this, enter a file name (including the path) in the appropriate text box and click on the Finish button. It is not necessary to include the XLS extension in the file name; the appropriate extension for the selected file type will automatically be added to the file name. **Figure 28** shows a partial listing of the Excel spreadsheet that was created.

	A	B	C	D	E
1	cname	cproduct_name	cenglish_name	yunit_price	yunit_cost
2	Beverages	Blah	Tibetan Barley Beer	19	13.3
3	Beverages	Chartreuse verte	Green Chartreuse (Liqueur)	18	12.6
4	Beverages	Chef Anton's Cajun Seasoning	Chef Anton's Cajun Seasoning	22	15.4
5	Beverages	Chicken Gumbo Mix	Chicken Gumbo Mix	500	379
6	Beverages	Côte de Blaye	Côte de Blaye (Red Bordeaux wine)	263.5	184.45
7	Beverages	Guaraná Fantástica	Guaraná Fantástica Soft Drink	4.5	3.15
8	Beverages	Ipoh Coffee	Malaysian Coffee	46	32.2
9	Beverages	Lakkalikööri	Cloudberry Liqueur	18	12.6
10	Beverages	Laughing Lumberjack Lager	Laughing Lumberjack Lager	14	9.8
11	Beverages	Mike's Cajun Spices	Mike's Cajun Spices	12	6
12	Beverages	Mike's Test Product	Mike's Test Product	1000	1
13	Beverages	Outback Lager	Outback Lager	15	10.5
14	Beverages	Rhönbräu Klosterbier	Rhönbräu Beer	7.75	5.425
15	Beverages	Sasquatch Ale	Sasquatch Ale	14	9.8
16	Beverages	Steeleye Stout	Steeleye Stout	18	12.6
17	Beverages	Toni's Secret Mushroom Sauce	Toni's Secret Mushroom Sauce	8	4
18	Condiments	Aniseed Syrup	Licorice Syrup	10	7
19	Condiments	Camembert Pierrot	Pierrot Camembert	34	23.8

Figure 28. *A partial listing of the spreadsheet that was created with the export output class.*

Controlling the tree view

The Reports and Queries selection form contains a tree view control that is populated with all of the reports and export/query objects created by the developer. The tree view control is populated from data that is stored in a table called REPOLIST.DBF. You have the opportunity to specify the location of this table when you create the first report or export object using VFE's wizards. Your choices are the data folder or the metadata folder.

If, after creating an output class, you decide to delete it, the entry in this table may not be removed. If the class is removed from the tree view control on the Classes tab of VFE's Application Builder, the entry will be deleted from the table. If the class is removed from the class library using VFP's Class Browser, the entry will not be deleted from the table. If this happens, you will have to open the table manually and delete the entry.

If you delete a report output class, the associated report files (FRX/FRT) will not be deleted from disk or removed from the project (if included). You will have to remove and delete these files as necessary.

> *If there are no records in the REPOLIST.DBF table or the REPOLIST table does not exist, the Reports & Queries option on the File menu will be disabled.*

Working with the report and export object classes

The report and export object classes have many options that are not exposed by the wizards. Also, when a developer creates a report, clients often request additional information on the report. This section describes some of the key properties and methods of the cOutputObject class, which is the parent class for the cReportOutputObject and cExportOutputObject classes. Report output objects and export objects are based on these classes, respectively.

The output objects work in one of two ways, and you should be aware of the differences when you are creating reports. If you are basing your report directly off of tables, or if you are using views and allowing the user to search on fields, the output objects build a SQL statement and execute it to get the data for a report. If you are working with a view and don't allow the user to search on any fields, or if you use view parameters to allow the user to select the data, the output objects simply use and requery the views.

SetFieldList()

This method determines the list of fields that will be included in the query. When an output object wizard is run, VFE actually inserts code into this method. VFE adds a call to the output object's AddFieldToList() method for each field that you included in the report to this method. Normally the VFE wizards simply set properties, but because the Visual Class Designer limits the length of a property value, the developers at F1 used a method to accomplish this in order to not place a limit on the number of fields to include in a report. If you wish to add a field to an existing report, you need to add a line to the SetFieldList() method like the ones generated by the wizard for the new field. Having extra fields in the SetFieldList() method won't cause the report any problems, so sometimes it's easier to simply select all of the fields and then remove the undesired fields from the report. Once the report has been finalized, extra fields should be removed from the SetFieldList() method for optimal performance.

lUseCurrentData

The lUseCurrentData property applies when the output object uses a view. The wizards set this property to indicate whether the output object should execute a SQL statement or simply use and requery a view. Although it is generally not good practice to execute a SQL statement against a view, sometimes this is a good option. If you're basing a report on a view, but you need to further control the data that's returned, you can set the lUseCurrentData property to False so that a SQL SELECT statement is executed and performed.

Executing reports from code

It is possible to create a report output object and call it from code. An example of this is attaching the code to a menu option. The code is very simple—all you need to do is create an instance of the report output object and then call the Execute() method. Here's an example:

```
Local loReport

loReport = createobject('v_productsreportoutputobj')
loReport.Execute()
```

Summary

The report and export object classes are very powerful features of a VFE application. We have just scratched the surface in this chapter. We encourage you to create a few of these classes and then examine the methods and properties of the classes that are created. There are several properties available that are not accessible via the wizards. There are also several methods that can be used to customize the classes. Have fun!

Chapter 19
Client/Server

Developing client/server applications takes n-tier development to the next level. The data is separated even further from the application—it resides on a network server and is accessed remotely over the network. Developing client/server applications is a bit different from developing with local data. However, if you have been developing with views up to this point, moving to client/server data is fairly easy.

VFE supports client/server data via remote views. Remote views are very similar to local views. The difference is that local views are views of VFP tables, whereas remote views are views of tables that are hosted by some other database. In most cases, you will need an ODBC (Open Database Connectivity) driver and configuration to get to the data. Sometimes there is more involved in developing client/server applications than accessing and modifying data. Client/server applications may need to call stored procedures (programs that reside and execute on the server). All of these things will be discussed in further detail in this chapter as we build a very simple client/server application. We'll assume that you have read the prior chapters and already know how to create a project, add a database, and create all of the required cursor, data environment, business object, presentation object and form classes. Here we will focus on the different procedures and techniques required for creating a client/server application.

Why (not) client/server?

As with most decisions we have to make as programmers, there are pros and cons to consider in deciding whether or not to develop your applications using the client/server model. There are some situations where client/server is obviously the right choice, and other situations where VFP tables will work best.

One example is if you are developing an application for a small office. In this situation, VFP tables are probably the best choice. Asking a small business to invest the money for the hardware and software required to implement a client/server system will not win you many friends, as this investment could run into several thousand dollars. Not many small businesses (or large businesses) are willing to invest that kind of money.

On the other hand, if a larger business has many potential users of the system (and they already have the hardware or can get it easily), and they need to integrate their data with their accounting software or share the data with their Web applications, client/server is probably the right choice.

Applications that use a client/server database management system such as SQL Server or Oracle have several advantages over file-based database systems. These advantages are security, reliability, speed and size restrictions. Each of these will be discussed further in following sections.

Security

One reason many companies want to develop client/server applications is because their data is more secure. Sure, we can password-protect our applications, but anybody with a little knowledge and an appropriate application (Access, Excel and so forth) can get to your table-based data.

You may also use one of the many encryption libraries to encrypt the data. The problem with this approach is that it makes the data inaccessible if it needs to be shared with other applications.

Most client/server applications have built-in security, allowing you to manage users and grant them appropriate rights to the data. Some users may be granted only read access to certain tables while having write access to others. Client/server security features are much more robust and fairly easy to manage.

Reliability (no more corrupt indexes)

How many times has this happened to you? A client calls and says that some of their data is missing. After talking to them for several minutes, you find out that while they were entering some data, the power went out in their building. As you know, with VFP tables, this almost always means corrupted index files. Now you must shut everyone down and rebuild the indexes.

Client/server software maintains indexes, but they rarely get corrupted. The main reason for this is that most client/server databases are on powerful network servers. These machines are backed up with batteries, so they rarely lose power when writing data. Also, the client machines are not connected live to the database; once the client requests the data, it is copied to the local machine. Because it's not connected to the data, if a client machine loses power, no trash can be written to indexes. In addition, the client machines do not actually process the saves. The client sends a save request to the server, along with the data to be saved, and the server actually processes the save request. This all results in more reliable data!

Speed

This is one issue that can be debated both ways. Accessing your data in VFP tables is very fast. Accessing your data in a client/server database is also very fast. There are situations where one may be better than the other. Consider the example of an application that uses VFP tables and has more than 75 users on an NT network. Most operations in the application are fairly fast. However, if some global updates need to be applied to a table or some complex queries need to be run, it really bogs down the file server and everyone complains about the speed. Upgrading this application to a client/server database that's on a dedicated server with quad processors and plenty of memory and disk space will allow the same global updates and complex queries to occur without the users even noticing a difference.

One of the primary differences between the two systems is that with VFP tables, the client machine has to fetch the data from the file server, transfer it over the network cable and then process it. In a client/server database, the client sends the request to the server, and the server processes the request and returns the results back to the client. With the data already on the server, the fetching is much faster. Most servers are multiprocessor machines with lots of memory. This makes the processing much faster as well.

Size restrictions

VFP tables are limited to 2 billion records and 2GB in size. Most systems will never have more than 2 billion records in a table, but it is realistic to exceed the 2GB size restrictions. Client/server databases have virtually no restrictions other than available disk space.

Tools used

There are a few tools that are required to create and maintain the databases used in the examples in this chapter. The examples are developed using a SQL Server 7 database management system. If you already have access to SQL Server 7, you're ready to go. If not, you may be interested in the next few paragraphs. If you are using a different client/server database management system, the examples may have to be modified slightly to work correctly.

We are actually using the Microsoft Data Engine (MSDE). This is a fully SQL Server-compatible database engine that can be used to develop desktop and shared databases. Applications built with MSDE can be distributed royalty-free. MSDE is based on SQL Server technology and is fully compatible with SQL Server 7.0. It is available free to any developer who is a registered user of any of the Visual Studio 6.0 products.

You can get more information about MSDE and download it from the MSDN Web site at http://msdn.microsoft.com/vstudio/msde/.

One problem with MSDE is that it does not come with any tools that can be used to create and maintain the databases. There are, however, several other tools that can be used. If you own Visual Studio 6, you can use Visual InterDev to create and maintain the tables. If you own Microsoft Office 2000, you can use Access 2000. If you have SQL Server, you can use the Enterprise Manager tool.

Another limitation of MSDE is that the physical database size is limited to 2GB. This is not a table limitation but rather a total database limitation. Microsoft also suggests that MSDE is optimized for 1-5 users. If the number of users exceeds five, performance may take a hit and get much slower as the number of users grows.

You can also use any of the popular commercial database modeling tools to design and maintain your databases. xCase, which is developed and marketed by Resolution Ltd., is a good choice. You can get more information about xCase from their Web site at http://www.xcase.com/. (xCase is distributed by F1 Technologies in North America. You can also find information on their Web site at http://www.f1tech.com/xcase/.)

You should also have MDAC (Microsoft Data Access Components) version 2.1 installed. This provides the latest ODBC drivers. If you do not have this installed, you can find it at http://www.microsoft.com/data/download.htm?RLD=377.

Application database

In this chapter, we will create a very simple client/server application that will demonstrate the basic concepts necessary for creating a full-fledged client/server application. This application will be a customer call log that would be used to keep track of notes about each call made to clients.

This database will only use three tables. These tables and their structures are described in **Table 1**. **Figure 1** shows the database drawing that was created using xCase.

Table 1. Table structures used in the client contact application.

Table	Field	Type	Length	Key
Customers	cCustomerID	Char	6	PK
	cName	VarChar	30	
	cAddress	VarChar	50	
	cCity	VarChar	30	
	cState	Char	2	
	cZipCode	Char	5	
	cPhone	Char	10	
	cFax	Char	10	
CallLog	cCallLogID	Char	6	PK
	cCustomerID	Char	6	FK
	cUserName	VarChar	30	
	dDateCalled	DateTime		
	cNote	VarChar	2000	
CtyStZip	cZipCode	Char	5	PK
	cCity	VarChar	3	
	cState	Char	2	

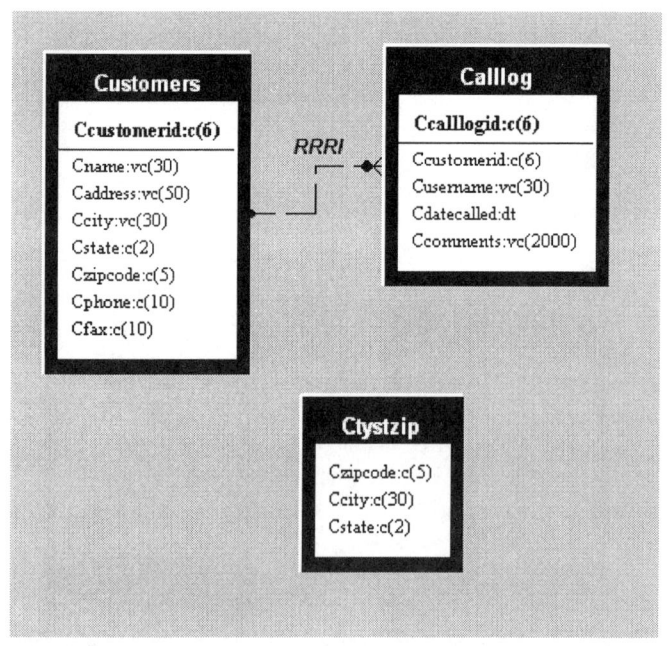

Figure 1. xCase drawing of the database used in this chapter.

An explanation of some of the field types in a SQL Server database is in order. First, SQL Server does not have a DATE field type. All dates are stored as DateTime fields. These fields can be formatted as DATE fields in the remote view if necessary. Also, SQL Server does not allow empty date values. Date values can be NULL or a valid date. If a date value is empty, SQL Server will store January 1, 1900 (1/1/1900) for the date.

SQL Server does not have a MEMO field type. In place of the MEMO field type, you can use either VarChar or Text. VarChar is a variable-length character field type. The length can vary from 1 to 8,000 characters. The advantage of using VarChar fields is that the storage requirements will vary depending on how many characters are in the field. You'll notice that we used VarChar fields for several of the fields in Table 1. By using the VarChar field type for the Customers cName field, if the customer name is only 10 characters, the field length for that row in the table will only be 10. This can save a lot of disk space in large databases.

The Text field type is more like the MEMO field type in VFP tables. The field is really a pointer into another table where the actual text is stored. Text fields can store up to 2,147,483,647 characters. Text fields, like MEMO fields, cannot be indexed. Therefore, unless you need the additional length, it is better to use the VarChar field type.

If you have a VarChar field that is longer than 254 characters accessed via a remote view, the field will be treated as a MEMO field in the client cursor. You will see this in the sample application as we get into creating the views.

Creating the database and tables

There are several ways to create the database and tables. The way you should do it depends on the tools you have available. If you have SQL Server's Enterprise Manager, Visual InterDev or Access 2000, you can create the database and tables interactively. If you have a commercial database modeling tool, you can use it to create the database and tables. If you don't have any of these, you can use VFP to create the database and tables. If you do not have any of the tools described here, you can create a VFP database and then use VFP's Upsizing wizard to upsize the database to a SQL Server or Oracle database. We will discuss the Upsizing wizard in a later section of this chapter.

ODBC/DSN

Once the database has been established and the tables created, you will need to create a DSN (Data Source Name) via an ODBC driver. Depending on the tools used in the previous section, you may have to have a DSN prior to creating the database and tables. For example, xCase requires a DSN in order for it to create the tables. A DSN is created using the ODBC Data Sources applet in the Control Panel. **Figure 2** shows the ODBC Data Source Administrator.

You can create a User, System or File DSN. Any of the DSNs can be used, but the User DSN is preferable for development for security purposes. This DSN is only available for the currently logged in user of the computer. We will discuss how to pragmatically create DSNs for the users of the application in a later section.

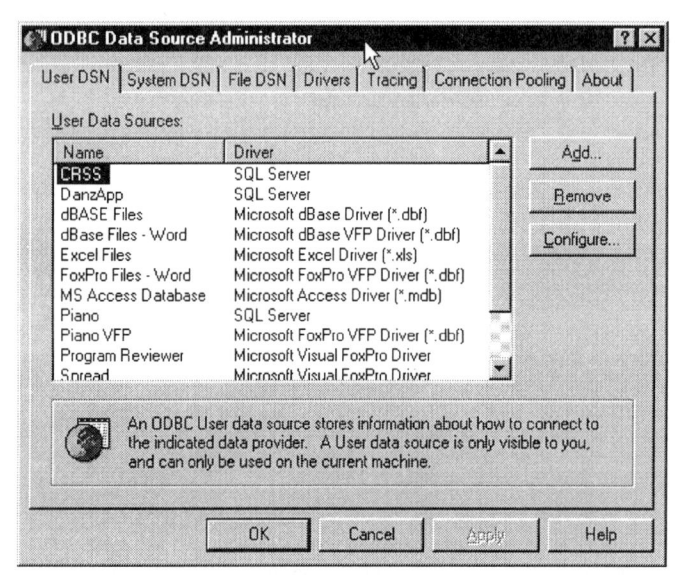

Figure 2. The ODBC Data Source Administrator used to create DSNs.

To create a User DSN, make sure the User DSN tab of the ODBC Data Source Administrator is selected. Click on the Add button. A list of available drivers will be displayed. Select the appropriate driver—SQL Server if you are using SQL Server 7 or the MSDE driver. Fill in a name and description, and specify the server to which you will be connecting. If you are using MSDE, the server should be (Local) if MSDE is installed on your computer. Otherwise, it should be the server name or IP address to the server. Click on the Next button to get to the next step, and specify your security options. We're using NT Authentication here.

In the next step, change the default database to your database. In the next step, accept all of the defaults unless instructed otherwise, and click on the Finish button. One more screen will be displayed for you to confirm all of your settings, and a Test Data Source button will be available here. We suggest clicking on this button to see whether you can connect to your database using the current settings. If it fails, go back and modify some settings (most likely security) until you can make a connection.

You now have your DSN that's going to be used in your VFP database to gain access to the SQL Server tables via remote views!

Creating your VFP database and remote views

Now that we have completed all of the background work, we're ready to create our VFP database and remote views. You will first want to create a VFE project for the sample app we will be creating. When creating a client/server application in VFE's Application Manager, note that in the third step of the Application wizard, there's a check box labeled Use Local Data. This sets an application property named lUseLocalData. This step is shown in **Figure 3**.

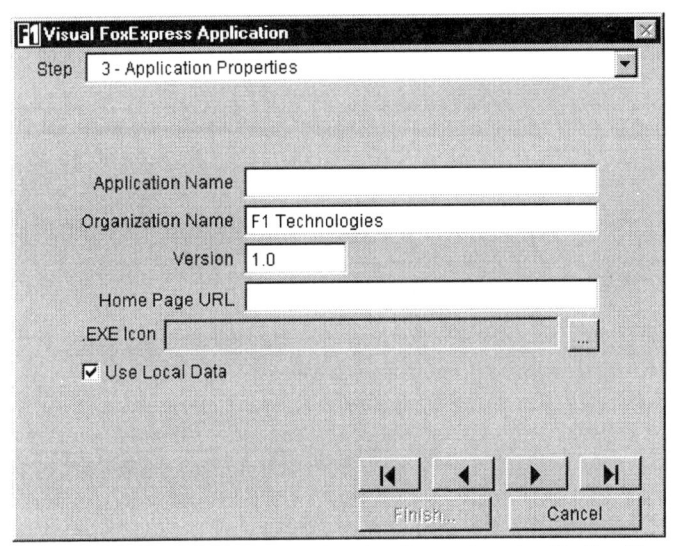

Figure 3. Step 3 of VFE's Application wizard with the Use Local Data check box.

Here's an excerpt from VFE's Help system that explains how VFE handles this property and provides details about naming your views:

> Visual FoxExpress includes a feature that allows the developer to specify globally whether or not an application should use local or remote views at run time. In order to use this feature, all local view names must begin with the prefix lv_ and all remote views must begin with the prefix rv_. The application object has a lUseLocalData property that defaults to True. Whenever an attempt is made to open a view that begins with either lv_ or rv_, the framework checks the value of the lUseLocalData property and will attempt to open the view whose name begins with lv_ if the property is True or rv_ if the property is False. **This feature is primarily provided for backward compatibility. Use of this feature is generally not recommended.**
>
> We don't recommend using the lUseLocalData property setting to determine if local or remote views are opened for a couple of reasons. The first reason is that this setting is global and impacts all views that have names beginning with lv_ or rv_. Not using this convention makes it easier to mix local and remote views within your application. The second reason is that DBCX stores properties related to views based on the view name. When both a local and remote view exist for the same purpose and the lv_ and rv_ naming conventions are used, this requires that separate metadata be created and maintained for both the local and remote view.
>
> If you are creating an application that can be used to access either local or remote data, we recommend using different data directories for the databases that will contain either the local or remote views. In other words, we recommend that you create a database that contains all local views in one directory and then a database with the same name that contains all remote views with the same name

as their local counterparts in another directory. This approach simply requires setting the cDataPath property of the application object to point to the directory that contains the desired database. No additional metadata is required. This approach also allows you to create a database that contains a mixture of local and remote views in another directory if necessary.

Remote and local views are treated identically in the Visual FoxExpress framework. All of the options in the data dictionary for default value generation, validation, lookups and so forth are available for views.

We like to use the lv_/rv_ naming convention with views. However, we do not mix local and remote views in the same DBC. Just remember, if you use this naming convention, VFE will remove the l or r from the name of the cursor. For example, if you name a view rv_Customers, the cursor will be named v_Customers in the application. Remote views are stored in a database container just as local views are, so we will need to add a database to the project.

Add a connection

The first thing that will be needed in the database container is a connection. This connection uses the DSN created earlier. With this information, the database container will be able to access the remote data tables. To add a connection to the DBC, it will need to be open. There are four ways to open the Connections dialog: via the Connections option on the Database menu; by right-clicking a blank area inside the Database Designer window and selecting Connections; by clicking on the Connections button on the Database Designer toolbar; or by entering CREATE CONNECTION in the command window. The toolbar is shown in **Figure 4**; the mouse pointer is pointing to the Connections button in the figure.

Figure 4. The Database Designer toolbar.

Use one of these methods to access the Connections dialog, which is shown in **Figure 5**.
Click the New button to add a new connection. The Connection Designer dialog will be displayed, as shown in **Figure 6**.

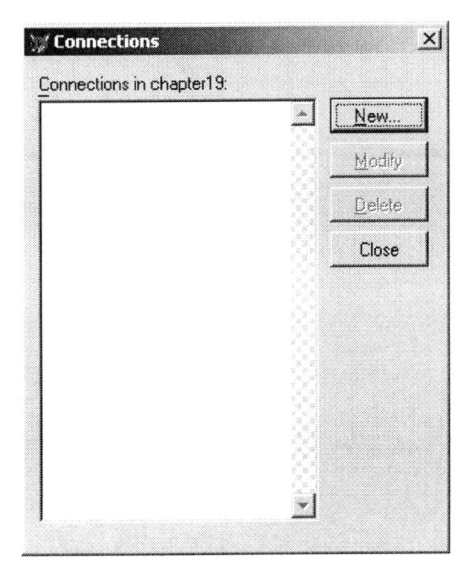

Figure 5. The Connections dialog.

Figure 6. The Connection Designer dialog.

The top section—Specify data source—is the most important section of the dialog. Make sure the "Data source, userid, password" radio button is selected. Then, in the Data source combo box, select the DSN that you created earlier. If necessary, specify the Userid, Password and Database name. If your SQL Server database is using NT Authentication, the Userid and

Password aren't necessary. After you've filled in these fields, click the Verify Connection button, and VFP will attempt to connect to the database using these settings. A message box will be displayed indicating success or failure. If the connection failed, verify your Data source, Userid and Password, and try again. If it was successful, click the OK button to save your connection information. You will have to give this connection a name. It is possible to have more than one connection in a DBC; this is useful if you need to access data that's stored in different databases, such as a company's accounting system.

For an explanation of the additional fields in the Connection Designer dialog, refer to the VFP Help system.

Creating remote views

Now we are ready to create our remote views. Again, there are four ways to add a remote view to the DBC: via the New Remote View option on the Database menu; by right-clicking a blank area inside the Database Designer window and selecting New Remote View; by clicking on the New Remote View button on the Database Designer toolbar; or by using the CREATE SQL VIEW command. The View Designer will ask which connection to use. Select the connection that was created in the previous section. You will then be presented with a list of tables in the remote database, as shown in **Figure 7**.

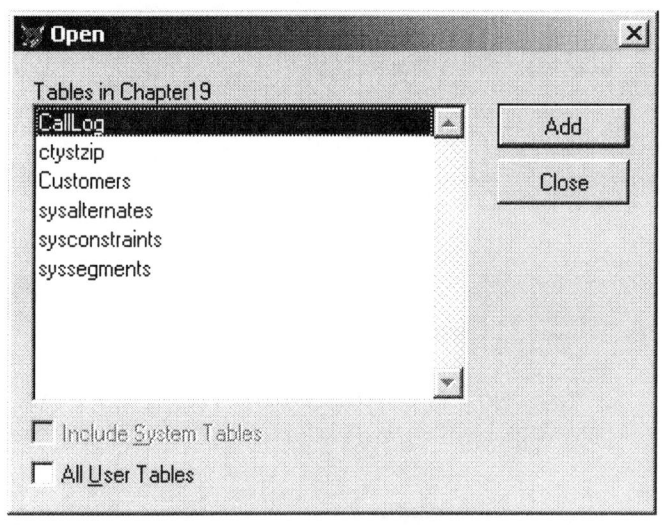

Figure 7. A list of tables in the remote database.

In client/server database applications, you will almost always want to create parameterized views. This will reduce the number of records that need to be copied to the workstation. Without parameterized views, all records will be copied to the workstation; this could take several minutes for large tables. The only time you should consider breaking this rule is with small (fewer than 100 records) lookup tables.

For our first view, select the Customers table. From this point the process of creating the view is the same as for creating a local view, with one exception, which we'll address in a moment.

First, on the Fields tab, select all available fields. Skip the Join tab, because we only have one table in this view.

The one exception we mentioned is on the filter expressions. SQL Server treats the = operator differently than VFP does. In VFP you can have the = do a leading edge comparison with SET EXACT OFF. This means that 'ABC' = 'A' will return True. With SET EXACT ON, this same expression returns False. SQL Server always treats the = as if we have SET EXACT ON. Because of this, you will need to use the LIKE operator when specifying your filter conditions.

The LIKE operator requires a wildcard character. The wildcard characters are % and _ (underscore). The % matches all characters, and the underscore matches a single character. For example, the following line will return all customers where the name starts with 'A':

```
SELECT * FROM Customers WHERE cName LIKE 'A%'
```

In VFP, with SET EXACT OFF, you will get the same results with this code:

```
SELECT * FROM Customers WHERE cName = 'A'
```

In SQL Server, this expression will return only those customers whose name is 'A'.

Another difference between SQL Server and VFP is that string comparisons are not case-sensitive. In VFP, this code will return nothing, unless you have some customers whose names start with a lowercase 'a':

```
SELECT * FROM Customers WHERE cName LIKE 'a%'
```

You would have to use the UPPER or LOWER functions to force the field to all uppercase or lowercase so that the condition will not be case-sensitive. This is not the case with SQL Server string comparisons; the preceding SELECT statement will return all customers whose names starts with 'A' regardless of case.

In our Customers view, we will add one filter condition:

```
cName LIKE ?vp_cName.
```

Make sure to add vp_cName to the view's parameters list. The view's parameters list is accessed by choosing View Parameters from the Query menu that's available when the View Designer is open. Note that we did not add the % sign here. VFE automatically adds the % when the LIKE operator is used in filter conditions.

On the Update criteria tab, make sure that all fields are marked as updatable and that the cCustomerID field is labeled as the key field. Also make sure that the cCustomerID field is marked as updatable, because we are going to use VFE's Default Value Generation Key to populate this field.

As always, be sure to check the Send SQL Updates check box. This is the most frequently forgotten step in creating views. If this is not checked, no data will be sent to the underlying tables to be saved.

Save the view and name it rv_Customers. In VFE's Database Explorer, set the default value for the cCustomerID field to be Base62, and set the initial value to 000000 (six zeros).

The other properties can be set as well—for example, forcing the cState field to all upper and using the (999) 999-9999 picture clause for the cPhone and cFax fields.

Create remote views for the CallLog (rv_calllog) and CtyStZip tables as well. In the CallLog view, add this filter condition:

```
cCustomerID = ?v_customers.cCustomerID
```

The call log table is a child table of the Customers table related on the cCustomerID field. Remember to mark the cCallLogID field as updatable. Specify the cCallLogID field to use the default key generation of Base62 with 000000 as the initial value. Also, enter a default value expression for the cCustomerID field in the CallLog view. The expression should be:

```
v_customers.cCustomerID
```

In the CtyStZip view, add two filter conditions:

```
cZipCode LIKE ?vp_cZipCode
```

and

```
cCity LIKE ?vp_cCity
```

Don't forget to add these two view parameters to the view's parameters list. Also make sure that the cZipCode field is marked as key and updatable.

Creating VFE's objects

With client/server applications, there is nothing different about creating the data objects (cursor and data environment classes), business object classes, presentation object classes, view parameter classes, and presentation object form classes. The only thing you need to remember is that when you base your cursor classes on parameterized views (rv_customers and rv_ctystzip), they are opened with no data by default.

Lookups and data validation

One of the goals of client/server development is to reduce the amount of data that is transferred to the client machine. One area of your applications that must be reviewed in order to accomplish this goal is your lookup tables (foreign key fields) and data validation. In our table-based systems, we would use a combo box control, populated with all possible values from the lookup table, or a text box control with a SEEK/LOCATE command in the LostFocus event to validate the data.

Unless your lookup tables are small, this is not a good practice to follow when creating client/server applications. Let's say you are writing an invoicing system. Your company has thousands of customers. On your invoice form, you use one of the methods described previously to validate that the customer entered is in your customer list. Both of these methods require that the entire Customers table be copied to the client machine.

Two possible solutions to this problem are to use a parameterized view or to use SQL pass-through. Either of these solutions (if constructed correctly) will greatly limit the amount of data retrieved from the server. We prefer using SQL pass-through via a quick-fill text box. The main reason for this is that we don't need the extra baggage of the view because we won't be using it to update data. It is much faster to retrieve the data using SQL pass-through, and we don't need all of the features provided by adding the view to the DBCX. We will discuss the quick-fill text box later. First, let's look at the specifics of SQL pass-through.

SQL pass-through

SQL pass-through enables you to send SQL statements directly to the server. The VFP function used to do this is SQLEXEC(). The syntax of this statement is:

```
SQLEXEC(nConnectionHandle, [cSQLCommand, [CursorName]])
```

This function will return –1 if the command fails for some reason or a positive number if it is successful. The positive number will indicate the number of record sets returned. In most cases, this will be 1. However, it is possible to execute a stored procedure on the server that returns more than one record set. The arguments for the function are described in **Table 2**.

Table 2. Arguments for the SQLEXEC() function.

Argument	Description
nConnectionHandle	Specifies the connection handle to the data source. This can be generated using the SQLCONNECT() function or the CURSORGETPROP() function. Each of these will be discussed later.
cSQLCommand	Specifies the SQL statement to be executed. This statement can contain a WHERE clause that contains a parameter creating a parameterized view.
CursorName	Specifies the name of the VFP cursor used to hold the result set. If this is omitted, the name of the cursor will be SQLRESULT.

The SQLEXEC() function requires a connection handle to the data source. This handle can be created in a couple of ways. One method uses the SQLCONNECT() function. Here's the syntax of this function:

```
SQLCONNECT([DataSourceName[, cUserID, cPassword]])
```

The function will return –1 indicating failure or 1 indicating success. The arguments are the name of the DSN and an optional user ID and password.

The other method is to use the CURSORGETPROP() function. This can be used if you are using remote views defined in a DBC. If a view is currently open (used), the CURSORGETPROP() function, with the proper arguments, will return the connection handle used by the view. The calling method used to get the handle is:

```
CURSORGETPROP("CONNECTHANDLE", [nWorkArea | cTableAlias])
```

Now let's look at some code that can be placed in the LostFocus event of a text box control to validate a customer name:

```
* LOSTFOCUS event
* Validate customer name entered into the control

LOCAL liConnectHandle, loSelect, lcCommand
LOCAL lcCustName, llReturnValue, liResult

* save current workarea
loSelect = CREATEOBJECT('cSelect')

* get connection handle
liConnectHandle = SQLCONNECT('chapter19') && chapter19 is the DSN

IF liConnectHandle > 0 && connection was successful
   * get value entered into control
   lcCustName = This.Value

   IF !EMPTY(lcCustName) && don't need to validate empty value
      * create SQL statement
      * remember, string comparisons are not case-sensitive
      lcCommand = "SELECT cName FROM customers WHERE cName = ?lcCustName"

      * pass command to server, name resulting cursor CUSTNAME
      liResult = SQLEXEC(liConnectHandle, lcCommand, "CUSTNAME")

      IF liResult > 0  && pass-through succeeded
         * CUSTNAME will be the selected workarea

         IF RECCOUNT() > 0 && we found one
            llReturnValue = .t.

            * You may want to find out if more than one
            * record was returned and provide a list box
            * or some other method to allow the user to
            * select the correct customer.

         ELSE && no customers were found
            llReturnValue = .f.
            <provide message to users>
         ENDIF

      ELSE  && pass-through failed
         llReturnValue = .f.
         <handle error>
      ENDIF

   ELSE
      llReturnValue = .t.
   ENDIF

   * disconnect from the server
   SQLDISCONNECT(liConnectHandle)
ELSE && connection failed
   llReturnValue = .f.
   <provide a message to the user>
ENDIF

RETURN llReturnValue
```

With a little thought and planning, you could create a text box subclass with the necessary properties and code similar to this in the LostFocus event to be used in this situation.

Quick-fill text box

VFE provides quick-fill text box capabilities in its text box control. It uses properties set up in the DBCX to accomplish this. The problem with using this control in a client/server application is that it opens the lookup cursor to do the search. If the lookup cursor is based on a remote view to a SQL table containing thousands of rows, the entire table is copied to the client to be used in the search. This is not a good practice in client/server applications.

We have created an alternative text box control that can be used in place of VFE's. This control only works with client/server data. It does not rely on the lookup properties defined in the DBCX. It uses SQL pass-through with a parameterized command using the LIKE operator wrapped around a couple of other SQL pass-through commands, so that there is only one record returned from the server. The process is similar to this:

```
SQLEXEC(liConnectHandle, "SET ROWCOUNT 1")
SQLEXEC(liConnectHandle, <search command>, <cursor name>)
SLQEXEC(liConnectHandle, "SET ROWCOUNT 0")
```

The first function tells SQL Server to return only one matching row. In our search command, we use an ORDER BY clause so that we'll get the first one. The last function sets SQL Server back to its default row count, which is all matching rows. The VCX that contains the control is available with the Developer Download files at www.hentzenwerke.com; it's named iSQLQFTextBox.VCX. Copy the VCX to your VFE ILIBS folder.

There are a few things that need to be done in order to use this control. The first is to create a custom property in your application class called iConnectHandle. Next, in the Init_Post() method of the application object, place the following code:

```
LOCAL llReturnVal

This.iConnectHandle = SQLCONNECT(<your dsn>[, <userid>, <password>])

IF This.iConnectHandle > 0
   llReturnValue = .t.
ELSE
   llReturnValue = .f.
ENDIF

RETURN llReturnValue
```

Then place this code in the application's DESTROY event:

```
SQLDISCONNECT(This.iConnectHandle)
DODEFAULT()
```

This will give us an application-level property that we can use anytime we need a connection handle to our data. Now we don't have to make a connection and disconnect every time we need a handle to our data. We just use This.oApplication.iConnectHandle.

Now all we need to do is drop the quick-fill text box on a presentation object, fill in a few properties and we're done! We have built in a few additional features of the text box control. After entering at least two characters, the user can enter the "?" character. This will display a list of all rows from the lookup table that match the characters that have been entered so far. The user can then pick a value from the list. Also, when the control loses focus, the control will query the lookup table to see whether more than one record matches the entered value. If so, it will display a list of all matching records so the user can pick the appropriate one. The fields that are displayed in these lists are configured by properties of the control.

You can also specify an additional filter clause. This lets you limit the selectable values. For example, if you only want to allow users to enter valid ZIP codes from the state of Texas, you can specify an additional filter clause like this:

```
cState = 'TX'
```

Another feature is that you can specify additional fields to be filled in from the lookup table. For example, in a ZIP code lookup, you may want to automatically fill in the City and State fields with the city and state of the selected ZIP code.

These additional fields, as well as the field list to be displayed in the lists, are properties of the control. They are to be entered in a comma-delimited list. As an extra bonus, we have created another class that is used to manage these comma-delimited lists, called StringToToken. This will take any delimited list of values and convert them to tokens. (Note that the cListParser class that comes with VFE could be used in place of the StringToToken class.) The following is an example of how to use this class:

```
LOCAL oTokens

* the first parameter is the delimited list
* the second is the delimiter
oTokens = createobject('stringtotoken', 'a,b,c,d,e,f' , ',')
?oTokens.nCount      && prints the number of tokens, in this case 6
?oTokens.GetToken(1) && prints the first token, 'a' in this case
?oTokens.GetToken(5) && prints the fifth token, 'e' in this case
?oTokens.GetToken(9) && prints '*Error*' since there are not 9 tokens
```

Table 3 lists the control's properties and descriptions.

Now we are ready to add the control to our presentation object. Open your customers presentation object and replace the ZIP code control with the quick-fill text box control. Set the properties as shown in **Figure 8**. You may also want to change the tab order so that the ZIP code field gains focus prior to the city and state fields.

Save the presentation object and run the application. Before testing this, be sure to add some ZIP codes to the CtyStZip table.

Table 3. The control's properties.

Property	Description
cAdditionalFields	The comma-delimited list of fields to be filled in with values from the lookup table. The additional fields will not be filled in if they already contain a value. This behavior can be changed on a field-by-field basis. To override this behavior, precede the field names with an asterisk (*).
cAdditionalFieldsSource	The comma-delimited list of field names. This is only needed if the field names in the lookup table are different from the field names in the main table.
cDisplayFields	The comma-delimited list of fields to be displayed in the list that is presented when the user enters a ? or when there is more than one record that matches the entered value. It is not necessary to put the cLookUpField in this list. It will always be displayed.
cField	This is a VFE property. It should contain the name of the field to which the control is bound.
cFilter	An additional filter condition to be added to the WHERE clause.
cFKField	The name of the foreign key field.
cLookUpField	The name of the field in the lookup table containing the display text.
cNotFoundMessage	The message to be displayed if no matching records are found. If it's left empty, a default message will be displayed.
cSourceTable	The name of the SQL table to be searched.
lProper	A logical property specifying whether additional fill field values should be converted to proper case.

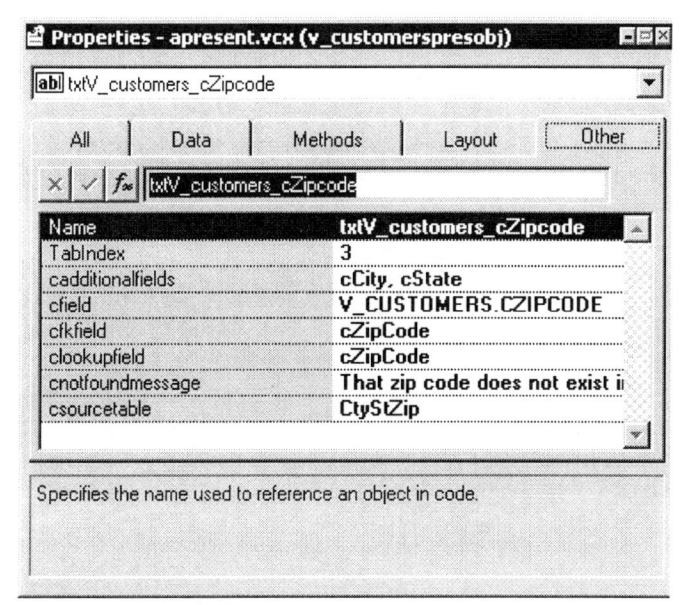

Figure 8. The Properties dialog of the quick-fill text box control showing properties for the ZIP code field.

Upsizing local data

VFP provides an Upsizing wizard that will upsize tables contained in a DBC to another data source that can be attached to using ODBC—namely, SQL Server. One advantage of using this tool is that if you have local views to your tables stored in the DBC, the wizard will convert them to remote views as well. However, it is not recommended by VFE that you store your local tables and views in the same DBC.

Our preferred method of upsizing a database is to convert the database design to SQL Server using a database modeling tool, and then let the modeling tool create the database on the server. We then follow VFE's recommendation of creating a separate data folder and create a new DBC to hold the remote views in the new folder.

An even better method, since we now have MSDE, is to create the application using SQL Server and remote views from the beginning!

> *At this time we don't recommend upsizing the security tables and the FESYS.DBC to SQL Server. VFE's builders do not currently support accessing the security table data via remote views. Your applications will work, but you will have to manually assign security names to the different objects, and the Login Journal (APPLOGINS.DBF) table does not record logging out or manually clearing logins.*

Summary

In this chapter we discussed the pros and cons of a client/server application—these included security, reliability and speed. We also explored the tools needed to create and maintain the databases, which included SQL Server 7.0, MSDE and xCase. We looked at the client/server features provided in the VFE framework. We also looked at some problems in the framework concerning data validations, and some solutions that are available using SQL pass-through. Now you have the knowledge and the tools you need to create client/server applications. Good luck, and have fun!

Chapter 20
Tips and Tricks

Here we will take a look at various techniques and some helpful information that will help you implement the kinds of processes and interfaces any programmer would be proud of.

As we find ourselves writing the last chapter, it seems that this book took on a life of its own. While we began with the intent to fill this book with examples and code, it became obvious that such isolated examples would have been useless if you didn't know how the framework operated. However, there is always a place for some small code snippets or discussions about why you should do something one way or another.

Keep in mind that the main "rule" for creating a program that works is, "If it ain't broke, don't fix it." Now, this may seem a little simplistic; however, you'll find that it's much more productive to spend your time getting many things to work properly, rather than getting one thing to work perfectly. Also, there are many different methods you can use in VFP to accomplish the same task, and since VFE is written with VFP this is true in this environment as well.

So, in writing this book we hoped to impart enough knowledge of the framework and its operation, rather than teach you how to load a TreeView with data. We hoped to keep you from writing 30 or 40 lines of code when a simple property switch on the business object would have done the trick.

Many times, we will see a question about the "VFE way" to perform a task. While there are general guidelines the creators had in mind when they wrote the framework, no one is going to yell at you if you write a business rule in the presentation object, for example. There is no need for you to use the cursor objects at all. While the metadata allows much of your label controls to be data-driven, it is not necessary. If you prefer to use the menu editor to create a menu item and not create a class for it, that's fine. In the event that you feel the VFE lookup is too slow or bringing in too much data, write your own validation. The finished product is going to be what you need. You may know that you will never have plans to go client/server and write your application to access tables directly—that's okay too, although we still think that views rule.

So, with that said, we would like to leave you with a few design ideas and samples to spark your imagination—steal or ignore as you wish.

Where's the project manager?

The VFE IDE is powerful and helpful. It is full of wizards and builders that speed you along your way. However, it is also modal, and it puts a lot of stuff out of your direct reach. The first and most apparent is the project manager. Most of us are so very comfortable with and accustomed to using this tool that we miss it.

The truth is that the project manager is there, it is just hidden in the background. When you are in the Application Builder, if you open the Window menu you will see that the project manager is listed. If you select it, you will have access to this window. When you are done with the project manager, be sure to "hide" it using the Window menu. If you close it, you will get many errors and will have to exit VFE and start again.

Drop the IDE

In the beginning of the book, we discussed the makeup of the product known as VFE. We indicated that there were two parts to this product: the IDE and the framework. It is possible to use the framework and not the IDE. As we mentioned earlier, the IDE includes a modal form that restricts your access to some VFP tools and causes problems with other third-party tools.

The solution here is to *not* load the IDE. We believe that this is preferable once you have created your classes or are debugging. We certainly use the IDE to build the classes, especially to build the presentation object. However, when debugging or working on the business objects, it is just an extra layer to use. We much prefer typing "modi class ?" at the command window to edit a class.

Here are a few other small tips if you are going to stray from the IDE.

Accessing builders

There are a couple of things you can do when you are working this way. The first is to set a path to the builders so you will have access to them. Granted, parts of the VFE builders will not work without the VFE Application Manager running, but some is better than nothing. The builders are in the Tools directory of VFE, so type the following in the command window:

```
set path to \vfe6\tools\builderb
```

DBCX Explorer

When you are working outside of the IDE, you also will not have access to the DBCX Explorer. This is too bad, because many of those items must be set during development. The way around this is to load VFP twice. In one session, you can load the IDE and open the DBCX Explorer. This application uses the data in a shared mode so that you can also run your application with it open. In the second session, you can work in the plain old VFP IDE that you have come to know and love, with all your third-party and other tools a click away.

Also, DBCX uses standard VFP tables to store its metadata. You can use these tables and the complete Visual FoxPro DML to manipulate them.

Running your application

Running the application is as simple as pushing a button in the VFE IDE. Because a VFE application runs by instantiating the application object, you can't just highlight MAIN.PRG in the project manager and press the Run button. You must type the code to instantiate the application object at the command line. This can become cumbersome if you are in a test, debug and fix cycle. To simplify running the application from the command window, create a program named RUN.PRG in the root directory of each project. This program only contains one line of code:

```
Newobject('NameOfProjectApplicationObject','libs\aapp')
```

This line of code will instantiate the application object (run the application), and you can call it just by typing DO RUN, in the command window. The name of the class to create is the name of your application object. By default this is the name of your project, followed by ApplicationObject. If you are unsure of you application object class name, you can find it in the "other classes" node of the Application Builder.

Using VFP Builders

Another issue to overcome is that the built-in VFP builders are not available for the VFE interface objects. This is due to the custom builders that have been provided for each class. While this is good and these builders are very helpful, it is also bad. There are still times when you'll want to use the VFP builders. The combo box builder is especially useful to create a hard-coded drop-down list of values, define the column sizes and specify the record source column. The VFP builder makes this much simpler.

Unfortunately, the VFE builders do not have a button to call the default VFP builder; perhaps in a future update we will see this feature. However, there is a quick way to access the VFP builders. In the Properties page, you can set the builderx property of the control to "(none)" by selecting the current value and pressing delete. The next time you choose Builder from the shortcut menu, the default VFP builder will run.

Once you have finished with the VFP builder, you can restore the builderx property value by pointing at it with the mouse, pressing the right mouse button and choosing Reset to Default from the shortcut menu.

Where do I put the code?

This is the age-old question you see on the VFE forums. The framework is divided into logical tiers, and most developers seem to know this but are unsure about which tier to put certain code in. This question can be both simple and difficult. Sometimes a business rule affects the user interface, while other times a business rule requires input from the user.

So, to put some of this in perspective—the perspective of one of the frameworks architects, that is—here is the text of an e-mail from Mike, a member of the F1 team, in regards to business rules, business objects and "where to put the code."

Hi Bob,

I was thinking about the sections on business rules and business objects last night, and I wanted to pass a few additional comments on to you. Since I've already sent the edited chapters, I thought I'd just shoot you e-mail.

The business rules section only talks about business rules in the context of using them in the bizrules collection of a business object. Obviously, this is good, because that's the default implementation. I noticed that you didn't mention how to get a business rule into the collection, but I assumed that's because you'll do this later when you actually implement one. I use business rules outside of the collection all the time. Many times it's really convenient to create a business rule that just scripts a bunch of method calls together in one place. Here's one that I have in an app now that's used for an automated billing process:

```
*===========================================================================
* Method: Execute
* Purpose: Kicks off the invoice generation process.
* Author: F1 Technologies
* Parameters:
* Returns:
* Added: 11/23/1999
*===========================================================================
WITH This

    * Create the necessary business objects.
    .CreateBusinessObjects()

    * Generate the invoices
    .GenerateInvoices()

    * Post the invoices to AR.
    .Post()

ENDWITH
```

They are also convenient anytime you want to create a generic reusable object—say, something that has a validate routine or something similar.

On the subject of where to put code, I suppose this could either go into the business object and presentation object sections or in the overview chapter:

A lot of people really seem to struggle with figuring out where to put their code in a VFE application. Because VFE's object model is layered and offers tons of hooks, and because there are often many ways to do things in VFE, where to put code can be confusing. Keep in mind that the VFE framework provides an n-tier architecture and that your applications should stick with that architecture. What does that mean?

If you are writing code that performs an interface operation, then the code most likely belongs in the presentation layer, either in a form, presentation object or control within a presentation object. Code in the presentation layer should simply concern itself with UI issues, and actual processing should be delegated to the business layer.

If you are writing code that enforces a business rule, performs a business operation or does any processing that in itself is not UI-centric, it belongs in the business layer, most likely in a business object or business rule. Code in the business layer should never perform UI operations. If operations require that notification be passed up to the interface, this should be handled by passing return values back to the interface or possibly by passing a UI object into the business layer. For example, it's common to display a thermometer to indicate progress when a time-consuming operation is executing. In situations like this, it's appropriate to pass a thermometer object to the business layer and to have the business layer call a method of the thermometer to update the progress. The interaction with the UI should be limited to a single method call. Why? The business object really doesn't care at all about interface; adding UI code to the business object breaks the n-tier model and also takes away from the reusability of the business object. Also, if you add code to the business object that specifically addresses UI objects, you've then limited the business object to only functioning with that UI. If you limit the communication to a single method call, you've created a contract that only requires one method of the UI. If you need a different UI, you only have one item (the method you're calling) to concern yourself with in order to let your business object work with multiple UIs. The following example code—a method called Process() in a business object—doesn't really do anything except provide a shell for this type of operation, but it illustrates the point well:

```
* Method: Process
LPARAMETERS toProgressIndicator

LOCAL ;
    lnPos, ;
    lnTotal, ;
    lnProcessed

WITH This
    lnTotal = .VisibleRecordCount
    lnProcessed = 0
    .Navigate("First")
    lnPos = FILE_OK

    DO WHILE lnPos <> FILE_EOF
* Processing Code Here
        lnProcessed = lnProcessed + 1
        IF VARTYPE("toProgressIndicator") = T_OBJECT
            toProgressIndicator.Update(lnProcessed/lnTotal)
        ENDIF
        lnPos = .Navigate("Next")
    ENDDO
ENDWITH

RETURN lnProcessed
```

Note that the code actually makes sure that toProgressIndicator refers to an object. This code isn't really necessary, but adding it will allow the method to function if a progress indicator is not passed to it. Adding this extra code keeps the business object available for situations where a UI object would not be passed to it—for instance, if it were called from an ASP page.

If you are writing code that manipulates or accesses data directly, such as a SQL SELECT statement, this code belongs in the data access layer, most likely in a cursor class. Generally speaking, the VFE cursor class is very robust and should shield you from writing data access code like you normally would in a VFP application. The preceding example code illustrates one way in which you're shielded from the data access. You'll notice that business object methods take care of traversing the file, which eliminates the need to use a DO WHILE or SCAN loop.

—Mike Feltman

From this letter we have learned a few things. The first is that a business rules class can be used as a good lightweight class to create what we call an "event" object. An event is a special business object that, instead of modeling a "thing" in the real world, models an event. One example of an event, as used by Mike's code, is Invoice Generation. The event type object generally has many methods but not much data. As a matter of fact, it may call on several business objects and collaborate with them to perform its task.

Second, Mike pointed out that the code should be located at the tier that matches its implementation. So, if you need to disable a text box, you would do that at the UI level. However, that text box may be disabled for a business reason, so the refresh of the text box might call a method in the business object, which will return information (a True or False) that the text box code will use to enable or disable the text box.

A third tip was how to manipulate data through the cursor object.

Data manipulation

A very common occurrence in a database application is the necessity of scanning through a record set and processing or updating each record based on some value or condition. But we are taught that in the business layer, you shouldn't write code that accesses your views or cursors. So, the business layer should access the data object to manipulate the value.

If you look at the code in Mike's e-mail, you will see the loop used to manipulate each record in the cursor. The code starts by calling the .Navigate("First") method. (You could also call the MoveFirst() method, which actually calls the Navigate() method and seems to be more readable.)

Next, the FILE_OK constant value is placed into the lnPos variable. At this point, the loop is started and should continue until the lnPos variable doesn't change to FILE_EOF. The return of the Navigate() method will return the FILE_EOF file when the end-of-file is encountered. *Don't make the mistake of checking for eof() because the framework will skip back to the last record if it encounters the eof.*

You can put any code into this loop that you see fit. (Consult Chapter 4, "Data Storage and Classes," for information on how to access the values of the field objects.) Also, you can use the GetValues() and SetValues() methods to move full records from one cursor to another.

Now, must you do it this way? Is there anything stopping you from using a SCAN… ENDSCAN? Absolutely not; the preceding method just conforms to the design of the framework layers. The goal here is to abstract out the data manipulation. The theory is that this code will work with any data type, as long as the cursor object knows how to deal with the data.

Mover alternative

A popular interface for selecting multiple items is a mover. This is a form with two lists of items. Usually, the list on the left contains the available items to be selected, and the list on the right displays the items that have been selected. Between the two lists you'll usually find arrows that users can press to indicate that an item should be moved from one list to another. **Figure 1** shows an example of a mover-type interface.

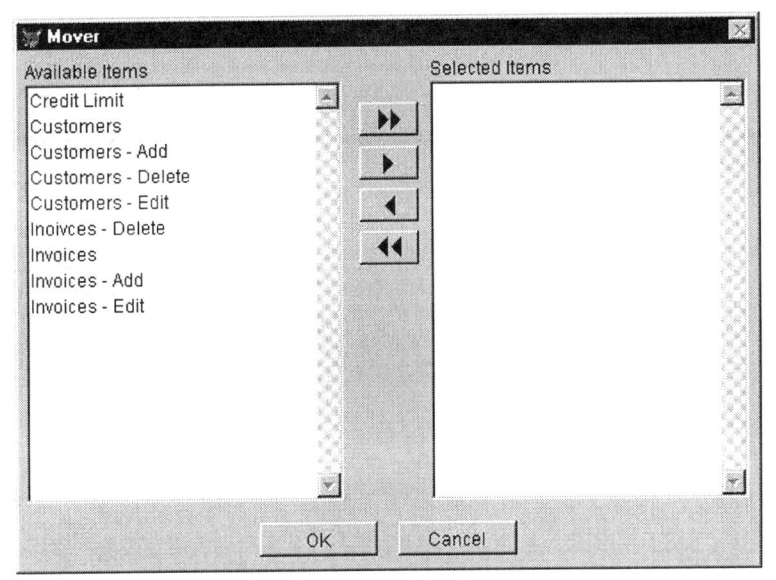

Figure 1. An example of a mover interface.

This is a fairly intuitive interface, but it has some drawbacks for the programmer. First, the lists are usually list boxes. This requires that you populate the list box or perhaps an array with the data you wish to display. Second, you have to access the array to determine which items have been selected.

Many times, the selections are to be made from a list of items in a data cursor. While we have preached that you stay away from grids for data entry, they are an interface alternative to the mover. If you create a view with a logical field added to it, you could have the user set the logical field to indicate that this record was selected.

The advantage here is that you will not need to write any code to populate your grid; just run the Grid Builder, putting your logical field in the first column and your description field in the second column. Set all columns other than the first one to read-only. Also, be sure to set the first column's "sparse" property to False.

To add the logical field to your view, you can utilize the "expression" field on the field page of the View Designer. After you have selected the fields needed to identify the selection, type something similar to this into the expression field:

```
.f. AS lProcessRecord
```

When you build your presentation object and use the Grid Builder, this lProcessRecord will be available for your use. Place this field into the first column of the grid with no heading. When the program is run, the grid will include a check box in every row. This type of interface looks more like a list if you turn the column rows off.

Once the user presses the Process button, your code can loop through the view and process each record with the lProcessRecord set to True. Be sure that you don't try to use a SELECT to get a record set, which only includes the selected records because, as you know, the SELECT statement will read the underlying tables and not the values from the view.

Figure 2 shows an example from an application that's currently under development. This is part of the termination screen on an HR application. Each employee can have one or more jobs that they perform. When you terminate the employee, the system will create a requisition for each job to replace the employee who is being terminated. As you can see, the user will select the jobs for which they would like to create a requisition. This example only shows one job, but it gives you an idea of how this interface works.

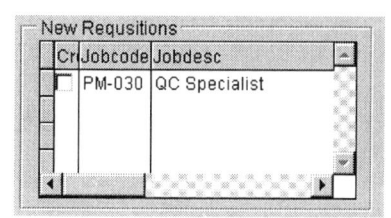

Figure 2. An example of a multi-select grid.

Views only database

When you are creating applications that many users will access, there could be a bottleneck when they all share the same DBC. It seems that when opening views from a DBC, FoxPro will temporarily lock the view definition. The common advice is to have two DBC files for your application. One DBC, along with the tables will be deployed on a shared network drive. A second DBC will contain only the view definitions, which will be deployed locally, on each client's hard drive.

If you wish, you can simplify the installation by including the DBC file in the EXE by "including" it in your project. Either method will provide a private "views" DBC for each user, which will alleviate the contention issues with view definitions. As long as your application has a path to the directory with each DBC in it, your files will be located.

Create an edit mode

While the default edit scheme is certainly satisfactory, some prefer that the screen be provided as read-only, requiring the user to press an Edit button to be able to modify an existing record. You can do this very simply with VFE.

The presentation object already has a property to disallow editing records. Setting this property (lAllowEdit) to False initially is the first step of meeting this requirement of an edit mode. The second step is to create an "action button" that will set the lAllowEdit property to True and refresh the presentation object. After a Save or Cancel is performed, you will need to set the property back to False. While this sounds simple, it gets a little more complicated because you also have to cascade the setting of the lAllowEdit property to any child presentation objects as well. But don't worry—we have done all the work for you, so all you have to do is set a switch to True in the presentation object and use our Edit button.

In the Developer Download files available at www.hentzenwerke.com, you will find a subdirectory named EditForm that has two class libraries in it. The iEditToolBarButton library contains the Edit button. This button is programmed to call the SetToEdit() method of the presentation object. You can put this button in a toolbar or directly on the presentation object. The iPresent library contains a modified iPresentationObj class. If you haven't made any changes to your iPresent library, you can just drop this one in its place. If you have modified it, you will have to retrofit the code changes yourself.

Once you have dropped this iPresent.VCX file into your iLibs directory, all of your presentation objects will have a new property, lUseEditMode. If you set this to True, your form will work as described previously without your writing any additional code. You don't even need to set the lAllowEdit property. This will also be integrated with security, so the Edit button will not be available if the user doesn't have adequate security to edit the record. Sorry, though—you will have to come up with your own icon for the button.

Debugging

Debugging your applications is generally a task on which you will spend many hours. The VFP debugger is one of the most robust available for a 4GL development environment. However, there are some tips you can use when debugging VFE applications.

First, set up your debugger layout before you need it. The debugger setup will be saved in your resource file. By default you should develop with your resource file set on. It's our preference to dock all the windows in the debugger and run in the debugger frame (see **Figure 3**). You may have different preferences, but it's nice to have all of the windows open. You can see from our layout that each window is available. One thing to note is that if you try to use the debugger's menus while working with VFE applications, they won't operate.

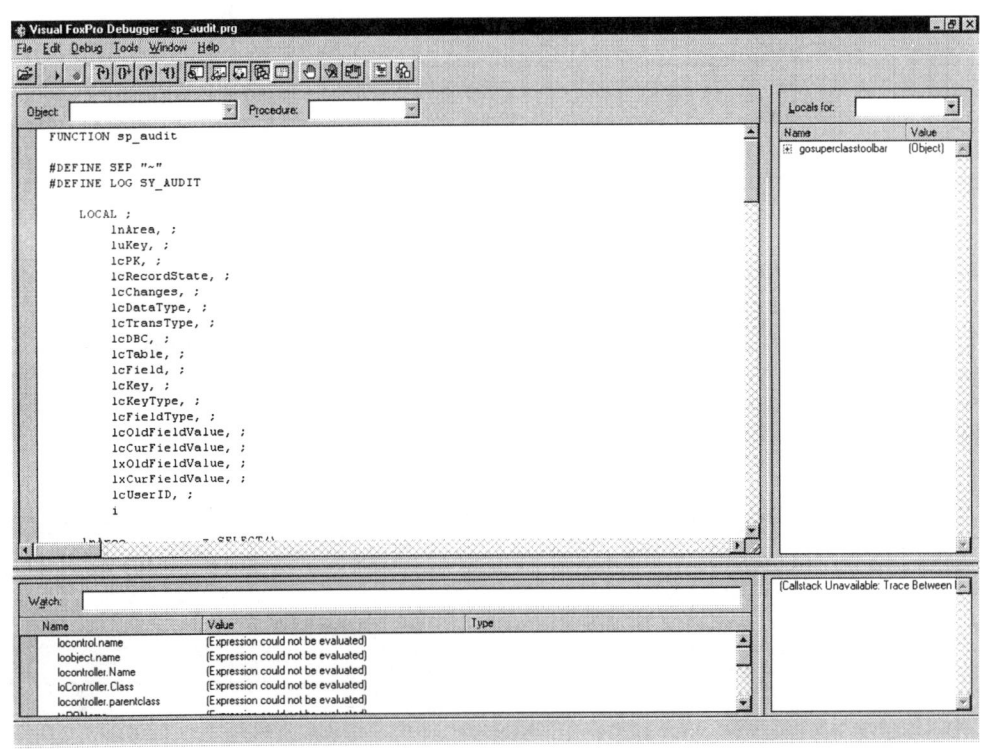

Figure 3. Set up your debugger layout ahead of time so that it is easy to navigate.

The second tip is to use a simple function that's provided by VFE to start the debugger. This function will display the object and the method that is running and ask whether you wish to start the debugger. This is helpful because you don't have to run the debugger every time you run your test, or on every iteration of your loop. Generally, you would put either the "set step on" or the "suspend" command in your code. Instead, put a call to DebugMode(). This function performs as described and is provided by the framework. Also, it will only prompt you if the DEBUG.TXT file is in your application directory. It is a most useful little function.

The third thing you should be aware of is how access methods affect your debugging session. Take the example of a line of code such as this:

```
This.oBizObj.oCursor.Fields.Item('MyField').Value = 'ABC'
```

This line of code has several properties that use access methods to resolve the value. Normally, when you point the mouse at an expression like this, it is able to resolve the value and display it as a ToolTip. But, with statements like this you should avoid hovering your mouse over it. The debugger will crash with a C0000005 error, and you will lose your whole session. So, make sure you avoid pointing at them with your mouse.

Another issue with a statement like this occurs when you trace through the code. If you "step into" this line of code, the debugger will trace all the access methods that fire. That's fine, if you are interested in how this particular value or reference was found, but usually it just gets you lost in all the access methods. A better choice is to use the "step over" function of the debugger as you are tracing the code, unless you are sure you want to follow the execution into an access or assign method.

UTILS.PRG

There are times when you need to do some type of manipulation with a string or array, or you want to know something about a variable, and there just isn't a native function to do it. Most of us have written a function library that we use in our day-to-day programming. You should also be aware of the function library included with VFE. The functions are stored in a file named UTILS.PRG, which is included in your project by default. **Table 1** shows a list of some of the functions you will find in this program. You should refer to the function code for parameters and usage information.

Table 1. Functions of UTILS.PRG.

Function	Description
DebugMode()	Provides a prompt that asks the developer whether to run the debugger during program testing. We discussed this function in a previous section.
FileSize()	Returns the size of a file.
ConvertToChar()	Converts any passed data type to a displayable character.
CSZ()	Properly formats a passed City, State, and Zip code for inclusion in an address.
FindApplication()	Returns a reference to the global application object.

Hopefully, you will find some use for the functions in this program. You should also use this tip to create your own function library.

Team programming

It is possible to have a team of programmers work on a VFE application if you follow some simple setup and project guidelines.

Source control

It's crucial that you use source control. Be sure to check in all the application class libraries. The problem with VFP and source control is that it is enabled at the file level, rather than at the class level. This means that if two classes are in the same library, only one person can have them checked out at once. The best way to solve this is to create a library (VCX file) for each entity's classes. We did this in our tutorial, storing the files for the Students entity in a specific students.VCX. There may be cases where you want to be more granular than this, though. Perhaps one person works on forms, and another works on business rules and objects; you can separate these aspects in separate libraries such as StudentUI, StudentData, StudentRules or something similar. Use your common sense when you are setting this up, and mirror the way your team works to avoid conflicts as much as possible.

The second problem with source control under VFE is that when you modify a class, VFE doesn't ensure that it is checked out. So, you will have to make sure your programmers check out the class lib manually first. The easiest way to do this is through the project manager. You can unhide the manager (as shown previously). If your programmers prefer, they can use the source control provider's front-end program. Keep in mind that when you are using a form wizard, it is most likely modifying the menu, so the developer should have the menu files checked out.

Project files

Once thing that no one we know of has ever been able to do is to get the project merge function to work properly. For that reason, it's wise for members of a team to each maintain their own project files. When a developer adds a library to the project, an e-mail will be sent stating that a new file has been added to the project. From there, each developer can check out the file from the source control program and add it to their projects. This seems to be the best method we have found to keep the project files synchronized.

Data

Another source of problems is how to deal with the data. There are two issues here: The first is the structure of the tables, and the second is your data. You may have test data, production data and perhaps training data. The best method we have found is to appoint a "DBA person." This person is in charge of all data structure and data changes for the project. The data can be stored on a shared network drive to which only the DBA can write.

The programmers can communicate changes that are to be made to the data to the DBA. If a programmer needs to add a view, they can provide the CREATE SQL VIEW code to the DBA. The DBA can maintain a library of programs to re-create these views, or perhaps after each modification of the DBC he can use GenDBCX to create a program. This program can also be checked into source control so that developers can run it to update their DBC files. (If you are using a tool such as SDT, this could simplify procedures.)

One developer on a forum took this a step further. He wrote code in a project hook so that when a developer modified the database, the code would copy the data from the shared network drive to the local drive, in addition to locking the file in source control. After the user had edited the data and checked in the DBC, the tables were copied back to the shared directory until the next developer checked out the files. A great idea.

Use some of these ideas, and also automate as much of it as you can—this will result in less overwritten and lost work.

Metadata

Many of the issues that apply to the data also apply to the metadata. For this reason, we recommend that you treat them as one. Any user who checks out the data should also check out the metadata.

A trick used by one developer is to set the "Next DBCX Id" to a higher value (such as adding 10000 to developers twos files). Each developer created tables, and the metadata records had unique IDs for each developer. When they brought the files together, they were able to merge them into one file without conflict. A great, but risky idea.

Communicate

This probably goes without saying, but communication is the most important part of a successful team project. As you can see, many of our methods rely on developer communication. If you are using a distributed team, make sure that each member has access to source control and e-mail at a minimum. A simple e-mail goes a long way toward avoiding having to redo something.

Remote data NewID()

When using the framework with local data, functions are provided to generate the surrogate values to use for primary keys. This applies if you are not using GUID values for your keys. To generate the next value, the last value used for each table is stored in a local table named APPIDS. However, if you are using remote data, you will probably prefer for this table to be remote and will thus need a method to generate keys.

The framework provides the code to call a stored procedure to generate these keys. A stored procedure is a program that is stored in the database and runs on the database server. By default, if you are using a remote view and you add a record, VFE will call a stored procedure named sp_NewID and pass it the name of the table needing the next key.

While this functionality is nice, VFE doesn't provide the stored procedure to generate these keys, so we have provided it for you. This function works and has been tested in SQL Server 7.0; however, it should work in SQL Server 2000 also. This method relies on the 7.0 ability to record lock, so you cannot use this in 6.5 as is.

This first thing you will need is a table to hold the last value. This table will hold the table name and the last value used. This function and table only supports integers; it doesn't support base62. Okay, so the first thing you need to do is create this table. You can run the following script from VFP or Query Analyzer to create the table:

```
CREATE TABLE appids (
   key_name varchar (30) PRIMARY KEY NOT NULL ,
```

```
      key_value int NOT NULL
)
```

This script will create an "appids" table in your database. Be sure you have selected the correct database prior to running the query.

This table will hold the last key used for each table that calls it. Next, run the following script to create your stored procedure:

```
create procedure sp_NewID
       @Name varchar(30)
as

set nocount on

declare @KeyValue int

set @Name = upper( @Name )

update appids
set key_value = key_value + 1
   ,@KeyValue = key_value
from appids
where key_name = @Name

select @KeyValue

return
```

This is a very simple procedure. It uses a correlated query so that the record that's read will be locked and then updated in the same query. This eliminates the need for a transaction. The procedure expects a name to be passed to it.—this will be the table name. The table name will be forced to uppercase so that only one record will exist that matches it. Notice the line that reads "select @KeyValue." This code creates a record set, which is returned to VFP, and the framework expects it to be returned in that manner.

As you can see, this is a simple procedure. If the key_value is not found in the table, a null will be returned. Also, there is no error handling. You could easily modify this to add a record to appids if the key_value didn't exist yet, and also add error handling to it. Hopefully this will help you if you plan to use SQL Server as your database.

Summary

The main point of this chapter is that there is more than one way to skin a cat. Just because the framework is basically designed to operate a certain way, this doesn't mean that you can't change its behavior or add to its behavior. Be sure to think outside of the box. *This is still VFP, and you can do anything in a VFE application that you can do in any VFP application.* Maybe SQL pass-through is a better choice than remote views; sometimes you might want to mix local data with remote data.

We hope that you have enjoyed reading this book as much as we have enjoyed writing it. We especially hope that the book has given you a greater understanding of the VFE framework and how to use it, or work around it when necessary. Now, go out there and *Create Visual FoxPro Applications with Visual Fox Express!*

Index

_ASSIST, 12
_GENMENU, 11
_INCLUDE, 11
Access 2000, 253
Access rights, 224
Action controls, 142
ActiveX list box, 15
Add form, single record, 185
Adding connections, 258
Adding custom code, 208
Adding data, 107
Adding files, 214
Adding security afterwards, 222
Adding security names, 218
AddNew, 44
ADO record set, 15
AllowDelete/Filter/List/Nav/Order, 98
AllowEdit/Filter/Cancel/Nav/New, 85
AllowNew/Delete/Edit/Save, 71
Application Builder, 2, 25
Application Manager, 2, 23
Application object, 112
Application, running, 270
APPSIDS.DBF, 62
ASSIST, 12
Base62-based primary key, 18
Behavior class, 201
Behavior page properties, 60
BindControls, 128, 134
BizObj, 7, 66
BizObj, 66
BizObjLoader, 123
BOF, 43
Buffering, 161
Builder, presentation object, 89
Builders, 28, 136
Builders, accessing, 270
Builders, VFP, 271
Business key, 33
Business object security, 219
Business objected, related, 175
Business objects, 65
Business rules, 68, 77
cAbstractDataItem, 47
Cancel, 44

Cancel, CancelPre/Post, 86
Cancel,CancelPre/Perform/Post, 72
cApp.VCX, 112
cApplication, 112
cBizObj, 68
cBusiness.VCX, 68
cCursor, 42
cData.VCX, 40
cDataEnvironment, 40, 67
cDeleteTriggerMessage, 43
cEditForm, 84
cFactoryClass, 118
cField, 48, 132
cForeignKeyExpression, 68, 176
cForms.VCX, 97
cGlobalHook, 133
cGrid, 15
Chain of Responsibility, 7, 79
Changing classes, 211
CheckFieldRule, 153
Child form security, 221
cInsertTriggerMessage, 43
cKeyField, 68, 176
Classes page, 25
Client-server mentality, 13
Client-Server, deciding, 251
cListFields, 84
cListView class, 15
cMenuPad, 84
Codebook, 1
Codebook naming conventions checkbox, 30
Collection data type, native, 66
Collectionfest, 6
Collections, 5
COM component, 67
COM object, 112
Complex views, 165
Component Gallery, 3, 31
CONFIG.FPW, 11
Configuring VFP, 11
Connections, 258
Containers, view parameter, 167
Control class builders, 136
Controls, 122
Copy, 86
cParentBizObjName, 69, 176
cPresent.VCX, 83
cPresentationObj, 83

cPresentationObjForm, 97
Creating business rules, 77
Creating VFE objects, 262
cRelationTag, 69, 176
cRightClickMenu, 131
CRUD (create, retrieve, update, delete), 7
cSetFocusTo, 84
cStartForm, 118
cUpdateTriggerMessage, 43
Cursor builder, 39
Cursor class, 5
Customize framework, 208
cVIewParameter, 132
Data binding options, 89
Data class, 5
Data classes, 37
Data edit controls, 131
Data environment, 6
Data manipulation, 274
Data session specific settings, 96
Data source, 33
Data Source Administrator, 256
Data Source Name, 255
Data validation, 147
Data validation, client-server, 262
Data, copies of, 279
Database utilities, 104
Database, views only, 276
Date text box, 139
DATE type, 254
DBCX, 4, 64
DBCX, 54
DBCX Explorer, 28, 54, 270
DBCX2, 4
DBCXMGR, 63
DCOM component, 67
DCOM object, 79
DEBUG.TXT, 106
Debugging, 277
Debugging notes, 106
Default Value Generation Key, 56
Defined range, 152
Delete, DeletePre/Perform/Post, 72
Delete, DeletePre/Post, 87
DELoader, 67
Developers menu, 105

Development Environment, 9
Display fields, 150
DoDefault, 208
DoForm, 120
DSN (Data Source Name), 255
DSN, creating, 255
Early binding, 136
Edit Default Menu Choices, 3, 32
Edit mode, 276
EOF, 43
Error log, 104
Event, raise, 205
eView, 170
Executing reports from code, 250
Export object class, 249
Export output class, 242
Export query wizard, 248
Express menu pad, 29
Express Tools, 3
Expression, lookup, 150
Expression-based primary key, 17
Extending the framework, 207
Factory class, 211
Factory, using, 212
Fetch, All, 167
Field level security, 223
Field objects, 48
Field rules, 153
Field value, 48
Field, search value, 150
Fields, 44
Fields collection, 48
FIELD_OK constant, 202
FIELD_POSTVALID constant, 202
FIELD_PREVALID constant, 202
File types, output, 245
Files page, 26
FILE_EOF, 46
Filter, 151
Filter tab, View Designer, 163
FindBizObj, 98
FindCursor, 41, 73
FindField, 73
FindViewParameter, 73
Form init, 128
Form load, 121

Forms, 93
GenDBC.PRG, 170
GenDBCX.PRG, 170
GENMENU.PRG, 101, 146
GENMENUX.PRG, 101, 146
GetBizObj, 98
GetClass, 119
GetController, 134
GetCriteria, 89
GetCursor, 42
GetMetaManager, 119
GetRecordSet, 73
GetValues, 73
Global Hook class, 133
Grids, 139
Group names, creating, 224
Grouping options, 234
Groups, user, 215
GUID, 50, 57
GUID-based primary key, 18
Hand coding views, 168
Hand-coding validation, 155
Hooks, not using, 209
I-class, 24
I-layer, 24, 207
iBizObj, 66
IDE (Integrated Development Env), 21
IDE, not loading, 270
iLibs, 24
Implementation class, 213
Incremental-based primary key, 17
Index tag, 149
Init, 112
InitialSelectedAlias, 41
InitPost/Pre, 119
Integrated Development Env (IDE), 21
interface controls, 131
Interface page properties, 61
Interfaces, related, 176
IsAdding/Changed/Cursor Empty, 46
IsAdding/Changed/Deleted, 74, 88
IsChanged, 48
Key name, 83
lActivateOnUIEnable, 84
lAllowDelete, lAllowEdit, lAllowNew, 69

lAllowDelete/Edit/Filter/List/ Nav/New, 85
lAlwaysDisable, 132
lAlwaysReadOnly, 132
Late binding, 136
lConfirmDelete, 85
lConfirmOnDelete, 69
lDisplayInterface, 119
lDisplayNoRecordMessage, 85
lGetHeaderCaptions, 142
List tool, 107
List value, 152
lMain, 85
lMaximizeOnStartup, 119
lNewOnParentNew, 69
lNoValidate, 132
Loader, BizObj, 123
Loader, session, 121
Look up add form, 151
Look up display form, 151
Look ups, client-server, 262
Lookup cursor, 149
Lookup issues, 154
Lookups, 147
LookUpSetup, 154
Lookup_Post, 204
LostFocusHook, 134
lPopulateOnInit, 142
lPrivateDataSession, 41
lRefreshParentOnRowChange, 142
lRequeryChildrenOnrowchange, 142
lRequeryChildrenOnSave, 70
lSaveAllRows, 70
lSelectRecordOnDoubleClick, 142
lUseCurrentData, 250
lUseLocalData, 257
lUseSecurity, 119
lv_ and rv_, 257
lWriteForeignKeyOnNew/Save, 70
lWritePrimaryKeyOnNew, 43, 63
lWritePrimaryKeyOnSave, 44
Maintenance, security, 229
Make, 119
Menu items security, 220
Menus, 145
Metadata, 4, 53, 280

Metadata storage, 58
Miscellaneous page, 30
Mixing lookup expressions, 152
Modifying reports, 239
MoveFirst/Last/Next/Previous, 46
Mover, 274
MSDE, 253
N-tier problems, 199
Names, security, 215
Naming conventions, 19
Naming conventions, Codebook, 30
Navigation menu, 107
New, NewPre/Perform/Post, 74
New, NewPre/Post, 87
NewID, 280
No data on open, 38
NoDataOnLoad, 44
Number of Records to Batch Update, 167
oApplication, 132
oBizObj, 48, 85
oBizObj Init, 127
oBizObjs, 71
oBizRules, 127
Object wrapper, 33
Object-based menu, 8
oCursor, 48, 70, 124
oCursorOpen, 125
oDataEnvironment, 70, 124
oDataEnvironmentInit, 124
ODBC, 255
oDELoader, 121
oField, 132
oGlobalHook, 133
oHost, 70
OkToMove, 74
oParentBizObj, 71
oPresentObj, 97
oPresentObjs, 97
oProperties, 48
Options dialog, 103
oResizer, 122
oSessionEnvironment, 121
oSessionEnvironmentLoader, 121
Output object, 231
Output options, 236
Parameter list, 163
Parameterize lookup, 155

Parameterized view, 15
Parameters, 44
Parameters, creating, 163
Parameters, view, 163
Parent-child forms, 196
Parent-child presentation object, 177
Path properties, 118
Post process expression, 151
Preferences, 29
Presentation object builder, 89
Presentation object init, 128
Presentation object, hosting, 93
Presentation object, multiple, 189
Presentation object, parent-dhild, 177
Presentation objects, 79
Primary key, Base62-based, 18
Primary key, expression-based, 17
Primary key, GUID-based, 18
Primary key, incremental-based, 17
Primary keys, 16
Project directory, 23
Project files, 279
Project manager, VFP, 269
Project, adding files, 214
PROPMAP.DBF, 59
Quick-fill text box, 138
Quick-fill text box, client-server, 263
Raise event, 205
Read-only, 38
Real-world entity, 7
RecNo, 43
RecNo, RecordCount, VisibleRecordCount, 71
RecordCount, 43
Related interfaces, 176
Related tables, 15
Relating tables, 16
Relations between views, 164
Reliability, client-server, 252
Remote data, 35
Remote View, Share Connection, 167
Remote views, creating, 260
Replacing VFE code, 209
Report object class, 249

Report output class, 231, 239
Requery, 45
Requery, RequeryPre/Perform/Post, 75
REQUERY_ERROR constant, 46
REQUERY_SUCCESS constant, 46
Required value, 152
Resizer class, 122
Revert, 48
RightClickHook, 134
rv_ and lv_, 257
Save, SavePre/Perform/Post, 75
Save, SavePre/Post, 88
SCAN WHILE, 16
Search, 89
Search expression, 149
Searchable Grid, 140
Security, 104, 215
Security groups, creating, 224
Security maintenance, 229
Security names, 215
Security names, adding, 218
Security, business object, 219
Security, child form, 221
Security, client-server, 252
Security, field level, 223
Security, menu items, 220
Security, turning on, 217
Send to back property, 82
Service Packs, 9
Services, 111
SET RELATION TO, 16, 173
SetControlSource, 135
SetField, 76
SetFieldList, 249
SetParameter, 76
SetSecurity, 120, 135
SetValues, 73
Share Connection, 167
Size restrictions, client-server, 253
Source control, 279
Speed, client-server, 252
Splash screen, 103
SPT (SQL pass-through), 263
SQL pass-through, 263
SQL Server, 253
SQLEXEC, 263
Standard menus, 106

START.PRG, 102
Startup, 112
Startup form, 120
Startup program, 9
Stonfield Systems, 53
Structural page properties, 61
Subclassing, 209
Summary options, 235
Surrogate key, 16, 17, 33
System level class, 96
System services, 111
Table rules, 153
Tarnation, 13
Team programming, 279
Third-party classes, implementing, 213
Toolbars, 98, 143
Tools menu, 107
Tree view, controlling, 249
UML, 4
Unified Modeling Language, 4
Update, 45
Update expression, 151
Upsizing local data, 268
User groups, 215
Users, 215
Users, creating, 228
Utilities, 104
UTILS.PRG, 278
UTILS.VCX, 133
ValidateControl, 133
Validate_Post, 205
Validation, 61
Validation views, 147
Validation, client-server, 262
Validation, custom, 202
Validation, tracing, 153
Validation, when, 153
Value, 48
Value_Access, 205
Version control, 168
VFE IDE, 21
VFE.h, 19
VFEMETA.DBF, 54, 59
VFENewKey, 62
View Designer, 161
View parameter class, 6
View parameter containers, 167
View parameters collection, 47
View, can't open, 166
View, Remote, 166
Views, 13, 161
Views only database, 276
Views vs. tables, 13
Views, creating, 35
Views, hand-coding, 168
Views, related, 173
Views, relating, 164
VisibleRecordCount, 43
Visual FoxExpress Service Pack 2, 9
Visual Studio Service Pack 3, 9
vp_, 261
Where does the code go?, 77, 271
Width of data, 13
Wizard Manager, 3
Wizards, 27
xCase, 253
XXXMETA.DBF, 55